Daniel Maul

The International Labour Organization

Daniel Maul

The International Labour Organization

100 Years of Global Social Policy

DE GRUYTER
OLDENBOURG

Published by
Walter de Gruyter GmbH
Genthiner Strasse 13
10785 Berlin
Germany
ISBN 978-3-11-061588-3
e-ISBN (PDF) 978-3-11-065072-3
e-ISBN (EPUB) 978-3-11-064666-5

In association with
International Labour Office
4 route des Morillons
1211 Geneva 22
Switzerland
ISBN 978-92-2-133043-1
e-ISBN (PDF) 978-92-2-133044-8

Library of Congress Control Number: 2019947687

Bibliographic information published by the Deutsche Nationalbibliothek
The Deutsche Nationalbibliothek lists this publication in the Deutsche Nationalbibliografie; detailed bibliographic data are available on the Internet at http://dnb.dnb.de.

Cover Image: Stained glass window at the International Labour Office © Max Pechstein.
Typesetting: Integra Software Services Pvt. Ltd.
Printing and binding: CPI books GmbH, Leck

www.degruyter.com

To Ricarda and Luis

Foreword

It is a rare privilege to review the priorities and achievements of an organization over a century. Understanding the past is essential for managing the present and preparing for the future. The International Labour Organization (ILO) and its constituents – governments, employers, and workers – have collaborated for 100 years to promote social justice and peace. The decades have been turbulent. Reconstruction has followed destruction, yet imbalances between poverty and prosperity have persisted. New challenges have arisen once old ones were resolved. Navigating between deeply entrenched interests, often in contradiction, has required special skills. Through the work of the ILO, tripartite cooperation and social dialogue have become the accepted method to meet basic human needs, contributing to economic growth and guaranteeing the freedoms and rights of nations and of people.

Through the joint decisions of governments and representatives of the employers and workers, the ILO has helped lay the basis for contemporary international labour and social legislation. It has sought to establish humane working conditions, balancing this goal with the rights and interests of workers and employers alike. The ILO's basic aims were set out in the ILO Constitution of 1919. The Philadelphia Declaration of 1944 confirmed the ILO as one of the indispensable actors of the multilateral system. The Organization's agenda is guided by international labour standards and policies to promote these standards on the ground, in an infinite variety of national and local circumstances.

This agenda has been put in practice in programmes for world employment, for fundamental rights at work, for setting decent work as a target for the Sustainable Development Goals of the United Nations, and for demonstrating that global markets can function in a fair way. Most recently, the ILO's aims were reaffirmed by the Centenary Declaration for the Future of Work, adopted by the International Labour Conference in 2019 and most recently by the General Assembly of the United Nations.

The decisions taken in 1919 gave the orientations for tripartite cooperation and established its practice. Fortunately, the founders of the ILO did not lack ambition and vision. They set in motion an organization that simultaneously addressed fundamental labour rights, such as freedom of association, equality, the abolition of child labour and forced labour as well as the elimination of all types of discrimination, and all aspects of social and labour policy. The Organization's methods have shaped the ways in which nations and people, individually and collectively, pursue and achieve economic and social security.

The goals of peace and prosperity through social justice are not easy to realize. Yet history has demonstrated that they can be achieved at the workplace and industry level as well as in countries aspiring to sovereignty or engaged in

https://doi.org/10.1515/9783110650723-202

nation building. The tripartite formula of the ILO provides universal guidance based on exchanges and negotiations between those directly concerned. The actors in turn have the responsibility to apply common standards in daily reality.

Daniel Maul, the author of this book, gives us a rich analytical overview of the ILO's history. A century is a long stretch of time. The period has seen political upheavals, the demise of imperial rule, democratization, and the recognition of independence and the rights of nations and individuals. Together with technological and structural change, these events have deeply transformed our societies, as well as the work that constructs them.

There is no one single story of the ILO. Many narratives spring from individual and collective experiences of workers, employers, and governments, and the ties of solidarity and common experience cut across national borders. These narratives are complemented by the perspectives of ILO officials and all those who have engaged with the ILO around the world. All have their own views on what the ILO has achieved. Naturally, these views do not always converge.

This book draws strength from research done from an external academic perspective. There is a growing scholarly interest in the multilateral system, global governance, and international organizations. This has informed an increasing amount of research on the ILO by historians and social scientists, which has contributed to this book. What makes the ILO particularly interesting for researchers is the link to the real world through employers' and workers' representatives. More recently, the role of civil society has further encouraged analysis of the ILO's synergies with cooperatives, social reform networks, human rights advocates, and other groups. Daniel Maul shows how the goals and principles of the ILO have shaped political and academic debate and how the ILO's research, technical cooperation, and the setting and supervision of international labour standards have contributed to social reform in many countries.

In the course of a century, the ILO has become a universal organization, with 187 member States. Its challenge is to cover, equally universally, all the evolving aspects of work. While its tripartite governance structure has remained constant, the ILO has reached out to increasingly diverse groups of workers, seeking to improve their living and working conditions and to help them assert their rights and gain protection. It has explored ways to adapt management methods, including negotiations and bargaining, so that the needs of workers and employers in all economic sectors are addressed.

The early years highlighted industrial and agricultural work and seafaring. However, commercial, clerical, and intellectual work also became a focus in the first decade of the ILO's existence. With decolonization and the thrust for development, the scope of activity expanded to various types of informal work, most recently domestic work. Addressing work in widely different situations, including some forms that we may not yet fully comprehend, remains an essential task of the ILO.

Setbacks and political tensions are inevitable in any story such as this. While it is useful to learn from successes, we should study the failures with equal care. The process of tripartite cooperation and social dialogue does not stop. Each solution achieved through negotiated settlements and new labour and social legislation is followed by new contradictions and new settlements. Herein lies the fascination of labour relations: they are part of the dynamics of life that touch workers, businesses, social institutions and, in the end, all components of humanity. The fact that each achievement is challenged and revisited is how social progress is wrought.

This said, the basic rights on which rests the dignity of workers, employers and nations should not be subject to the fluctuations of growth and income levels. The rights to equal opportunity, association, negotiation, social security, and occupational safety and health are not negotiable. Beyond the floor set by international labour law and practice, various forms of negotiations and collaboration demonstrate that social dialogue is not a zero-sum game and that it can deliver benefits for all. If this were not so, the ILO could not function.

Daniel Maul constantly draws our attention to the moments in history, often in times of war and crisis, where the ILO successfully adapted its methods, reached out to potential allies, and took courageous decisions. Remaining at the forefront of global social policy – with regard to both policy debate and concrete action – is the main challenge for the ILO at the outset of its second century.

History not only shows us what can be achieved, it also makes us realize the cost of our failures. When the world has faced economic and political crises, it has too often been reluctant, or incapable, of honouring the goal of social justice. Transformations of the economy and of work require sustained action to strengthen the social infrastructure of all countries. New threats arising from climate change and evolving methods of work organization demand immediate and effective action.

At the same time, the basic promises of decent work are still beyond the reach of large numbers of working people. The need for social justice and peace is as great today as at any point in the last century. The lessons from the last 100 years deserve careful consideration and study. This book offers an analytical account of the creativeness of the ILO and its constituents. Combining the strength of its principles with the imagination of workers, employers, and governments is the best guarantee for the future of the Organization.

Guy Ryder
Geneva, September 2019

Acknowledgements

I would like to thank De Gruyter and Rabea Rittgerodt for taking this book on board. I am also very grateful to the ILO and its Director-General Guy Ryder for their support for the Global Social Policy Project at the University of Oslo. This gave me the time to write the book, the project's most important outcome.

From the International Labour Office, I must first thank historian Dorothea Hoehtker and the ILO Century Project of the ILO Research Department. Dorothea pushed the project forward from its initial stages. Her thorough expertise on ILO history paired with her poise in resolving all hurdles big and small has been a *sine qua non* for this book. Kari Tapiola, former Deputy Director-General and special adviser at the ILO, also gave invaluable support. His great institutional knowledge and critical comments have helped me to get my arguments straight.

I am grateful for the support from the ILO Research Department and its Director Damian Grimshaw as well as from Chris Edgar, in charge of ILO publications, who from the beginning significantly contributed to the book's production and managed the collaboration with De Gruyter. Special thanks is due as well to the translators and the production team at the ILO, who were responsible for the French and Spanish versions of this book published in parallel by the ILO.

Many thanks to Remo Becci and Jacques Rodriguez of the ILO Archives, who were always accessible for my questions. Not only this book but nearly two decades of research on the ILO is indebted to the Archives' open and outstandingly researcher-friendly attitude. I am equally grateful to the ILO Library for the same reasons.

The path of this book followed the Nordic turns my academic career has taken in recent years. I was lucky to have the necessary institutional support from my university departments all along the way. Special thanks go to Thorsten Borring Olesen and Signe Larsen at the School of Culture of Society (CAS) at Aarhus University and to the Dean of the Department of History, Archaeology and Conservation at Oslo University, Tor Egil Førland, as well as to Hilde Henriksen Waage and Erlend Haavardsholm.

I was privileged to have the support of three very able student assistants. Stefan Haagedoorn at Aarhus University and Mads Drange at the University of Oslo have been part of the Global Social Policy Project from its beginnings, and Anna Marie Nesheim refined sections of the manuscript during the last phase. Additional thanks in this regard go to Hyo Jeong Jung, Dorothea Hoehtker's assistant at the ILO in 2018.

I was delighted to have a fine group of readers. My friends and colleagues Dietmar Süss and Tobias Winstel read the entire manuscript, while Eileen Boris, Lorenzo Mechi, Corinna Unger and Emmanuel Reynaud, a benevolently critical

https://doi.org/10.1515/9783110650723-203

follower of my work throughout, shared their expertise with me on substantial parts of it. I am deeply indebted to them all. The text also profited substantially from the comments of two anonymous peer reviewers. Thorough and knowledgeable copy-editing by Manfred Boemeke and by Suruthi Manogarane for DeGruyter made the text much more readable.

I cannot hope to do justice to all the friends and colleagues who inspired me, shared their work with me, and discussed my findings at conferences and in private conversation. One such experience was the "Fair is Fair: International Perspectives on Social Justice" conference in Padua in 2016, which I had the pleasure to organize with Lorenzo Mechi and Dorothea Hoehtker as part of the Global Social Policy Project. This book profited enormously from my participation in two major research projects supported by the Independent Research Fund of Denmark: "Laying the Foundations: The League of Nations and International Law", led by Morten Rasmussen of Copenhagen University, and "The Invention of International Bureaucracy: The League of Nations and the Creation of International Public Administration, ca. 1920–1960", led by Karen-Gram-Skjoldager of Aarhus University.

Over the years many scholars, archivists and practitioners have commented on my work, filled knowledge gaps and generously shared their research with me. I am especially grateful to Victoria Basualdo, Stefano Bellucci, Camille Bolivar, Martin Breuer, Laura Caruso, Thomas Cayet, Andreas Eckert, Ulf Edström, Norberto Ferreras, Birte Förster, Jill Jensen, Sandrine Kott, Marieke Louis, Opolot Okia, Laure Piguet, Fiona Rolian, Michele Sollai, Gabriella Scodeller, Andres Stagnaro, Veronique Stenger, Marcel van der Linden, Yannick Wehrli, Theresa Wobbe and Aurelien Zaragori.

At Oslo, I had many opportunities to discuss my findings and get new perspectives. Special thanks goes to Marta Bivand Erdal, Sunniva Engh, Hanne Hagtvedt Vik, Kim Priemel, Doug Rossinow and Mathias Hatleskog Tjønn, as well as to the students in my International Organizations in History classes taught as part of the Master Programme in International and Transnational History (MITRA).

These acknowledgements would surely be incomplete without an expression of my gratitude to Marcelo and Torsten Lösel-Caruso, who at various critical points hosted writing retreats in their beautiful Berlin-Pankow guest apartment. Their friendship and great hospitality, including fine dinners and conversation, surely left a mark on this book.

Finally, a heartfelt thanks to my family, my wife Verona and my children Ricarda and Luis, who have long lived in the shadow of "the book" (*das Buch*). I am immensely grateful for their continuous support and affection, for their patience and also for their healthy impatience.

Contents

Introduction

> *The social factor must take precedence over the economic factor; it must regulate and guide it in the highest cause of justice.*
>
> Albert Thomas, 1931[1]

The International Labour Organization (ILO) is a fascinating object of study for historians from more than one point of view. Born in 1919 out of the political and social turmoil of the First World War and its aftermath, it is today one of the oldest organizations of the United Nations system. Its unique tripartite structure, in which decisions are taken by representatives of governments, employers and workers, adds to its distinctive status. But that is not all, and it may not even be half, of the explanation of why the ILO is such a rich resource. The main reason is that the ILO opens up windows through which we catch a view of a vast field of themes that have dominated the twentieth and early twenty-first centuries. A study of the ILO offers a longitudinal perspective on the conditions under which people have been working; the changing modes of production and the response by workers and governments; the struggles for social justice both within nations and in their relationships with other nations; and, finally, the answers that states have found, or tried to find, during the past hundred years to the social problems of their day, in the wider context of international cooperation and competition.

While the ILO as an organization is at the heart of this book, the institutional aspect is but one important part of a larger story, in which the numerous aspects of people's work experiences and the quest for labour and social rights have been reflected in the Organization's history. In this sense, the ILO's attempts to create "global social policy" are at the core of this analysis. It provides a perspective on the ways in which the Organization, over a hundred years, has sought to influence the debates on this issue. It examines the ILO's practical contributions to improving the conditions of work and to promoting social policies that have gone beyond the strict confines of the labour environment – above all, but not only – through the definition and adoption of international labour standards.

In the following account, the ILO appears in a dual role: On the one hand, from the times of its first Director, Albert Thomas, the ILO's permanent secretariat, the International Labour Office (the Office for short), has been an actor in its

---

1 ILO, *The International Labour Organisation. The First Decade.* Preface by Albert Thomas (Geneva: ILO, 1931), 12.

https://doi.org/10.1515/9783110650723-001

own right in the field of global social policy. On the other, the ILO has provided an arena for direct and open debates among the representatives of governments, workers and employers. In this latter regard, the story of the ILO mirrors the continuous interest of governments, trade unions, business groups and a variety of other actors. They have had manifold and varied motives for engaging with the transnational dimension of social policy and using the Organization to debate matters of social justice, development, the alleviation of poverty, social mobility, and the distribution of wealth in an international context. These actors have often followed intertwined humanitarian, economic, political and geopolitical, as well as ideological rationales. This has involved contests for power and influence as well as a constant struggle to define what the ILO should truly be and what purposes it should serve.

Against this background, the story that this account will tell evolves around three central questions. Whose organization was and is the ILO? What characterizes the ILO as an international organization? And finally, in light of the importance attributed to the ambiguous goal of "social justice" both within and among its member States: what has been the ILO's specific contribution to the social justice debates that have spanned an entire century – from the meeting rooms at the Paris Peace Conference in 1919 to the exploration of the future of work in our day? These three questions form the narrative that runs throughout this study.

Whose Organization?

Despite its universalist approach, the ILO has never represented the world of work in all its dimensions and aspects. Struggles with inclusion and exclusion, and with the question what kind of workers and what kinds of work are within or outside of the ILO's mandate, have been part of the Organization from its very beginnings. It is crucial to recognize that the boundaries of the ILO's scope of action are continuously shifting, because then we can use the ILO as a prism, through which we can see the inequalities, injustices, and power struggles, as well as the profound socio-economic transformations that take place in the world surrounding the Organization.

The question of "whose organization" the ILO is has always had many facets. What activities qualify to be treated as "work" within the scope of the Organization? Who has the primary claim on the ILO's attention, work and resources? The debates have covered dichotomies such as industrialized vs. developing countries, market vs. planned economies, formal vs. informal sector, men vs. women, industrial vs. rural labour, migrants vs. nationals, production vs. service economy, blue vs. white collar work, and Fordist vs. post-Fordist production. The conjunctures of inclusion and exclusion and the dynamics behind the ILO's work have been fluctuating, depending on specific political, social, and economic contexts. In this sense the question of who or what should be represented in the ILO's meeting rooms, in its work programmes and its research activities, has always reflected the struggle of ideologies – East vs. West, North vs. South, imperial vs. colonial, Keynesian vs. neoliberal. It has equally been affected by shifting conceptions of gender roles and changing perceptions of race at the national and international levels. These considerations provided the background for including colonial and indigenous labour within the sphere of standard-setting. They accompanied the discussions on equal pay for men and women, on development, and the ILO's exploration of the so-called informal economy.

To read the ILO's history as one of constant expansion, however, would miss the point. None of these new paths were uncontested at the time, and they were accompanied by demands for a re-focusing and prioritizing of the Organization's activities. The same has been true for the ILO's repeated endeavours to expand its mandate beyond the field of labour policy into the broader social and, in particular, economic areas.

What and, above all, who has driven these discussions? The questions of who was in charge, and who set the direction are instructive to the understanding of the workings of the Organization. The ILO has never been – as some might have wished – the "enchanted palace" of internationalist ideals, to borrow from Mark Mazower's assessment of the hidden imperial roots of the United Nations (UN).[2] It has rather served as both a mirror and a vessel for power relations within the international system at any given time. As this account will show, the particular treatment of colonial labour matters in the interwar years clearly reflected the dominant position that the imperial powers, especially Great Britain and France, occupied within the ILO at the time. Similarly, the strong influence of the United States as the Western superpower can be traced all over – from the debates on human rights during the 1950s, through the venture into technical cooperation and the ILO's 1998 Declaration on Fundamental Principles and Rights at Work. Through which channels have influence and power manifested themselves? The questions of who pays the bills obviously plays an important role. The withdrawal of the United States from the ILO from 1977 to 1980 put this on full display, inasmuch as it deprived the Organization of US membership contributions, which

2 Mark Mazower, *No Enchanted Palace: The End of Empire and the Ideological Origins of the United Nations* (Princeton, NJ: Princeton University Press, 2009).

accounted for a quarter of the ILO's regular budget. Money, however, is not the only way how states exert influence or "hegemony".[3] Recruitment within the ILO and the design of its programmes of work come into play. In turn, in many fields of the ILO's activities the primacy of national prerogatives of powerful states becomes tangible.

At the same time, power relations within international organizations are seldom static; mainly they constitute rather fluid and dynamic structures. Claims to hegemony never remain unchallenged, as several debates during the ILO's history, and in particular those on human rights, have shown. Lest we forget, tripartism and the participation of trade union and business representatives serve as a corrective to the influence of states – although the extent to which they do so is relative, as is the degree to which the International Labour Office itself has influenced debates and decisions.

An International Organization among International Organizations?

What defines the ILO as an international organization? Its story cannot be told in isolation from the wider history of internationalism and international organizations in the nineteenth and twentieth centuries. The Organization's roots can be traced back to the crossroads of (social) liberal and Socialist aspirations in the nineteenth century. Like the League of Nations, the other great experiment in international governance rising from the ashes of the First World War, the ILO was a supreme expression of liberal traditions of internationalist thought and action. At the same time, it incorporated the central aims of the Second (Socialist) International (1889–1916) and the international trade union movement, which was an important – if not the most important – driver behind the ILO's founding.[4] As an organization, the ILO would help to merge those traditions to become the standard bearer of a new social liberal branch of internationalism, defined and re-defined in an ever shifting political and social environment. The most dramatic challenges to the ILO's social liberal principles came both from inside and

3 Robert W. Cox, "Labor and Hegemony", *International Organization* 31, no. 3 (1977): 385–424.
4 Sandrine Kott, "From Transnational Reformist Network to International Organization: The International Association for Labour Legislation and the International Labour Organization, 1900–1930s", in *Shaping the Transnational Sphere. Experts, Networks and Issues from the 1840s to the 1930s*, ed. Davide Rodogno, Bernhard Struck, and Jakob Vogel (New York: Berghahn Books, 2015), 239–259; John W. Follows, *Antecedents of the International Labour Organization* (Oxford: Clarendon Press, 1951).

outside the Organization with the allure of fascism and communism. Still, the ILO has always served in less dramatic ways as a sounding board for alternative ideas of internationalism. It provided room for those ideas on a regional level – for example, pan-Americanism and pan-Africanism – and it provided space for expressions of solidarity among groups of states or transnational movements, such as the countries of the global South or indigenous internationalism in the post-1945 era.[5]

What distinguishes the ILO from the bulk of international organizations whose activities today cover nearly all dimensions of people's lives? Is it all that different? In some ways the ILO has arguably been an international organization among others from its inception. This is particularly true regarding its relationship with governments and the world of nation states that founded and sustained the system of international organizations throughout the twentieth century.[6] The ILO was born at the historical moment when three empires – the Austro-Hungarian, Ottoman and Russian – collapsed, giving way to a new political landscape where the nation state became the standard international actor. The demise of European colonial empires after 1945 led to a further strengthening of the principle of national sovereignty in international affairs. As much as any other international organization, by definition the ILO is first and foremost dependent on the states that constitute its membership.

The ILO has been an international organization among international organizations in another sense. Emerging from the Paris Peace Conference, it started its work as part of the League of Nations system. In 1946, it became the first "specialized agency" of the United Nations. The ILO has thus been from its beginnings institutionally linked to the wider family of international organizations. Even though it has at all times kept a degree of autonomy within this family, competition and cooperation in this network of institutions, as well as with other regional and sectoral organizations outside this framework, have always defined features of the ILO's work.[7] The history of the Office, too, cannot be separated from a broader internationalist milieu of governmental and non-governmental actors. Many of the dynamics behind the ILO's actions is due to its position within this

5 Glenda Sluga and Patricia Clavin, eds., *Internationalisms: A Twentieth Century History* (Cambridge: Cambridge University Press, 2017).
6 Glenda Sluga, *Internationalism in the Age of Nationalism* (Philadelphia, PA: University of Pennsylvania Press, 2013).
7 For the history of international organizations in a long-term perspective, see Mark Mazower, *Governing the World: The History of an Idea* (New York: Penguin Press, 2012); Bob Reinalda, *Routledge History of International Organizations: From 1815 to the Present Day* (London: Routledge, 2009).

broader network which is composed of parts of the United Nations family as well as of transnational actors such as the cooperative movement or organizations dealing with children's welfare, social insurance, health issues and the rights of migrant and domestic workers.

From the beginning, the International Labour Office was part of this broader network and its officials, especially its Director (later Director-General), played a central role. Albert Thomas perceived of the Organization as an important instrument in maintaining peace in Europe after the First World War. He saw the ILO as well positioned to fulfil a role in securing peace, both within societies and among nations, based on international labour standards and by bringing political issues down to the level of "technical", labour-related problems in order to initiate contact and cooperation. His successors have by and large maintained Thomas' proactive stance to the role of international bureaucracies.

The unique position of the ILO within the international framework is due first and foremost to its tripartite structure. Its institutional make-up, in which governments, employers (the representatives of business interests), and workers (trade unions) share in the decision-making process shapes the ILO's work and its organizational "ideology". Tripartism has played an important yet ambiguous part in the history of the ILO's venture into new fields of action. It has worked as a powerful tool for inclusion and expansion in the ILO and opened a space for the representation of societal interests from the world of work. Yet, to the degree that tripartism is based on the concept of formal (industrial) employment, it has sometimes been an obstacle to including other groups of working people outside this norm within the scope of the Organization. On the whole, however, the tripartism which the ILO has fostered on the international level and actively sought to put in practice "on the ground" is the ILO's signature characteristic and asset within the sphere of international organizations.

An Organization for Social Justice

The ILO has been constructed around the idea of social justice. While the term itself may have had different connotations over the years, it has remained a guiding principle in the ILO's work. However, the exact meaning in terms of concrete policies is as controversial as ever. There has never been a clear definition, let alone a stable consensus, on what social justice entails; nor has there been agreement on the means by which it could (or should) be attained. Perhaps the very fact that social justice evokes quite different understandings of its content and implications has served to make the term a point of reference in the ILO's work for 100 years.

The first paragraph of the preamble of the ILO's Constitution, written in the aftermath of the First World War, asserts that "peace can be established only if it is based upon social justice".[8] While references to social justice as a means for the establishment and maintenance of a lasting peace, both within and among nations, were frequent during the very first days of the Organization, the 1944 Declaration of Philadelphia connected it to the idea of individual rights. Written in the final phase of another World War, in which the ILO sided with the cause of liberal democracy, the Philadelphia Declaration also defined social justice as a precondition for the stability of democratic government. The most recent prominent appearance of the term can be found in the Declaration on Social Justice for a Fair Globalization of 2008, usually referred to as the "Social Justice Declaration". Social justice now features as a "universal aspiration", under pressure from market imperatives and rapid technological change. The Declaration defines the term indirectly, *ex negativo*, as the need to remedy "income inequality, continuing high levels of unemployment and poverty, vulnerability of economies to external shocks, and the growth of both unprotected work and the informal economy, which impact on the employment relationship and the protections it can offer".[9] What social justice could mean in a more positive sense, whether, for instance, it involves redistributive elements on the national as well as the international levels, is as open to interpretation and controversy as at any earlier time in the ILO's history.

While there has never been a clear-cut concept of social justice at the heart of the ILO's work, there are distinctive recurring motives. One of them, present from the start in the ILO's work for social justice, was built on the assumption that the ILO was able, through standard-setting and other means, to help ensure social cohesion within open market economies. Founded against the background of political and social revolution, a major impetus for the ILO's establishment – and even for the attempts of social reform preceding its founding – was to rein in the excessive forces of capitalism without removing the capitalist system itself. The preferred means to achieve this was state regulation, whether through legislation, social policy, or economic and social planning.

By its calls on governments to take preventive action, the founders of the ILO tried to subdue the socially (and politically) destructive tendencies of unfettered capitalism. In this sense, the ILO, more than any other international institution, was part of and affected by the "great transformation" observed by Karl Polanyi

---

8 "Whereas the League of Nations has for its object the establishment of universal peace, and such a peace can be established only if it is based upon social justice ... ". ILO, *Constitution of the International Labour Organisation* (Paris, 1919).

9 ILO, *Declaration on Social Justice for a Fair Globalization*, Adopted by the International Labour Conference at its Ninety-seventh Session, Geneva, 10 June 2008 (Geneva: ILO, 2008), 5.

in the middle of the twentieth century.[10] In the same year that Polanyi published his book, 1944, the ILO would in Philadelphia for the first time explicitly proclaim an overarching social objective for all, particularly regarding economic and financial policies. The thought that the ILO had a mandate to pursue such a social objective had been there from the start. From this perspective, it was only recently, in the course of the "neoliberal turn" starting in the late 1970s, that the basic assumptions behind this quest were radically challenged, while the myth of self-regulatory markets, deconstructed by Polanyi, was restored.

In this regard, the story of the ILO opens two particularly panoramic windows on the history of the twentieth and twenty-first centuries. Firstly, it offers a view on the conjunctures of economic thought and the history of capitalism and capitalism's varieties, its adherents, and its opponents. The ILO is an appropriate place to analyse the different ways how open economies have been organized and the equally manifold ways in which the social challenges and disruptions accompanying the capitalist mode of production have been addressed by various actors. Secondly, the ILO has been a major participant in an on-going debate on the boundaries of the "social realm" and, consequently, on what exactly constitutes "social policy". This study will repeatedly show the ILO as a major force in the struggles to apply concretely the outcomes of these debates, frequently through outwardly technical matters of occupational safety and health or working time. Very often they touch on such fundamental issues as the share which the state and the individual, respectively, should assume with regard to social protection or the regulation of productive versus "reproductive" (care and domestic) work.

The ILO's quest for social justice has always been marked by a dual approach, where the national and international levels are complementary and interdependent. The Organization promoted labour legislation and social policy measures that would benefit workers and thus strengthen social cohesion within societies, and this goal was to be achieved through the adoption and implementation of international labour standards. The 190 Conventions and over 200 Recommendations that the ILO has adopted have expressed the strategic objective of ensuring that progressive social legislation at the national level would not turn into a competitive disadvantage in the international environment. International labour standards and the often controversial discussions surrounding their adoption testify to the struggles over the boundaries of social policy mentioned before, which are mirrored in the ILO's other activities, from research to technical cooperation.

Decolonization and the growing weight of the developing countries gave a new direction to the debate. In the eyes of many governments from the global

---

10 Karl Polanyi, *The Great Transformation* (New York: Rinehart & Company, 1944).

South, ILO standards were transformed from a means to achieve social justice across national borders into a protectionist tool used by the rich industrialized countries to maintain the inequalities of the international system. In this perspective, social justice needed to be established *between* nations first. For this, the ILO was above all expected to provide practical help. As the Social Justice Declaration of 2008 revealed, developments usually summarized under the term "globalization" have added another dimension to the debate. Against the background of a rising tide of right-wing populism, which combines criticism of globalization with illiberal and openly xenophobic policy proposals, the on-going debate about the state of the world has also brought back onto the agenda the link (or the lack thereof) between social justice and democracy.

Histories of the ILO

For a long time, historical studies on the ILO were few and far between. Except for research from political scientists and scholars in international relations,[11] Antony Alcock's account, published in the wake of the ILO's fiftieth anniversary (1969), was the only monograph available that dealt with the organization from an explicitly historical point of view.[12] This situation has changed radically in recent years. Many of the gaps in research that Jasmien van Daele (2008) and the authors of a pioneering *ILO Histories* anthology (2010) identified a decade ago have been filled.[13] Many articles and contributions have discovered the ILO's activities as a fruitful field of study. Three anthologies, coordinated by the ILO, have contributed to this development: *Globalizing Social Rights* (2013),[14] *The ILO from Geneva to the*

---

11 Ernst B. Haas, Beyond the Nation-State. Functionalism and International Organization (Stanford, CA: Stanford University Press, 1964); Viktor-Yves Ghébali, The International Labour Organisation: A Case Study on the Evolution of UN Specialised Agencies (Dordrecht: Martinus Nijhoff, 1989); Robert W. Cox, "ILO–Limited Monarchy", in *The Anatomy of Influence. Decision Making in International Organizations*, ed. Robert W. Cox and Harold K. Jacobson (New Haven, CT: Yale University Press, 1973), 102–138.

12 Antony Alcock, *History of the International Labor Organization* (New York: Octagon Books, 1971).

13 Jasmien Van Daele, "The International Labour Organization in Past and Present Research", *International Review of Social History* 53, no. 3 (2008): 485–511; Jasmien Van Daele et al., eds., *ILO Histories. Essays on the International Labour Organization and Its Impact on the World During the Twentieth Century* (Bern: Peter Lang, 2010); Magaly Rodríguez García, "Conclusion: The ILO's Impact on the World" in *ILO Histories*, ed. Van Daele et al., 461–478.

14 Sandrine Kott and Joëlle Droux, eds., *Globalizing Social Rights. The International Labour Organization and Beyond* (Basingstoke: Palgrave Macmillan; Geneva: ILO, 2013).

Pacific Rim (2015)[15] and *Women's ILO* (2018)[16] assemble contributions that cover a wealth of thematic areas: from unemployment to nutritional standards and food policy, maritime to domestic labour, and women's representation at the ILO to children's welfare. In parallel, numerous articles have been published that address certain aspects of the ILO's work, regional activities, or its interaction with other international actors.[17] Scholars like Sandrine Kott[18] have played an important role in this recent research, well on display in the 2018 special issue of *Le mouvement social* about "La justice sociale dans un monde global", which covers 100 years of

15 Jill M. Jensen and Nelson Lichtenstein, eds., *The ILO from Geneva to the Pacific Rim: West Meets East* (Basingstoke: Palgrave Macmillan; Geneva: ILO, 2015).

16 Eileen Boris, Dorothea Hoehtker, and Susan Zimmermann, eds., *Women's ILO: Transnational Networks, Global Labour Standards and Gender Equality, 1919 to the Present*, Studies in Global Social History (Leiden: Brill; Geneva: ILO, 2018).

17 Amalia Ribi Forclaz, "A New Target for International Social Reform: The International Labour Organization and Working and Living Conditions in Agriculture in the Inter-War Years", *Contemporary European History* 20, no. 3 (2011): 307–329; Christophe Verbruggen, "Intellectual Workers and Their Search for a Place within the ILO during the Interwar Period", in *ILO Histories*, ed. Van Daele et al. 271–292; Jill Jensen, "From Geneva to the Americas: The International Labor Organization and Inter-American Social Security Standards, 1936–1948", *International Labor and Working-Class History* 80, no. 1 (2011): 215–240; Norberto Osvaldo Ferreras, "Europe–Geneva–America: The First International Conference of American States Members of the International Labour Organization", in *Beyond Geopolitics: New Histories of Latin America at the League of Nations*, ed. Alan McPherson (Albuquerque, NM: University of New Mexico Press, 2015), 83–96; Lorenzo Mechi, "Economic Regionalism and Social Stabilisation: The International Labour Organization and Western Europe in the Early Post-War Years", *International History Review* 35, no. 4 (2013): 844–862; Patricia Clavin, "What's in a Living Standard? Bringing Society and Economy Together in the ILO and the League of Nations Depression Delegation, 1938–1945", in *Globalizing Social Rights*, ed. Kott and Droux, 233–248; Paul Weindling, "Social Medicine at the League of Nations Health Organisation and the International Labour Office Compared" in *International Health Organisations and Movements, 1918–1939*, ed. Paul Weindling (Cambridge: Cambridge University Press, 1995), 134–153.

18 From the wealth of publications by Sandrine Kott, see: "Fighting the War or Preparing for Peace? The ILO during the Second World War", *Journal of Modern European History* 12, no. 3 (2014): 359–76; "From Transnational Reformist Network to International Organization: The International Association for Labour Legislation and the International Labour Organization, 1900–1930s", in *Shaping the Transnational Sphere. Experts, Networks and Issues from the 1840s to the 1930s*, ed. Davide Rodogno, Bernhard Struck, and Jakob Vogel (Oxford: Berghahn Books, 2015), 239–58; "Towards a Social History of International Organisations: The ILO and the Internationalisation of Western Social Expertise (1919–1949)", in *Internationalism, Imperialism and the Formation of the Contemporary World. The Pasts of the Present*, ed. Miguel Bandeira Jerónimo and José Pedro Monteiro (Basingstoke: Palgrave Macmillan, 2018), 35–57; "OIT, justice sociale et mondes communistes. Concurrences, émulations, convergences", *Le Mouvement Social* 263, no. 2 (2018): 139–151.

ILO history.[19] The ILO has encouraged a variety of academic studies and published a number of books on the history of the Organization. In addition to contributions in English and French, an increasing amount of literature is available in other languages.[20] Nonetheless, there certainly are some missing parts and unchartered territories. With regard to the post-1945 era, and in particular after the 1970s, as well as on some regional aspects (Africa, East and South-East Asia) research has only just begun to dig deeper. In other fields, too, there is still room and demand for further study, especially for the period after 1945.[21] The trend, however, is clear: historians have discovered the ILO as a worthwhile field of study.

This renewed interest for the ILO seems to be part of a bigger phenomenon. The significant rise in interest in international organizations was already noted in 2008 in the review articles on the recent historiography of the League of Nations[22] and the United Nations.[23] Debates on globalization have raised an

19 *La justice sociale dans un monde global. L'Organisation Internationale du Travail*, Special Issue of *Le Mouvement Social*, 263, no. 2 (2018). Kott has not only covered many aspects of the ILO's history herself but has helped and encouraged a new generation of ILO scholars to come forward. See Véronique Plata-Stenger, "Une voie sociale pour le développement. Le Bureau International du Travail et les débuts de la coopération technique (1919–1949)" (PhD diss., Université de Genève, 2016), Véronique Plata-Stenger, *Social Reform, Modernization and technological Diplomacy. The ILO Contribution to development* (1930-1946), Series: Work in Global and Historical Perspective 8 (Oldenbourg: DeGruyter, forthcoming 2020); Olga Hidalgo-Weber, "Dimensions transnationales des politiques sociales britanniques: Le rôle de la Grande-Bretagne au sein de l'OIT, 1919–1946" (PhD diss., Université de Genève, 2015).

20 See, e.g., Theresa Wobbe, "Das Globalwerden der Menschenrechte in der ILO. Die Umdeutung von Arbeitsrechten im Kontext weltgesellschaftlicher Strukturprobleme von den 1930er bis 1950er Jahren", in *Menschenrechte in der Weltgesellschaft. Deutungswandel und Wirkungsweise eines globalen Leitwerts*, ed. Bettina Heintz and Britta Leisering (Frankfurt am Main: Campus Verlag, 2015), 283–316; Cédric Guinand, *Die Internationale Arbeitsorganisation (ILO) und die soziale Sicherheit in Europa (1942–1969)* (Bern: Peter Lang, 2003); Isabelle Lespinet-Moret and Vincent Viet, eds., *L'Organisation internationale du travail: origine, développement, avenir* (Rennes: Presses Universitaires de Rennes, 2011); Jean-Michel Bonvin, *L'Organisation internationale du travail: Etude sur une agence productrice de normes* (Paris: Presses Universitaires de France, 1998); Laura Caruso and Andrés Stagnaro, eds., *Una historia regional de la OIT: Aportes sobre regulación y legislación del trabajo latinoamericano* (La Plata: Universidad Nacional de La Plata. Facultad de Humanidades y Ciencias de la Educación, 2017).

21 There is no comprehensive study of the ILO's post-1945 technical assistance programmes. Other areas where research is still in its early stages are, for instance, the ILO's treatment of automation and technological change and the debate on structural adjustment. There is also no work that covers the ILO's efforts in the field of labour migration since its beginnings.

22 Susan Pedersen, "Back to the League of Nations", *American Historical Review* 112, no. 4 (2007): 1091–1117; Sunil Amrith and Glenda Sluga, "New Histories of the United Nations", *Journal of World History* 19, no. 3 (2008): 251–274.

23 Sluga and Clavin, *Internationalisms: A Twentieth Century History.*

interest in movements of people, goods, and ideas beyond national borders, and international organizations provide a "seductive and underutilized focus" for such transnational perspectives.[24] Moreover, it is probably no coincidence that the interest in international institutions increases at the very moment when existing institutions of international cooperation are under growing pressure in the face of a resurge of nationalist policies and unilateralism in international affairs. Some of the "new histories" of the international organizations published in the 2000s, above all those that addressed primarily US audiences, were influenced by the 9/11 terrorist attacks and the bypassing of the United Nations in the handling of the Iraq controversy by the George W. Bush administration.[25] If we accept the premise that one source of inspiration behind the renewed interest in how international cooperation has functioned in the past is the perceived threat to its purpose in the present, then we can expect a whole range of fresh research in the coming years.

Yet there are more specific reasons why the ILO has lately garnered the attention of a growing number of historians. The topics the ILO addresses are of major concern in today's world. The debate on the social dimension of globalization and the impact of trade liberalization on working conditions, the internationalization of production, and the accompanying trend towards deregulation and labour market flexibility have heightened the interest in an organization founded to contain the effects of an earlier phase of global capitalism. In the same sense, the financial crisis of 2008 and the rise of right-wing populism in many places around the world have sparked renewed interest in an organization that embodied – through its Declaration of Philadelphia – the social and economic lessons of two World Wars, the crises years in between, and the subsequent recovery of liberal democracy based on the spirit of welfare reform. The attention to an organization that ever since has promoted a social objective for all policies, including economic policies that respect rights at work and the rule of law, further resonates with the "social turn" that historiography on international human rights has recently taken.[26]

The following chapters are building on the abundant research on the ILO and its broader international context. The intention of this study goes beyond pre-

24 Amrith and Sluga, "New Histories of the United Nations", 252.

25 Mazower, *Governing the World*, IX–XVI; Susan Pedersen has made a similar point on the scholarship on the League, in which the interwar years feature as another era of blossoming internationalism against an increasingly gloomy unilateral background of interstate relationships. Pedersen, "Back to the League".

26 Samuel Moyn, *Not Enough: Human Rights in an Unequal World* (Cambridge, MA: The Belknap Press of Harvard University Press, 2018).

senting a synthesis of the existing scholarly findings. It comes instead with its own aims and surely also with its biases. It starts from my own broader research interests, which have focused on the history of decolonization, internationalism at large, development aid, and human rights policies, as well as on the history of globalization discourses.[27] These perspectives have unquestionably influenced the way in which I portray the ILO in this book.

The following story of the ILO's hundred years is organized quite pragmatically, in a chronological order. Most of the narratives described above, however, run through the entire history of the ILO. Some are more visible than others, but they all provide the red threads of this study. Following a short introduction of the pre-history of the ILO, the analysis moves through four major periods. From the inter-war years, it proceeds to the period of the ILO's "second founding" during and immediately after the Second World War with the 1944 Declaration of Philadelphia at the heart of events. The history of the ILO since the Second World War is organized along several sometimes overlapping time lines: The first period, defined by the Cold War and decolonization and subsumed under the headings of "Human Rights" and "Development", runs from 1948, which saw both the arrival of a new Director-General, David Morse, and the launch of the ILO's technical cooperation activities, to 1976 and the highly publicized World Employment Conference. The second period, which finally locates the ILO in the transition to the post–Cold War era and the looming age of globalization, starts with the end of the "Morse-era" in 1970 and extends to the 1998 Declaration of the Fundamental Principles and Rights at Work, which can be regarded as the ILO's answer to the systemic changes mentioned before. To the end of the book, I venture into the most recent period and suggest possible lines along which future accounts of the ILO might be written.

27 Daniel Maul, *Human Rights, Development and Decolonization: The International Labour Organization, 1940–70* (Basingstoke: Palgrave Macmillan; Geneva: ILO, 2012); "The International Labour Organization and the Struggle against Forced Labour from 1919 to the Present", *Labor History* 48, no. 4 (2007): 477–500; " 'Help Them Move the ILO Way': The International Labor Organization and the Modernization Discourse in the Era of Decolonization and the Cold War", *Diplomatic History* 33, no. 3 (2009): 387–404; "The ILO, Asia and the Beginnings of Technical Assistance, 1945–60", in *The ILO from Geneva to the Pacific Rim*, ed. Jensen and Lichtenstein, 110–33; "The International Labour Organization and the Globalization of Human Rights, 1944–1970", in *Human Rights in the Twentieth Century*, ed. Stefan-Ludwig Hoffmann (Cambridge: Cambridge University Press, 2010), 301–320.

Antecedents

> *Universal and lasting peace can be established only if it is based upon social justice.*
> ILO Constitution

The frequent references in the early days of the International Labour Organization (ILO) to its peace-building function point to a simple historical fact: The ILO was "a daughter of the war".[28] Its creation at the Paris Peace Conference of 1919 was in many ways a direct consequence of four years of bloodshed and of the revolutions and the social, economic, and political turmoil that had followed the First World War. However, too close a focus on the circumstances of the ILO's foundation easily obscures the fact that the roots of the Organization go back much deeper in time. When the members of the Commission on International Labour Legislation met in Paris in February 1919, entrusted with a mandate by the victorious allied countries to shape the features of the future ILO, they built on almost half a century of discussions on international social policy. Against the background of accelerating industrialization and the massive expansion of global trade, social reformers and trade unionists from countries in Europe and North America had entered a debate on how to best control the undesired effects of these driving forces of industrial capitalism.

Early Traditions

The first ones to introduce the idea of international labour standards into the public debate in Europe in the early nineteenth century were philanthropic entrepreneurs, whose primary interest lay in the material and moral betterment of the working classes. Robert Owen, a Welsh industrialist and utopian socialist who had experimented with building egalitarian communities of workers at his Scottish textile mill at New Lanark, sought to improve working conditions, especially with regard to child labour and working time, on national level through international agreements. His ideas were picked up and introduced in the political debate by others, such as the English cotton mill owner Charles Hindley, who clearly saw in international labour laws a means to prevent economic disadvantage for socially

28 Bruno Cabanes, *The Great War and the Origins of Humanitarianism, 1918–1924*, Studies in the Social and Cultural History of Modern Warfare (Cambridge: Cambridge University Press, 2014), 79.

https://doi.org/10.1515/9783110650723-002

progressive nations such as Great Britain, or a little later the Swiss-Alsatian manufacturer Daniel Legrand.[29]

When governments first started to regulate minimum work ages for children, to introduce state-led systems of factory inspection, and to initiate social insurance schemes that protected workers against the hazards of accidents, old age, or unemployment, they had not only humanitarian but also political and economic reasons to do so. A central aim of the Bismarckian social legislation initiated in Germany during the 1880s was to quell the revolutionary potential of the labour movement and to integrate workers into the new nation. At the same time, regulations directed against the exploitation of workers and social benefits were introduced by most Western European governments during the second half of the nineteenth century, and they followed an economic rationale. In countries that embraced the free trade doctrine, the protection of workers by the state was seen as a means to cushion the potentially socially and politically hazardous effects of international competition between open economies. Even parts of the labour movement were in favor of a combination of strong "labour compacts" and free trade.[30] The attempt to harmonize social standards internationally in order to avoid competition by means of lowering these standards –the "race to the bottom" – was seen at least by some as a logical next step.[31]

Around the turn of the century, governments took the initiative to harmonize labour legislation on an international scale. In some cases, they tried to arrange for multilateral treaties governing particular social and labour issues. For example, in 1890, the German government convened a group of European states in Berlin in a first attempt, although ultimately unsuccessful, to establish international regulations concerning women's and children's work. Smaller countries like Switzerland[32] were in the forefront of even more far-reaching initiatives in order to position themselves in the international diplomatic arena.[33] Some governments, like those of France and Italy, chose to conclude bilateral agreements

29 Follows, *Antecedents of the International Labour Organization*, 1–57.

30 Michael Huberman, *Odd Couple: International Trade and Labor Standards in History*, Yale Series in Economic and Financial History (New Haven, CT: Yale University Press, 2012).

31 Reinalda, *Routledge History of International Organizations*, 169–170.

32 Switzerland could, in addition, draw on its experience of regulating economic competition between its cantons.

33 Martin H. Geyer and Johannes Paulmann, eds., *The Mechanics of Internationalism. Culture, Society, and Politics from the 1840s to the First World War* (London: Oxford University Press and German Historical Institute, 2001); Madeleine Herren, *Hintertüren zur Macht: Internationalismus und modernisierungsorientierte Außenpolitik in Belgien, der Schweiz und den USA* (Munich: Oldenbourg, 2000).

that guaranteed labour migrants equal access to social benefits in both countries in 1904.[34]

A second source of inspiration for international social policy measures was the socialist labour movement, loosely united in Second International founded in 1889. Although the Second International was deeply divided between a Marxist (revolutionary) and a reformist wing for most of its existence, it provided important impulses to the debate. In countries with the strongest labour movements – Germany, France, England, Switzerland, and Belgium – opinions initially differed widely on whether an improvement of working conditions could be achieved by legislative means. However, around the 1890s the merits of such a strategy became obvious.[35] Especially those parts of the socialist movement and their trade union allies, which were prepared to work within the existing capitalist system and supported the introduction of social legislation on the national level, were more open to cooperation with other political forces in order to push governments to harmonize this legislation internationally. However, by and large, the main focus of trade unions remained a national one.[36]

It was during the same time that international labour law became the concern of a growing transnational network of mostly liberal social reformers – in the main lawyers, political economists, and others – who called for the state to use its power of intervention. Labour law was promoted both as a philanthropic undertaking and as a body of scientific knowledge and scientific methods by which social progress could be achieved through peaceful means. Reformers built upon and indeed entertained symbiotic relationships with the equally expanding field of social statistics, which provided the necessary data and helped to create categories like "unemployment" as a precondition for the creation of models for successful intervention.[37]

An important venue for this approach and the major testing ground for some of the ideas and practices that later came to characterize the ILO was the International Association for Labour Legislation (IALL), founded in 1900. The IALL

34 Reinalda, *Routledge History of International Organizations*,167.

35 Van Daele, "Engineering Social Peace: Networks, Ideas and the Founding of the International Labour Organization", *International Review of Social History* 50 (2005): 435–466, here 439–442; Follows, *Antecedents of the International Labour Organization*, 70–119.

36 Michel Dreyfus, "The Emergence of an International Trade Union Organization (1902–1919)", in *The International Confederation of Free Trade Unions*, ed. Anthony Carew et al. (Bern: Peter Lang, 2000), 27–71.

37 The broader background was provided by what the historian Lutz Raphael has called the "scientization of the social". Lutz Raphael, "Die Verwissenschaftlichung des Sozialen als methodische und konzeptionelle Herausforderung für eine Sozialgeschichte des 20. Jahrhunderts", *Geschichte und Gesellschaft* 22, no. 2 (1996): 165–93.

constituted, first and foremost, an umbrella organization for the different groups of reformers united by the common goal of transforming society by means of legal intervention. Social liberals like the Belgian law professor Ernest Mahaim or the German political economist Lujo Brentano were most influential. But the association also appealed to representatives of the social Christian (Catholic) doctrine as well as to the reformist wing of the Second International and parts of the international trade union movement.[38]

The IALL was in many respects a typical representative of late nineteenth-century internationalism. It was no coincidence that the association was founded in the wake of the Paris World Fair of 1900, an exposition that was in itself a quintessential expression of the internationalist spirit of the age, situated as it was between the ideals of peace, progress, and cooperation among states and peoples on the one hand side and a world of competing empires and nation states on the other.[39] Equally characteristic was the specific mixture of private initiative and government involvement that defined the work of the IALL and that could be found in similar constellations in other internationalist undertakings of the age such as the International Red Cross movement.[40] Even though the IALL was a private association and its members consisted mainly of academics – university professors at law and economics faculties – the nation state was its primary point of reference from the start. The IALL and its permanent secretariat, the International Labour Office, founded 1901 in Basel, were financed through the contributions of its national sections. The members of these sections also occupied the double role of experts and representatives of their respective countries. Civil servants from the fledgling social administrations of European countries – such as Arthur Fontaine, French Director of the *Office du Travail* from 1899 to 1920 – played a prominent role.[41] This added weight to national sections from major industrial countries, like the German *Gesellschaft für Soziale Reform* or the American Association for Labor Legislation, and made the IALL a place where different models of social reform competed with each other. Most importantly, the association's major aim and its *raison d'être* – the international dissemina-

38 Van Daele, "Engineering Social Peace", 442–446; Kott, "From Transnational Reformist Network to International Organization"; Alcock, *History of the International Labor Organization*, 239–246; Bruno Cabanes, *The Great War and the Origins of Humanitarianism*, 86–89.

39 Geyer and Paulmann, *The Mechanics of Internationalism. Culture, Society, and Politics from the 1840s to the First World War*; Sebastian Conrad and Dominic Sachsenmaier, eds., *Competing Visions of World Order: Global Moments and Movements, 1880–1930* (New York: Palgrave Macmillan, 2007); Sluga, *Internationalism in the Age of Nationalism*.

40 John F. Hutchinson, "Rethinking the Origins of the Red Cross", *Bulletin for the History of Medicine* 63, no. 4 (1989): 557–578.

41 On Fontaine, see Cabanes, *The Great War and the Origins of Humanitarianism*, 87–88.

tion and application of labor law – rested upon the ability of the association to convince national governments to take action at home and internationally. In order to achieve this goal, the Basel Office maintained relations between its national sections and among reformers in a broader sense, collected information, and promoted the study and harmonization of labour law through its own publications. Its work overlapped with several other international institutions, such as the Permanent Committee for Social Insurance or the International Association for the Prevention of Unemployment, as well as social statistics associations in many countries. They all belonged to the same broad reformist internationalist milieu and provided the input for the IALL's work.

At the heart of the IALL's activities lay the effort to establish international labour conventions. Before 1914, the Association was successful in two cases, chosen deliberately for their symbolic value and because they touched on issues that already commanded a high level of agreement. The first one was a convention prohibiting the use of white phosphorus in the manufacture of matches, adopted in 1906, which brought the long struggle against one of the most infamous industrial poisons to a conclusion. It stood for the broader fight against hazardous conditions at the workplace, which was regarded as emblematic for an unregulated exploitative capitalism and which had long mobilized the labour movement and public opinion in many countries.

The other example, a convention on the prohibition of night work for women, could count on broad support, because it appealed to liberal and conservative governments alike. In addition, it could count on the support of the socialist movement, which, during the 1890s, had also come around in favour of special protection for women workers. After the breakthrough in these two areas, further conventions were envisaged. In 1913, a new conference discussed an instrument that would have prohibited night work for children under the age of fourteen. Another planned convention concerned the reduction of working hours for women and young persons to 10 hours a day, thus addressing demands of the trade union movement.[42] However, before a diplomatic conference scheduled for September 1914 could adopt these new instruments, the war broke out.[43]

Conventions were not the only legacy the IALL left to the ILO. Significant personal lines of continuity connected the IALL and the ILO. A majority of the members of the Commission on International Labour Legislation (Labour Commission) at the Peace Conference in Paris that would work on the contours of the

42 Stephan Bauer, "International Labor Legislation and the Society of Nations", *Bulletin of the United States Bureau of Labor Statistics*, Washington, DC: Government Printing Office, 1919, No. 254, 134.
43 Reinalda, *Routledge History of International Organizations*, 162–177, here 169.

future ILO knew each other through the IALL. Some of its protagonists would later work for the ILO: Arthur Fontaine, as Chairman of the ILO's Governing Body from 1919 to 1931, and Albert Thomas, the ILO's first Director, were but two prominent examples. Maybe an even more important asset that the IALL passed on to the ILO was the mechanisms it had developed and tested for the creation of international social legislation in cooperation with national governments. Hard won experiences in identifying and promoting issues that would win the support of a critical mass of governments in adopting international standards and in getting those standards implemented provided a valuable body of information both to the Labour Commission in Paris and the later ILO. This was particularly relevant with a view to the setbacks which the IALL had suffered with regard to the conventions on white phosphorus and on the night work of women. Although they were relatively uncontroversial, some nations were reluctant and others simply not willing to implement them. But it was no small accomplishment that the IALL had benefitted from the growing participation of reformist trade unionists and a number of progressive industrialists, which broadened the association's political influence and made it appear, especially in the years before the war, as "both an epistemic community and a tripartite organization in the making".[44]

The First World War

At the beginning of the First World War, the initiative shifted. Now, the international trade union movement began to take on a much more important role in the promotion of international social policy.[45] While trade unionists in many European countries had taken an active part within the IALL's national sections in the years preceding the war, the same could hardly be said about the international trade union movement as such. Its most important representation was the International Secretariat, founded in 1901 and located in Berlin, which was renamed International Federation of Trade Unions (IFTU) in 1913.[46] The International Secretariat was a rather loose association of mainly socialist and syndicalist national trade union federations. While it was generally appreciative of the IALL's work and the concept of international social policy in general, it did not support it directly. One of the reasons for the lack of support was the mainly middle-class,

44 Kott, "From Transnational Reformist Network to International Organization", 244.
45 Reiner Tosstorff, "The International Trade Union Movement and the Foundation of the International Labour Organization", *International Review of Social History* 50, no. 3 (2005): 399–433.
46 On the IFTU, see Geert van Goethem, *The Amsterdam International*: The World of the Intenational Fedeation of Trade Unions (IFTU), 1913–1945 (Aldershot: Ashgate Publishing, 2006).

bourgeois, and politically liberal character of the IALL. Even more important was that many of the IFTU's members, in particular the powerful German Trade Union Federation, opted for a division of labour between trade union and political work, the latter being regarded as the realm of the Socialist International and the national Socialist Parties. The American Federation of Labor (AFL), which joined the IFTU in 1909, in turn represented yet another, "voluntarist", concept of trade unionism and was highly apprehensive of any kind of involvement with state or political party politics. There were many reasons, why the IALL and the IFTU kept at friendly distance from each other. That changed with the outbreak of the war.[47]

The first effect of the war was that the IFTU split along national lines, and the trade union federations sided with their respective governments, with the federations from neutral countries from Scandinavia or Switzerland torn between the two sides of the conflict. While the IFTU's secretariat remained in Berlin, the associations from the Allied countries began to build up parallel structures. Against this background, the idea of international social policy and the project of establishing an international organization to pursue it on behalf of workers' interests moved on top of the agenda for a post-war settlement. The reasons were manifold: The necessities of war production and the aim to mobilize the support of the workers' movement for the war and to avoid strikes and social unrest put trade unions in a position of relative strength. In many countries, reformist trade union leaders and socialist politicians moved into responsible positions. In Great Britain, George Barnes, a former trade unionist and Labour politician, became Minister of Pensions in the government of David Lloyd George. In France, Albert Thomas, a reformist socialist and disciple of Jean Jaurès, became Minister of Artillery and Munitions. On the side of the Central Powers, trade unionists like Carl Legien, head of the Social Democrat *Generalkommission der Gewerkschaften Deutschlands*[48] and President of the IFTU, and his Austrian counterpart closed ranks with their governments at war.[49]

Common to all was the expectation that workers' participation in the war came at a price, and that labour would want to be heard in return during the negotiations of a future peace treaty. In 1916, trade union representatives from the Entente countries of France, Great Britain, and Italy, as well as from German-occupied Belgium, met in Leeds in order to discuss labour's demands for a future peace order.[50]

---

47 Dreyfus, "The Emergence of an International Trade Union Organization (1902–1919)".
48 The *Generalkommission* was the predecessor to the *Allgemeiner Deutscher Gewerkschaftsbund*, which was founded after the end of the war.
49 Tosstorff, "The International Trade Union Movement and the Foundation of the International Labour Organization", 402.
50 Ibid., 402–408.

The Leeds Programme was the first international trade union document that publicly endorsed both the concept of international labour legislation and the work of the IALL. It contained a list of measures for international regulation with regard to freedom of association, social insurance, hours of work, factory inspection, occupational health, and labour migration. The Leeds Programme also proposed the establishment of an international commission that would prepare a governmental conference to carry out this programme and to strengthen the role of the IALL's Basel Office, with the declared goal of putting it in a position where it could effectively monitor the adherence of governments to the agreed-upon standards. Intended partly as a challenge to the German-led IFTU office in Berlin, the Leeds Programme caused an immediate reaction from Legien, who tried to regain control. Within a couple of months after Leeds, in February 1917, trade union federations from the Central Powers came up with a counterproposal, which essentially confirmed the international social policy parts of the Leeds document but argued for a significantly strengthened Basel International Labour Office, with permanent IFTU representation. This would have put the international trade union movement in a supervisory role with regard to the creation and implementation of international labour legislation. It also would have given this legislation a more binding character, since it would have obliged governments to directly apply the standards adopted by government conferences.

These proposals set the stage for the international trade union movement to push, once the war was over, for international labour legislation and a strengthened International Labour Office in Basel to oversee and put in effect this legislation. When it came to the implementation of this programme however, the situation had already changed significantly. Firstly, the American entry into the war in April 1917 gave more importance to the AFL's views on international trade union matters. Within the Allied camp, it soon became clear that the Americans were not only skeptical of the socialist leanings of most of the other IFTU members, but they strongly opposed all proposals that placed too much emphasis on state intervention. Later on in the year, the Bolshevik takeover in Russia threatened trade union unity from yet another angle, when it brought the anti-capitalist and revolutionary option to the fore. During the last year of the war, and the closer the conflict came to a close, governments once again began to reassert their primacy in negotiating peace and constructing the international order of the post-war era. Against this background, trade unions remained observant but increasingly took a back seat in the discussions of international social policy.[51]

51 Ibid.

The Labour Commission in Paris

When the war entered its last year, the preparations for the peace began in earnest. On 8 January 1918, President Woodrow Wilson addressed Congress on the war aims of the United States. In the last of his "Fourteen Points", in which Wilson outlined his ideas of a durable peace based on a new diplomacy, he called for a "general association of nations" to be formed as part of a future peace treaty. Although Wilson did not make any specific mention of labour or social issues, other governments' considerations about a future "League of Nations" soon connected it to the ongoing debate on the place of international social policy in the post-war order. When the hostilities eventually ceased in November 1918, the preparations for the creation of an international labour organization were already well under way.[52]

France, which had been first in creating a committee as early as 1917 to work on proposals for the social policy clauses of a future peace treaty, was among those who tried to bring their ideas in line with Wilson's principles. However, the work of the committee, in which members of the French IALL section occupied the key positions, was still ongoing when the armistice was declared in November 1918.[53] The Germans, by contrast, who had shown no particular interest in the matter for a long time, were quick to incorporate social policy demands into their peace agenda once the liberal government of Max von Baden had taken over in the face of a looming German military breakdown.[54]

Among the major war powers, however, it was in Britain that planning was by far the most advanced. This was one of the reasons why the British delegation became the decisive force behind the creation of an international labour commission and of many of the major features of the future ILO. The British government had two major reasons to be supportive of an international organization. First, as Europe's leading industrial power, it had a genuine interest in international social

52 On the preparations for the League of Nations see Mazower, *Governing the World*, 116–153.
53 In France, committees were set up to deal with the questions of labour conditions, wages, food rationing, etc. Representatives of the *Confédération générale du travail* (General Federation of Labour–CGT) and management participated in these commissions. In reaction to a wave of strikes in the armament industry in the winter of 1916–1917, Albert Thomas, Minister of Artillery and Munitions and later the first Director of the ILO, issued, among other measures, a decree to set up state-led joint arbitration commissions to solve industrial conflicts. Petra Weber, *Gescheiterte Sozialpartnerschaft – Gefährdete Republik? Industrielle Beziehungen, Arbeitskämpfe und der Sozialstaat. Deutschland und Frankreich im Vergleich (1918–1933/39)* (Munich: Oldenbourg, 2010), 140.
54 Tosstorff, "The International Trade Union Movement and the Foundation of the International Labour Organization", 415.

legislation. In order to maintain its high standard once economic competition was restored, it was necessary that standards were applied to other competitors as well. The second reason was political. As in other leading nations, in Britain, the trade union movement had been closely incorporated into the war effort. Through the so-called Whitley councils, industry-based bipartite institutions had been created during the war, in which employers' and workers' representatives met on an equal footing.[55] There was a broad political consensus that the contribution which the trade union movement had made during the war would have to be rewarded in the post-war period by meeting some of its demands.

Against this backdrop, a small group of British officials began to work on a proposal for the future labour organization which would be presented at the peace negotiations. Three individuals became of particular importance in this regard, two of which would later serve as heads of the ILO: Harold Butler (ILO Director, 1931–1938), then an official in the Ministry of Labour who was working on plans for the state's long-term labour policies; and Edward Phelan (ILO Director-General, 1941–1948), an Irishman and member of the Intelligence Section of the Ministry of Labour, who was tasked with monitoring trends in the labour sector.[56] The third official was Malcolm Delevigne of the Home Office, who had been a representative of the British government at several IALL conferences and was in close contact with other IALL members. It was mainly Phelan who authored various memoranda that would become the main bases for debate in Paris. Since the other powers were far behind in their preparations, the British draft gained additional weight. In its latest version, which had already incorporated the results of consultations with other Allied powers, two items stood out: The British draft strongly argued for the establishment of an international labour *organization* rather than the IALL model of only occasional conferences and in contrast to the alternative idea of merely incorporating a set of labour standards in the overall peace treaty. Another important proposal was that the new organization would be tripartite and would thus bring together governments, trade unions and employers to decide together on the adoption of international labour standards.[57]

When the delegates to the Paris Peace Conference took up their work on 18 January 1919, they placed "international labour legislation" on the agenda of

---

55 Olga Hidalgo-Weber, "Social and Political Networks and the Creation of the ILO: The Role of British Actors", in *Globalizing Social Rights*, ed. Kott and Droux, 17–31.
56 ILO, *Edward Phelan and the ILO: The Life and Views of an International Social Actor* (Geneva: ILO, 2009).
57 Hidalgo-Weber, "Social and Political Networks and the Creation of the ILO: The Role of British Actors."

their first meeting. Great Britain proposed to set up a special commission to work out a binding agreement on the creation of a future organization as part of the peace treaty. An agreement was reached after the United States pointed out that it wanted the new organization to become part of the League of Nations, which was yet to be founded during the peace talks. Only two weeks later, on 31 January 1919, the members of the commission were appointed, and the next day it took up its work.

The Labour Commission conferred for about two months (1 February–24 March 1919). Its 15 members, who were appointed both as national representatives and as experts, comprised two delegates each from the Big Four – the United States, Great Britain, France, and Italy – as well as Japan and Belgium.[58] The remaining three seats were granted to Cuba and two other European countries of "chief industrial importance" – the newly established Czechoslovakia and Poland. Most of the members of the commission were social reformist academics, a majority of whom were lawyers with liberal or moderate socialist political leanings. Almost all of the members had been linked in one way or another to the IALL. The Commission also included a handful of politicians or higher civil servants like Arthur Fontaine, but counted only two trade unionists – Samuel Gompers, the president of the AFL, and Leon Jouhaux, the leader of the French CGT – and a single employers' representative among its members and advisers.[59] Gompers' position, however, was elevated by the fact that he was elected chairman. His choice was first and foremost a gesture to Wilson and the United States, but it was surely also meant as an attempt to neutralize his opposition to the very task that the Commission was set to accomplish in the minds of the overwhelming majority of its members and the governments that had nominated them: the creation of a permanent tripartite organization that would define, adopt, and promote international labour legislation. Even though Gompers, in the end, went along with the majority opinion, the main dividing line in the Commission ran between the chairman and the rest of its members, with occasionally shifting alliances on various questions of detail. Instrumental as brokers of compromises between the varying camps were the two Belgian delegates, the social scientist and jurist Ernest Mahaim, and the reformist socialist Emil Vandervelde.[60] Another key player was the second US delegate, the historian and director of research of the Carnegie Endowment for Peace, James T. Shotwell. Before the war, Shotwell

58 Van Daele, "Engineering Social Peace", 449.
59 This representative was Henry Mauris Robinson, a banker from California and a member of the US Council of National Defense; however, Robinson hardly attended any of the meetings. H. B. Butler, *Confident Morning* (London: Faber and Faber, 1950), 165; ILO, *Edward Phelan and the ILO.*
60 Van Daele, "Engineering Social Peace".

had been associated with the US section of the IALL, and he helped to ease the frictions between Gompers and the other members. He would become a lifelong supporter of the ILO.[61]

Gompers' opposition to an organization in which governments would gain a major influence shaped the discussion on the question of representation within the envisaged tripartite framework. The British memorandum proposed to give governments a double representation vis-à-vis that of workers and employers (2-1-1). Gompers, who predicted that, under such an arrangement, governments and employers combined would outvote workers, pleaded for equal representation (1-1-1). The British view prevailed by a slim margin, because the majority of the Commission, in line with the IALL tradition, thought that strong government representation was inevitable if the future organization's decisions should carry any weight. In practice, most agreed, it would be the national governments that, in the end, would have to implement these decisions in practical politics.[62]

Much of the substance of the discussion concerned the legal status of the future organization's labour standards. The core question was: How binding would those standards be for the governments? Would the organization function as a "world parliament of labour" whose decisions on labour standards would become national law without additional intermediary steps. This solution, favoured by the French, British, and Italian delegations, would have been a revolutionary one and a fundamental break with the pre-war practice. The compromise that was found after long debate was based on the distinction between voluntarily ratified Conventions, which became binding only after their ratification, and non-binding Recommendations. The ratification of Conventions would come with an obligation to translate them into national law and to periodically report on the progress made towards their application. The other form of standards, the Recommendations, were in turn designed as non-binding guidelines, which may or may not be linked to a Convention. The US delegates, which opposed binding instruments, found themselves once again in a minority position, this time not only because of Gompers' anti-statist inclinations, but also because of the political structure of the United States as a federal republic, where social legislation was predominantly the domain of its individual states. This issue has remained a stumbling block in the US relationship with norm-creating international institutions, including the

61 Harold Josephson, *James T. Shotwell and the Rise of Internationalism in America* (Rutherford, NJ: Fairleigh Dickinson University Press, 1974).

62 On this and other discussions in the Labour Commission, see Alcock, *History of the International Labor Organization*; James T. Shotwell, "The International Labor Organization as an Alternative to Violent Revolution" *Annals of the American Academy of polical and Social Science* (1933): 18–25; Van Daele, "Engineering Social Peace".

ILO, ever since. In the end, the compromise that was found allowed the United States and other federal states to treat Conventions like Recommendations for the purpose of legislation by their individual states.[63] The shared aim to secure the states' participation in the new organization and, accordingly, to refrain from building hurdles that were too high for them to join also influenced the debate on the question of sanctions. The compromises reached with regard to the filing of complaints and the use of economic sanctions against countries that did not fulfil their commitments were all of a relatively mild nature. After all, ratification of Conventions remained entirely voluntary, and if governments did not live up to their commitments after ratification, the ILO did not command any means other than persuasion to ensure their compliance.[64]

A politically controversial issue was the question of membership in the organization, which was closely connected to the yet to be defined relationship of the ILO to a future League of Nations. For an organization that would primarily exist to establish international labour standards, universality of membership – at least that of the major industrial powers – had to be an important goal. However, at the time when this issue was discussed in the Commission, several questions regarding League of Nations membership were still unresolved. The most important problems in this regard concerned Germany (and the other defeated nations) and Japan. It soon became clear that Germany and Austria would not be immediately admitted to the League. The socialist members of the Labour Commission, in particular, were highly critical of this attitude towards the new republican governments of these countries, whose trade unions were ready to rejoin their wartime opponents. Excluding the two major Central European industrial powers would have seriously compromised the significance of the new organization.

Many of the members of the Labour Commission therefore pleaded for immediate German membership. The Japanese case was a further argument for separating the discussion on ILO membership from that about the membership in the League. Japan was an emerging industrial power and had entered the negotiations in Paris with the declared aim to inscribe the principle of racial equality in the peace treaty. When it found its proposal rejected by a coalition of the Europeans and Americans, with Wilson as the major obstacle, its government

63 See Daniel P. Moynihan, "The United States and the International Labor Organisation, 1889-1934", PhD diss., Fletcher School of Law and Diplomacy, Medford, MA, 1960; James T. Shotwell, *The Origins of the International Labour Organization* (New York, 1934).

64 Until 1946, Article 33 of the Constitution provided that member States could take "economic measures" against each other, upon recommendation by an independent commission of inquiry. See Bernhard Boockmann, "The Ratification of ILO Conventions: A Failure Time Analysis", in *ZEW Discussion Papers*, ed. ZEW – Zentrum für Europäische Wirtschaftsforschung (2000) .

considered to not join the new international organizations. This would have been a serious blow with regard to the ILO, especially for British dominions like Australia and New Zealand, which considered Japan as a direct competitor in Asia. In light of this situation, it was not surprising that a majority of the Commission voted to separate League and ILO membership.[65]

When this and most other issues of form and structure had been resolved, the Commission turned to the vital question of a Labour Charter and a set of items that a new organization should prioritize with regard to its initial Conventions and Recommendations. Next to the various British drafts, the input for this Charter came from different sources. One was the IALL, which had started to collect support from the states even before the outbreak of the war for the creation of labour standards in specific areas. Another source was the international trade union movement's declarations of Leeds (1916) and Berne (1917). Another trade union conference in Berne in February 1919, which took place in parallel to the meetings of the Commission, confirmed the major demands of these documents. In fact, one of the motivations of the Entente powers for including trade unionists and their demands in the work of the Labour Commission was to prevent the trade unions – including those from Germany and Austria – from holding a parallel trade union conference at the time of the peace negotiations.[66]

The decision about the principles that should be incorporated in the final document lay with the Labour Commission. For the trade unions, they clearly were of capital importance, because without a statement of core principles, the Constitution would merely consist of procedures without any content. For some government representatives, these claims rather belonged to the realm of rhetoric. After lengthy discussion and consultations among its members and the respective state governments, the Commission finally came up with nine core principles and a preamble, which reflected both the tradition of international social legislation of the nineteenth century and the caesura of the war.

The preamble opened with the proclamation that "universal and lasting peace can be established only if it is based on social justice". The subsequent text did not contain a more specific definition of what social justice entailed. The first of the following set of principles, however, gave an indication, when it asserted that "labour is not merely a commodity". In a nutshell, this phrase incapsulated the liberal social premises on which the ILO rested. "Labour is not a commodity" was part of a minimum consensus among the ILO's founders, who realized

65 Alcock, *History of the International Labor Organization*, 31.
66 Tosstorff, "The International Trade Union Movement and the Foundation of the International Labour Organization", 418–420.

that the survival of open market economies ultimately depended on the gradual de-commodification of labour[67] – a consensus enforced to a large degree by the revolutionary threat posed by the Russian October revolution.[68] The second point proclaimed a "right of association for all lawful purposes" for not only workers but also for employers. This was a confirmation of basic trade union freedoms and a significant gesture towards the labour movement. Yet, the understanding of what exactly were regarded as "lawful purposes" was left to the discretion of national governments. What this point reflected, first and foremost, was the fact that certain trade union activities, in particular strikes, were far from being considered generally accepted means of action.

The next three points, which called for an eight-hour working day and a 48-hour work week, a weekly rest time of at least 24 hours and wage policies that would allow workers to maintain a "reasonable" living standard were, by comparison, all responding to long-standing trade union demands. Point six, which called for the abolition of child labour and the "limitation on the labour of young persons" was following up directly on the pre-war activities of the IALL and brought to a conclusion the struggles of social reformers since the latter part of the nineteenth century. To a certain degree, this was also true for the eighth point, which called for equal treatment of migrant workers in their countries of residence; it created an international platform for an area in which hitherto only a number of bilateral agreements existed.[69] The principle of "equal remuneration for work of equal value" for men and women, by contrast, was a remarkable departure from the past and can be credited to the intense lobbying efforts from women's rights groups around the Paris Peace Conference. Even though it was put in the most general terms possible, and therefore left much room for interpretation with regard to its practical implications, the fact that the principle featured at all, was nothing less than revolutionary and provided a basis for future debates. Further indication for a change in the perception of the role of women

67 The term "de-commodification" is of a more recent age. It goes back to Karl Polanyi and has been popularized in the 1990s by sociologist Gøsta Esping-Andersen. It refers to social entitlements to reduce the exposure of workers to market forces and the resulting economy insecurity. Gøsta Esping-Andersen, *The Three Worlds of Welfare Capitalism* (Princeton, NJ: Princeton University Press, 1990).

68 On the origins of the term, see Paul O'Higgins, " 'Labour Is Not a Commodity' – An Irish Contribution to International Labour Law", *Industrial Law Journal* 26 (1997): 225–234; Stein Evju, "Labour is not a Commodity. Reappraising the Origins of the Maxim", *European Labour Law Journal* 4 (2013): 222–229.

69 Reinalda, *Routledge History of International Organizations*, 167.

was given by the last point, which called for the installation in all countries of public systems of labour inspection "in which women should take part".[70]

All principles and the preamble were incorporated into part XIII of the Treaty of Versailles and included in all subsequent peace treaties. Altogether consisting of 41 articles, these sections would later become the first ILO Constitution. Despite this major achievement, the final outcome of the Labour Commission's work was not greeted with unanimous enthusiasm. The IFTU in particular, which reconstituted itself at a Congress in August 1919 in Amsterdam, was widely disappointed with the way in which the Labour Commission had left future international legislation to the discretion of the states at all stages of the process. The new "Amsterdam International" instead put emphasis on trade union unity and opened itself to German and Austrian membership.[71] Some governments joined the chorus of skeptics: Germany, which saw itself humiliated by the conditions of peace imposed by the victors at Versailles, was equally resentful towards the Labour Commission's decisions, in which it had had no say; nevertheless, it instantly tried to attain membership in the ILO. The most worrying voices came from the United States. Samuel Gompers had left Paris pledging to promote the new organization with all his authority back home. Yet, in light of the criticism of international rules potentially overriding national legislation, his defense of the ILO was at best half-hearted. What Gompers had sought to achieve was a Labour Charter, not an institution that would produce international legislation. At the same time, opposition to the outcome of the peace negotiations built up in Congress, and the United States did not ratify the Treaty of Versailles.[72]

As a result, and despite the groundwork having been done, much of the road towards a functioning international organization remained uncharted. What seemed the fulfillment of a long-held ambition for some of the IALL members of the Commission was, from another perspective, still a distant and nebulous goal.

---

70 The League of Nations, *Treaty of Versailles*, opened for signature June 28, 1919. Part XIII, Section II: *General Principles*. Article 427 is reproduced, for example, in Gerry Rodgers et al., *The International Labour Organization and the Quest for Social Justice, 1919–2009* (Ithaca, NY: Cornell University Press; Geneva: International Labour Office, 2009), 250–251.

71 See van Goethem, *The Amsterdam International*.

72 Ibid., ch. 6: Isolationism or Leadership. The American Federation of Labor and the International Federation of Trade Unions; Moynihan, "The United States and the International Labor Organisation".

Part I An Experiment in Social Justice: 1919–1939

Thus, inequality in labour conditions seems itself to mean a possibility of international discord, and it is our duty to try to find some solution. Both our Constitution and the nature of work therefore require us to try to introduce into the world certain of the conditions necessary for peace.

Albert Thomas in a letter to the *Maison du Peuple*, Brussels, 22 April 1929[73]

73 Albert Thomas, *International Social Policy*, trans. Monica Curtis (Geneva: ILO, 1948), 140.

https://doi.org/10.1515/9783110650723-partI

1 Beginnings

After the Paris Peace Conference, the International Labour Organization (ILO) got down to work. Much of what happened during its first years was in many aspects unprecedented and unchartered territory. An international bureaucracy had to be built up from scratch, and the position of the ILO with regard to the scope of its work, and its position in the new world order emerging from the war, had yet to be defined. In order to secure the survival of the Organization in the volatile international environment of the post-war era, Albert Thomas, the ILO's first Director, interpreted his role in a diplomatic and political, as well as in a technocratic, way. He set out to position the ILO within a broad network of social actors beyond its immediate tripartite constituents.

Despite the outwardly universal language of its Constitution, one question accompanied the ILO from the very first day: whose organization, exactly, would and could it be; and what kinds of workers and what forms of work would it represent? Both geographically and with regard to the problems it addressed, the ILO was far from being an organization that covered all the global realities of work but rather started from a clear European and industrial bias.

The Washington Conference

Events taking place in the months following the end of the Paris Peace Conference renewed the sense of urgency that had carried the foundation of the ILO. Revolution, civil strife, and the plight of hundreds of thousands of refugees had left vast parts of Europe a social and political powder keg. The Bolshevik takeover in Russia and like-minded revolutionary upheavals in Hungary, Germany, and other European countries provided a tangible alternative to social and political reform, stirring up fears of a complete political and economic meltdown. The demobilization of millions of soldiers, many of them mutilated and traumatized, and the return of staggering numbers of prisoners of war added to these fears. Massive unemployment, strikes, and social unrest became almost inevitable consequences of the transition from a war to a peace economy. Against this backdrop, governments, trade unions, and employers from 42 nations now set out to implement the decisions of the peace conference and make the ILO become a reality.

The decision to hold the first Session of the International Labour Conference (ILC) in Washington, D.C., was motivated by the desire to secure the continued American interest in, and cooperation with, the ILO; this hope, however, was soon dashed. Upon their arrival in the capital of the United States in late

https://doi.org/10.1515/9783110650723-003

October 1919, the conveners quickly realized that they could hardly have found a less welcoming environment for the Organization's constituting Conference. After his return from Paris, President Wilson had suffered a severe stroke, which further diminished his ability to influence the discussion. Only days before the meeting, the budget for the Conference was still not secure. Provisional offices could be found only after an intervention by the then Assistant Secretary of the Navy, Franklin Delano Roosevelt. In Congress, arriving European delegates were denounced as trouble-rousers, and when it was eventually decided to let the ILC take place, it did so only under the explicit condition that no US commitments as to future membership would be made.[74]

Figure 1: First International Labour Conference, Washington, D.C., United States, 1919.

The meeting eventually started on 29 October, with 40 delegations present. The most urgent matter to be settled was the unresolved status of the former Central Powers, Austria and Germany. The International Federation of Trade Unions (IFTU), with which the majority of the Workers' representatives at the Washington Conference were affiliated, had made it a condition of their participation that the Organization would be open to all nations. The Supreme War Council, which was consulted by the government delegates from the Allied Powers, agreed that it would be up to the Conference to decide on the question of German and Aus-

74 Alcock, *History of the International Labor Organization*, 38.

trian membership. It eventually did so by nearly unanimous vote, although this decision came too late to actually allow German and Austrian representatives to participate in the Conference. However, it paved the way for their future membership in the ILO – in sharp contrast to the League, which would deny Germany membership for another seven years.[75]

The Conference further confirmed the composition of the Governing Body as the executive organ of the ILO, with eight of the 12 government seats assigned to countries of "major industrial importance" – Great Britain, France, Italy, Germany, Japan, Belgium, Switzerland, and Denmark (substituting for the United States) – and four seats allocated to Argentina, Spain, Poland, and Canada, respectively, as representatives of the "other" countries. Even though over half of the delegations came from outside Europe, the composition of the Governing Body clearly reflected the existing power relations. A strong European bias permeated all groups – governments, workers, and employers alike, which drew some critical comments already in Washington. The election of Arthur Fontaine, who embodied the traditions of the International Association for Labour Legislation (IALL) as the first Chairman of the Governing Body, in turn, reflected the strengthened position of France.[76]

Once the Governing Body had been established, it decided to elect not only its Chairman but also the Director of the International Labour Office. To the surprise of many observers, the choice fell on another Frenchman: Albert Thomas. From the beginning, Harold Butler had been regarded the frontrunner; as a British citizen, he seemed to have a natural claim to the position after the French had already been given the top post in the Governing Body. However, Butler, a government official, lacked the connection to both the trade union and socialist movements, as well as to the social reformist network around the IALL, which Thomas, whose name was brought forward by the Workers' group, had in abundance.[77]

Albert Thomas had been a leading member of the French Socialist Party (SFIO) since 1905. As a representative of the party's reformist wing, he had been a supporter of the *Union Sacrée*, joined the French war government under Raymond Poincaré in 1915, and became Minister for Artillery and Munitions one year later.

75 Ibid., 38–39.

76 Ibid., 41–42.

77 Among the rich literature on Albert Thomas, on his ILO years, see in particular Denis Guérin, *Albert Thomas au BIT, 1920–1932: De l'internationalisme à l'Europe*, Euryopa Etudes (Geneva: Institut européen de l'Université de Genève, 1996); Jean-Michel Guieu, "Albert Thomas et la paix. Du socialisme normalien à l'action internationale au Bit", *Les cahiers Irice* no. 2 (2008), 65–80. On his role in the war, Adeline Blaskiewicz-Maison, *Albert Thomas. Le socialisme en guerre 1914–1918* (Rennes: Presses Universitaires de Rennes, 2016).

In this position, which he held until 1917, he worked closely and mostly successfully with both industrialists and trade unions to secure wartime production. This was a valuable practical experience with tripartism. Although he had not been a member of the Labour Commission in Paris, nor in any other way involved in the creation of the ILO (he had not been present at the Washington, either), his candidacy was no coincidence. He was the very personification of class cooperation: a moderate socialist, anti-revolutionary, close to the international trade union movement and the cooperative world, and, thanks to his wartime activities and his long-standing connection with the IALL, an acceptable candidate for most governments and employers as well. Still, as the British were not prepared to concede the position, a vote had to be taken, which Thomas won after two rounds and by a very narrow margin. That way, he started his first term as the first Director of the ILO, a post he would occupy until his death in 1932, from a somewhat weak position. Few might have imagined the great imprint he would leave on the Organization.[78]

An International Organization in the Making

Virtually everything was new when the International Labour Office started its work. Premises had to be found, staff had to be hired, and work had to be organized. To secure the survival of the fledgling organization, to stake out and, if possible, expand its areas of activity were the primary tasks during the ILO's first decade.

The Governing Body confirmed Thomas as Director at its first regular meeting on 20 January 1920. Next, practical matters had to be settled. An immediate question was where the Organization would take up its headquarters. Article 7 of the Treaty of Versailles had designated Geneva as the headquarters of the League of Nations. This implied that the ILO should be in the same place. In June 1920, the ILO rented its first premises in La Châtelaine (Pregny) on the northern side of Lake Geneva, before moving into a new building at the lake shore, built for that purpose in 1926. This building would become the ILO's official headquarters for almost 50 years (1926–1974) until the need for more space led to the construction of the current Office building in Geneva. The old premises, with their

78 In the second round, the appointment of a "provisional director" was put to the vote. The result was: "Mr. ALBERT THOMAS, 11 votes; Mr. Butler, 9 votes; blank votes, 1". See ILO, Minutes of the Governing Body, 1st Session, Geneva, 1919, 3.

labour-themed murals, became the seat of the General Agreement on Tariffs and Trade (GATT) and later of the World Trade Organization (WTO).[79]

Within a new post–world war order emerging from the peace conferences, the ILO found itself in a highly volatile environment. Not only had the United States declined to become a member, but an increasing group of countries in- and outside the Organization downright challenged the post-Versailles order. Consequently, it was crucial to tie the remaining allies closely to the Organization. Smaller nations appreciated the legitimacy they gained through participation in an international forum like the ILO. But neither France nor Great Britain, the two most important member countries, initially showed any enthusiasm for the new organization. On the contrary, the conservative government of Great Britain regarded the ILO with a great deal of scepticism, suspecting to compromise the sovereignty of its Empire.[80] The relationship with France was not any easier, despite the strong position French nationals occupied at all levels of the Organization and the close relationship Thomas maintained with French government circles. In fact, concerns that the ILO might encroach upon national sovereignty had grown strong in Paris, too, and the French government was initially in the forefront of countries that tried to restrict and curtail the ILO's competences. French opposition to the ILO's attempts to expand its standard-setting to agricultural work ultimately led Thomas to bring the case to the Permanent Court of International Justice, which, in 1922, confirmed the ILO's competence in agricultural matters.[81]

This lent support to Thomas' view that the ILO had to demonstrate its usefulness to governments in order to secure the success and even the survival of the organization. His strategy was both diplomatic and technocratic in nature. On the one hand, he continuously tried to promote the idea of international labour standards through direct contacts with political authorities, but also by creating broader networks that could help to influence public opinion and put some degree of pressure on national governments. He therefore tried to strengthen the reformist trade unions and win the support of "modern" employers who had a certain awareness of social issues. Other groups whose support he courted included the cooperative movement, social reformist networks inside and outside academia,

---

79 The buildings, which had served as a boarding school for young women before the Office moved there, today house the headquarters of the International Committee of the Red Cross.

80 Hidalgo-Weber, "Dimensions transnationales des politiques sociales britanniques".

81 The International Court of Justice also decided in favour of expanding the ILO's competences in other matters, for example with regard to questions of productivity in industry. See Nicolas Valticos, *International Labour Law* (Deventer: Kluwer, 1979), 39–41; on Thomas' relationships with France, see Cabanes, *The Great War and the Origins of Humanitarianism*; Guieu, "Albert Thomas et la paix", 75–76.

civil society organizations, and religious groups, most prominently the Catholic trade unions and the Vatican itself.

A central issue during the extensive travels of Thomas and other ILO officials all across Europe, parts of Asia, the United States, and Latin America during the 1920s was the slow pace of ratifications of the ILO's Conventions. Thomas himself would in 1930 refer to his own role as that of a "traveling salesman of social policy".[82]

Travel diplomacy alone, however, was not enough to secure the ILO's survival. It needed to demonstrate its usefulness – not through standard-setting alone, but also in providing its members with a comprehensive pool of information and comparative analysis of social policy measures taken by different countries. In his own words, Thomas wanted the ILO to become nothing less than "the great clearing house for information on social questions world wide".[83] From the IALL and its Basel Office, the Organization had inherited mechanisms to collect and process data on working conditions and labour legislation which it institutionalized and expanded during the interwar years under the umbrella of a specific Scientific (later Research) Division. It included a statistical unit, which over the years became a department. It has convened since 1923 regular International Conferences of Labour Statisticians. The ILO could thus provide to governments, trade unions, and employers' organizations valuable statistical information, expert knowledge, and best practices, which they would not have been able to find elsewhere. This allowed for the first time a comparative analysis of international social policy practices. Research was a necessary first step for the development of new labour standards. It also had a diplomatic function since it gave an opportunity to reach out to non-members, such as the United States, Mexico (a member since 1931), and Soviet Russia (later the Soviet Union), for which a separate "Russian Section" was created as early as 1920.[84]

When a deep economic crisis hit Europe and other parts of the world in the immediate aftermath of the First World War, the ILO could first demonstrate its capacity to help governments to better understand the social impact of the economic downturn and to provide information on measures taken in other coun-

---

82 On his travels in Europe, see Dorothea Hoehtker and Sandrine Kott, eds., *À la rencontre de l'Europe au travail. Récits de voyages d'Albert Thomas* (Paris: Publications de la Sorbonne; Geneva: ILO, 2015); Sylvie Massart, "Les Voyages d'Albert Thomas Directeur du BIT (1919–1932)", Master's thesis, Université Paris-I, Sorbonne, 1993. The quotation from Cabanes, *The Great War and the Origins of Humanitarianism*, 112.

83 Albert Thomas, Address to the Reichstag, Berlin, 29 March 1930.

84 Charles Prince, "The U.S.S.R. and International Organizations", *The American Journal of International Law* 36, no. 3 (July 1942): 425–445.

tries to overcome its consequences. This also raised awareness of the transnational character of the crisis and the unemployment problem.[85] One example of this kind of work was the Technical Commission on Unemployment, established by the Washington Conference, which until 1924 undertook a broad investigation of the employment situation in ILO member States and some non-member countries (most prominently the United States). Reports on social insurance, working conditions, and living standards further enhanced the ILO's reputation as a "social library" – a depository of publications in the social field and a "locus of expertise and authority on social regulation".[86]

These activities belonged to the "technical functions" which the ILO had inherited from the IALL. They were particularly helpful in building and maintaining a constituency among its smaller member States. Especially in Eastern and Central Europe, new nation states like Poland and Czechoslovakia, products of the Paris peace treaties and the dissolution of the defeated Austro-Hungarian, Russian, and German empires, looked for help to create unified social legislation out of different national traditions.[87] Here, the ILO would also contribute to regional harmonization with regard to social policy and labour relations. A similar case could be made for the Nordic countries. While, for instance, trade unions in these countries had widely different approaches towards industrial conflict, the ILO provided a forum that helped to form a common model of the "Scandinavian class compromise", which emphasized collective bargaining and agreements negotiated between labour and business.[88] The ILO has triggered similar processes in other parts of the world through regional conferences, starting in the Americas in 1936 and spreading to Asia, Africa, and Europe after the Second World War. With regard to the establishment of the principles and practices of social insurance, the ILO apparently laid the foundation for a Western European "Social Model" during these early years.[89]

Within the diplomatic-technocratic framework provided by the ILO, Germany occupied a special position. Admitted to the ILO and awarded a permanent seat in the Governing Body as a country of "major industrial importance" by the 1919

85 Olivier Feiertag, "Reguler la mondialisation: Albert Thomas, les débuts du BIT et la crise économique mondiale de 1920–1923", *Les cahiers Irice*, no. 2 (2008), 127–155.

86 Cabanes, *The Great War and the Origins of Humanitarianism*, 125.

87 Natali Stegmann, "The ILO and East Central Europe. Insights into the Early Polish and Czechoslovak Interwar Years", *Acta Universitatis Carolinae. Studia Territorialia* no. 1 (2017), 11–34.

88 Pauli Kettunen, "The ILO as a Forum for Developing and Demonstrating a Nordic Model", in *Globalizing Social Rights*, ed. Kott and Droux, 210–230.

89 Sandrine Kott, "Constructing a European Social Model: The Fight for Social Insurance in the Inter-War Period", in *ILO Histories*, ed. Van Daele et al., 173–196.

Conference in Washington, D.C., Germany assumed an important role in the ILO from the start. Thomas, who spoke German, actively fostered this cooperation. In 1921, the ILO branch office in Berlin became the first one outside the former Allied countries. The next step was to fill strategic positions with officials from the German Ministry of Labour and other social institutions, in order to promote the internationalization of the "German model" of social insurance.[90]

For the government of the Weimar Republic, the cooperation with the ILO was important from a diplomatic point of view as well. Social policy had long served the German state as a "powerful affirmative instrument of national identity and international reputation", but the promotion of its "social model" – and in particular of its advanced system of social insurance – through the ILO offered Germany alternative diplomatic capital in a time of national weakness.[91]

The importance attached by the Office to strengthening relations with the ILO member States was reflected in the network of correspondents and branch offices created during the 1920s. The functions of these correspondents were both diplomatic and technical. They were supposed to maintain contacts with national labour ministries, trade unions, and employers' organizations and also to gather information and statistical data for the ILO on the social policy in a given country or region. The persons deemed to qualify for the post of a national correspondent normally had a close connection to the relevant government circles. They were often academics with good political contacts or former members of the government or social administration. The spread of correspondent offices was a good indicator for the geographical and political emphasis of the ILO's work during the early period. The first offices were opened already in 1920, initially in the capitals of the Allied Powers (London, Paris, Rome, and Washington, D.C.), followed by Berlin and Vienna. Outside of Europe and North America, the ILO was much slower in casting its net of contacts. Branch offices were set up in Tokyo and Delhi

---

90 Friedrich Rietzmann headed the industrial safety section from 1921 onwards. Andreas Grieser, who was the head of the social insurance department at the Ministry of Labour in Berlin, participated as an expert on the Commission on Social Insurance as of 1926 and was a regular member of the German delegation to the ILC in the 1920s. As Sandrine Kott has shown in various places, German officials were instrumental, for example, in the "internationalization of the German social insurance system". See "Dynamiques de l'internationalisation: l'Allemagne et l'Organisation internationale du Travail (1919–1940)", *Critique internationale* 52 (2011), 69–84. In a broader context, see also Kott, "Towards a Social History of International Organizations: The ILO and the Internationalisation of Western Social Expertise" (1919–1949), in *Internationalism, Imperialism and the Formation of the Contemporary World. The Pasts of the Present*, ed. Miguel Bandeira Jerónimo and José Pedro Monteiro (Basingstoke: Palgrave Macmillan, 2017), 33–58.
91 My own translation from the French "*puissant instrument d'affirmation de l'identité nationale et de rayonnement international de Allemagne*", in Kott, "Dynamiques de l'internationalisation", 72.

as well as in Rio de Janeiro in the 1920s, but in other parts of the world, it would take a decade or more (and in sub-Saharan Africa until 1959) before the first ILO offices were established.

The most important task faced by the ILO in order to become operational was to build an international bureaucracy from scratch and without a blueprint. Between 1920 and 1925, the number of employees at the Geneva headquarters grew to roughly 250. Where, how, and according to which criteria where these people recruited? When the ILO and the League started their work, little experience was available on how to create a body of committed international civil servants that would carry out the daily work. The secretariats of nineteenth-century international institutions had only rarely exceeded a handful of permanent staff members. Only a small portion of the first generation of ILO staff could be directly transferred from the Basel office or the national sections of the IALL.[92]

Albert Thomas' first decision after taking up his mandate was to appoint Harold Butler as his Deputy and Edward Phelan as head of the Diplomatic Division, responsible for the ILO's relation with its constituents. For some of the other senior posts he relied heavily on his own networks, mostly built before the war, but also during his time as a member of the French government. Most governments, however, were initially reluctant, in particular after the massive losses of young men to the First World War, to let the ILO draw from the ranks of their own national administrations, and France was no exception. Younger recruits sometimes came directly from universities, often on a recommendation of their academic institutions, with reform-oriented institutes like the London School of Economics assuming a special role.[93]

From 1921 onwards, the ILO established an examination system similar to the one commonly used at the national level for careers in public administration. The criteria of selection were mainly twofold: in addition to education and expertise, the question of nationality featured prominently. Early recruitment clearly reflected the power relations within the Organization's membership. Although the ILO's staff in 1921 comprised citizens of 19 countries, a majority was of British, French, or Swiss nationality. The ILO leadership was from the start dedicated to creating a sense of cohesion among its staff and to fostering commitment to the Organization's objectives. Internationalism and loyalty to the ILO's goals, however, did not equal cosmopolitanism. On the contrary, inasmuch as the post-First World War order was built on the concept of the nation state, the ILO

92 Véronique Plata-Stenger: "Europe, the ILO and the Wider World (1919–1954)", in *European History Online (EGO)*, published by the Leibniz Institute of European History (IEG), Mainz 2016-03-09.

93 Ibid.

was looking for staff members who were firmly rooted in their respective national places of origin. Far from being detached from the world of nation states, international organizations were, on the contrary, to a large extent the supreme manifestation of the very principle of the nation state. International civil servants were supposed to have a clear understanding of the mechanisms of this world.[94] The ILO itself, despite its tripartite structure, reflected the shifting nature of internationalism which became more state-centred after Versailles.[95] In those early days, when good relationships to governments were essential, the potential of international officials fulfilling a quasi-diplomatic role vis-à-vis their own countries of origin virtually became a matter of life or death for the Organization.

The Invention of Tripartism

With its tripartite structure and practice, the ILO, in particular in its early years, became a laboratory for an essentially new format of cooperation between workers' and employers' organizations. Tripartite cooperation, or tripartism for short, was a mostly untested idea when it was introduced into the debate, prior to the establishment of the ILO, by the authors of the British proposal to the Labour Commission in Paris.[96]

Some countries had introduced mechanisms and institutions for cooperation between governments, trade unions, and employers during the First World War. As part of the *Union Sacrée* in France and the *Burgfrieden* in Germany, governments had been eager to secure the political allegiances of the greater part of the trade union movement, and they had been mostly successful. Yet, the corporatist arrangements made during the war were mainly ad hoc provisions,[97] imposed by governments, often against the resistance of the two other parties, and their continuation in peace time was highly contested. This was the case not only for business representatives, who usually resented the social-

94 Sluga, *Internationalism in the Age of Nationalism*, 45–78.
95 Kott, "From Transnational Reformist Network to International Organization", 246–253.
96 A good discussion of the origins of tripartism can be found in the unpublished work of Kari Tapiola, "A Wild Dream. A Century of Tripartite Cooperation and Social Dialogue", (2017). For a concise overview, see Claire La Hovary, "A Challenging Ménage à Trois? Tripartism in the International Labour Organization", *International Organizations Law Review* 12, no. 1 (2015): 204–236.
97 Even before the war, trade unions and industry leaders were already consulted in several countries on both social legislation and conflict resolution. The very creation of the British Trades Union Congress (TUC) in 1868 had aimed at a better coordination of the workers' various views on social policy. In Europe, in particular, trade unions had close links to labour parties, which in turn was reflected in social reforms and the spread of parliamentarism.

ist undertones of the measures, but also for some trade unions. For many of them, the idea of tripartism gave governments an undue voice in labour relations, something of which the American Federation of Labour (AFL) was highly critical.[98] As a matter of fact, in hardly any of the ILO's member countries did the tripartite cooperation established in the new organization reflect the reality on the ground. Nor were trade unions fully recognized everywhere. Their legal status varied widely even in the highly industrialized countries of Europe and North America.[99]

Tripartism, then, rather than being a recognized practice adopted by the ILO on the basis of national experiences, has to be seen as something developed and practised first on the international level before being promoted as a model in the ILO's member States.[100] For the ILO, the tripartite principle became another tool to secure its own survival, to anchor the Organization in various national environments, and to gain additional access to public opinion within its member States.[101] At the same time, and from a diplomatic point of view, Albert Thomas considered that the strengthening of the Office's ties within the tripartite network of constituents was vital – not least in light of the often lukewarm support by governments during the Organization's early years.

This was particularly true with regard to the international trade union movement which had refounded itself in July 1919 in Amsterdam and became known as the "Amsterdam International". Despite the considerable disappointment among the IFTU about the results of the Paris Peace Conference, discontent about the general features of the new organization soon gave way to a more pragmatic stance. The main reason for this change was that, although the IFTU was not officially given the representative monopoly in the Workers' group that it had originally claimed, it dominated the group during the entire interwar period to a degree that would have made non-cooperation absurd.[102]

Much of the Amsterdam International's openness to the ILO had to do with the personality and the previous trade union links of Albert Thomas, whose election at the Washington Conference of 1919 could be regarded as a major success

---

98 A systematic overview: Marcel van der Linden, "Trade Unions" in *Handbook Global History of Work*. ed. Karin Hofmeester and Marcel van der Linden (Berlin: DeGruyter Oldenbourg, 2018), 551–570.

99 Ibid.

100 On the highly diverse situation in the Nordic countries, see Kettunen, "The ILO as a Forum for Developing and Demonstrating a Nordic Model", in *Globalizing Social Rights,* ed. Kott and Droux, 210–230.

101 There are no records of Albert Thomas having attended or even promoted tripartite meetings during his travels, but usually met with trade union and employers' representatives separately.

102 On the IFTU, see van Goethem, *The Amsterdam International.*

by the IFTU. Especially during the early days of the ILO, the Amsterdam International entered into a close cooperative relation with the Director of the ILO, which formed a key element in Thomas' strategy to secure the Organization's survival. The trade unions were supportive of the ILO's major projects, that is, the advancement of international social legislation and the expansion of the Organization's competences beyond a narrow social mandate. The ILO Director attended, in an informal but plainly visible capacity, the IFTU's congresses as well as the meetings of some of its national affiliates, and he occasionally mediated conflicts between members or between the IFTU and federations outside of its framework (such as the AFL). He also entertained close personal contacts with the International's Dutch Secretary, Jan Oudegeest. To some Thomas on occasions appeared to be acting as a "de-facto additional member of the IFTU leadership".[103]

Yet, in some cases, conflicts arose, for example when Thomas courted IFTU competitors like the Christian trade union movement or entertained official relations – considered at times too cordial by IFTU leadership – with countries that suppressed trade union activities, such as Fascist Italy or Spain under the dictatorship of Primo de Rivera.[104]

Albert Thomas' overall approach was pragmatic, guided by the conviction that the collaboration with governments of whatever political orientation was the first step to get international labour standards ratified. Occasional turbulences could not distract from the fact that the relationship between the leadership of the ILO and the most important international trade union federation was sometimes even symbiotic. Although this close and personal cooperation did not continue with Thomas' successor, Harold Butler, who took a much more neutral stand towards the ILO's constituents, the trade unions maintained a privileged position.[105]

The cooperation with the employers was different from the very beginning. The International Organisation of Industrial Employers, soon to be renamed International Organisation of Employers (IOE), was founded in 1920 for the purpose of representing the world of business and coordinating the views of employers in the ILO, in an attempt to match at least partly the unity that existed among the Workers' group. An international association that united business interests had existed before the war, and there was also a continuity when it came to the people

103 Reiner Tosstorff, "Albert Thomas, the ILO and the IFTU. A Case of Mutual Benefit?", in *ILO Histories*, ed. Van Daele et al., 91–114.

104 The travel diaries on Thomas' visit to Italy 1925, 1928, 1930, 1932, and to Spain 1928; Hoehtker and Kott, *À la rencontre de l'Europe au travail. Récits de voyages d'Albert Thomas*, 215–255, 255–273.

105 Tosstorff, "Albert Thomas, the ILO and the IFTU: A Case of Mutual Benefit?", 111–112.

involved. Some of the protagonists of the IOE in the interwar years – such as the Belgian Jules Lecocq, the French Robert Pinot, or the Italian Gino Olivetti – had known each other from earlier attempts to organize employers' interests on the international level. Yet, it was the British proposal to set up the ILO as a tripartite organization that brought this international association into being. The existence of the ILO and the employers' participation in the Organization was and remained the raison d'être of the IOE.[106]

By and large, in 1919, the employers' attitude towards the ILO was sceptical. Many perceived of the ILO as "an unsolicited gift". At the same time, they acknowledged the potential of a cooperation with the trade unions in order to keep what they saw as the regulatory zeal of governments under control.[107] The employers felt that in welcoming them, the ILO's arms were not as open as they had expected, given the recognition that the Organization's structure gave them formally an equal position with the trade unions. Many employers soon complained that the environment of the new Organization was hostile towards the representatives of business. From the beginning, the Employers' group found itself accused of obstructionism. Employers may not have been the "brake" in the machinery of the ILO, as Thomas' oft-quoted dictum would have it (in opposition to the workers, whom he saw in the role of the "motor" or "locomotive"[108]), but they did work as a corrective to all ambitions to expand the ILO's mandate. Until the Second World War, the employers regularly voted against the budget proposals. They expressed a clear preference for the adoption of non-binding Recommendations on almost all questions concerning standard-setting that were put on the agenda of the Conference, and they took generally a defensive position whenever the debate turned to "new topics" to be explored by the ILO. This was even true in cases in which employers had taken a more positive approach on the national level, such as in the discussion on "public works" programmes in

---

106 Marieke Louis, "Building a Transnational Business Community. Insights from the International Labour Organisation", unpublished working paper for the ILO Century Project, 4–8.

107 This cooperation manifested itself at the International Labour Conference of 1919, where Workers and Employers started deliberating first in groups and often between themselves. At the first Session of the Governing Body, it led to the election – by majority vote – of both Arthur Fontaine and Albert Thomas. Jean-Jacques Oechslin, *The International Organisation of Employers. Three-Quarters of a Century in the Service of the Enterprise (1920–1998)* (Geneva: IOE, 2001).

108 An actual reference for this often quoted comparison could not be traced. The closest one gets to it is taken from Oechslin, *The International Organisation of Employers*, 36, who refers to a speech of 1928 in which Albert Thomas likened the ILO to a train of which the employers were "the brakemen". "This may indeed be your role", he told the employers. "But you have climbed aboard a train and a train ... goes inexorably towards a destination. A little more slowly, a little faster, but inexorably we shall proceed towards social justice and peace."

the 1930s. One of their main concerns was that the ILO would promote measures which could become an incentive for governments and workers to team up in favour of more regulation and state intervention in the economy. As the Danish employer delegate Hans Christian Oersted pointed out in 1927, employers saw it as their "duty not to compromise the economy of their countries by making unconsidered concessions to workers' claims".[109]

The problem with the employers' position within the ILO architecture was from the beginning political and structural, and it could not be solved through a search for some kind of a formal balance. The objective of standard-setting even before the ILO existed had been to improve the situation of workers. Labour standards were not designed to deal with, let alone advance, the interests of the business community. Consequently, what could be seen as an overall defensive and even at times obstructionist attitude by the Employers' group was an unavoidable consequence of the very idea of international social legislation which the ILO was built upon. After all, the employers' organizations had their roots in a desire to counter the demands that were expressed especially by the Second International. Later on, once social legislation started being put in place, the employers realized the need for coordinating their positions.[110]

On closer examination, the employers' approach to the ILO was considerably more differentiated and complex. The first generation of employers' representatives, some of whom had been members of the IALL, had a genuine interest in international social legislation as a means to reduce unfair competition and to diminish the risk of social unrest. From this perspective, the ILO seemed to be the right place to look for non-confrontational and negotiated solutions to the social question. Employers voted in favour of Conventions on unemployment or sickness insurance. They preferred instruments on social insurance coverage for accidents rather than on work-related illnesses where the financial obligation could be less well controlled. They voted for standards to protect women's work (for instance, maternity conventions) since there was a common understanding of the primary role of women as mothers.[111] The majority of them even voted in favour of the first ILO Convention on the reduction of working hours (the principle of the eight-hour workday) in 1919, although this attitude was tied to the specific context of the Washington Conference and was later replaced by strong and per-

109 Louis, "Building a Transnational Business Community", 6.
110 Ibid., 10–12.
111 Isabelle Lespinet-Moret, "Promouvoir la santé au travail comme droit social (1919–1940)?", *Le Mouvement Social* 263, no. 2 (2018): 61–76.

sistent opposition against any other attempts to such regulations.[112] In the first two decades, the IOE did not actually have a mandate to coordinate the positions of the individual Employer delegates, and certainly not to the same degree as the IFTU with the Workers.[113]

Especially in the early days, the political position of the members of the IOE was mostly liberal-conservative, and they saw the ILO as a bulwark against the Bolshevik threat. While parts of the business community equally perceived of the ILO as a threat to their interests, the IOE learned to appreciate the ILO as a valuable source of information about social legislation in other countries, which they could pass on to their members. The ILO also served as a kind of early warning system that would help employers to anticipate trends in international social legislation. This seemed useful to strengthen their "vigilance" and give them a better chance to "nip it in the bud".[114] Last but not least, the IOE had its own genuine interest in an association with the ILO, inasmuch as its very legitimacy rested on its position as a "privileged channel of information between the ILO and national business organizations".[115] However, in the perception of the ILO leadership and its allies, both among governments and trade unions, the employers increasingly assumed less the role of a partner than that of an obstacle to be overcome.[116]

Despite these tensions, Albert Thomas showed genuine concern about questions of management and the broader issues regarding economic and industrial organization. An early example of this was his interest in "scientific management", which as a term combined ideas of economic planning within a capitalist order and the Taylorist organization of industrial production. Thomas shared with many socialists and social democrats of his era a fascination with Taylorism which started to spread in Europe, especially in car manufacturing, after the war.[117] From his perspective, scientific management offered an opportunity to build up expertise in a field from which the ILO had been largely excluded due to the resistance of employers and most governments. Scientific management opened up a space to pursue a broader vision of social and labour problems and

---

112 Ingrid Liebeskind Sauthier, "Modern Unemployment: From the Creation of the Concept to the International Labour Office's First Standards", in *Globalizing Social Rights*, ed. Kott and Droux, 67–84.

113 Louis, "Building a Transnational Business Community", 10–12.

114 Quoted from a strategic paper of the IOE, 1928; see ibid., 6.

115 Ibid.

116 Ibid.

117 For the German case and the German Social Democrats' fascination with Taylorist principles, see Mary Nolan, *Visions of Modernity: American Business and the Modernization of Germany* (Oxford: Oxford University Press, 1994).

to keep the ILO in touch with economic discussions in the League of Nations and elsewhere.

In the early 1920s, Thomas started a cooperation with the US Twentieth Century Fund and its President, Edward A. Filene. Filene, a progressive philanthropist businessman who had long promoted scientific management as a means to both rationalize industrial production and mitigate social conflict, was mostly interested in the economic planning aspect. He saw the cooperation with the ILO as a way to access the Organization's broad network of governmental and non-governmental actors. For the ILO, in turn, the cooperation offered opportunities both in terms of funding and outreach. The major outcome of this cooperation was the establishment, in 1926, of the International Management Institute (IMI), with Paul Devinat, an ILO *chef de service*, as its Director.[118] The IMI was funded by the Twentieth Century Fund and staffed mainly from the ranks of the ILO. For Thomas, the IMI would serve as a spearhead in the international movement for scientific management, with the ILO bringing a social aspect to the debate.[119] After 1930, the Institute was built up as an "international clearing-house of modernizing ideas linking Taylorist experts to reformist networks".[120] At the same time, the Twentieth Century Fund, together with the Ford Motor Company, sponsored a study on living standards by the ILO.[121]

When the economic crisis hit after 1930, the IMI's emphasis on social and economic planning first seemed to gain in relevance. Yet, the IMI proved to be short-lived. Eventually, the Twentieth Century Fund lost interest, and, in 1934, the Institute had to close its doors due to a lack of funding. The IMI nevertheless had helped the ILO to build up expertise and earn some recognition. Part of its work was continued during the 1930s in the Office's newly established Economic Planning Section. At the same time, the ILO had gained recognition for its economic expertise, tangible, for example, in its work with the League's Economic and Financial Section.[122] Thus, the IMI episode had effects that proved useful in the longer run.[123]

118 Thomas Cayet, "The ILO and the IMI: A Strategy of Influence on the Edges of the League of Nations, 1925–1934", in *ILO Histories*, ed. Van Daele et al., 251–270.

119 Another result was the introduction of simultaneous interpretation at the 1927 Conference, which was financed by Filene.

120 Cayet, "The ILO and the IMI", 263.

121 Victoria De Grazia, *Irresistible Empire: America's Advance through Twentieth-Century Europe* (Cambridge, MA: The Belknap Press of Harvard University Press, 2005), 78–84.

122 Patricia Clavin, *Securing the World Economy: The Reinvention of the League of Nations, 1920–1946* (Oxford: Oxford University Press, 2013), 11–46.

123 Cayet, "The ILO and the IMI".

Casting a Wider Net

The ILO's attempts to broaden its influence exceeded the tripartite framework also in other aspects. During its early years, it was constantly seeking to mobilize public opinion within the member countries. As a result, the ILO acted as part of a broader international network. Its relationship with the League of Nations was marked by a mix of cooperation and competition.[124] Although the ILO was jealously trying to secure its autonomy with regard to the League, both organizations found fields of common interest in areas like health policies or living standards which led to mutually beneficial joint actions. Equally important, the ILO's interactions with the international milieu surrounding the League of Nations in Geneva and with internationalist circles of lawyers, pacifists, and social reformers elsewhere provided additional sources of support that helped to secure its position.[125]

In parallel, the ILO itself became an umbrella for organizations whose activities and interests partly overlapped with its agenda. Here, the ILO often played an active role in fostering and sometimes even initiating ostensibly private initiatives that were deemed to carry the potential of supporting its goals. Obvious partners in these endeavours could be found among the international associations that had preceded the ILO in its work, in particular the IALL. However, there was a problem with this cooperation. The foundation of the ILO had drained most of these associations of both their public funding and their personnel. In the case of the IALL, the ILO had taken over its library and most of its archives. Many prominent members of both the Basel Office and the IALL's national sections were appointed to positions in the ILO. For example, Sophy Sanger, a leading member of the British IALL branch, became head of the ILO's Labour Legislation Section.[126] The ILO established an equally symbiotic relationship with the Inter-

---

124 Magaly Rodríguez García, Davide Rodogno and Liat Kozma, eds., *The League of Nations' Work on Social Issues. Visions, Endeavours and Experiments* (New York: United Nations Department of Public Information, 2016).

125 On the Geneva international milieu, see Sluga, *Internationalism in the Age of Nationalism*, 45–78. On the broader internationalist environment during the interwar years, see also Daniel Gorman, *The Emergence of International Society in the 1920s* (Cambridge: Cambridge University Press, 2012); and Daniel Laqua, *Internationalism Reconfigured: Transnational Ideas and Movements between the World Wars*, International Library of Twentieth Century History (London: I.B. Tauris, 2011).

126 However, Sanger only stayed for three years and left the Office after disagreements with Thomas, as in the early days the reality of gender equality in the Office did not yet match the progressive principles of the Constitution. See Olga Hidalgo-Weber, "Femmes britanniques et pratiques internationales de justice sociale dans la première moitié du XXe siècle", in "La jus-

national Association for the Fight against Unemployment, which merged with the IALL in 1924 to become the International Association for Social Progress (IASP). The influence of these associations did not disappear in the shadow of the ILO, because Albert Thomas saw their national sections as valuable allies in reaching out to the public. These national sections also represented an opportunity to maintain a dialogue with social reformers in countries that were not members of the ILO, most importantly the United States. The ILO, therefore, actively supported the IASP, which served as an intermediary and conducted research on the impact of ILO Conventions. For the same purpose, the ILO promoted the foundation of non-governmental organizations that supported its own agenda. An example was the International Association for Social Insurance (1927), in which two senior ILO officials – Oswald Stein of Czechoslovakia and Adrien Tixier of France – played a major role as experts.[127]

From the beginning, the ILO showed a keen interest in the international cooperative movement. It opened its own cooperative branch, set up an International Committee on Inter-Cooperative Relations, and sought to join forces with the movement's main umbrella organization, the International Cooperative Alliance (ICA). To Thomas – who had been linked to the cooperative movement before the war – and some of his close collaborators, the cooperative principle was not only a mode of production. It was a social laboratory that would eventually bring about better living conditions for workers, a more humane and democratic organization of the economy at large, and ultimately peace within societies and on the international level.[128] As early as 1920, the ILO took a decision to establish firm relationships with what Thomas saw as a "mass movement" and a "movement of ideas", capable of providing solutions to "almost all general problems of labour".[129] From this point of view, cooperatives were a means to pursue a "*révolution silencieuse*"[130] which would be beneficial especially in a number of areas, ranging from housing to consumption, and from insurance through agriculture to fisheries. In the wake of the economic downturn following the First World War, cooperatives became also to be seen as institutions that were

tice sociale dans un monde global. L'Organisation internationale du travail (1919–2019)", special issue, *Le Mouvement Social* 263, no. 2 (2018): 77–92; here 80–81.

127 Kott, "From Transnational Reformist Network to International Organization", 251.

128 Hagen Henry, "The Contribution of the ILO to the Formation of Public International Cooperative Law", in *Globalizing Social Rights*, ed. Kott and Droux, 98–114; Claudia Sanchez Bajo, "Work and Cooperatives: A Century of ILO Interaction with the Cooperative Movement", in *Cooperatives and the World of Work*, ed. Bruno Roelants et al. (London: Routledge, forthcoming).

129 Sanchez Bajo, "Work and Cooperatives".

130 Marine Dhermy-Mairal, "L'unification du mouvement coopératif au BIT: la 'revolution silencieuse' d'Albert Thomas (1919–1932)", *Le Mouvement Social* 263 (Jan. 2018): 15–29.

relatively robust in times of cyclical depression. According to his travel diaries, Albert Thomas always sought meetings and collaboration with the cooperative movement during his official visits to Europe (and also to the Soviet Union in 1928).[131] In 1921, the ILO hired Georges Fauquet, a French leader of the consumer cooperative movement, as head of the ILO's cooperative branch. In the following years, Fauquet, who had worked under Thomas in the Ministry of Artillery and Munitions during the war, would personify the close relationship with the cooperative movement.[132]

From the beginning, the ILO saw itself as part of the wider liberal internationalist milieu, which had been energized by the founding of the League of Nations. In this respect, an important medium to gain wider public support was the *Union internationale des associations pour la Société des Nations* (UIASDN), an umbrella organization for the national League of Nations Associations. Despite its ambiguous relationship with the League, the ILO tried to mobilize the wider network of civil society groups, international lawyers, and pacifists of various shades that supported and promoted the League both in Geneva and within its member States. Notwithstanding their rivalries and occasional turf wars, for Thomas, the League and the ILO were complementary instruments for peace. As a member of the central committee of the French *Ligue des droits de l'homme*, he had been instrumental in the foundation of the French League of Nations Association (*Association française pour la Société des Nations*) in 1918. Once in Geneva, Thomas used both the French Association and the UIASDN to boost public support for the organization. During the 1920s, the UIASDN and its French president, Théodore Ruyssen, issued resolutions that were addressed to its national sections and asked them to influence their governments in favour of the ratification of ILO Conventions.[133] Some national sections became tools for the promotion of the Organization, too. In Britain, the League of Nations Union (LNU) was the ILO's key ally, second only to the trade unions. The LNU, which had over 100.000 members during the mid-1920s, gained the support of liberal internationalists like Alfred Zimmern and Leonard Woolf, as well as prominent conservatives like Robert Cecil and Austen Chamberlain. To secure the support of the most important ILO member State of the time was regarded as one of the main assets.[134]

From the late 1920s onwards, the ILO entertained a relationship of a similar kind with the Institute for Pacific Relations (IPR), an American-based interna-

131 Hoehtker and Kott, *À la rencontre de l'Europe au travail. Recits de voyages d'Albert Thomas.*

132 Fauquet maintained close relationships with the ICA (and became a leading member of the organization after his time at the ILO).

133 Guieu, "Albert Thomas et la paix", 76–80.

134 Ibid.

tional NGO which acted as a think tank on problems shared by countries of the Pacific Rim. Through its contacts with the IPR, the ILO gained further access to the Institute's wide net of contacts, which extended from liberal internationalists in the United States to affiliates and contacts in countries such as Japan and the Soviet Union. The IPR contact would prove extremely helpful, particularly during the Second World War, when the ILO relocated to Canada and relied on the support of the United States, which was facilitated by the Institute's close relations to the Roosevelt administration.[135]

A major institutional contact with these networks was provided from 1926 onwards through the ILO's Committee of Experts on the Application of Conventions and Recommandations (CEACR),[136] which was a crucial feature of the developing supervisory mechanism for standards. Within half a decade, it had become clear that the ILC could not deal with the increasing number of reports on ratified Conventions without some kind of a preparatory mechanism that would assist the Office and the Conference. As of 1927, a report summarizing the information provided by national governments was prepared by a committee of independent experts. Their task was to review the annual reports of the various national governments on the implementation of ratified standards. The members of the Expert Committee, who were appointed by the Governing Body, were mostly internationally renowned jurists and other experts in labour law, like Paul Tschoffen from Belgium or William Rappard from Switzerland.[137] While the mandate adopted by the Governing Body did not limit the Committee's membership to jurists alone, in practice, it became the most prestigious body of legal expertise in the ILO. Its members played a significant part in clarifying and establishing international labour law in all member States. Through the different national legal traditions and political systems they represented, the experts also fulfilled a role as translators and emissaries for the ILO within their own national and regional contexts.[138]

---

135 Paul F. Hooper, "The Institute of Pacific Relations and the Origins of Asian and Pacific Studies", *Pacific Affairs* 61, no. 1 (1988), 98–121.

136 Guy Fiti Sinclair, *To Reform the World: International Organizations and the Making of Modern States*, The History and Theory of International Law (New York: Oxford University Press, 2017), ch.1.: From Standard-Setting to Technical Assistance.

137 Membres et réunions de la Commission d'experts pour l'application des conventions et recommandations et décisions du Conseil d'administration 1927–1939. The list of members and meetings was made available to me through the ILO Archives.

138 On the ILO's relationship with international jurists, see Dzovinar Kévonian, "Les juristes et l'Organisation internationale du Travail 1919–1939. Processus de légitimation et institutionnalisation des relations internationales", *Journal of the History of International Law* 12, no. 3 (2010): 227–266; see also the research project "Laying the Foundations. The League of Nations and International Law, 1919–1945" Københavns Universitet, and its various publications:

The high rank and independent status of its members also made it difficult to dismiss or ignore the Committee's findings. The success of the Committee, which has arguably remained one of the most effective instruments for the monitoring of international standards, has set a precedent for the ILO, which would in the future use committees of independent experts also with regard to several other controversial issues, such as forced labour or freedom of association.[139]

Another prime example of the ways the ILO, under Albert Thomas' leadership, broadened its appeal beyond its tripartite framework was its relationship with the Catholic Church. Thomas had shown an early interest in the Catholic social doctrine, which had long played a strong role in the French social reformist milieu. He saw the Holy See as a key ally in building good relations not only with various governments and the Christian trade union federations but also with some members of the Employers' group, who were committed Catholics. Pope Pius XI generally encouraged Catholic laymen to get involved in all aspects of social life both nationally and internationally, and despite his socialist background, Thomas could encounter a certain degree of responsiveness.[140]

Despite the importance of Christian – and especially Catholic – trade unionism, the Vatican, as a state entity, did not have any organizational link to, or representation of, trade unions and employers. Consequently, it did not fit in the tripartite structure of the ILO. Thomas circumvented this problem by creating a new position within the ILO, occupied by a representative of the Catholic Church who would act as a special advisor to the Director on social and religious matters. Based on an unofficial agreement between the ILO and the Vatican, this post was filled for the first time in 1926 with the Jesuit priest André Arnou. The institution of a special ecclesiastical advisor to the Director-General has been maintained to

---

www.internationallaw.ku.dk. For a history of the establishment of the Committee, see Kari Tapiola, "The ILO System of Supervision on the Application of Conventions and Recommendations: A Lasting Paradigm", in *Protecting Labour Rights as Human Rights: Present and Future of International Supervision*, Proceedings of the International Colloquium on the 80th Anniversary of the ILO Committee of Experts on the Application of Conventions and Recommendations, Geneva, 24–25 November 2006, ed. George P. Politakis (Geneva: International Labour Office, 2006), 29–36.

139 Bob Reinalda, "Organization Theory and the Autonomy of the International Labour Organization: Two Classical Studies still Going Strong", in *Autonomous Policy Making by International Organizations*, ed. Bob Reinalda and Bertjan Verbeek, 42–62; here 49–52.

140 Zaragori, "Missions et l'Organisation internationale du Travail (OIT)"; Liliosa Azara, "*The Holy See and the International Labour Organization:* The Origins of a Special Relationship", *in Christian Democrat Internationalism. Its Action in Europe and Worldwide from post-World War II until the 1990s. Volume II: The Development (1945–1979). The Role of Parties, Movements, People*, ed. Jean-Dominique Durand (Bern: Peter Lang, 2013), 42–56.

the present day, and seven Jesuits have so far held the position. The nature of the ILO's relationship with the Catholic Church has obviously fluctuated over time, but, on more than one occasion, it has served as a broker of ILO politics in the Catholic world.[141]

Standard-setting in the 1920s

From its inception, the ILO started working on what was – according to the mandate issued at Versailles – the Organization's most important task: the elaboration and adoption of international labour standards. The questions were: what kinds of problems would these standards address, and which would be their primary target groups? Restricted by both traditions and its mandate, the ILO initially focused on (male) industrial labour based on regular employment contracts. Most other forms of labour, and, in fact, the work of a great majority of the world's population, lay outside the scope of the Organization. At the same time, the boundaries of the ILO's normative actions were constantly contested and extended. This process was driven by the interplay of two forces: on one side stood the International Labour Office under Albert Thomas' leadership and its allies within the tripartite structure of the Organization; on the other side were groups from outside, which sought access to the ILO in order to make their voices heard and to find recognition for their demands. Standard-setting during the 1920s reflected the struggle between the protective tradition present, for example, in the fields of women's work and in particular with regard to children and youth on the one hand and an ever broadening understanding of the ILO's "social mandate" on the other.

Four of the six Conventions adopted by the first ILC continued the protective tradition of the IALL's pre-war standards and dealt with women's night work, maternity protection, minimum age in industry, and night work of young persons. However, the other two Conventions, on hours of work and unemployment, were more ambitious in scope and also an indicator of the future path of the ILO, its

141 See, for example, on the role of the Catholic Church in the context of the ILO's Andean Indian Programme of the 1950s Aurélien Zaragori, "L'OIT, Le Saint-Siege et les milieux catholiques africains et latinoamericains dans les années 1950 et 1960", *Le Mouvement Social* 263 (2018), 123–138. In an audience with Pope John XXIII, Director-General David Morse sought the support as a "soldier in your army losing my battle" against conservative clerics resisting the programme (Oral History Interview David A. Morse, Harry S. Truman Library/OHIM-C 248). On another occasion Director-General David Morse sought the help of Pope John XXIII and Pius XII in order to overcome Cold War impasses vis-à-vis the American trade unions during the 1960s, and the Catholic Church played a role in the controversy surrounding the independent trade union Solidarnosc in Poland in the 1980s at the time of Pope John Paul II.

drive for enlarged areas of competence, and the power relations within the newly established tripartite structure.

The ILO's first Convention dealt with the regulation of working hours.[142] This had significant symbolic value, although legislation on this issue had already been adopted in many countries. It also marked the start of a general debate on working time that essentially continued for the following hundred years. From the trade unions' perspective, the eight-hour working day was seen as a litmus test for the fulfilment of wartime promises. The limitation of working time had been the central claim of the labour movement since its beginnings, in addition to the demand of a living wage. Shorter working days would significantly improve workers' lives by giving them more time for physical recreation and family and leisure time. Most importantly, reduced working hours would offer new opportunities for political participation and further education and thus open the road for individual and collective advancement. It was, in this sense, also a highly symbolic issue, in particular from the point of view of the reformist parts of the workers' movement. Moderate socialist and Christian workers showed the same dedication to the limitation of working time in order to prove that their non-revolutionary gradualist strategy would ultimately be successful.[143]

Against this backdrop, the Workers' group of the ILO could indeed see the results of the Washington Conference as a victory, even if it was not a complete one. The wording of the Hours of Work Convention and some of its provisions – both agriculture and wholesale commerce were omitted from the arrangements – reflected the demand of employers for more flexibility.[144] Working hours and related issues, such as paid leave, leisure time, and night work regulations, remained on the agenda of the ILO throughout the interwar years. During the 1930s, these questions were increasingly debated in a Keynesian framework, in which the reduction of working hours was promoted by some analysts as a means to fight unemployment.[145]

---

142 Hours of Work (Industry) Convention, 1919 (No. 1) For a general debate on working hours, see Gerry Rodgers et al., *The ILO and the Quest for Social Justice* (Geneva: ILO, 2009), 110–111; Alcock, *History of the International Labour Organization*, 42–43.

143 Lex Heerma van Voss, "The International Federation of Trade Unions and the Attempt to Maintain the Eight-Hour Working Day 1919–1929", in *Internationalism in the Labour Movement, 1870–1940*, ed. Marcel van der Linden and Frits van Hoolthon (Leiden: Brill 1988); Gary Cross, "Les Trois Huits: Labor Movements, International Reform, and the Origins of the Eight Hour Day, 1919–1924", *French Historical Studies* 14, no. 2 (1985): 240–268.

144 Although the eight-hour day constituted the symbolic aim, the Convention itself focused on the 48-hour week, including a weekly rest day and room for a second day off (Saturday). With regard to the eight-hour target, it contained much more flexibility.

145 See Chapter 2.

By contrast, a discussion of unemployment within a broader social and economic framework was still a distant goal at the Washington Conference.[146] But since it was to many the most pressing problem of the immediate post-war years, it was subject to a Convention and a Recommendation. They called for the establishment of free public employment services and the payment of unemployment insurance benefits to all workers, including foreign workers. At the Washington Conference, some delegates already thought that the ILO should extend its mandate beyond the struggle against the mere social consequences of unemployment and deal with the root causes of the problem and thus with economic, financial, and trade policies.[147] In the end, however, and even though the Convention established the basis for the Organization to work as a clearing house for unemployment policies in the future, the broader economic dimension of unemployment was not regarded to be within the scope of the ILO's mandate.[148]

Women

During its first decades, the ILO's standard-setting constantly oscillated between the nineteenth-century protective tradition and expanding notions of social policy. One of the key issues which challenged the limits of the protective framework was the situation of women in the world of work. Arguably, women's work and the feminist fight for the inclusion of women and their fair representation in the ILO have been the most important and long-lasting struggle within the larger story of ILO standard-setting. During the interwar years, the Organization responded to those claims by adopting four women-specific protective labour standards based on the prevailing conceptions of gender difference. However, these norms were met with opposition from feminists, especially from Northern Europe and the United States, who argued for full legal equality between men and women in the workplace. It would take until the 1930s and the aftermath of

146 Liebeskind Sauthier, "Modern Unemployment", 74–83.

147 Some governments and trade unions, for instance, promoted the foundation of a permanent commission to oversee the equitable international distribution of raw materials as a means to revitalize production and to avoid unemployment. A majority of governments, however, resisted this idea as an infringement on national sovereignty. Countries rich in raw materials were particularly unenthusiastic, and the proposal was defeated by a clear majority. A year later, the Council of the League of Nations decided that this question lay outside the competence of the ILO. See Alcock, *History of the International Labor Organization*, 45.

148 There were only small hints of this aspect in an accompanying Recommendation to the economic dimension of the problem, which mentioned that public works programmes were to be reserved for times of unemployment.

the Great Depression for their protests to slowly gain some ground. Even then, governments, trade unions, and employers favoured to an overwhelming degree protective legislation aimed specifically at women.

It is only recently that the active part which women played in the Organization from the very outset has received more attention.[149] Women's organizations showed a keen interest in the Organization. They spoke on behalf of women workers who had entered employment in unprecedented numbers in many countries as a consequence of the First World War, and they wanted to make their voices heard. Feminist organizations, representing women who had just won the right to vote in a number of European countries, lobbied national governments at the Paris Peace Conference and the Washington Conference in 1919 to secure female participation in the new Organization and to establish women's work as a central field of its activities. In Washington, about 200 women from 19 countries attended the first International Congress of Women Workers (ICWW), in order to develop a common strategy for the first Session of the ILC.[150]

Women, however, did not speak with one voice, and the idea of what social justice meant for women diverged according to the social and cultural frame of reference. Some women, like Betzy Kjelsberg, a women's rights activist and Norwegian government delegate to the ILC from 1923 to 1935, saw their fight for equality in the workplace as part of a bigger struggle for full equality with men. Thus, they were largely against women-only protective legislation. Conservatives and Christian women's associations, on the other hand, embraced protective legislation. The latter also found support among many women trade unionists, often socialists, who prioritized the objective of better working conditions for women through special legislation. Many of them had supported the 1906 IALL convention on women's night work, which was protective in nature, and which again came up for discussion in Washington. In 1919, these ideological and strategic differences within the women's movement particularly limited the ability of legal equality feminists to influence the decision-making process in any significant way. This was even more tragic given the difficult economic conditions in Europe and the return of millions of soldiers from the trenches caused fears of mass unemployment, which in turn fueled a general objection against women's work.[151]

---

149 See, for example, Boris, Hoehtker, and Zimmermann, eds., *Women's ILO*.

150 Dorothy Sue Cobble, "The Other ILO Founders: 1919 and Its Legacies", in *Women's ILO*, ed. Boris, Hoehtker, and Zimmermann, 27–49; Ulla Wikander, "Demands on the ILO by Internationally Organized Women in 1919", in *ILO Histories*, ed. Van Daele et al., 67–90.

151 Wikander, "Demands on the ILO by Internationally Organized Women in 1919".

Figure 2: The Norwegian government delegate Betzy Kjelsberg (centre) with technical advisers. Kjelsberg was the first and only woman delegate with voting rights when she attended the third Session of the ILC in 1921.

The two Conventions that dealt specifically with women`s employment were, for most part, an expression of the protective mainstream thinking. For legal equality feminists the Night Work (Women) Convention (No. 4) was the quintessential expression of the attempt to perpetuate a social order through ILO standard-setting which gave men priority in access to jobs and relegated women to the role of housewife and mother.[152] By contrast, the Maternity Protection Convention (No. 3) had wider support among women's organizations, because it also contained provisions for compulsory benefits that went beyond the merely protective frame. The protection of women workers during pregnancy and after childbirth has been the least controversial area of protective standard-setting for women, and it has

152 Nora Natchkova and Céline Schoeni, "The ILO, Feminists and Expert Networks: The Challenges of a Protective Policy", in *Globalizing Social Rights*, ed. Kott and Droux, 49–66, here 53; see also Brigitte Studer, Regina Wecker, and Gaby Sutter eds., *Die "schutzbedürftige Frau". Zur Konstruktion von Geschlecht durch Mutterschaftsversicherung, Nachtarbeitsverbot und Sonderschutzgesetzgebung* (Zurich: Chronos, 2001).

remained to this day the only women-specific feature in the ILO's standard-setting. Throughout the interwar years, the ILO continued its predominantly protective standard-setting. It adopted mainly conventions with gender-specific orientation, for example with regard to underground work, or it included women-specific paragraphs in gender-neutral Conventions.[153] The debate continued into the 1930s, especially after the world economic crisis starting in 1929 exacerbated the situation and narrowed down women's access to skilled jobs. At the same time, new feminist groups like Open Door International, founded in 1929, renewed the campaign for gender equality centred on the issue of equal pay.[154]

Closely related to the debates on women's position in the world of work was the question of female representation in the ILO. Early attempts to have women represented on equal terms with men in the tripartite political bodies of the ILO came to naught. Not one of the 40 national delegations in Washington in 1919 contained a female delegate with voting rights. Instead, the 23 women present were advisers or assistants to male delegates. While some of them interpreted their role quite actively – like the Japanese feminist and scholar Tanaka Taka, whose unauthorized speech at the Conference on behalf of low-income women provoked a scandal in Japan – most women remained marginalized.[155] Yet, women advisers like Margaret Bondfield from Great Britain managed to have an impact on Conventions through their work in the committees. Still, during the entire interwar period, only 4% of all delegates to the ILC were women. During the same period, the employers' delegations did not include a single woman.[156]

At the International Labour Office itself, the situation was not much different, even though women were initially better represented in the ILO than in the League of Nations' Secretariat, due to their relatively strong position within the

153 The Old-Age Insurance (Industry, etc.) Convention, 1933 (No. 35) contained a passage to the effect that pensions had to include a fixed sum, regardless of the time covered by the insurance. This worked particularly to the benefit of women, since they were more likely to receive lower wages and work for shorter periods because of maternity. Unemployment Provision Convention, 1934 (No. 44), in comparison, allows for the exemption of domestic work (predominantly female).

154 On Open Door International, see Francoise Thébaud, "Difficult Inroads, Unexpected Results: The Correspondence Committee on Women's Work in the 1930s", in *Women's ILO,* ed. Boris, Hoehtker, and Zimmermann, 50–74.

155 Dorothy Sue Cobble, "Japan and the 1919 ILO Debates over Rights, Representations and Global Labour Standards", in *The ILO from Geneva to the Pacific Rim,* ed. Jensen and Lichtenstein, 55–79.

156 Natchkova and Schoeni, "The ILO, Feminists and Expert Networks: The Challenges of a Protective Policy"; Marieke Louis, "Women's Representation at the ILO: A Hundred Years of Marginalization", in *Women's ILO,* ed. Boris, Hoehtker, and Zimmermann, 202–225.

pre-war international network of social reformers around the IALL. Still, only a very small number of these women worked in senior positions. If they did, they were typically positioned in areas deemed to be "female" domains, dealing, for example, with children and young persons. The world economic crisis provided an impulse for the establishment, in 1932, of a Correspondence Committee on Women's Work, whose primary task was the collection of information on the situation of women workers in the ILO's member States. Although it provided a valid "solidarity network",[157] the predominance of Christian groups in the Committee, many of which were opposed to women's employment in the first place, reflected the protective paradigm. The Committee's activities thus formed a "fragile backbone" for the ILO's work for women in the 1930s.[158] The opening of an ILO Division for Women and Young Workers in 1933, led by the French socialist feminist Marguerite Thibert, however, already pointed in a different direction. In "balancing conflicting visions of women's equality" Thibert's small division prepared the ground for future work. Most importantly, it produced the first comprehensive report on the working conditions of women in 40 member States, which provided a point of reference for legal equality activists, and established a basis for the ILO to move beyond the protective approach in later years.[159]

Children and Youth

The topic of child labour, by contrast, which was also mainly treated from a protective point of view, drew much less controversy. Legislative action directed towards the well-being of children had long worked as a door opener for broader humanitarian and social projects, and it seemed particularly well suited to mobilize public support for the ILO's work. During the second half of the nineteenth century, a new understanding of childhood and the protection of children from hazardous living conditions had gained increasingly currency.[160] Against this backdrop, the fight against the exploitation of children and for minimum age

157 Thébaud, "Difficult Inroads, Unexpected Results", 50–74.

158 Ibid.

159 Thibert's division was understaffed compared to other divisions, but she still managed to compile the first legislative summary: *Le statut legal des travailleuses* – a 750-page-long description of working conditions of women in 40 countries, including various aspects, such as equal pay, unemployment, and the right to work.

160 Joëlle Droux, "From Inter-Agency Competition to Transnational Cooperation: The ILO Contribution to Child Welfare Issues During the Inter-War Years", in *Globalizing Social Rights*, ed. Kott and Droux, 262–279.

regulations carried enormous symbolical weight and rallied reform movements across political dividing lines. Here, the ILO could build on the preparatory work of the IALL, which had taken up the issue of minimum age in industry already before the war. In this respect, Convention No. 5 that set the minimum age for starting work in industry at 14 years, adopted by the first ILC in 1919, was seen as a landmark success of a decade-long struggle. During the interwar years, the ILO adopted altogether 15 more Conventions and Recommendations that dealt with the protection of children and young persons from various angles.[161]

Paradoxically, these Conventions on minimum age clearly demonstrated the ILO's limitations. Many countries refrained from ratifying those Conventions, not primarily because they favoured child labour at an earlier age, but because compulsory education in their countries ended at the age of 12. Consequently, the adopted instruments would have created a gap of two years until the adolescents would have been allowed to take up employment. In order to overcome this hurdle, a more comprehensive approach to the whole issue was needed, but matters of education lay clearly outside the competence of the ILO. This was one of the reasons why in the beginning the ILO did not prioritize child protection in its work. Instead, it sought an alliance with early NGOs like the Save the Children International Union (SCIU) and the International Association for Child Protection (IACP). By working with these transnational voluntary organizations, the ILO tried both to assert its own competence and, at the same time, to neutralize "powerful and potential rival networks", a pattern that would repeat itself in other fields. This was all the more important with regard to child protection after the IACP developed closer ties with the League of Nations' social section in the course of the 1920s. With the SCIU – which turned in the 1930s from its beginnings as a provider of emergency aid into an organization advocating child welfare in a more comprehensive social policy sense – the ILO entered, in particular in Central and Eastern Europe, into a symbiotic working relationship, with the SCIU which became "an efficient spokesman" for ILO standards.[162]

During the 1930s, the focus of this network started to shift from children to young workers. The issue of youth protection was regarded a particularly pressing one, as young workers had belonged to the most vulnerable groups since the years of the economic crisis. Following traditional theories of youth protection, some saw the integration of young people into the labour market as the best means to save them from sliding into delinquency and moral decay. Others attached a

---

161 Among the Conventions were the Minimum Age (Industry) Convention (No. 5) of 1919, the Minimum Age (Agriculture) Convention (No. 10) of 1921, and Minimum Age (non-industrial employment) Convention (No. 33) from 1932.

162 Droux, "From Inter-Agency Competition to Transnational Cooperation".

political mission to the task, based on the observation that young people, permanently cut off from the labour market, were an easy prey for anti-democratic movements. This led to a series of Conventions and Recommendations between 1935 and 1939, including a Recommendation on youth unemployment. It triggered a controversial discussion about the degree to which the state should take on a more decidedly interventionist role and even use to a certain degree coercion to overcome the problem. The debate centred on the use of work camps as a means to get young people out of unemployment as practised in Nazi Germany and Fascist Italy; however, work camps for young people also existed in some democratic countries, most prominently in the United States where they were as key element of the New Deal. In 1935, when a Recommendation on youth unemployment was adopted by the ILC, the US delegation, represented by the renowned child welfare activist Grace Abbott, succeeded to have work camps included in the provisions. Concerns that such schemes could well degenerate into political indoctrination and military mobilization were, however, not easily dispelled.[163]

War Veterans, Disabled Workers, Refugees

The ILO's early activities regarding the protection of three other groups of workers were directly related to the immediate historical background against which the Organization had been founded. The first of them concerned disabled workers. The occupation with disabled men originated from the Organization's efforts to address the large-scale problems of physically mutilated war veterans. In charge of disabled veterans' affairs at the ILO, the Frenchman Adrien Tixier was instrumental in the work with associations supporting disabled veterans of the First World War, having himself lost his left arm in one of the first battles of 1914.[164] In 1921, the Governing Body convened an advisory commission to study problems related to the employment of disabled former soldiers. Subsequently, in 1923, an ILO meeting of experts was held to study "methods of finding employment for disabled men". The report of the meeting was the first in-depth international comparative study on the employment of persons with disabilities. Concern for war veterans spilled over into concern for the employment of all injured workers. Two years later, the Workmen's Compensation (Minimum Scale) Recommenda-

---

163 Ibid.

164 On Tixier's role see also Jay Winter and Antoine Prost, *René Cassin and Human Rights: From the Great War to the Universal Declaration*, Human Rights in History (Cambridge: Cambridge University Press, 2013), 52–58.

tion, 1925 (No. 22), was adopted by the ILC and became the first international recognition of the vocational needs of persons with disabilities.[165]

The second group the ILO became involved with were refugees.[166] The war, the Russian Revolutions, and the collapse of three empires (the Austro-Hungarian, Russian, and Ottoman) forced people to leave their homes on a hitherto unprecedented scale: Russians fleeing from revolution and civil war; Armenians who had escaped the genocide in Ottoman Turkey; Ruthenians, Ukrainians, and Belorussians who had become minorities in the newly created nation states of Eastern and Central Europe, which were striving for ethnic homogeneity. Together with Jews fleeing endemic persecution, they were on the move. In the host countries, themselves haunted by the war and economic crisis, they often encountered resentment and were perceived as a political and social threat. The issue of employment soon moved to the centre of the debate.

It was under these circumstances that the League of Nations High Commissioner for Refugees, the Norwegian Fridtjof Nansen, who had from 1921 onwards organized help for Russians and Armenians, in particular, turned to the ILO for help. In 1924, he submitted a proposal to the League's Council to transfer the services of the High Commissioner to the ILO, which had both the permanent structures and the resources that he was lacking. In addition, the transfer of the refugee issue to the ILO was a way, from Nansen's point of view to, to "de-politicize" a highly controversial and politically complex problem. After some debate in the Governing Body in June 1924, the High Commissioner's staff was transferred to the Office, where a small Refugee Service was created in January 1925. The Refugee Service, which formally remained part of the League, collaborated with the ILO's Migrant Service and with the Organization's national correspondents in a number of countries. The ILO set up a special committee to deal with refugee issues in 1926. While this committee assumed the day-to-day responsibilities, the League retained the political management of refugee affairs. In all its work for refugees, the ILO inherited the strictly defined mandate of the High Commissioner, which meant that, in practice, it was dealing exclusively with Russians and Armenians and a number of Christian minorities from the former Ottoman territories.[167]

---

165 Gildas Brégain, "Un problème national, interallié ou international? La difficile gestion transnationale des mutilés de guerre (1917–1923)", *Revue d'histoire de la protection sociale* 9, no. 1 (2016): 110–132.

166 Dzovinar Kévonian, "Enjeux de catégorisations et migrations internationales. Le Bureau International du Travail et les réfugiés (1925–1929)", *Revue européene des migrations internationales* 21, no. 3 (2005): 95–124.

167 Edita Gzoyan, "The League of Nations and Armenian Refugees. The Formation of the Armenian Diaspora in Syria", *Central and Eastern European Review* 8 (2014); Kévonian, "Enjeux de catégorisations et migrations internationales".

The function of the ILO's Refugee Service was to research and centralize employment offers, to carry out statistical research about the refugee population, and to select refugees according to their qualifications for employment – a complex task, since it needed the cooperation of the host countries. Another important aim was to investigate resettlement possibilities, for instance in Latin America. Although Thomas insisted on the technical nature of the ILO's work, the problems were numerous: the problematic legal status of the refugees; their need for visas; and the diversity of the refugee populations, with all age groups represented. The work produced mixed results. The ILO placed some 50,000 refugees between 1925 and 1928, but many of them were settled in France, which was in need of migrant workers at the time, or in territories under French mandate (in fact, 52% of all placed refugees in 1925 and 1926). In Latin America, however, where Argentina was seen as the most promising destination, the efforts were unsuccessful for legal and financial reasons. States did not renew so-called Nansen passports for stateless persons; they tightened immigration controls; and employers refused to issue work contracts. Another problem was that, while the ILO was able to place industrial and, to a certain degree, agricultural workers, it was generally not in a position to find employment for white-collar workers, nor could it take action for people outside its mandate, such as children, old persons, and the disabled.[168]

Critical voices in the Governing Body accompanied the ILO's work for refugees from the start. Some insisted that it should continue to be regarded as provisional and temporary. States did not want the ILO to be engaged in resettlement issues, which they thought lay outside the Organization's mandate. Since the problem could not be restricted easily to employment issues alone, in time, those voices grew in strength.[169] Finally, in 1928, Thomas proposed to transfer the functions of the Refugee Service back to the High Commissioner at the League, which happened in 1929.[170]

The ILO's work for refugees, although exceptional in character, highlighted a more general pattern with regard to the ILO's strategy against unemployment – organized migration to countries with labour shortages. In this respect, the 1920s refugee crises constituted a time of experimentation. Unemployment was increasingly seen as a question of structural imbalance between work offers and job seekers. Organized migration was justified with the need to maintain regu-

168 Kévonian, "Enjeux de catégorisations et migrations internationales".

169 ILO, Minutes of the Governing Body, 38th Session, Geneva, 1928, 66, 67.

170 After Nansen died in 1930, the League of Nations created a regular organ, the Nansen International Office for Refugees. Claudena Skran, *Refugees in Interwar Europe. The Emergence of a Regime* (Oxford: Oxford University Press, 1995).

lated and protected labour markets and social systems in countries where a high concentration of refugees had led to wage dumping, increased burden on social systems (health care for refugees), competition among the poorest, and, eventually, grave social tensions.[171]

Beyond the Industrial Bias: Seafarers, Agriculture, and Intellectual Labour

Most standard-setting during the interwar years was tailored to the needs of industrial workers. Other ILO activities, such as the research undertaken into living standards, tended to even further emphasize this bias. At the same time, the sole emphasis on the problems of industrial workers did not remain uncontested. On the contrary, it was challenged both from above, that is, by the leadership of the ILO, which constantly tried to widen and diversify its sphere of action, and from below, from those excluded from or marginalized by the ILO's work.

A group of workers that acted as trailblazers in this respect were seafarers. Maritime labour was regarded, because of its thoroughly transnational character, as an area in which the ILO could make a valuable contribution to the improvement of working conditions. Due to its special character, it was the only area of the Organization's work that was subject to separate, maritime labour conferences, starting with the second – maritime – Session of the ILC in Genoa in 1920.[172] The task to find common standards was, however, complicated by the huge differences in salaries and working conditions that separated European seafarers from their counterparts in South or South-East Asia or Africa. Neither the European governments nor shipowners or sea farer trade unions were too keen to tackle these differences along racial lines, for instance, when it came to the regulation of working hours. On the other hand, Asian seafarers criticized universal standards as a protectionist tool imposed by Western countries. Despite these controversies,

---

171 On the wider implication of the ILO's work in the field during the era, for example the development of the very category "international migration", see Yann Stricker, "'International Migration'" between Empire and Nation. The Statistical Construction of an Ambiguous Global Category in the International Labour Office in the 1920s, *Ethnicities*, March (2019).

172 The Genoa Conference was the first ILC with the full machinery in place. Seafarers' issues might have been singled out because they had been dropped from the nine points of the Labour Charter under article 427 in the original Constitution and had not been included in the Washington agenda, largely due to resistance of the US sailors' union leader, Andrew Furuseth, who was initially a fierce opponent of the ILO. Later, Furuseth became an important supporter of the Organization. See Leon Fink, "A Sea of Difference: The ILO and the Search for Common Standards. 1919–1945", in *The ILO from Geneva to the Pacific Rim*, ed. Jensen and Lichtenstein, 15–32.

the ILO managed to adopt not less than 12 Conventions between 1920 and 1936, regulating mainly less controversial issues like minimum age, repatriation, or medical examination.[173]

The case of agricultural labour followed a different path. Whether, to what degree, and what kinds of workers in the huge and heterogeneous agricultural sector should fall within the scope of the ILO's standard-setting were permanent issues throughout the interwar period and basically remained so far into the post–Second World War era.[174] The first two ILCs decided that some of the Conventions adopted – for instance, those relating to unemployment and the protection of women and children – should also apply to the agricultural workers. A French government intervention in 1921, which challenged the ILO's competence, offered an opportunity for clarification. After the Permanent Court of International Justice had settled the matter in favour of the ILO's position, it also paved the way for a total of seven Conventions adopted before the Second World War.[175] Yet, neither the court's decision nor the agricultural standards adopted, covering, for example, the right to freedom of association, minimum age, and sickness insurance, could conceal the fact that the ILO was moving on uncertain ground. There was already another agency in place, the International Institute of Agriculture (IIA) in Rome, which claimed responsibility for all matters related to agriculture. In 1922, the ILO and the IIA built a Mixed Advisory Agricultural Committee, which never became a strong voice in international agricultural discussions. The cooperation would soon also be overshadowed by the IIA's transformation into a foreign policy instrument of the Italian Fascist government.[176]

A much more fundamental problem was hidden behind the very term "agricultural labour" itself, because of the enormous diversity of agricultural labour and the equally vast variety of conditions – with regard to property, distribution of land, climate, social and cultural differences – under which this labour was performed throughout the world. To find common standards that would adequately reflect this diversity was a giant task, and it was a real concern that this very diversity would render any standards practically meaningless. In addition,

173 Today, there are 36 maritime Conventions, with the 2006 Maritime Labour Convention as a new legislative umbrella. On the ILO's treatment of maritime labour, see Fink, "A Sea of Difference".

174 Ribi Forclaz, "A New Target for International Social Reform".

175 Alcock, *History of the International Labour Organization*, 55.

176 Guiseppe de Michelis, head of the IIA from 1925–1933, served for many years also as a delegate both in the League of Nations and the ILO. See Stefano Gallo, "Dictatorship and International Organizations: The ILO as a Test Ground for Fascism", in *Globalizing Social Rights*, ed. Kott and Droux, 160–161.

agricultural labour did not easily fit into the ILO's tripartite structure, as agriculture belonged to the least unionized parts of the world of work, and the leading trade union federations did not take a genuine interest in the matter, either. The lower status of agricultural labour was reflected in the limited resources dedicated to it on the institutional level. As in most other areas, the world economic crisis marked a turning point for the ILO's treatment of agricultural labour. The crisis put a spotlight on low living standards and dire working conditions in rural areas both inside and outside Europe, which had suffered immensely from the effects of the depression and, in particular, from the decline in demand and prices that followed. In 1936, the ILO called in a tripartite Permanent Agricultural Committee, which included representatives of agricultural employers and trade unions as well as experts in the field. Through its composition and its work, the Committee displayed, for the first time, what Amalia Ribi Forclaz has called an "understanding of global social problems in agriculture", which laid the foundation for the fuller integration of agricultural labour into the realm of the ILO's work after the Second World War, with regard to both standard-setting and technical assistance.[177]

Similar to the case of agricultural labour, part of the problem faced by "intellectual" or "white-collar" workers in seeking recognition as a group through the ILO was the very vagueness of these categories. The term "intellectual worker" included a kaleidoscope of professions, from artists, musicians, and writers through journalists to academics. "White-collar work" referred to middle management employees and clerks, but it was basically a catch-all term for those who were employed without performing manual labour in the narrower sense. Some of these sub-groups had long-standing transnational representations like the *Association litteraire et artistique internationale*, founded in 1878, or the *Bureau central des associations de presse* (1894). To find common ground for trade unions spanning all different categories was, therefore, not an easy task, as their primary stakes in a professional representation differed significantly. While some where interested in copyright law issues or standard contracts for freelance work, others, such as academics or salaried employees, were more concerned with classical trade union issues like wages or working time.

To become part of the ILO's standard-setting framework was therefore the most important motive behind the founding of the *Confédération internationale des travailleurs intellectuels* (CITI) in 1923 – the first association that crossed professional boundaries. Thomas promoted this step, as the new association once again strengthened the ILO's international network. The ILO

177 Ribi Forclaz, "A New Target for International Social Reform", 323.

also had to find a mode of cooperation with the International Committee on Intellectual Cooperation (ICIC), an advisory organization for the League (and predecessor of the United Nations Educational and Scientific Organization, UNESCO) founded in 1922. A division of labour between the two institutions was relatively easy to establish, since the ICIC focused on intellectual work and the promotion of intercultural exchange, while the ILO and the CITI (which also cooperated with the ICIC) were interested primarily in the intellectual worker as such.

While the ILO welcomed intellectual workers, fitting such a broad and amorphous group into an Organization with a strong industrial bias was challenging. This was reflected, for instance, in the creation of different subcommittees for "salaried employees" and a consultative commission for intellectual workers, which represented all other categories. More important than this division was the fact that the integration of intellectual workers raised questions about the broader meaning of intellectual work, the significance of "habitus", professional cultures, and the tension between individualized work processes and the quest for collective representation.[178]

Entering the Broader Social Field: Occupational Health, Housing, and Spare Time

While the ILO thus expanded its scope of action with regard to new groups of workers, it also took an interest in an ever-widening notion of what constituted genuine social policy issues. Some of the discussions ultimately led the ILO into areas that lay originally outside its immediate scope of competence. This was certainly not the case for the area of social insurance. During its first two decades, the ILO adopted conventions dealing with social insurance schemes covering old age, sickness, injury, and unemployment. These standards were based on the "German model" of contributory insurance schemes tied to the individual worker's employment contract, and they reflected the ILO's orientation towards industrial work. Only in the 1930s, under US influence, did broader ideas of social security begin to gain ground in the Organization.[179]

One of the most innovative areas of the ILO's standard-setting work that opened the door to broader social questions was related to minimum wages.

178 Verbruggen, "Intellectual Workers and Their Search for a Place within the ILO During the Interwar Period".
179 Kott, "Constructing a European Social Model", 181–193.

Since the beginning, the provision of an "adequate living wage" had been listed among the ILO's objectives and was seen as a means to avoid unfair competition on the basis of low wages. At a time when strong mechanisms of collective bargaining were still few and far between, minimum wages were considered the best way to secure workers' living standards and thus to promote both economic stability and social peace. Normative action, in this sense, followed both a protective and a "proto-Keynesian" rationale. In 1928, the ILC adopted the Minimum Wage-Fixing Machinery Convention (No. 26), which belongs to the most widely ratified of all ILO Conventions. The ILO's research on living standards that accompanied normative action from the 1920s onwards was equally credited for its innovative nature and served as a yardstick for social policies.[180] By defining abstract categories to measure living standards, the ILO contributed to – and, in a sense, created – the preconditions for social and economic planning, including the field of development policies, which could thus start from a solid empirical basis. In the same way, the ILO's research on living standards and its elaboration of social statistics helped to build a concept of social and economic rights during this early period.[181]

A supreme example of the broadening understanding of the ILO's social mandate and the very notions of the boundaries of social and labour policies was the treatment of health issues. During the first years of its existence, the ILO and its industrial hygiene section were mainly concerned with matters of occupational health and safety and followed the path opened by the first international convention banning white phosphorus from 1906. In the course of the 1920s, however, the ILO developed a more inclusionary approach and increasingly framed industrial health issues with regard to their broader social context. But there were clear limits as to how far it could incorporate a comprehensive approach to occupational health in its standard-setting process. To define "occupational diseases" as diseases "contracted at work" was a difficult task, for the very reason that these diseases could not always be neatly isolated from the worker's broader living conditions. While the ILO helped to create a list

180 See Emmanuel Reynaud, *The International Labour Organization and the Living Wage: A Historical Perspective*, Conditions of Work and Employment Series No. 90 (Geneva: ILO, 2017).
181 Laure Piguet, "Establishing Social Justice through International Quantification: The International Labour Organization and Labour Statistics (1919–1939)", unpublished conference paper submitted at the conference *Fair is fair. International Historical Perspectives on Social Justice*, Padua, 2016; see also Laure Piguet, "La justice sociale par les statistiques? Le cas des accidents d'attelage des wagons de chemins de fer (1923–1931)", *Le Mouvement Social* 2 (2018), 31–43; Dzovinar Kévonian, "La légitimation par l'expertise: le Bureau international du travail et la statistique international", *Les cahiers Irice* 2, no. 2 (2008): 81–106.
Wobbe, "Das Globalwerden der Menschenrechte in der ILO".

of recognized occupational diseases in 1925, standard-setting in this field inevitably raised some delicate questions about responsibility and financial compensation. Governments and employers were, therefore, often hesitant to commit to standards that might result in considerable costs for them. Luigi Carozzi, the head of the ILO's Industrial Health Section, applied a cautious and multi-layered approach, including research and advocacy, to overcome this resistance. Under his guidance, the ILO chose a strategic cause, the struggle against silicosis – a respiratory disease typically related to the mining industry – and mobilized its international networks. In 1930, the ILO organized an international conference in Johannesburg, South Africa (the first-ever ILO Conference outside Europe), which produced results that built a platform allowing the inclusion of silicosis in the Workmen's Compensation for Occupational Diseases Convention, 1934 (No. 42).[182]

Early on, the ILO entered into cooperation with the League of Nations Health Organization (LNHO) and its Polish Director Ludwik Rajchman, who tried to establish "social medicine" as a paradigm in international health politics. Throughout the interwar period, the ILO and the LNHO cooperated on a series of committees and conferences, which examined the relationship between health and general living conditions, rural hygiene, and child welfare. Both organizations promoted innovative research on the effects of malnutrition on the working population, as well as on the positive effect of sunlight, and the health risks related to smoke and noise at the workplace. In the 1930s, at the height of the economic crisis, both organizations conducted surveys on the psychological effects of unemployment. The ILO's cooperation with the LNHO reflected more than anything a renewed sense of concern with the socio-economic bases of health,[183] which was a hallmark of this time period. It was one of the least conflict-ridden of the many partnerships the ILO entered into during its first decades.[184]

A similar point about the limits of the ILO's social policy scope could be made about its treatment of housing, which, on the surface, was not less a part of workers' welfare than public health or employment services. Many countries suffered from

182 Lespinet-Moret, "Promouvoir la santé au travail?"; Thomas Cayet, Marie Thébaud-Sorger, and Paul-André Rosental, "How International Organisations Compete: Occupational Safety and Health at the ILO, a Diplomacy of Expertise", *Journal of Modern European History* 7, no. 2 (2009): 174–96.

183 Gerry Rodgers et al., *The ILO and the Quest for Social Justice*; Lespinet-Moret, "Promouvoir la santé au travail comme droit social?".

184 When eugenics emerged as an increasingly powerful competitor during the latter part of the interwar period, both organizations shared a recognizable position as a common stronghold of the social medicine paradigm. See Weindling, "Social Medicine at the League of Nations Health Organization and the International Labour Office Compared", 147–148.

a severe housing crisis, with a great majority of workers in industrialized countries living in cramped and unhygienic conditions. Proactive public housing schemes, like those implemented in the "Red Vienna" of the 1920s, with houses built that provided living space for tens of thousands of people, were still an exception to the rule. For Albert Thomas and many others, housing clearly belonged within the scope of the ILO's standard-setting, but all attempts to put it on the agenda of the ILC met with stiff resistance from governments and employers. For the employers, housing was a problem that had to be solved by private initiative; governments, for their part, resisted the adoption of an appropriate convention because it would have committed them to comprehensive and potentially costly public housing programmes. Due to the lack of political will and funding, much of the International Labour Office's work in the field during the interwar period remained small-scale. The ILO saw itself compelled to use indirect channels to continue promoting its housing policies. For instance, housing was included in the Utilisation of Spare Time Recommendation of 1924 (No. 21), where it featured next to recreational activities and the fight against alcoholism. In addition, the ILO tried to mobilize public opinion by means of cooperation with non-governmental organizations like the International Town Planning Federation. It also helped to launch an International Housing Association (located in Frankfurt am Main, Germany), which was closely linked to the ILO in institutional terms. The networks created through these cooperations were intended to raise the awareness of both the problem and the preparedness of the ILO to provide solutions.[185]

Yet another area in which the ILO became very active during the interwar period was leisure time policy. The Utilisation of Spare Time Recommendation reflected the broad and comprehensive social reformist approach that the ILO took towards workers' leisure time.[186] The Recommendation was also in its wording a direct follow-up to the Hours of Work (Industry) Convention of 1919 and was connected to the debate on workers' living standards. Rather than defining spare time as merely time spent off work, it perceived of leisure time as a tool to further class-crossing private consumption and workers' individual development. In the Recommendation's own words, "during such spare time workers have the opportunity of developing freely, according to their individual tastes, their physical, intellectual and moral powers". As a consequence, "such development is of great value from the point of view of the progress of civilisation". Spare time, in this broad understanding, fulfilled various material and immaterial, individual and

185 Pierre-Yves Saunier, "Borderline Work: ILO Explorations onto the Housing Scene until 1940", in *ILO Histories*, ed. Van Daele et. al., 197–220.

186 Liebscher, *Freude und Arbeit*.

societal goals. During leisure time, workers should be able to "do as they please", but if spare time was "well-directed", it could also help increase the workers' productivity and fulfill an economic function at the same time.[187] During the interwar years, the ILO provided the most important international forum for debate on spare time policies. As will be shown later, this was also an area of work in which the ILO's social liberal model competed with authoritarian models of spare time policy represented by Fascist Italy and Nazi Germany.[188]

How successful was the ILO's work in the area of standard-setting during these early years? Measured by the numbers, the balance was mixed. During the interwar years the ratification rate with regard to all international labour standards rose steadily, but not in the same way for all standards.[189] Of all the Conventions adopted, the Equality of Treatment (Accident Compensation) Convention, 1925 (No. 19), aimed at migrant workers, was the most successful with 35 ratifications, followed by the Medical Examination of Young Persons (Sea) Convention, 1921 (No. 16), the Workmen's Compensation (Occupational Diseases) Convention, 1925 (No. 18), and the Marking of Weight (Packages Transported by Vessels) Convention, 1929 (No. 27), which all drew 34 ratifications.[190]

The relative success of some of these standards might be explained by their rather technical nature (as the lack of ratifications for other standards may be explained by their controversial or otherwise political character). In the case of the Equality of Treatment Convention, its adoption was due to the fact that it could build on bilateral agreements from the time before the First World War, regulating the treatment of labour migrants on a mutual basis between individual nations. It is still remarkable how uncontroversial the equal treatment of migrant workers and the international regulation of the issue was during this early period.

Numbers, in any case, have to be taken with a grain of salt. They alone might not tell the whole story with regard to "success" or "failure". They might conceal both the revolutionary nature and the transformative power that some of the ILO's standard-setting activities had, despite slow and low ratification. With regard to some of the standards for which this was the case (like the ones on the eight-hour working day, on unemployment insurance, or on women's protection),

187 Utilisation of Spare Time Recommendation, 1924 (No. 21).

188 Liebscher, *Freude und Arbeit;* see also the chapter 2 on "Fascism", below.

189 Nicolas Valticos, "Fifty Years of Standard-Setting Activities by the International Labour Organisation", *International Labour Review* 135, no. 3–4 (1996), 393–414, here 408.

190 There were conditional ratifications, for example by France, since some countries did not want to fully ratify until other countries, such as Great Britain, had not done so. In all, there were 13 ratifications subject to such a condition. Francis Maupain, *The Future of the International Labour Organization in the Global Economy* (Oxford: Hart Publishing, 2013), n. 50.

the debates they encouraged on the international and national levels had long-lasting effects.

The ILO and the World(s) of non-European Labour, 1919–1930

While the ILO's mandate was not restricted to any region of the world or any political or social environment, its work was deeply biased, both politically and geographically. Despite all proclamations to the contrary, for most of the interwar years, the Organization kept a pronounced European profile, with the greater part of its activities directed at workers in the industrially advanced countries of the West.

This bias was not immediately obvious from the composition of the ILO´s first Conference. Of the 40 delegations present in Washington, D.C., in 1919, less than half came from Europe and North America. Latin America alone accounted for 16 participating nations, but also five Asian countries (China, India, Japan, Persia, and Thailand) and one from Africa (the British Dominion of South Africa) took part in the ILO's inaugural Conference. During the interwar years, when more non-European countries such as Mexico, Afghanistan, Egypt, Liberia, and Ethiopia joined the Organization, their numerical weight increased further.

Numbers, however, did not equal influence. The European bias was above all reflected in the composition of the Governing Body. When it first met in 1919, not less than 20 of its 24 members came from European countries, with Japan, Argentina, and Canada as the only non-European Government members. Between 1919 and 1922, the Workers' and Employers' groups in the Governing Body had no members from outside Europe (and Canada) at all.[191] The financial and logistical difficulties of most non-European nations in sending full delegations to the ILC further constrained their ability to exert any influence. This was the case for countries like Liberia or Persia, but it was even true for economically advanced members such as New Zealand or some of the Latin American countries. They were often

191 In the period from 1919 to 1930, the Workers' and Employers' groups of the Governing Body had only a few members from outside Europe and Canada, despite an amendment which already in 1922 increased the number of Governing Body members from 24 to 32 (16 Government, eight Employers' and eight Workers' delegates). In 1922, an Indian delegate joined the Workers' group for many years as a deputy member. A South African delegate became a regular member of the Employers' group where we find later also a deputy member from Argentina (1925) and Japan (1928). See ILOA, "List of Employers' and Workers' Members and Deputy Members of the Governing Body Since 1919 and Their Countries of Origin".

represented by their permanent representatives in Geneva, who had little specific knowledge of ILO matters.[192]

The lack of representation of the non-European world was also reflected at the level of the Office. Until way into the 1950s, there were very few staff members from Asia and Latin America and none from Africa. During the interwar years, the average ratio of European vis-à-vis non-European employees was 10:1. Given the aforementioned double role – experts and diplomats vis-à-vis their countries of origin – which these international bureaucrats were often supposed to fulfill, this was a clear indicator of the marginal position certain regions of the world occupied in the ILO's realm during this period. The same was true for the network of correspondents, which was highly developed in Europe, while no official representation at all existed, for example, in sub-Saharan Africa until the end of the 1950s.

The most substantial obstacle to the integration of the non-European world into the ILO's framework was inextricably tied to standard-setting. In 1919, the Labour Commission in Paris had already admitted that the new Organization's focus on industrial labour would make its labour standards not easily, if at all, applicable to the conditions in economically less advanced regions of the world. The formula found to deal with this situation and that was eventually incorporated in the ILO's Constitution read:

> In framing any Convention or Recommendation of general application the Conference shall have due regard to those countries in which climatic conditions, the imperfect development of industrial organization, or other special circumstances make the industrial conditions substantially different and shall suggest the modifications, if any, which it considers may be required to meet the case of such countries.[193]

During the inaugural Conference, the paragraph was applied for the first time with regard to the Hours of Work Convention, for which some countries such as China and Persia were granted exceptions or special regulations (Japan: 57 hours per week; India: 60 hours per week). During the discussion which led to the adoption of Convention No. 33 on the minimum age in non-industrial employment in 1932, employers and governments argued successfully against the workers' position, which favoured abolition of child labour without distinction, and came out instead in defence of a "gradual" approach to be applied in non-Western countries.[194]

192 Jeremy Seekings, "The ILO and Welfare Reform in South Africa, Latin America, and the Caribbean, 1919–1950", in *ILO Histories*, ed. Van Daele et al., 145–72.
193 ILO, Constitution of the International Labour Organisation, art. 19 (3) (Paris, 1919).
194 Rodgers et al., *The ILO and the Quest for Social Justice*, 70, 101.

The ILO's position in this regard was ambivalent. It clearly acknowledged that, even in countries where industrialization was gaining ground, such as in India, the bulk of ILO standard-setting still affected only a tiny proportion of workers. With regard to the Organization's standards, Harold Butler, who was the first ILO Director to visit India in 1938, appreciated that, while industrialization bred the same problems in India as in the West, the problems of industrialized countries, such as wages, working time, social insurance, and relations between workers and employers, were secondary to India's more urgent problems of population growth, illiteracy, and health.[195]

The ILO was, at the same time, not indifferent to the world outside Europe, although with a clear hierarchy. In Latin America, in particular, the ILO tried to build up contacts and widen its geographical scope early on. From Albert Thomas' perspective, the region provided a potentially fruitful field for ILO action. Like many of his contemporaries, he saw in Latin America a sort of "strategic reserve in the defence of democratic values and social justice", an outpost where European, and therefore universal, values were defended. In addition, many countries in the region started to industrialize in the period after the First World War. Their economies were dynamic and attracted labour migration from Europe and other places. Some, such as Brazil, Argentina, Chile, Uruguay, or Mexico (which, however, became a member of the ILO only in 1931), had already implemented social legislation comparable to European schemes. Albert Thomas was therefore keen to convince Latin American countries to ratify ILO conventions and to send full delegations to the ILC. The ILO collected data on social developments in the region and hired Latin American staff to the International Labour Office. In 1925, Thomas went on a five-week-long trip across the Southern Cone, passing through Brazil, Argentina, Uruguay, and Chile in order to make the work of the ILO better known.[196] Despite these efforts, relationships between Latin America and the ILO only developed slowly. While parts of the political elites were suspicious of the "leftist" character of the Organization, a greater part of the Latin American labour movement, with its strong anarcho-syndicalist and communist currents, found the ILO model of class cooperation not very attractive, to say the least. In addition, the ILO competed with pan-Americanism as an alternative to an exclusively continental form of internationalism. The dominant role of the United States in this framework, and its position outside the ILO, made these two internationalisms hardly reconcilable during this period. Yet, the network the

195 Plata-Stenger, "Une voie sociale pour le développement", 191–205.

196 Ferreras, "Europe-Geneva-America: The First International Conference of American States Members of the International Labour Organization".

ILO steadily built up among social reformers, administrators, and parts of the trade unions raised the credibility of the Organization's claims to universality. It would pay off a few years later, when the ILO, in the years of crisis under Albert Thomas's successor, Harold Butler, would shift its attention away from Europe to the western hemisphere.[197]

The white British settler dominions of Australia and New Zealand shared some similarities with the Latin American countries in this respect. Australia's social policy, in particular, was in many ways more advanced than the ILO conventions, but its governments and trade unions also showed a genuine interest in international labour standards. Among the reasons for the appeal of the standards were the country's highly restrictive immigration policies, epitomized by the slogan of "White Australia". ILO conventions were seen as a means of protecting white Australian workers against "unfair" competition by cheap Asian labour, particularly from China. Adherence to ILO policies also suited Australia's self-perception as an outpost of European civilization in the Asia-Pacific region. However, in spite of their support of the Organization, Australia and New Zealand, with their vast distances from Europe, remained marginal in the ILO's cosmos during the early decades.[198]

The situation in East Asia differed in some ways from those in Latin America and the Asian Pacific. Japan had been the only Asian country accepted among major powers at the Paris Peace Conference and assigned a permanent seat in the ILO's Governing Body from its inception. The ILO's early interest in Japan stemmed from many sources. Both politically and economically, it was the leading power in the East, and in order to secure Japan's hegemonic position, the country's elites initially showed a keen interest in international cooperation.[199] In the economic field, although Japan's industry was still in an infant state, the country had embarked on a rapid and highly ambitious programme of industrialization and economic expansion after the First World War. State-directed economic planning in the Japanese industrialization model soon caught the attention of ILO officials. Moreover, Japan presented an interesting opportunity to promote ILO labour standards, as many advanced industrial countries increasingly felt Japanese competition and accused it of "social dumping". Poor working conditions

---

197 Yannick Wehrli, "ILO and Latin America: A Bibliographical Synthesis", unpublished working paper for the ILO Century Project (Geneva: ILO, 2017).

198 Marilyn Lake, "The ILO, Australia and the Asia-Pacific Region: New Solidarities or Internationalism in the National Interest", in *The ILO from Geneva to the Pacific Rim*, ed. Jensen and Lichtenstein.

199 Thomas W. Burkman, *Japan and the League of Nations: Empire and World Order, 1914–1938* (Honolulu: University of Hawai'i Press, 2008).

Figure 3: Albert Thomas, first Director of the ILO (left), and ILO official Marius Viple during their visit to Japan in 1928.

in Japanese industry had already been a topic debated by the first ILC, and countries like Australia would repeatedly attack Japan's low wages and social standards, which, in their view, constituted unfair competition. Japanese Workers' delegates in return used the forum of the ILC to call attention to their country's low standards.[200] From the beginning, the ILO tried to intensify its contacts with Japan, and, as early as 1922, it opened a correspondent office in Tokyo. In 1928–1929, Albert Thomas made the country the last and longest stop of his journey to the East, and ILO technical missions were sent to Japan in the following years.[201]

China, by contrast, although among the founding members of the Organization, opened up much later to the ILO. A three-month ILO mission led by Pierre Henry, which investigated labour conditions in China in 1924, remained an excep-

200 Sluga, *Internationalism in the Age of Nationalism*; Cobble, "Japan and the 1919 ILO Debates over Rights, Representations and Global Labour Standards", 65–69.

201 Veronique Plata-Stenger, "L'OIT et le problème du sous-developpement en Asie dans l'entre-deux-guerres" *Le Mouvement Social* 263 (2018), 109–122.

tion. During the 1920s, China sent only Government delegates to the annual sessions of the ILC, and it provided very scarce information on its labour and social policy. Repeated calls from the ILC for China to accept additional ILO missions to investigate child labour and working conditions led to even stiffer resistance. This attitude changed only when the Nationalist (Nanjing) government assumed power in 1925. China gradually shifted to a more active and forthcoming policy, and it increasingly used the ILO as a venue for pursuing its foreign policy goals. The ratification of ILO standards thus became part of a strategy to enhance China's international status, in particular after the start of the Sino-Japanese War in 1932 and Japan's exit from the League and the ILO the following year. China was first elected to the Governing Body in 1934 and became a permanent member in 1944.[202]

India was yet another special case. Formally still a British colony, it became the only non- independent member of the ILO in 1919, and, in 1922, occupied one of the permanent seats in the Governing Body as a "country of major industrial importance". The composition of its delegations and its overall standing within the ILO were undoubtedly determined by its status as a British colony. Its ratification of certain international labour standards, as well as its non-ratification of others, always reflected to some degree the interests of British industry, which sought to exclude low-cost labour competition from India. Nevertheless, the very fact of India's prominent presence at the ILO contributed to the legitimacy of an independent Indian position. It also provided a point of departure for being recognized – in addition to Japan – as a voice of the Asian continent in the international arena at large.[203] The ILO, much more so than the League, offered India an opportunity to assert an autonomous stand even before independence. In 1928, the ILO opened a branch office in Delhi, the first in continental Asia, which further underscored India's particular status. Membership in the ILO also had effects at the local level. It gave an incentive to both workers and employers to overcome intra-Indian divisions in an effort to build strong national representations.[204] Yet, in the light of the fact that the number of workers in the industrial

202 Chen Yifeng, "The International Labour Organization and Labour Governance in China 1919–1949", in *China and ILO: Fundamental Principles and Rights at Work.* Special Issue of *Bulletin of Comparative Labour Relations* 86, ed. Roger Blanpain, Ulla Liukkunen, and Chen Yifeng (Alphen aan den Rijn: Kluwer Law International, 2014), 19–54; Aiqun Hu, *China's Social Insurance in the 20th Century: A Global Historical Perspective* (Leiden: Brill, 2015).

203 The first initiatives for an Asian Regional Conference were launched by India as early as the 1920s.

204 Gerry Rodgers, J. Krishnamurty, and Sabyasachi Bhattachary, "India and the ILO in Historical Perspective", *Economic and Political Weekly* XLVI no. 10 (2011).

area was still very small, this remained little more than an "elite's leisure" – an observation that could easily be applied, *cum grano salis*, to the situation of the great majority of ILO member States from Asia.[205]

If Asia remained in the backwaters of the ILO's activities and interests throughout the interwar years, the Organization's presence in Africa was by far weakest. Apart from the South African Union, which, due to its status as a "white" British Dominion and its relatively advanced industry, occupied a unique position, only two sub-Saharan African countries, Liberia and Ethiopia, were members of the Organization before the Second World War.[206] As to the countries in North Africa, the situation was little different, except for Egypt, which developed early relationships with the ILO. In both cases, the ILO's room for action was tightly restricted by the colonial status of the vast majority of African territories during the interwar years.[207]

A World Apart – Colonial Labour

Nowhere, then, was the European bias of the ILO more pronounced than in the field of colonial labour. When the ILO was founded, hundreds of millions of people, a significant part of the world's population, lived and worked under the colonial domination of European powers. Yet, their problems hardly ever reached the agenda of the ILO's meetings.

The reasons could be found in the nature of the international system that emerged from the First World War and the imperial nature of its most powerful protagonists. When the League of Nations was founded, the major European powers did not consider it a threat to their imperial ambitions but as a means to renew and stabilize their claims to colonial rule. British imperialists like Winston Churchill or Jan Smuts saw the League as a kind of extended Commonwealth, and thus as a tool to ideologically tighten the grip of the colonial powers on their imperial subjects by evoking a legitimate international mandate to spread (European)

205 Madeleine Herren, "Global Corporatism after the First World War – the Indian Case", in *Globalizing Social Rights*, ed. Kott and Droux; Rodgers, Krishnamurty, and Bhattachary, "India and the ILO in Historical Perspective".
206 Jeremy Seekings, "The ILO and Welfare Reform in South Africa, Latin America and the Caribbean, 1919–1950", in *ILO Histories*, ed. Van Daele et al.; Daniel Maul, Luca Puddu, and Hakeem Ibikunle Tijani, "The International Labour Organization", in *General Labour History of Africa: Workers, Employers and Governments, 20th–21st Centuries*, ed. Stefano Bellucci and Andreas Eckert (Woodbridge: James Currey, 2019), 223–264.
207 On Egypt, see Plata-Stenger, "Une voie sociale pour le développement", 301–303.

civilization.[208] The League's mandate system changed little of substance in that respect: on the one hand, the creation and the work of the League's Permanent Mandates Commission (PMC), in which the ILO also held a seat, formally placed the administration of the mandates – the former German and Ottoman possessions in the Middle East, sub-Saharan Africa, and the Pacific – by the mandatary powers (the victors of the First World War) under international supervision. It tied the custody over those mandates to a catalogue of criteria, asked the powers to provide reports on the progress of the mandates towards ultimate independence, and added an element of accountability that was absent in the old-style colonial system. On the other hand, the PMC consisted almost exclusively of European members, the majority of which held colonial possessions themselves. The PMC's composition and its limited competences virtually ensured that the mandate system would not interfere with the colonial powers' discretionary authority over these territories.[209]

In the ILO, the situation was very similar. During the first two decades of its existence, the claim of the colonial powers to sovereignty over the affairs of their colonial subjects was essentially never disputed within the bodies of the Organization. The reasons for this were obvious: all major colonial powers held permanent seats on the ILO's Governing Body. The initial absence of the United States and the Soviet Union, two powers potentially critical of (European) imperialism, meant that the colonial powers encountered very little resistance in their attempts to keep their territorial possessions out of the international limelight.[210]

One of the most important decisions regarding the ILO's constitutional treatment of the colonies was taken at the Second Session of the ILC in 1920. The issue under debate was whether and how the provisions of international labour standards could be applied to overseas territories as stipulated in Article 35 of the ILO's Constitution. This article, known as the "colonial clause", gave the colonial powers freedom to exempt their colonies from certain international labour standards, without these territories automatically falling outside the scope of ILO standard-setting in general. In practice, the "colonial clause" provided the colonial powers with an effective means to ensure, up to the Second World War, that all initiatives aimed at larger-scale ILO involvement, let alone the implementation of ILO standards, would have very little impact.[211]

208 Mazower, *No Enchanted Palace.*

209 Susan Pedersen, *The Guardians: The League of Nations and the Crisis of Empire* (Oxford: Oxford University Press, 2015).

210 Susan Zimmermann, "'Special Circumstances' in Geneva: The ILO and the World of Non-Metropolitan Labour in the Inter-War Years", in *ILO Histories*, ed. Van Daele et al., 221–250.

211 Maul, *Human Rights, Development, and Decolonization*, 19.

The exclusion of colonial issues from the ILO's proceedings was further highlighted by the absence of direct representation from the colonies in the Organization's meeting rooms. India was the only exception to the rule.[212] In no other case prior to 1939 did metropolitan governments ever include a representative of a colonial territory in their delegations, although prominent figures from the colonies were sporadically called upon in an advisory capacity to help with the ILO's standard-setting work.[213] In the absence of direct representation from the colonies during the annual sessions of the ILC, it was mainly up to the Workers' group to place colonial issues on the agenda.[214]

In contrast to the situation after the Second World War, the few independent countries from Asia or Africa were rarely ever able to act on behalf of colonial peoples, and they even had problems in sending complete delegations to the ILC. The small space given to the discussion of colonial labour issues during the interwar years was mirrored in the lack of resources committed to the study of colonial labour issues by the Office. A tiny Native Labour Section of only one to three persons accounted for all of the Office's colonial work.[215] Given this situation, when the ILO first became active on behalf of colonial labour, it did so under predominantly humanitarian premises. These efforts focused on the worst abuses of "native labour" in the colonies and centred on the problem of forced labour.[216] The systematic use of forced labour in many parts of colonial Africa (and some parts of Asia) during the interwar years was the result of a complex interplay between the colonial powers' aim to make their colonies more profitable (*mise en valeur*) and their parallel unwillingness to commit resources for a social infrastructure that would be capable of ameliorating the damaging effects of this policy.[217] This reluctance was not based on financial considerations alone. According to the prevailing colonial doctrines of the time, it was seen as a mistake, for example, to promote a policy that provided the indigenous pop-

---

212 India was represented from the very beginning. However, up to 1929, its delegations were instructed by the British delegation. Afterwards, they became increasingly independent. On India's early role, see Gerry Rodgers, "India, the ILO and the quest for social justice since 1919". *Economic and Political weekly*. Mumbai: EPW Research Foundation. Vol. 46, no. 10 (March 2011), 45–52.

213 See ILO, *Social Policy in Dependent Territories* (Geneva: ILO, 1944), 56ff., nn. 2, 3.

214 The best overview of the treatment of colonial issues in the ILO during the early years is provided by Zimmermann, "'Special Circumstances' in Geneva", 221–250.

215 Ibid.

216 J.P. Daughton, "ILO Expertise and Colonial Violence in the Interwar Years", in *Globalizing Social Rights*, ed. Kott and Droux, 85–97.

217 For the case of Kenya, see Opolot Okia, *Communal Labor in Colonial Kenya: The Legitimization of Coercion, 1912–1930* (Basingstoke: Palgrave Macmillan, 2012).

ulation with an incentive to leave the rural areas and move permanently into "European" working conditions. Wherever the need for labour arose, short-term, migratory forms were favoured, and the social costs were left to be shouldered by the indigenous workers' "natural environment" – the rural areas and the "tribal" structures from which they came and to which they were expected to return when their labour was no longer required. Until the Second World War, at least in the British Empire, the general policy was to prevent "stabilization" at the place of work and permanent migration to the cities. Labour shortages were often bridged by coercive measures, and private and public interest went frequently hand in hand in order to meet the demand in the labour force. The brutality of the recruitment methods and working conditions, and the socially disruptive effects that the mass recruitment of men of employable age inflicted on the indigenous communities, repeatedly caught the attention of the public in Europe and North America. As a result, the topic of forced labour pervaded all aspects of the contemporary debate on colonial policy. From the early 1920s onwards, the ILO and Albert Thomas acted as part of an "international colonial issue network" opposing forced labour in the colonies.[218]

When the League of Nations began preparations for a convention against slavery in 1924, the ILO seized the chance to use this as a lever for its own campaigns. In the wake of the League's debates on the Slavery Convention, which was passed in 1926, the ILO was given the task of conducting a study into possible steps "to prevent compulsory labour or forced labour from developing into conditions analogous to slavery".[219] Its mandate was constrained, however, by the colonial powers' unwillingness to expose their ruling practices to any significant degree of international scrutiny, and the ILO went a long way to accommodate them. The appointment of a non-tripartite Committee of Experts on Native Labour underpinned the patronizing character of this work. The Committee consisted mainly of colonial administrators and colonial economic interests.[220]

Four Conventions and a whole series of Recommendations which the ILO adopted between 1930 and 1939 as a result of this work addressed in one way or

---

218 Daughton, "ILO Expertise and Colonial Violence"; Luis Rodríguez-Piñero, *Indigenous Peoples, Postcolonialism, and International Law: The ILO Regime (1919–1989)* (Oxford: Oxford University Press, 2005). For a summary of the debate, see Maul, "The International Labour Organization and the Struggle against Forced Labour".

219 Alcock, *History of the International Labour Organization*, 85–87.

220 Among the members of the Commission were Sir Frederick (later Lord) Lugard, British colonial administrator and Governor-General of Nigeria (1914–1919); Albrecht Gohr from the Belgian Ministry of Colonies; Martial Marlin, former governor of various French colonies; and Albrecht Freiherr von Rechenberg, former Governor of German East Africa. Zimmermann, "Special Circumstances in Geneva", 237.

another the problem of forced labour. For the ILO colonial labour was a special form of labour – referred to as "native" or "indigenous" labour – to which applied separate standards. As a consequence, the ILO developed a special "native labour code" that was distinct from the International Labour Code comprising all ILO conventions.[221] The discourse which culminated in the development of this special labour code underpinned this distinction. It rested on the widely shared assumption that colonial policies had to "educate" the native population. The main area of controversy was the question of whether the abolition of forced labour and related phenomena helped or hindered the performance of this educational duty. Albert Thomas, who was arguing for far-reaching measures to abolish forced labour, saw the ILO's role in "lift[ing] the chains that still bind the native so as to prepare him for the next educative step"[222] – a position that was widely supported by the Workers' group within the ILO. Among the colonial powers, however, only Great Britain supported the immediate abolition of forced labour for private purposes. In contrast, the French, Belgian, Dutch, Portuguese, and South African delegations were rather critical of the distinction between forced labour for public purposes and forced labour for private interests, as both seemed acceptable to them, at least for a transitional period.[223]

The Forced Labour Convention No. 29 of 1930 called for the abolition of forced labour "in all its forms" and permitted only transitional periods with regard to work performed for "public purposes". However, provisions stipulating the conditions that were *not* to be considered forced or compulsory labour (among them military service and forced labour as a consequence of a court conviction) provided loopholes for the colonial signatories. The Convention also exempted any work or service forming part of the "normal civic obligations of citizens" as well as of "minor communal services". This offered further opportunities to make exceptions for certain coercive practices widely used in colonial Africa.[224] Notwithstanding their indisputable humanitarian achievements, the ILO Conven-

---

221 In addition to the 1930 Forced Labour Convention, ILO instruments dealing with recruitment practices and working contracts – Recruitment of Indigenous Workers' Convention, 1936 (No. 50) and Contracts of Employment (Indigenous Workers) Convention, 1939 (No. 64) – tackled the problem of long-term contracts, the latter mostly aiming at widespread systems of indentured labour.

222 Quoted in Maul, *Human Rights, Development and Decolonization*, 24.

223 For a summary of this discussion, see Maul, "The International Labour Organization and the Struggle against Forced Labour", 480–485; see also Alcock, *History of the International Labor Organization*, 81–93.

224 Despite these far-reaching concessions that all parts of the native labour code made to the demands of the colonial powers, very few of them, apart from Great Britain, were prepared to ratify the ILO instruments until the early1950s. See K.K. Norsky, *The Influence of the International*

tions on indigenous labour, which more or less explicitly dealt with forced labour, underlined that Africa and other parts of the colonial world were still deemed areas where a different set of rules applied. It would take the world economic crisis and its destabilizing effects on the economic, social, and political fabric of colonial empires, and ultimately the Second World War, to trigger changes in colonial social policy.

Labour Organization on Principles of Social Policy in Non-Metropolitan Territories (Oxford: Oxford University Press, 1951), 88–103.

2 Facing the Crisis

The disastrous crisis that hit the world economy in the wake of the 1929 New York stock market crash deeply affected the International Labour Organization (ILO) in a variety of ways. Confronted with a global economic downturn of an unprecedented dimension, Albert Thomas – who died at the height of the crisis in 1932 at age 53 – and his successor, Harold Butler, vigorously promoted the social *and* economic benefits of social legislation. Under Butler's leadership, the ILO took a distinct economic turn, committed itself to a Keynesian programme of reforms, and brought the fight against mass unemployment once again to the centre of all the Organization's activities. The sense of urgency with which the ILO acted during this period was heightened by the presence of powerful authoritarian alternatives to the liberal model represented by the Organization. The mostly antagonistic stand of the Soviet Union towards the Organization and the withdrawal of Nazi Germany and (later) Fascist Italy from membership were reminders of the increasingly hostile environment in which the ILO operated.

Under Butler, the ILO answered this challenge with a geographical reorientation towards the western hemisphere. The entry of the United States in 1934 and the first Labour Conference of American member States of the ILO in Santiago de Chile in 1936 were important steps in this regard. Under Butler and his successor from 1938, the American John Gilbert Winant, the United States rapidly turned from an outsider to one of the Organization's most important supporters. The engagement with the United States and the intellectual and practical input received from the Roosevelt administration's New Deal policies constituted a source of inspiration and gave new impetus to the political project of providing legitimacy to the (re-) organization, in the context of the crisis, of capitalist economies under liberal democratic premises. At the same time, the Organization took steps to discard its narrow European focus, which, in the later part of the 1930s, resulted in a closer cooperation with Latin America, especially on issues like social insurance. It also affected other regions and spilled over onto the question of colonial labour. All these developments gave further leeway to expanding the ILO's portfolio of activities beyond standard-setting and to building a nucleus for developing into an agency of technical cooperation.

https://doi.org/10.1515/9783110650723-004

Figure 4: Chilean President Arturo Alessandri Palma and ILO Director Harold Butler (centre) leaving the inaugural session of the First American Regional Conference, Santiago de Chile, 1936.

The World Economic Crisis and the ILO's Keynesian Turn

For the great majority of people affected by the Great Depression, their personal crisis arrived brutally in the form of unemployment.[225] At the peak of the crisis, in 1932, about 25% of Americans and 32% of Germans were out of work. Similar situations existed in most other European and North American industrial societies. Welfare schemes, if they existed at all, were not in the least prepared to alleviate the effects of the crisis. For workers and their families everywhere, unemployment thus posed an immediate threat of poverty. The depression hit industry the hardest, but its repercussions were also felt in agriculture, where overproduction in the United States combined with Soviet price-dumping to finance Stalin's five-year plans. With the breakdown of international trade, this started a downward

225 Dorothea Hoehtker, "The ILO's Role in the Economic Debate (from 1919 to the 1990s)" (unpublished note for the IILS, ILO, Geneva, 2013); Stephen Hughes and Nigel Haworth, "A Shift in the Center of Gravity: The ILO under Harold Butler and John G. Winant", in *ILO Histories*, ed. Van Daele et al., 293–312.

economic spiral. The situation was further aggravated by the fact that no consensus existed on the right economic policies to deal with the crisis. Some governments began to experiment with Keynesian ideas of stimulating the economy by means of countercyclical spending; others – like the German government under Chancellor Heinrich Brüning – did the exact opposite, promoting austerity and cutting down on social programmes, which soon made the situation in the labour market only worse and led to disastrous social and political destabilization.[226]

The opinions on how to contend with mass unemployment also differed widely among the ILO's constituents. The lack of consensus among trade unions and employers became particularly visible in the discussions preceding the adoption of a "Convention concerning the Reduction of Hours of Work to Forty a Week" in 1935.[227] While trade unions, however wholeheartedly, supported the 40-hour week as a means of distributing employment more equally and made the case for wage increases to stimulate consumption, employers were staunchly opposed to both. When the project for a Convention concerning a 40-hour work week had first been put on the agenda of the ILC in 1934, the employers had refused even to discuss the draft proposals prepared by the International Labour Office. Against this background its eventual adoption was a success for the workers. But the contested nature of the question was clearly reflected by the fact that, although many governments supported the Convention in principle, almost none of them was prepared to ratify it. It took, therefore, until 1957 before it entered into force.

The discussion about working hours was but one example of the debates on the appropriate economic strategy to overcome mass unemployment. In this controversy, the International Labour Office took a position that, over time, became increasingly more explicit. Attempts on the part of the ILO to gain recognition as a player in international economic and monetary debates were as old as the Organization itself. In the 1920s, the ILO had started to conduct research on the connections between economic and social issues, in particular with regard to employment. Based on his own wartime experience, Albert Thomas had long been a proponent of international economic planning, and he always considered the separation of the economic and the social realms to be an artificial one. He had tried to make the ILO's voice heard at international economic conferences, such

226 Zara Steiner, *The Lights that Failed. European International History 1919–1933* (Oxford: Oxford University Press, 2005), 640–42.

227 The preamble of Forty-Hour Week Convention, 1935 (No. 47) made a direct connection to the immediate economic and social context, by stating that "unemployment has become so widespread and long continued that there are at the present time many millions of workers throughout the world suffering hardship and privation for which they are not themselves responsible and from which they are justly entitled to be relieved".

as the World Economic Conference of 1927, organized by the League of Nations. However, while the Organization's contributions were generally acknowledged, the ILO was invariably relegated to a subaltern position by the League's Economic and Financial Section, which clearly saw the ILO as a competitor.[228] Quite apart from this, Thomas had to reckon with strong resistance from within the Organization's own ranks: employers, in particular, and most governments were strongly opposed to the ILO expanding its competences into the economic field.[229]

The world economic crisis offered a chance to the ILO to renew its claim. In 1930, Deputy Director Harold Butler pleaded to "take this opportunity of shifting our centre of gravity, so to speak, from the purely social to the economic sphere, by devoting the whole of our attention to the effects on the workers oft the world depression".[230] The next year, the Governing Body followed up on this appeal, offering a catalogue of measures to fight the crisis. It promoted, among other means, the reinforcement of public works, the coordination of labour migration, the extension of unemployment insurance schemes, and a limitation of the hours of work, which, taken together, amounted to a Keynesian programme of state-led active employment creation and the stabilization of consumption through income security.[231]

Even if Keynesianism was still in its infancy in the early 1930s (Keynes' *General Theory of Employment, Interest and Money* was only published in 1936), the ILO had, in fact, endorsed its basic ideas at an even earlier time. ILO economists like Percival W. Martin can be considered proto-Keynesians in the 1920s and 1930s. They were part of a network of economists who had either worked directly with Keynes or shared his core ideas. Keynes' approach compellingly asserted the positive interdependence between social and economic progress and promoted economic planning and state intervention within an open market setting. In 1931, Thomas had already referred directly to Keynes in his ILC report to justify public works as a remedy for the crisis. Later, the ILO's relationship to Roosevelt's New Deal administration further deepened this connection. During the 1930s, the ILO began to enter into a quasi-symbiotic relationship with Keynesianism. It became instrumental in spreading Keynes' ideas, building an international epistemic community around them, and ultimately establishing Keynesianism as the new economic paradigm that was valid until far into the 1970s.[232] At the same time,

228 For a broader perspective, see Clavin, *Securing the World Economy*.

229 Hoehtker, "The ILO's Role in the Economic Debate (from 1919 to the 1990s)".

230 Quoted in Hughes and Haworth, "A Shift in the Centre of Gravity", 301

231 Hughes and Haworth, "A Shift in the Center of Gravity", 299–303.

232 In 1936, Abba Lerner, an American economist, published an article in the *International Labour Review*, in which he summarized the main arguments of the "General Theory", which was

Keynesianism, as an economic theory based on the integration of economic and social policy, played an important role in making the ILO's activities in the field acceptable. Moreover, it prepared and legitimized the expansion of these activities not only in the economic area but, in the following decades, also in the field of development policy.

In the 1930s, however, these developments were hardly predictable, and Keynesian ideas remained highly contested. Nevertheless, the promotion of a "scientific" way to organize the economy and the promotion of state-led economic and social planning as tools to avoid the kind of employment crises that had followed the Great Depression became the ILO's new trademark under Director Harold Butler.[233] In his reports to the ILC, Butler did not miss the chance to point to underconsumption as the most important reason for the persistence of the economic crisis. Butler would reorganize the ILO in a way that it would fit more closely the demands of this Keynesian framework. A new economic section was created, which engaged in research and the collection of relevant data, and which included several regional specialists. Butler thus fostered a process in which the International Labour Office developed into a highly differentiated body of expert-bureaucrats, with competences in a broad range of fields. In this way, the ILO built expertise and carried out landmark research in the fields of workers' living conditions, wages, and family incomes – all under the new Keynesian paradigm.[234] To some degree, standard-setting also reflected a Keynesian turn during Butler's time at the helm of the ILO. Conventions adopted included the aforementioned one on the 40-hour work week (1935), on holidays with pay (1936), and on various social insurance regulations (1933), all of which could also be read as parts of a programme intended to stimulate consumption during a time of crisis.

The most prominent part of this programme concerned unemployment insurance. The concept had been part of a Recommendation, which had accompanied the Unemployment Convention of 1919, the latter stipulating especially the set-up of public employment agencies. In the 1930s, however, unemployment insurance acquired a new meaning as a way of maintaining purchasing power and thus stabilizing the economy in a time of economic downturn. Although some countries had already introduced voluntary or compulsory schemes directed mostly at industrial workers during the period, resentment against the introduction of

---

an important step in popularizing Keynes' ideas. See Abba P. Lerner, "Mr. Keynes' 'General Theory of Employment, Interest and Money'", *International Labour Review* 34, no. 4 (1936): 435–54.

233 Jaci Leigh Eisenberg, "Butler, Harold Beresford", in *IO Bio: Biographical Dictionary of Secretaries-General of International Organizations*, ed. Bob Reinalda, Kent J. Kille, and Jaci Leigh Eisenberg, www.ru.nl/fm/iobio.

234 Plata-Stenger, "Une voie sociale pour le développement", 41–102.

far-reaching unemployment insurance systems had not been overcome by far. Some argued that unemployment insurance diminished workers' willingness to seek work, and employers often opposed unemployment schemes because of the increased cost of production and the detrimental effect on international competition. The ILO's argument that unemployment insurance schemes would help to overcome the social and economic crisis did not catch on easily. An ILO Convention (No. 44) that required member States to provide benefits or allowances for involuntarily unemployed workers was eventually adopted in 1934.[235] Although the instrument acknowledged the widely differing unemployment schemes in place and allowed substantial exceptions for such groups as agricultural workers, public services, or young persons, it only attracted the bare minimum of two ratifications (Great Britain and Switzerland) before the outbreak of the Second World War.[236]

Arguably, the most innovative element emerging during the unemployment debate concerned the area of (international) public works. The use of public works to counter fluctuations in the private sector had been promoted before, but, in 1931, the ILO issued a report entitled "Unemployment and Public Works", which lifted the discussion on a new intellectual level. It was in this context, and in Thomas' reference to this report in 1931, that the connection to Keynesian thinking became most obvious.[237] The report advertised public works as a way to counter the economic crisis. It not only included calls for national schemes but also featured an ambitious plan for public works that expressed an early form of a pan-European vision (in the construction of railways, electricity networks, and other infrastructure projects). These plans pursued the double aim of combating unemployment and, at the same time, contributing to European economic recovery. The issue of public works was also put on the agenda of the 1933 World Economic Conference, in which the ILO participated. Peacebuilding, too, was an objective here, as the ILO's ideas included infrastructure projects in areas like electricity and transportation that would have promoted international cooperation through their border-crossing character.[238] In the same year, the League of Nations launched its own Committee on Public Works. These steps notwithstanding, the discussion did not yield the results which the ILO had hoped for. In 1937, the ILC adopted two Recommendations that dealt with public works, on both the

235 Unemployment Provision Convention, 1934 (No. 44).
236 Liebeskind Sauthier, "Modern Unemployment", 82.
237 ILO, Unemployment and Public Works, *Studies and Reports, Series C*, No. 15. (Geneva: 1931).
238 Johan Schot and Vincent Lagendijk, "Technocratic Internationalism in the Interwar Years: Building Europe on Motorways and Electricity Networks", in *Journal of Modern European History* 6, no. 2 (2008), 196–217.

national and international levels. The International Labour Office interpreted these adoptions as an acknowledgement and a confirmation of the Organization's competence in discussing matters that were predominantly economic in nature. However, this was as far as the Organization could get before the outbreak of the Second World War, which interrupted all plans for the implementation of international schemes.[239]

A third area in which the ILO tried to make its voice heard was international migration. This was another example of the Organization's growing disposition for economic planning on a global scale. Except for the short episode of working for refugees in the late 1920s, the ILO had so far treated migrant workers mainly from a protective point of view. The depression led to a sharp decrease in migration flows; it fanned the flames of xenophobia and cut back on the acceptance of labour migrants even in countries such as France that hitherto had shown a great demand for workers.[240] Against this background, and on the strength of its refugee work experience, the ILO tried to lift the debate out of its national framework, carried out statistical research, and developed a plan for an international agency whose task was the management of migration streams by channelling, in a rational way, the flows of labour from areas with a surplus to those with demand. Very few governments, however, caught on to the idea of an international agency regulating access to national labour markets, and the scheme was not popular among the Workers' group, either. Instead, a majority of European governments, and also Latin American countries and Australia, insisted on quotas on labour immigration.[241]

In this difficult environment, the ILC of 1939, in its last meeting before the war, adopted a Convention and two Recommendations dealing with "Migration for Employment". The circumstances of this Conference could hardly have been less favourable for a generous accord on the international regulation of labour migration. While the economic considerations were still looming large, the migration issue was overshadowed by parallel debates on the acceptance of a massive number of German and other refugees fleeing from intensified Nazi persecution. An international conference in Evian, France, a year earlier, that had sought to find havens for Jewish refugees from Germany had exposed the reluc-

---

239 Public Works (International Co-operation) Recommendation, 1937 (No. 50); Public Works (National Planning) Recommendation, 1937 (No. 51).

240 On the issue of international migration, see Paul-André Rosental, "Géopolitique et Etat-providence. Le BIT et la politique mondiale des migrations dans l'entre-deux-guerres", *Annales HSS* 61, no. 1 (2006): 99–134; W. R. Böhning, "The ILO and Contemporary International Economic Migration", *International Migration Review* 10, no. 2 (1976), 147–156.

241 Alcock, *History of the International Labor Organization*, 71–74.

tance of many governments to open their borders. Among other reasons, their reluctance was due to fears that the acceptance of the refugees would further aggravate the employment situations in their countries and strengthen xenophobic sentiments.[242]

With this in mind, the very fact that the ILO adopted three standards dealing with migration had to be seen as a success. Still, at closer look, the wording of the instruments demonstrated the narrow limits of international action. The Convention focused on recruitment and working conditions of labour migrants only, and, while the Recommendations also included some paragraphs that promoted the cooperation among states, the result was a far cry from previous plans, which would have given the ILO the role of an international clearing house for labour migration.[243]

There was thus more than one reason why the comprehensive plans the ILO, promoted in order to fight unemployment internationally, never really got off the ground. A good deal of the blame could be given to the deteriorating international environment of the 1930s, which generally constricted the space for international action. With Germany, Japan, and Italy leaving the organization one by one, the willingness of the remaining powers to enter into international agreements shrank to a minimum. The retreat to economic nationalism, in turn, left few opportunities for programmes that promoted the kind of cooperation across national boundaries that the ILO had in mind with regard to migration and public works.

Facing Alternative Internationalisms: Fascist Italy, Nazi Germany, and the Soviet Union

The ILO's project of socio-economic reform to counter the effects of the global economic crises assumed a heightened sense of urgency because of the growing strength and appeal of totalitarian regimes. The Organization's relations with Italian Fascism and Soviet Communism had long been marked by ambiguity. Both surely were competitors and were essentially diametrically opposed to the social liberal model represented by the ILO.[244] Nevertheless, some of the features

242 Gatrell, *The Making of the Modern Refugee*, 77.

243 Rosental, "Géopolitique et État-providence"; Böhning, "The ILO and Contemporary International Economic Migration".

244 Recent historiographical literature has warned against the narrow focus on liberal internationalism as the only true expression of internationalist thought. The authors point instead to the multiple origins (socialist vs. liberal) and to the multifaceted character of internation-

of these regimes – the corporatist organization of industrial relations or Soviet economic planification – seemed to provide answers to the pressing problems of the time – answers that attracted interest and even admiration beyond the political and ideological dividing lines. At the historical juncture of the 1930s, however, and in the wake of the Great Depression when liberal democracy seemed on the defensive everywhere, Italian Fascism (and German National Socialism) posed a serious and potentially deadly threat to the ILO's philosophy and policy. At the same time, Soviet Communism challenged the ILO from a different direction, as it divided the labour movement along ideological lines. It was crucial that, against this backdrop, the ILO found an ally in the United States under President Roosevelt. The entry of the United States not only gave the ILO the necessary diplomatic support to survive in an increasingly hostile international environment. Roosevelt's New Deal policies helped as a source of inspiration and a blueprint for the ILO's programme of social and economic intervention under liberal democratic auspices.

Italy, as one of the ILO's founding members and countries of "major industrial importance" in the Governing Body early on, began to pose a problem for the Organization, as it gradually turned from a liberal democratic into a full-fledged dictatorial regime after Benito Mussolini's "March on Rome" in October 1922. Despite of its ultra-nationalist overtones, the Fascist regime, from the start, showed a strong interest in international networks. Mussolini's regime, in fact, went to great lengths within the League of Nations to promote its alternative "third way" vision of modernity, between liberal democracy and communism.[245] The ILO became a prime venue for the strategy of "Fascist internationalism": to gain legitimacy through international cooperation and to transform international institutions from the inside along the lines of its own ideas. Italy fully embraced the idea of ILO standard-setting and was among the countries with the most ratification of ILO Conventions (21), second only to Belgium. The Fascist regime even took a lead in the adoption of the 40-hour week Convention of 1935 (No. 47), which was widely seen as a landmark success for the Workers' group. In the wake of the world economic crisis after 1930, Italy also became an ally in the effort to expand the ILO's competences in such fields as migration and public works. In the latter case, in particular, the position taken by the liberal democracies – with

alism during the interwar period, in particular, when various "internationalisms" – liberal, socialist-communist, but also a genuinely fascist brand – existed in parallel and in competition with each other. See Glenda Sluga and Patricia Clavin, "Rethinking the History of Internationalism", in *Internationalisms: A Twentieth Century History*, ed. Sluga and Clavin, 3–14.

245 Madeleine Herren, "Fascist Internationalism", in *Internationalisms: A Twentieth Century History*, ed. Sluga and Clavin, 191–212.

the notable exception of the United States – often seemed lukewarm in comparison to the demonstrative projects realized under strictly authoritarian terms and militaristic premises in Fascist Italy and Nazi Germany.[246]

A further indicator for the friendly approach the Fascist regime took for most of the period towards the ILO was the selection of delegates to the ILC, especially of Angelo Cabrini and Giuseppe de Michelis, who were promoting the regime's "third way" approach but were also experts with a degree of independence and long-standing links to the ILO from the time before Fascism.[247] The same was true for the well-known statistician, demographer, and sociologist Corrado Gini, the inventor of the "Gini index".[248]

Thomas had a somewhat ambiguous attitude towards the Fascist regime. Personally, he despised Fascism's violent and anti-democratic features, but he shared with many of his contemporaries a fascination for the corporatist organization of the Italian world of work. Once stripped of its coercive nature, which he initially perceived as a children's disease, Thomas saw corporatism as reconcilable with and even potentially invigorating to the tripartite principle. Even though his optimism about the possibility to eventually democratize the regime rapidly diminished in his later years, he kept up a dialogue with Rome. His attitude was perfectly in line with the treatment of Mussolini's government by the majority of the ILO's mostly liberal democratic member States. Far from being treated as a pariah, Italy enjoyed wide recognition, reflected among other indicators by the fact that an Italian government delegate was elected president of the ILC in 1933.[249]

Less surprisingly, the stiffest resistance to a "normalization" of the Fascist regime came from the Workers' side. At the ILC in 1923, the credentials of the Italian Workers' delegate were challenged for the first time. In the unanimous view of the other Workers' delegates, Edmondo Rossoni, who belonged to one of the Fascist corporatist organizations that included both workers and employers, did not represent a genuine workers' organization. This move was, however, rejected by the vote of the great majority of governments and employers – a procedure that would be repeated at each session of the ILC until 1935. During the same time, Italian Workers' delegates found themselves excluded from the Workers' group and all conference committees, but their right to participate and represent Italian Workers was nevertheless upheld. As the Fascist regime at home steadily

246 Gallo, "Dictatorship and International Organizations: The ILO as a Test Ground for Fascism", 158–160.

247 Ibid., 160–162.

248 Corrado Gini served as a member of the Committee on the Application of Conventions and Recommendations for over a decade.

249 Gallo, "Dictatorship and International Organizations: The ILO as a Test Ground for Fascism".

narrowed the space of the trade unions to act freely, and violence against them increased, the situation led to a great deal of frustration among the IFTU and its representatives in the Workers' group. This situation only worsened after the attempt to put a convention dealing with freedom of association on the agenda of the ILC in 1927–1928 had failed. While the Workers' group initially intended to define the principle of freedom of association in such unequivocal terms that would make it possible to attack the Fascist regime for its suppression of trade union activities, the ensuing debate highlighted the absence of a consensus on this question even among liberal democratic states.[250] A lasting legacy of the debate was the publication of a comprehensive five-volume report on the state of freedom of association across the world. The material had been compiled by the ILO during the late 1920s and would serve as a resource once the discussions were reinitiated after the Second World War.[251]

Pragmatism on the part of the ILO and major democratic states was only one reason, albeit probably the most important one, of why the Fascist regime met with relatively little open resistance in the ILO during the first 15 years of Mussolini's *ventennio*. In some of its features, Fascism seemed to provide an attractive alternative to liberal solutions. This was certainly true for corporatism, but it applied also to other social policy areas. A case in point was the field of leisure time policy. Here, the Fascist regime had created a widely appreciated national recreational organization, the *Opera Nazionale Dopolavoro,* which would later become the blueprint for the Nazi counterpart, *Kraft durch Freude*. While it was clearly part and parcel of an indisputably Fascist programme of popular mobilization for a coming war, Italy used the *dopolavoro* as an instrument for national image building and the promotion of its "third way" approach. As recent research has shown, leisure time policy could work as an "icebreaker" for Fascist internationalism in the field of social policy, because it rested on the same "productivist" assumptions that Italy had in common with its liberal democratic competitors, which, in turn, were largely influenced by American ideas. Both approaches conceptualized leisure time as a period of regeneration and thus primarily as a precondition for productivity. Even if the Fascist model clashed with social reformist concepts pursued by the ILO or, for that matter, with the French Popular Front government, there was still enough common ground to make it seem like an option, for the very reason that it favoured collective over individualistic aspects.[252]

---

250 A summary of the debate can be found in Valticos, *International Labour Law*, 60.
251 Alcock, *History of the International Labor Organization*, 75–80; ILO, *Freedom of Association*, Studies and Reports, Series A, Nos. 28–32, 5 vols. (Geneva: ILO, 1927–1930).
252 Liebscher, *Freude und Arbeit*.

Although similar on the surface, the case of Nazi Germany differed from the Italian one in some important respects. Despite its weakened position within the post-Versailles order, Germany had occupied an important position within the ILO since its admission in 1919. When the National Socialists assumed power in 1933, however, they showed little interest in good relations with the ILO. They regarded the Organization, just like the League of Nations, as representative of the despised "Versailles system" that they sought to destroy.[253] In parallel, the wholesale elimination of democratic institutions and the crushing of trade union organizations during the first months of the Nazi terror made it clear enough that the relations between the ILO and Germany were heading for troubled waters. The ILC in June 1933 proved these predictions to be true. It saw violent verbal clashes between the representatives of the new regime and other delegates. Robert Ley, head of the Nazi corporative organization *Deutsche Arbeitsfront* (DAF), which had come to replace independent trade unions, used the forum to launch fierce attacks on various other delegations. He met with staunch resistance from Worker's representatives like Leon Jouhaux of France, who, in turn, denounced the anti-Jewish measures and the persecution of trade unionists by the new regime.[254]

Only a short time after the Conference, the Nazi regime declared its intention to leave both the League and the ILO. In 1934, the ILO office in Berlin, too, had to close, when the German employees of the Office were obliged to pledge allegiance to the Nazi regime. The International Labour Office first reacted with caution to the new situation and, during the following years, was motivated by the basic aim of avoiding a total breakdown of relationships with Nazi Germany. After the shutdown of the Berlin office, it still maintained contact through the Christian trade unionist Wilhelm Claussen, who acted as a correspondent to Geneva in Germany. In order to enter into an agreement with the German state, the ILO, however, had to accept that Claussen produce proof of his "Aryan descent" and pledge his

---

253 Sandrine Kott, Competing Internationalisms: "The Third Reich and the International Labour Organization", in *Nazism across Borders. The Social Policies of the Third Reich and their Global Appea*l, ed. Sandrine Kott and Kiran Klaus Patel (Oxford: Oxford University Press, 2018), 29–52.

254 The IFTU considered the German social-democratic politician Wilhelm Leuschner, an opponent of the Nazi regime, to be the legitimate trade union representative. Although he was present at the Conference, Leuschner abstained from public statements. Before the Conference could pronounce itself on the credentials of Robert Ley, the German government decided to withdraw from the Conference. See Reiner Tosstorff, "Leuschner Vs. Ley. Der gescheiterte nationalsozialistische Auftritt auf der Internationalen Arbeitskonferenz im Jahre 1933", *Jahrbuch für Forschungen zur Geschichte der Arbeiterbewegung* (2004), 70–90. For an English version, see Reiner Tosstorff, *Workers' Resistance against Nazi Germany at the International Labour Conference 1933* (Geneva: ILO, 2013).

loyalty to National Socialism. The ILO also had to agree to receive all future information on social policy in Germany through Joseph Goebbels' Ministry of Propaganda. In 1934, Walter Reichhold, a staff member of the Berlin office at the time of the Nazi takeover and an early supporter of the regime (he had replaced a picture of Albert Thomas with one of Hitler in 1933), was transferred to the ILO's Geneva headquarters on the recommendation of the German government.

If the aim to maintain contacts with one of the major industrialized countries and a leader in social policy measures was a strong motive for the ILO's cautious diplomatic policy vis-à-vis the Nazi regime, there was certainly also a genuine interest in some of the policies pursued by the Nazi regime, in particular with regard to public work schemes and other programmes initiated to reduce unemployment in the German Reich. However, the German side decided exclusively where, and to what degree, it would seek cooperation or share information with Geneva. Leisure time policy was one area where the Nazi regime used the ILO platform for the international promotion of its social policy, in particular its *Kraft durch Freude* organization, which was in competition not only with the liberal-democratic approach but also with the Italian Fascist *dopolavoro* described above.[255]

With the eventual withdrawal of Italy from the League in 1937 and the contours of an alternative Fascist–National Socialist internationalism becoming clearer, Germany lost what little interest it had ever had in the cooperation with the ILO. Even before the Second World War, the DAF started preparations – as part of a larger programme of the internationalization of Nazi social policies in support of German hegemony – for a new agency that would replace the ILO altogether as the leading international social policy organization. These plans materialized during the war, when the Nazis not only launched a Central Office for International Labour (*Zentralamt für internationale Arbeitsgestaltung*) but also started publishing its own journal, the *Neue Internationale Rundschau der Arbeit*, which was intended to take the place of the German version of the ILO's *International Labour Review*.[256]

While the ILO's dealings with Italian Fascism were, at least in the beginning, marked by ambiguity, the relationship with the Soviet Union started from open hostility. From its very foundation, many of the ILO's supporters saw the Organization's commitment to class cooperation as the best available alternative to the threat presented by the Bolshevik Revolution. The Soviet leadership, in turn, did not tire from portraying the ILO and the IFTU, which dominated the workers'

255 Liebscher, *Freude und Arbeit*, 351–549.
256 Kott, "Dynamiques de l'internationalisation", 82.

groups, as stooges of capitalism and traitors of the working class.[257] At the same time, the IFTU faced the opposition internationally of the Moscow-oriented Red International of Labour Unions.[258] The ILO, nevertheless, took an early interest in the situation in Soviet Russia, and a special Russian Section, set up in 1920, collected information on Soviet Russian social life.[259] Its purpose was to prepare a mission of investigation, which the Soviet authorities refused to admit.[260] First contacts with the Soviet authorities were established in 1924. In the latter part of the 1920s, when diplomatic relationships between the West and the Soviet Union entered a period of normalization, the ILO stepped up its endeavours. Invitations were issued to Soviet representatives to take part as observers in technical meetings and in the ILC. Although a staunch opponent of the Bolshevik experiment, Albert Thomas shared with many of his contemporaries a fascination of the rapid industrialization process and the dynamic social development in the Soviet Union. In 1928, he visited Moscow on an official mission (as the first part of his trip to the Far East), where he met government officials, visited social institutions, and gathered information on the Russian cooperative movement.[261] There would, however, be no follow-up, and ideas for a further rapprochement, like the opening of an ILO office in Moscow, ultimately came to naught. Thomas faced criticism in his own organization for being, in the words of a Portuguese government delegate, "too friendly disposed toward the Soviet [*sic*]", a country "which desires to destroy society as we understand it".[262] Soviet resentment against the ILO was fuelled by these kinds of attacks. They intensified during the debate on the (colonial) forced labour Convention in 1929 and 1930, when some of the colonial powers tried to deflect attention from their coercive practices by pointing to the systematic use of forced labour for political purposes in the Soviet Union. At the same time, the Great Depression seemed to confirm Moscow in its view

257 Harold Karan Jacobson, "The USSR and ILO", *International Organization* 14, no. 3 (1957), 402–28.

258 Van Goethem, *The Amsterdam International*, ch. 2: The discordant clamour for international unity. The Red Temptation of the International Federation of Trade Unions; Specifically, on the Red International see Reiner Tosstorff, *The Red International of Labour Unions (RILU) 1920–1937* (Leiden: Brill, 2016).

259 In 1920, it produced a tentative account of the Bolshevik industrial system entitled *Organisation of Industry and Labour Conditions in Soviet Russia*. Studies and Reports. Series B: Economic Conditions. No. 11 (Geneva: ILO).

260 Prince, "The U.S.S.R. and International Organizations".

261 Albert Thomas, *A la recontre de l'Orient. Notes de voyage 1928–1929.* (Geneva: Societe des amis d'Albert Thomas, 1959).

262 ILO, *Record of Proceedings*, International Labour Conference, 14th Session 1930 (Geneva: ILO, 1930), 154.

that capitalism was doomed, and the Soviet government saw little need to enter into cooperation with the representative of a dying system. Thomas answered his critics in the ILO by pointing to the "important economic developments in Soviet Russia" and made the case for reaching out to the Soviet Union, because European countries "may be faced in the near future with dangerous competition from Russia", which had, in fact, emerged relatively unscathed from the economic crisis of 1929.[263]

The relationship, however, remained tense, even after the Soviet Union joined the ILO in 1934. This step was motivated less by a change of mind on the part of the Soviet leadership concerning the usefulness of the Organization, but it was rather a consequence of Stalin's change of tactics in the face of the Fascist advance in Europe and Japan's expansion in China.[264] In 1935, Georgi Dimitrov, head of the Communist International (Comintern), issued a new directive, which suggested that Communist parties should enter into broad alliances ("popular fronts") with all national anti-fascist political forces. In parallel, the Soviet Union joined the League of Nations in order to develop this strategy on the international level. As a consequence, it automatically became a member of the ILO, where, as a country of "chief industrial importance", it was immediately given a seat in the Governing Body.

Soviet membership, however, did not mean full cooperation. In fact, in the 1930s, the Soviet Union only rarely participated in the sessions of the Conference and the Governing Body, and it did not ratify any ILO conventions or follow up on any recommendations. After 1937, when the Spanish Civil War and other international developments quickly caused popular front policies to fade, the Soviet leadership lost what little interest it might have had in the ILO and ceased its participation altogether. The expulsion of the Soviet Union from the League of Nations, following the country's attack on Finland in late November 1939, confirmed the end of the short rapprochement between the Soviet Union and the ILO. Soviet Union – which was by then tied to Nazi Germany through the August 1939 Non-Aggression Pact –was declared vacant. The full consequences of this episode would resonate only a few years later, when the ILO would face the hostility of the Soviet Union, which, since 1941, was fighting the war against Nazi Germany as one of the major Allied powers.[265]

The participation of the Soviet Union in the ILO, short-lived though it would prove to be, still raised some fundamental questions about the ILO's nature and

263 ILC, 14th Session (1930), *Record of Proceedings*, 214.

264 Other, altogether pragmatic, reasons were the set-back of Communism in China and the need of loans from Western countries.

265 Jacobson, "The USSR and ILO", 404.

composition. As one Dutch representative of the Christian trade unions explained the problem in 1937: "The provision for tripartite representation will be useless if it is sufficient for Governments simply to consult organisations which are part of their own machinery or which are subject to their own instructions or influence. It is useless to have tripartite representation which, in fact, is simply a triple representation of a Government."[266] In what seemed like a mirror image of the year-long debates on the Fascist workers' representatives, it was now the Employers' group that challenged the credentials of the Soviet Employers' delegate. Since, under the Communist system, the state acted as the sole employer, and trade unions were to implement the policies of the Communist Party, the Soviet Union, in fact, sent four Government representatives to the Conference. The question of credentials was settled in favour of the Soviet Union, but the discussion was only a mild prelude to what was to become one of the most heated confrontations on the overall character of the Organization in the Cold War era. Given the highly volatile international context of 1937 and the centrifugal forces working against the Organization, many felt that the ILO could not afford to alienate any more members. Thus, the workers, with the exception of the Christian trade unions, did not object to the Soviet Workers' delegates but rather welcomed them to their group. They also harshly criticized the employers' attitude, because they had never objected to the credentials of the Fascist delegates.[267]

The "Americanization" of the ILO: The Entry of the United States

In the increasingly hostile environment that the ILO encountered during the 1930s, the entry of the United States acted as a counterweight that can hardly be overestimated. The active role which the world's most important industrial power finally decided to play gave a new impetus to the ILO that went far beyond the diplomatic level. The Organization drew from the New Deal not only inspiration but proof for the need to broaden its scope of activities to include the influencing of economic policy.

Throughout the 1920s, the absence of the world's largest industrial power was painful for many reasons, since it compromised the value of ILO standard-setting from the point of view of all industrial powers competing with US businesses. This alone was enough reason for Thomas, who held the US model of social and

266 ILO, *Record of Proceedings*, International Labour Conference, 23rd Session 1937 (Geneva: ILO, 1937), 299.
267 Ibid.

economic organization in high esteem, to keep the door open for the United States to participate in the Organization's work even as a non-member. In order to maintain the dialogue with the American administration and with representatives of capital and labour, the ILO had opened a branch office in Washington, D.C., as early as 1920. Despite of the fact that he did not speak any English, Thomas also toured the United States from December 1922 to January 1923 and kept close contacts with ILO sympathizers like James Shotwell. The establishment of the International Management Institute (mentioned in the previous chapter) was yet another way in which Thomas sought to continue the exchange of information across the Atlantic. However, in the face of stiffening isolationist tendencies in the United States during the 1920s, courting the Americans was not an easy task for an essentially francophone socialist. While the State Department turned down all invitations to send observers to ILCs, the American Federation of Labor (AFL), too, quickly resorted to its previous ambivalent position. After Samuel Gompers' initial endorsement of the ILO, the AFL soon reverted to its apprehensive view of the "statist" and "socialist" nature of the Organization, a notion that was widely shared by American business leaders. Since the AFL had left the IFTU, only loose connections existed to the members of the ILO's Workers' group.[268] Despite all attempts, there was, on the whole, little progress in ILO–US relations until the early 1930s. It would ultimately take the election of Franklin D. Roosevelt as president in 1932 to bring about a decisive turn.[269]

Roosevelt's election at the height of the economic crisis would prove to be a gift to the ILO. In hindsight, it is not an exaggeration to say that it was probably the single most important reason for the ILO's survival in the following decade. In 1930, a high-ranking ILO delegation that included both Albert Thomas and Harold Butler met with Roosevelt, then Governor of the State of New York. He had just begun to launch public works schemes in his state and was looking into unemployment insurance as a means to counter the effects of the Depression. He thus took a great interest in the concepts developed by the ILO. When he became president two years later, Roosevelt almost instantly initiated a process of rapprochement with the ILO which eventually led to the entry of the United States as a member in 1934.[270]

The interest of the Roosevelt administration in the ILO throughout the coming years went through various stages. During the early years, it saw the ILO first and foremost all as a valuable source of information to support its ambitious programme of

268 Hughes and Haworth, "A Shift in the Center of Gravity".
269 Edward C. Lorenz, *Defining Global Justice: The History of U.S. International Labor Standards Policy* (Notre Dame, IN: University of Notre Dame Press, 2001).
270 Jensen, "From Geneva to the Americas", 217–218.

economic and social reforms commonly known as the New Deal. Beyond this aspect, many New Dealers saw ILO standards as a means of containing the potentially negative effects that domestic social reforms could cause for the United States in international economic competition. For social reformers like Frances Perkins, Roosevelt's Secretary of Labor and one of the staunchest supporters of the ILO and US membership for many years, the Organization provided a forum for the internationalization of New Deal policies.[271] This argument caused even proponents of trade liberalization, such as Secretary of State Cordell Hull, to join the ranks of ILO supporters. Women's rights activists like Frieda Miller, who later served as the US government delegate to the ILC for many years, perceived the Organization as an opportunity to carry the progressive domestic agendas of the New Dealers onto the international scene.[272]

In the years after 1935, the ILO and the United States entered into an almost symbiotic relationship. ILO experts advised the New Deal administration on a range of problems, from social insurance and employment services to public works. In return, the ILO received much-needed political support at a time when it increasingly lost ground in Europe.

Harold Butler was aware of this fact, and he deliberately sought to build a close association between the Organization and the United States. From the early 1920s onwards, he had been a central figure when it came to maintaining contacts with the Americans. His personal connections with Roosevelt, which dated back to the Washington Conference of 1919, and his good relationship with Frances Perkins were key elements of the process that led to the entry of the United Sates in 1934.[273] The turn to the United States under Butler's leadership also translated into the recruitment of Americans to senior positions in the ILO, reflecting to a large degree the reorientation which the Office underwent during this time. From the New Deal, the ILO took inspiration in implementing an ever-closer conceptual combination of economic and social policy. A prime example was the recruitment, in 1935, of Lewis Lorwin, a political economist, who became economic advisor to the ILO's Director. Lorwin personified the ILO's orientation towards economic planning, and he represented a new type of ILO official distinguished by technocratic expertise and an orientation towards Keynesian economics.[274]

---

271 On the global dimension of the New Deal see Kiran Klaus Patel, *The New Deal. A Global History* (Princeton, NJ: Princeton University Press, 2016).

272 Ibid.; on Frieda Miller's role, see also Jensen, "US New Deal Policy Experts and the ILO, 1948–1954", in *Globalizing Social Rights,* ed. Kott and Droux, 172–189.

273 He had a first meeting with the new president as early as November 1933.

274 Plata-Stenger, "Une voie sociale pour le développement", 144–147. See also Lorwin's book Lewis Lorwin, *The International Labor Movement: History, Policies, Outlook* (New York: Harper and Bros., 1953).

The most important and certainly the most consequential among the American recruitments of the time was John Gilbert Winant, who was appointed Assistant-Director by Butler in 1934. After returning to the United States soon thereafter at Roosevelt's request, he came back to Geneva as a US government delegate, then took up his Assistant-Director again, and was elected as the first American Director of the ILO in late 1938. Winant was a Republican, but he had been one of the most important allies of Roosevelt's New Deal policies. As a former governor of New Hampshire, he had served as the first chairman of the newly established US Social Security Board from August 1935 until February 1937. Winant's time at the helm of the ILO lasted only three years, but it would be mostly remembered for his role in leading the Organization into exile in Montreal and thus clearly on the side of the Allies during the Second World War.

In addition to providing new and different personnel, the United States' entry was a caesura with long-term consequences in yet another regard. Since United States became a member of the ILO but still remained outside the League of Nations, the special relationship which the ILO enjoyed with the US government constituted one more step in the growing estrangement between the ILO and the League. A resolution issued by the Selection Committee of the 1934 ILC on the occasion of the American entry had sealed the League issue for the time being, as it explicitly confirmed that membership in the ILO "shall not involve any obligation under the Covenant of the League of Nations". This move would bear unintended fruit during the war, when any connection to the "failed" and rapidly fading League could have further endangered the ILO's existence.[275]

The ILO Laboratory – Latin America and the First Technical Assistance Missions

At the same time that the United States joined the Organization, the ILO took steps towards a geographical expansion and regionalization of its work. Not surprisingly, the prime location of this process was Latin America. The motivation behind this move, which was accompanied by the establishment of a Special Section within the Office dedicated to the problems of non-European countries,

---

275 For the text of the resolution see ILO, *Record of Proceedings*, International Labour Conference, 18th Session 1934 (Geneva: ILO, 1934), 463. The emancipation from the League became clearly visible, when in 1934 the numbering of articles of the ILO Constitution was disconnected from that of the Treaty of Versailles. See ILO, *Constitution and Standing Orders of the International Labour Organisation* (Geneva, 1934).

was threefold. First of all, Butler was sensitive to a growing discontent among the non-European members of the ILO, which felt that their countries were underrepresented in the ILO's political structure and that their interests received too little attention in the Organization's general programme of work. The demands for better representation also expressed the more assertive role that non-European actors took during the period.[276] Secondly, by responding to these voices, Butler hoped to gain a new constituency that would help the ILO to counter the centrifugal forces that were working on the Organization in an evermore unstable international environment that was marked by political and economic nationalism. Finally, the quest for geographical expansion was not isolated from the wider context of the ILO's shift towards the western hemisphere marked by the entry of the United States.[277]

To move the Organization closer to Latin America was not an easy task, however. Many countries of the region doubted whether the ILO was sufficiently equipped to serve their needs. Pan-Americanism was a serious competitor, and there were several initiatives in place to build alternative structures and arenas to discuss labour and social issues at a purely regional level.[278] The underlying question was whether ILO standards, tailored as they were to the situation in industrialized countries, would fit the needs of the situation in Latin America. Countries like Chile, Uruguay, or Argentina had developed a degree of industrialization, and their trade unions were organized in similar ways as those in Europe. Social insurance schemes were in place in some of these countries, while, in other parts of the continent, an overwhelming majority of the population earned its living through small-scale agriculture.[279]

276 Marc Matera and Susan Kingsley Kent, *The Global 1930s: The International Decade* (London: Routledge, 2017).

277 Plata-Stenger, "Europe, the ILO and the Wider World (1919–1954)"; Ferreras, "Europe-Geneva-America: The First International Conference of American States Members of the International Labour Organization".

278 Wehrli, The ILO and Latin America, 11; Norberto Osvaldo Ferreras, "La construcción de una *Communitas* del Trabajo: las relaciones de la Organización Internacional del Trabajo (OIT) y América del Sur durante la década de 1930", *Dimensões, Revista da Universidade Federal do Espírito Santo*, vol. 29, 2010, 3–21.

279 Here, the ILO built on existing contacts with established networks, both through its recruitment of Latin Americans to the Office and a number of correspondents and contacts positioned in strategically important countries of the region, such as Mexico, Argentina, and Chile. See Yannick Wehrli and Fabián Herrera León, "Le BIT et l'Amérique latine durant l'entre-deux-guerres: Problèmes et enjeux", in *L'Organisation internationale du Travail*, ed. Lespinet-Moret and Viet, 157–166.

After a number of missions to Latin America by high-ranking ILO officials, which aimed above all at inducing Latin American governments to ratify ILO Conventions, Butler accepted a proposal by the Chilean government in 1935 to hold a conference of the ILO's American member States in Santiago de Chile in the following year. In the Organization, there was a good deal of scepticism about such a gathering, which, as some feared, could easily lead to an erosion of importance of ILO Conventions and strengthen notions of regional labour standards instead.

As it turned out, the Regional Conference in Santiago was a success, with repercussions that exceeded the geographically limited nature of the meeting. As the first ILO Regional Conference, it created an entirely new framework for community-building within the ILO. Regional Conferences gained a steady place in the ILO's calendar and, before long, spread to Asia and Africa. They developed into venues that would confirm the universal scope of the ILO's work, while allowing enough space for the discussion of problems that were specific to the particular region. In this latter sense, they also became a kind of safety valve for more localized concerns among the ILO's member States, a space where these concerns could be voiced without directly putting into question the ILO's labour standards. In Latin America, in particular, where pan-Americanism at this time posed a powerful challenge to the ILO's claims for universality, Regional Conferences worked as an insurance against the potential split of the organization along continental lines.[280]

The Santiago Conference discussed social insurance schemes, minimum age regulations, women's work, and the reduction of working hours in the textile industry. The agenda also included debates on international labour migration, which was an important topic for many Latin American countries. The Conference addressed specific regional issues, such as agriculture and the abolition of the truck system (based, for instance, on the payment of wages in kind), in certain industries like mining and for indigenous labour. The gathering gave Latin American countries, furthermore, an opportunity to voice their demands with the ILO. They asked for better representation in the Governing Body, the recruitment of more Latin Americans to the ILO's staff, and the publication of ILO documents in Spanish and Portuguese. In addition, groups that were part of the broader reformist milieu in Latin America used the conference to connect their agendas with the ILO's. One example was the area of nutrition, which occupied many governments and reformers in Latin America. They showed a keen interest in the ILO's work

---

280 Wehrli, "The ILO and Latin America", 11. Véronique Plata-Stenger, "'To Raise Awareness of Difficulties and to Assert Their Opinion'. The International Labour Office and the Regionalization of International Cooperation in the 1930ies", in *New Histories of Latin America at the League of Nations*, ed. Alan McPherson (Albuquerque, NM: University of New Mexico Press, 2015), 97–113.

with regard to living standards and wage policies.[281] Last but not least, the first two Regional Conferences of the Americas in Santiago de Chile and Havana (1939) did much to strengthen the ILO's regional network. It brought the Organization closer to the workers' movement, which, in turn, gained a greater sense of unity through cooperation within the ILO.[282]

Notwithstanding all fears and predictions, the two Regional Conferences did not raise the question of regional standards. To the relief of the ILO, they served to confirm the universal nature of the ILO's Conventions, while, at the same time, reminding the Organization of the limits of normative action more generally. One of the most significant outcomes of these first step towards regionalization was the encouragement it gave to ILO to develop new, more practical means of promoting its Conventions.

A method increasingly used during the 1930s to prepare the further dissemination of ILO standards was sending "technical assistance" missions to South-Eastern Europe in the beginning of the 1930s (Greece and Romania), China (1931), Egypt (1932), Cuba (1934), and, following the Santiago Conference in 1936, to various Latin American countries (Venezuela and Brazil). Those missions reflected both the geographical expansion of the ILO's work and the broader shift in the ILO's programme, paying more attention to economically "backward" countries and emphasizing the relationship between economic planning and social legislation.[283]

The purpose of most of these early missions was to help governments to implement specified social legislation and, in particular, social insurance schemes intended to support industrialization. This was certainly the case in Latin America. Populist governments that were pursuing ambitious projects in this regard – like the ones led by Getulio Vargas in Brazil or Lazaro Cardenas in Mexico – were looking to the ILO, because they thought that social insurance would help them to build strategic alliances with segments of the trade union movement that organized the often relatively small group of industrial workers. In other cases, ILO experts were called upon to help with the creation of institutions like labour inspectorates (China) or the Department of Labour itself (Cuba and Egypt).[284]

---

281 Corinne Pernet, "Developing Nutritional Standards and Food Policy: Latin American Reformers between the ILO, the League of Nations Health Organization, and the Pan-American Sanitary Bureau", in *Globalizing Social Rights*, ed. Kott and Droux, 249–261.

282 Patricio Herrera González, "El pacto por la unidad obrera continental: sus antecedentes en Chile y México, 1936", *Estudios de Historia Moderna y Contemporánea de México* 46 (Dec. 2013): 87–119.

283 Plata-Stenger, "Une voie sociale pour le développement", 257–312.

284 Seekings, "The ILO and Welfare Reform in South Africa, Latin America and the Caribbean, 1919–1950".

The early missions were mostly led by ILO officials, sometimes supported by external experts. The group of people sent on missions constituted a very peculiar hybrid form of *experts-fonctionnaires*,[285] whose technical and professional expertise was generally accompanied by a strong commitment to the ILO's ideas and methods of work, for which they acted as virtual conveyor belts. In some cases, as in Egypt, the Director himself or other high officials participated in a mission, which gave it a quasi-diplomatic undertone.[286]

In parallel, these first ventures into technical assistance also paved the way for new and more comprehensive ways of thinking about social problems in the European colonial territories. In the shadow of the forced labour debate, the ILO began to associate itself with an increasing body of reformist thinking on colonial social policy. A major impulse for this course of action came from the economic crisis, since the Great Depression hit export-oriented areas within the colonial world particularly hard. Social unrest and strikes, which affected strategically important functions of the colonial economy, broke out in several places, from the British Caribbean to the Dutch East Indies. They became the motivation for the measures taken by the French Popular Front government (1936–1938), as well as by the British government in its Colonial Development and Welfare Act of 1940. The measures adopted moved in the direction of an active colonial development policy and, for the first time, admitted financial responsibility for the welfare of all the people of the Empire.[287] To be sure, these initiatives were modest in scale and thoroughly paternalistic in outlook. However, taken together, they provided a platform which, soon afterwards, enabled the ILO to become a driving force for a change of attitude and for targeted actions in addressing the social problems of colonial territories.[288]

For most of the 1930s, the ILO's Native Labour Section tried to sustain this official change of attitude with its own activities. While its initial task consisted mainly of supporting the struggle against forced labour, it began to gradually collect data and produce surveys on African social affairs in general, in order to be prepared to support an eventual reform of colonial social policy.[289] Thus, the ILO was part of a changing international perception of the colonies' social and economic problems, which came to be analysed increasingly in a global(izing) framework. In this light, industrialization and the implementation of social

285 Plata-Stenger, "Une voie sociale pour le développement", 313–406.
286 Ibid.
287 Frederick Cooper, *Decolonization and African Society: The Labor Question in French and British Africa* (Cambridge, MA: Harvard University Press, 1996), 58–65.
288 ILO, *Social Policy in Dependent Territories*, 32–42.
289 Zimmermann, "Special Circumstances", 242–244.

policy measures, accompanied by projects to enhance the efficiency of agriculture, were increasingly seen as necessary means to elevate the colonial territories out of their "backward" state. In addition to social and political considerations, these measures were also seen as a way to better integrate the colonies into the world economy and thus, ultimately, to make them more profitable. This cautious but clear change is, accordingly, part of the early history of international development and of what has been labelled as the internationalization of colonial policies. These efforts would bear full fruit in the post-Second World War world under the auspices of the United Nations. Seen that way, the ILO's activities also open a perspective on the high degree of continuity in terms of imperial conceptions of colonial and post-colonial Africa and Asia that has been reflected in the work of international organizations across the watershed of 1945.[290]

290 Marc Frey, Sönke Kunkel, and Corinna R. Unger, "Introduction: International Organizations, Global Development, and the Making of the Contemporary World", in *International Organizations and Development, 1945–1990*, ed. Marc Frey, Sönke Kunkel, and Corinna R. Unger, 1–22 (Basingstoke: Palgrave Macmillan, 2014); Klaas Dykmann, "Only with the Best Intentions: International Organizations as Global Civilizers", *Comparativ* 23, no. 4/5 (2014): 21–46.

Part II The Second Founding: 1940–1948

> *I suggest that tonight you should each take this declaration and put in front of each paragraph the two words "I believe". If when you have done that, you feel that you believe what it says, vote for it. If you don't I ask you in the name of conscience, to stand up here and tell us where you differ, and we will try to come to terms with each other. We don't want any half-hearted people in this movement.*
>
> Sir John Forbes Watson, Employers' delegate, British Empire, 1944[291]

291 ILO, *Record of Proceedings*, International Labour Conference 26th Session 1944 (Montreal: ILO, 1944), 96.

https://doi.org/10.1515/9783110650723-partII

3 The Road to Philadelphia

The 1944 Declaration of Philadelphia stands out as a turning point in the history of the International Labour Organization (ILO). After the painful experiences of the immediate past – the social and political upheaval caused by the Great Depression, the rise of Fascism and Nazism, and the world's descent into war – the Declaration embodied the hopes for and the will to renewal of the liberal democracies gathered under the Organization's auspices. Its central demand, derived from the lessons of the past, was as simple as it was radical. The value of all future ILO policies should be measured exclusively in the light of whether they contributed to the realization of an overriding social objective designed to serve all people. Most importantly, "all policies" explicitly included the areas of the economy, finance, and trade and linked the national to the international dimension.[292] The ILO, equipped with such an extended mandate, would act as the guardian of this general social objective. What was more, the Declaration's claim to be valid for "all men irrespective of race, creed or sex" made it a key document for the groundswell of support for international human rights, and its main points were taken up a few years later by the United Nations Charter and the Universal Declaration of Human Rights.[293]

The Declaration of Philadelphia became one of the blueprints for the establishment of the welfare state in the post-war years, because it successfully combined the ideas of the New Deal and the concepts of European social reformers, such as William Beveridge of Great Britain. At the same time, its appeal extended beyond Europe and the North Atlantic, since it gave the less industrialized parts of the world, and, at that time, particularly Latin America, a voice to raise their demands for "economic security" in an international context.

In hindsight, the Philadelphia Conference turned out to be a "second founding" of the ILO. This was, however, in no way foreseeable, and only one of many possible outcomes of the ILO's wartime experience. For longer periods, it had not even been the most probable one. More than once during the war, the very survival of the ILO was called into question. The Declaration of Philadelphia eventually provided the ideological and programmatic plat-

292 Alain Supiot, *The Spirit of Philadelphia: Social Justice vs. the Total Market*, trans. Saskia Brown (London and New York: Verso, 2012).

293 Alcock, *History of the International Labor Organization*; Kott, "Fighting the War or Preparing for Peace? The ILO During the Second World War"; Geert van Goethem, "Phelan's War: The International Labour Organization in Limbo (1941–1948)", in *ILO Histories*, ed. Van Daele et al., 313–340.

https://doi.org/10.1515/9783110650723-005

Figure 5: ILO Director-General Edward Phelan signing the Declaration of Philadelphia with Franklin D. Roosevelt, President of the United States, at the White House, 1944.

form upon which the ILO could secure its place in the post-war order, as the result of factors that its leadership and its most devoted supporters could only partly control.

From Geneva to Montreal

With the start of the Second World War, dark clouds gathered over the ILO's headquarters in Geneva. When France signed a ceasefire in June 1940 that turned large areas of its territory over to German occupation, neutral Switzerland found itself surrounded on all sides by the Axis powers. The international organizations that had remained in Geneva thus became a political burden in the eyes of the Swiss government. Staying in the country was not a particularly attractive option for the ILO's leaders, either. For John Winant and most of his colleagues, leaving Switzerland seemed to be the only option for the ILO if it wanted to continue to act freely.

Staying on would inevitably have meant severe limitations on travel and communication for ILO employees. Indeed, ever since Germany's *Anschluss* of Austria 1938, there had been plans and simulations in place for relocating, in an emergency, the ILO's headquarters to neighbouring France. At the beginning of 1940, and following an agreement with the French government, the ILO's archives had already been transferred to Vichy.[294]

After the fall of France, however, this was no longer an option. Winant now reached out to the US government. To his surprise and disappointment, his approach was met with rejection. Given the widely held neutralist position, both by Congress and the American public at large, Secretary of State Cordell Hull considered it impossible to host the ILO, since this could be interpreted as openly taking sides in the European conflict. After a short debate, London was ruled out as an alternative due to its exposed position in the war. In the end, the Canadian Prime Minister, William Mackenzie King, offered the ILO temporary accommodation in his country. In private conversations with Winant, Mackenzie King issued an invitation to the Organization to transfer its headquarters to the premises of McGill University in Montreal.

Relocating the International Labour Office to Canada, and to Montreal in particular, held many advantages. As part of the British Commonwealth, Canada, too, was officially at war, but it was distant enough from the conflict to be a safe choice. Because of its bilingualism, and as a booming centre of the Canadian war industry, Montreal was an attractive location for the Organization. Furthermore, McGill University had one of the best economics libraries in the world, which was an important criterion for the ILO under Winant.[295]

In July 1940, Winant, using a previously agreed code, sent an encrypted telegram from the United States to his deputy, Edward Phelan, instructing him to begin immediate preparations for the Organization's relocation overseas. Some difficult decisions had to be taken, since only a small staff could accompany Winant to Montreal. While a handful of staff remained in Geneva, with the Organization's French press officer Marius Viple taking care of the ILO's property and staying in contact with the remaining League of Nations staff,[296] the great major-

294 Ironically enough, the building that housed the archives, the Pavillon Sévigné, became only a few months later the residence of the French collaboration government under Marshal Pétain. See Edward Phelan, "Some Reminiscences of the International Labour Organization", in *Edward Phelan and the ILO. The Life and Views of an International Social Actor*, ed. ILO (Geneva ILO, 2009 (1954 Studies: an Irish Quarterly Review, Vol. 43, No. 171), 241–270).

295 Edward Phelan, "The ILO sets up its Wartime Centre in Canada", in *Edward Phelan and the ILO. The Life and Views of an International Social Actor*, ed. ILO (Geneva ILO, 2009 (1955 Studies: an Irish Quarterly Review, Vol. 44, No. 174), 152–170).

296 Phelan, "Some Reminiscences of the International Labour Organization".

ity had to be laid off. All in all, about 40 members of the ILO's staff travelled secretly through French and Spanish territories to Lisbon. From the Portuguese capital – where thousands of people fleeing persecution and war were desperately waiting for passage to a safe haven overseas – the group eventually boarded the steam liner *Excambion*, leaving Europe for an uncertain future.

Figure 6: Group of ILO staff in Lisbon, waiting to board a ship to Canada, 1940.

The conditions under which the ILO was expected to start working in Montreal came as a shock to many of the new arrivals. The rooms McGill University was initially able to offer were basic in comparison to the spacious offices of the Geneva headquarters. Phelan's memoirs contain a vivid description of the huge open space which the Organization's skeleton staff had been allocated – a "disused chapel" with high windows, a gallery, and rows upon rows of plain wooden tables. As Phelan points out, in this one big room, with its "faintly ecclesiastical air", "roneotypists, typists, accountants, statisticians, editors, translators, experts and all the rest were camping out sheltered by four bare walls and a roof".[297] As time went by, additional rooms were found and conditions improved. More importantly, however, the ILO had retained its freedom of action. Butler's and

297 Phelan, "The ILO Sets up Its Wartime Centre in Canada", 259.

Figure 7: Morrice Hall, McGill University, Montreal, Canada, 1941.

Winant's strategy to move the ILO closer to the Americas now paid off, helping to pave the way for the Organization's survival. From its base in Montreal, the ILO was quickly able to retake the initiative. Because of his excellent contacts with the Roosevelt administration, Winant himself played a decisive role, and this allowed the ILO to reinvent itself. Winant made sure that the technical assistance missions to Latin America continued uninterrupted despite the Organization's limited budget.[298] This capacity to act, coupled with Winant's conviction of the ILO's potential role as a "spearhead of social and economic freedom" in dark times and an instrument to internationalize New Deal-style politics, significantly contributed to its survival.[299] They also outweighed flaws of Winant's leadership style, which was described by many as distant and erratic, sometimes bordering on a refusal to communicate even with his closest associates.[300]

298 Jensen, "From Geneva to the Americas", 228.

299 Quoted in ibid., 228.

300 Phelan, "The ILO Sets up Its Wartime Centre in Canada", 265.

In view of this, Winant's surprise decision, in February 1941, to leave his post with immediate effect to become the US ambassador to Great Britain, was met all round with dismay and consternation. His resignation threatened, during a critical phase of consolidation, to leave a vacuum. For all practical purposes, Edward Phelan, the Deputy Director, had been managing the Organization in Montreal, but in the circumstances he could not obtain the necessary legitimacy, which only a regular election by the Governing Body could have granted. Phelan, whether justified or not, had the reputation of being a bureaucrat, and he lacked Winant's charisma. As an Irishman, and thus a citizen of a neutral nation, he was also subject to some scepticism as to whether he was the right choice to head an organization that was moving more and more openly into the anti-Hitler camp. The US government and in particular the chairman of the Governing Body, John Carter Goodrich, were initially lukewarm in their support of Phelan. On the other hand, Phelan, as Secretary of the Labour Section of the British delegation at the Paris Peace Conference, had been instrumental in establishing the ILO in the first place.[301] Part of the ILO's leadership since its very beginnings, he embodied more than anyone else continuity. This was certainly no small asset in a time of crisis and turmoil. Within a few months, Phelan was able to overcome the resentments of his critics. He won the support of the most important groups in the ILO, including the US government and the trade unions. Eventually, the Emergency Committee, which had been established to take the place of the Governing Body in wartime, decided to appoint Phelan as Acting Director,[302] thus conferring on him the appropriate authority to head the Organization for the time being.

New York, 1941

Upon their arrival in Montreal, Winant and Phelan agreed that the ILO could not simply continue its activities in exile. To survive the war, it had to convince its member States of its continuous usefulness, in order to make its voice heard once the post-war planning could actually begin. It was particularly with this latter aim in mind that, in the spring of 1941, all efforts went into the preparation of an extraordinary meeting of the ILO, the first since the outbreak of war. In the summer, Phelan secured an invitation from the US Secretary of Labor Frances Perkins, who suggested in the name of President Roosevelt that a conference be

301 ILO, ed., *Edward Phelan and the ILO*, 19.

302 Phelan retained this status until 1946 when he was awarded the rank of Director-General until his retirement in 1948 in appreciation of his services to the ILO during wartime.

convened in the United States. New York was chosen as the most accessible place. Feverish preparations began.

When the Conference began at the end of October 1941 at the premises of Columbia University's Butler Library, the ILO could celebrate a first success. Despite all transportation restrictions due to the war, over a hundred delegates and a further hundred advisers from 35 countries had made the perilous journey – a clear sign of the significance which many of the participants attached to the Conference. The high rank of many delegates underlined this fact. For the United States, Frances Perkins herself and Assistant Secretary of State Adolph Berle led the delegation, while Great Britain sent Clement Atlee, second in line in Winston Churchill's war cabinet. Other prominent participants included the former Czechoslovak Foreign Minister Jan Masaryk, the former President of the Norwegian Parliament Carl J. Hambro, and Paul-Henri Spaak of Belgium, who later became a co-founding father of the European Economic Community. The Latin US contingent, which accounted for 13 of the 35 delegations in New York, also arrived with ministers and other high-ranking officials, including the 33-year-old Chilean Health Minister Salvador Allende.

In his Conference report, "The I.L.O. and Reconstruction", Phelan set out a programme of action which intended to secure a place for the Organization in the international order after the end of the war. It committed the ILO in clear terms to the cause of liberal democracy and called for its inclusion at an early stage in post-war planning. It invited governments to provide the ILO with a broad social mandate that would include in its remit economic and financial policy. The report suggested that such a mandate would reflect the growing acceptance that, after the war, policies should be guided by an overriding social objective. Governments everywhere should no longer be interested just in the conditions of work and the protection of the workers. They should embrace the notion of "economic security" and the "better organisation of the life of the community as a whole, in the interest of the community as a whole".[303]

The report drew its inspiration from many sources. It built heavily both on Roosevelt's Four Freedoms speech of January 1941 and on the Atlantic Charter of August 1941, in which Roosevelt and the British Prime Minister, Winston Churchill, had laid out a range of common goals for the period following an Allied victory. The Atlantic Charter's promise of a peace "which will afford the assurance that all the men in all lands may live out their lives in freedom from

303 ILO, "The I.L.O. and Reconstruction. Report by the Acting Director of the International Labor Office to the Conference of the International Labor Organization" (Montreal: ILO, 1941), 88–89, 97ff.

fear and want" and in which "the fullest collaboration between all nations in the economic field" would be brought about "with the object of securing for all improved labour standards, economic advancement and social security" became also the underlying theme of "The I.L.O. and Reconstruction".[304] A joint declaration by the Commonwealth nations and the European governments-in-exile that endorsed the Atlantic Charter was quoted as well.

Substantial space was dedicated to the social policies of many Latin American governments, as they could provide further proof that the "economic security of the citizen must be a central point of policy and [of] how completely it has been accepted by those responsible for the government of the peoples of the world".[305] The report was rounded off by references to statements ranging from the international trade union movement to the Catholic Church, all seemingly confirming that a new spirit had emerged during the war.

The social policy measures of the Axis powers did not go unmentioned, either. The report made it clear how big the challenge was that the liberal democracies were facing in this field. The memories of the Depression years and the failure of democratic governments to forcefully counter its devastating social effects still haunted the Conference participants in New York. Social policy, the report noted, would be "ultimately at the core of the issues which the war will decide". The ILO pleaded for a positive vision as an alternative to the gloomy prospects of a Nazi-ruled Europe. It acknowledged the social measures taken by Nazi Germany but reminded the members of the ILO that the goal to which they were bound was broader and brighter still – "economic security for all citizens, achieved in a manner which respects individual dignity and liberty". Economic security, in the view of the ILO, would never be an end in itself. It was the "precondition of a fuller, richer, and, above all, a freer life" and thus in direct contrast to the conditions of the Nazi "slave State" based on racist premises.[306]

"The ILO and Reconstruction" already contained concrete post-war measures. Predictably, among the future concerns, unemployment featured prominently. With the experiences of the First World War in mind, securing employment was seen as the single most important problem looming after the end of the war. It was regarded the major threat to political and social stability that had to be avoided at all costs. Vocational training, social insurance, wage policy, minimum living wages, better nutrition, housing, recreation, and improved conditions of work were also on the list. Greater equality of occupational opportunity was

304 Ibid., 89, 110–111.
305 Ibid., 90.
306 Ibid., 92, 95.

a (relatively feeble) nod to the women's movement, and the call for increased employer–worker collaboration on economic and social issues appealed to the trade unions. At the very end of the list of elements defining the "social mandate" which the ILO was seeking, we find international public works policy and the organization of migration – the core components of the programme for which the ILO had made an unsuccessful claim in the 1930s in the struggle to mitigate the consequences of the Great Depression.

The almost unanimous support the ILO received from the Conference for its post-war programme was due, at least in part, to the unusual circumstances of the Conference itself. Many of those present in New York were united by a common interest in making the Conference a success and in strengthening the ILO.[307] This was surely true for the American hosts themselves. Since the beginning of the war in Europe, Roosevelt had been leading the country, both rhetorically and practically, towards an ever-closer collaboration with the anti-Hitler Coalition. Both the Atlantic Charter and the Lend-Lease Act of March 1941, which permitted the United States to supply arms to Great Britain (and later the Soviet Union), clearly pointed in this direction. Despite these steps, at the time the Conference started, just a few weeks before the Japanese attack on Pearl Harbor, a significant part of the American public still opposed the direct involvement of the country in the European conflict. Against this backdrop, a conference on American territory provided an opportunity to promote greater US commitment to the Allied war effort. It also presented an occasion for the President, in particular, to win the support of the American trade unions to the prospect of war, which was regarded as an extremely important step for the transition to a war economy with its heavy implications for both production and labour relations. More generally, the Conference was seen as another propaganda platform to demonstrate the success and universal appeal of the social and democratic model embodied by the New Deal.[308]

In this context, John Carter Goodrich described the Conference in his opening speech as an "act of faith" born out of the belief that "social justice and social security and basic elements of economic democracy" formed the "essence of the conflict" and were "the very stuff for which free men fight".[309] The position of the United States was a clear signal to the other governments to come out in support

307 Alcock, *History of the International Labor Organization*, 161–170.

308 Kott, "Fighting the War or Preparing for Peace? The ILO During the Second World War", 365–367; Jensen, "From Geneva to the Americas"; For the broader project of an internationalization of the New Deal see Patel, *New Deal*; Elizabeth Borgwardt, *A New Deal for the World: America's Vision for Human Rights* (Cambridge: Cambridge University Press, 2005).

309 ILO, *Record of Proceedings*, International Labour Conference, 1941, New York and Washington, D.C. (Montreal: ILO, 1941), 2.

of the ILO – particularly to Great Britain, for which an ILO Conference had been low on the list of priorities given the more pressing concern of German air raids. The same was true for the group of London-based governments-in-exile that had come to New York: Free France, Belgium, the Netherlands, Poland, and Norway. For them, the Conference was an important opportunity to support the United States in its commitment to the joint fight against the Axis powers. For these governments, it was a question of life or death. The Norwegian government delegate and former labour leader Olav Hindahl echoed these feelings, when he supported the Report's claim that "without complete Allied victory over the Nazi aggressors, the ideals for which the International Labour Organization and its Labour Office stand cannot be reached". An Allied victory was for all representatives of Nazi-occupied countries the "absolute condition for the proper solution of all other problems confronting us in our efforts to create a better future".[310] A wealth of expressions of solidarity with recently occupied Greece, which had also sent a delegation, highlighted the urgent need for action.

Similar considerations motivated the trade union representatives present in New York.[311] Those who had gone into exile or underground to escape persecution in Europe, whose organizations had been shattered under German occupation, and whose colleagues had been murdered or sent to concentration camps felt strongly that it was time for the United States to enter the war. The British and American trade unions, on the other hand, were already thinking beyond the immediate circumstances of the day and saw the ILO as a means to secure the participation of labour in post-war planning. The Workers' group called emphatically on the Government representatives to provide Phelan with the necessary mandate and, on the basis of the Atlantic Charter, to "resolve that the ILO, with technical advisers selected on the tripartite principle, shall partake in the coming peace conference".[312]

Should any doubts have remained about the seriousness of the ILO's commitment to the Allied camp, they quickly evaporated in the course of the Conference. One particular question of great symbolic significance in this respect was that of the French representation to the ILO. Following the defeat of France in 1940, the country's seat had formally passed to Marshal Petain's Vichy collaboration regime, which, tolerated by Nazi Germany, governed the unoccupied part of France and most of France's colonial possessions. Nothing about this status

---

310 ILC, New York and Washington, D.C. (1941), *Record of Proceedings*, 49.

311 Bernard Delpal, "Le refuge américain de l'OIT (1940–1946). De l'esprit de Genève à l'esprit de Philadelphie, place du syndicalisme dans la stratégie de reconstruction", in *L'Organisation internationale du Travail*, ed. Lespinet-Moret and Viet, 107–120.

312 Ibid., 86.

had changed following the ILO's move to Montreal, partly because it affected the ILO's financial interests, since the Organization was not keen on dispensing with the French contribution. Marius Viple, the ILO's head press officer who had remained in Geneva, had maintained, with Phelan's approval, official contacts with the Vichy government despite the latter's increasingly repressive labour and social policies modelled on those of Fascist Italy. This course had drawn criticism from many sides. Adrien Tixier, in particular, the French Assistant-Director of the ILO, had long pleaded for the Organization to cut ties with the Vichy regime and to assign the French seat to the Free France government-in-exile under General Charles de Gaulle. Tixier himself had close ties with Free French representatives, such as René Cassin and De Gaulle's Minister of Labour Henri Hauck.

In New York, the question of French representation became the subject of a showdown. Both the Vichy regime and Free France had sent delegates, but the first group quickly found itself isolated and exposed to sharp condemnation on the part of various government and workers' representatives. When the French seat was eventually transferred to De Gaulle's government-in-exile a few months later, it just officially confirmed a state of affairs that had existed de facto since the Conference. Thus, by the end of 1941, even the last formal limitation on the ILO's support for the Allies had been removed.[313]

Latin America also played a key role in New York. In fact, for the second time since the 1930s, Latin America became an essential pillar in the Organization's survival. The United States had courted its southern neighbours intensively before the Conference, eager to keep them in the Allied camp. The Latin American countries, in turn, had their own motives for supporting the ILO. Mexico, Brazil, and Chile were all on the course to industrialization and hoped to gain the United States' commitment to a regionally coordinated policy of economic security. In their eyes, the ILO would provide a suitable platform for this. As in the 1930s, when the Roosevelt administration had been open to such agreements as part of its Good Neighbor policy, the Latin Americans were seeking the ILO's help in securing the international harmonization of social security policies. The Chilean delegation rightly pointed out that "the welfare of the working class of America depends chiefly on the economic conditions existing in our countries". To Latin American countries, what however mattered were "trade and economic relations satisfactory to both parties".[314] They supported the ILO because they hoped it would strengthen their position internationally, and because they regarded the

313 Jaci Leigh Eisenberg, "Laquelle était la vraie France? France and the ILO during the Second World War", in *ILO Histories*, ed. Van Daele et al., 341–364.
314 ILC, New York and Washington, D.C. (1941), *Record of Proceedings*, 91.

Organization as the best forum to achieve internationally coordinated social and economic policies, with the overriding aim of economic security.

Against this background, it did not come as a surprise that the Conference concluded with the adoption of several resolutions. As Carter Goodrich pointed out solemnly, it was the ILO's "duty and responsibility to give authoritative expression to the social objective, both in the decisions on reconstruction and in the creation of the permanent framework of international order".[315] The ILO deserved a new and extended mandate not only because it represented governments, industry, and labour but also because it had "the confidence of the free peoples, and more than that, of men of free spirit everywhere."[316] For the symbolic final act of the Conference, President Roosevelt invited the participants to hold their last session in the White House, thus signalling both his personal respect and US support for the ILO, calling it a "parliament for man's justice" and a cornerstone in a future "stable international system of social justice for all peoples everywhere".[317]

The ILO's first Conference since the beginning of the war went well beyond merely proving that the Organization was not dead or fading away. It succeeded in securing a mandate that acknowledged many of the ideas of the 1930s linked to the goal of "economic security". At the same time, Phelan's report on "The ILO and Reconstruction" provided a concrete social policy vision to complement the general promises of the Atlantic Charter. For a short and historic moment, then, the Organization found itself in New York at the forefront of international post-war planning. The euphoria surrounding this success was not to last long, however. Just a few months after the United States had joined the war in December 1941, disillusionment kicked in as post-war planning became more concrete, and the ILO found itself again facing the threat of being sidelined.

Post-war Planning

At the end of 1941, the US State Department created a new Division of Special Research, led by Leo Pasvolsky, later dubbed the "father of the United Nations". When the Division began to set out ideas for the future architecture of international organizations, the ILO played a reasonably prominent role. The initial ideas that were circulated granted the ILO responsibility not just for social policy but

---

315 Conference of the ILO, New York and Washington D.C. (1941), *Record of Proceedings*, 136.
316 Ibid.
317 Ibid., 156, 158. See for the background Jensen, "From Geneva to the Americas", 229–230.

also for the entire economic dimension of the reconstruction programme. This would have transferred to the Organization practically all the economic functions previously carried out by the League of Nations. However, after the United States had entered the war, diplomatic and military concerns soon pushed these considerations to the background, and the ILO quickly began to lose ground.[318]

On the first two days of 1942, representatives from 26 countries gathered in Washington, D.C., to sign what would later become the Declaration of the United Nations. The signatories agreed to join forces in the fight against the Axis powers and, on the basis of the principles set out in the Atlantic Charter, to work together on a joint system of international security, which would take effect once the war had ended. The Declaration made the Soviet Union a partner on an equal footing with the United States and Great Britain, and both of them had an interest in actively involving their new partner in all post-war planning. In Montreal, this news must have set off some alarm bells, since the attitude of the Soviet Union towards the ILO was openly hostile. The Soviet Union, which had never been very active since its joining in 1934, had left the ILO after its expulsion from the League of Nations following its attack on Finland in the fall of 1939. In the following years, Moscow would use every opportunity to question the ILO's legitimacy as a representative of workers' interests.[319] Instead, it aimed at establishing a unified international of trade unions which, it hoped, would eventually replace the ILO altogether. This approach would also have the side effect of driving a wedge between the major Western trade unions. The British Trades Union Congress (TUC), acting to some degree in the name of British foreign policy, was open to trade union unity, while the AFL fought it tooth and nail. As a result, labour, one of the ILO's most important advocates, did not speak with one voice when the Organization needed its support.[320]

In the United States, the ILO's main supporters in the Department of Labour were losing ground to the foreign policy makers in the State Department. It became clear quite quickly that Cordell Hull, while appreciating the potential of the ILO as an instrument for advocating American war aims, gave priority to the liberalization of world trade and did not consider the ILO to be suitable for that purpose. He, therefore, resisted the proposals to extend the ILO's economic and financial competences.[321]

318 Van Goethem, "Phelan's War", 322–324.

319 Jacobson, "The USSR and ILO", 404.

320 Geert van Goethem, "Labor's Second Front: The Foreign Policy of the American and British Trade Union Movements During the Second World War", *Diplomatic History* 34, no. 4 (2010): 663–680.

321 Ibid., 669.

The ILO continued to try, from its Montreal base, to use the momentum of the New York Conference to become actively involved in the post-war planning that its main member States had embarked upon. Its focus lay on unemployment, and the policy "prescriptions" that the ILO issued to its members for addressing this problem contained echoes of the Great Depression. Once again, the ILO argued for active employment policies based on international treaties in the fields of labour migration and public works, organized both nationally and at an international level. A new aspect was the focus on the expansion of vocational training, which was increasingly seen as a major tool in rebuilding the labour force. Refugees, too, were explicitly included in the ILO's considerations. This development was the result of the Organization's collaboration with the Inter-Allied Committee on Post-War Requirements under Sir Frederick Leith-Ross, which established estimates on the needs for essential goods and transport after the war.[322] Due to this connection, the ILO was involved, at least initially, in all the labour- and employment-related aspects of the Allies' post-war planning.

Along these lines, the ILO's experts pursued the international promotion of social security, with almost missionary zeal. Oswald Stein, Deputy Director of the ILO and Director of its Social Security Division, maintained relations with many of the British and American experts who, during the war, were working on expanding social security in their respective countries. William Beveridge, whose report on "Social Insurance and Allied Services" became the foundation of the British welfare state, consulted Stein regularly. He made broad use of the information the ILO put at his disposal, particularly with regard to social security systems in other countries.[323] The same applied to Arthur Altmeyer, Director of Roosevelt's Social Security Board, who was working at the same time as Beveridge on a similar report ("Security, Work, and Relief Policies"), which, however, never attained the prominence or the impact of its British counterpart.[324]

Latin America remained, for the entire duration of the war, one of the ILO's main fields of activity in the area of social security. Stein and other ILO experts undertook a series of technical assistance missions to Mexico, Argentina, Uruguay, Chile, Peru, and Bolivia. In July 1943, the ILO was able to bring Beveridge and other renowned social security experts to a pan-American Conference

---

322 Alcock, *History of the International Labour Organization*, 172.
323 William Beveridge, "Social Insurance and Allied Services", London: HMSO, 1942; reprinted in *Bulletin of the World Health Organization* 78, no. 6 (2000): 847–55.
324 On Altmeyer's report, see Jensen, "From Geneva to the Americas", 230. The full title of the report was "Security, Work, and Relief Policies. 1942: Report of the Committee on Long-Range Work and Relief Policies to the National Resources Planning Board", United States Government Printing Office, Washington, DC, 1942.

on Social Security in Montreal, which resulted in the draft of an "International Charter of Social Security" that called for the establishment of national social security systems worldwide and for international agreements to coordinate the measures.[325]

A less visible, but not less consequential, ILO field of action resulted from the work it had performed on colonial social policy. In September 1940, when the ILO had moved to Montreal, Winant had decided to attach a representative to the ILO's Liaison Office in London, who would act as a commissioner for colonial issues. This post was occupied by Wilfrid Benson, a relatively low-ranking official who had been part of the ILO's Native Labour Section throughout much of the interwar period. His London outpost may have seemed insignificant at the beginning, but it became the intellectual powerhouse from which much of the ILO's post-war colonial work originated. At the New York Conference the ILO received an extended mandate to draw up a programme of colonial reforms as part of the wider process of reconstruction.[326] In early 1943, Benson published an article in the *International Labour Review*, which contained a detailed proposal for colonial social reforms. Its title "A People's Peace in the Colonies" was programmatic inasmuch as it cited the famous dictum by Ernest Bevin, the British war-time Minister of Labour, stating that the "people's war" that the democracies were fighting had to be followed by a "people's peace". The article thus connected the colonial situation to the general debate on post-war social policy. The article presented the following basic pillars of the people's peace in the colonies: the subordination of all colonial policy to a superordinate social objective; a move away from the laissez-faire politics of the pre-war period to a commitment by the colonial state to active economic and social development; the safeguarding of participation by the indigenous populations as a contribution to social development "from the ground up" (with the effect of promoting trade union freedoms in the colonies); and the increased "internationalization" of colonial social policy, that is the

325 Jensen, "From Geneva to the Americas", 230–231. See for the broader debate also Martin H Geyer. "Social Rights and Citizenship during World War II", in *Two Cultures of Rights: The Quest for Inclusion and Participation in Modern America and Germany*, ed. Manfred Berg and Martin H. Geyer, Publications of the German Historical Institute (New York: Cambridge University Press, 2002), 143–166, esp. 157–166.

326 Benson had prepared this move in conversations with colonial circles in London (both official and non-official), including a number of colonial representatives within the exile governments of France, the Netherlands, and Belgium. Benson had also engaged in discussions with US government officials and research institutions with an interest in colonial affairs.

strengthening of the ILO's role in defining the main direction of colonial social policy.[327]

Although its conceptual work and its practical activities in the field of employment policy and social security gave the ILO some recognition and, on occasion, visibility, close observers were concerned that the Organization did not appear to be playing much of a role, if any, in the negotiations on the post-war policy pursued among the Allies. One particularly alarming signal was the ILO's exclusion from the United Nations Conference on Food and Agriculture in Hot Springs, Virginia, in May 1943. The meeting focused on a number of topics – such as living standards, nutrition, and agricultural labour – that, according to a resolution passed at the New York Conference, lay within the ILO's competence. When the United Nations Relief and Rehabilitation Administration (UNRRA) was established later in the same year, which took over some of the functions of the Leith-Ross Committee, the ILO was sidelined again. It gradually became clear to the majority of the ILO's supporters that the Organization was at risk of losing all influence over post-war planning and that, if this were to happen, many of the initiatives already embarked upon would end up going nowhere. While the ILO's expert advice and technical services continued to be sought after, at the diplomatic level, the Organization was fighting for its survival. When the ILO was excluded from a meeting of Allied foreign ministers scheduled for October 1943, which foresaw the establishment of the basic architecture of international organizations, the writing was clearly on the wall. At a specially convened meeting of the Governing Body in London in December 1943, its members agreed that the best way to regain the initiative would be to convene a regular session of the ILC. This time, though, just passing new resolutions would not be good enough. What was needed was a bold affirmation of the ILO's basic principles, which could return the Organization to the forefront of post-war planning and serve as a basis for claiming a broad social mandate.[328]

The US government declared itself once again willing to host the Conference, and this time the choice fell on Philadelphia, the deeply symbolic site of the American Declaration of Independence. In the run-up to the Conference, the Western Allies, the Workers' group, and the employers were all in agreement that a new Conference would offer the ILO the perfect forum to renew its claim for full involvement in post-war planning. Frances Perkins recorded in her notes on a meeting with Winston Churchill their shared satisfaction that the new Confer-

327 Wilfrid Benson, "A People's Peace in the Colonies", in *International Labour Review* 47, no. 2 (1943): 141–168.
328 Van Goethem, "Phelan's War", 328–331.

ence would, like the one two and a half years earlier in New York, be an "excellent piece of psychological warfare".[329] With a view to the future profile of the Organization, not everyone was as receptive of the ILO's ambitions as the Labour Department and the New Dealers in line with Perkins. Neither the British Foreign Office nor the US State Department nor the UN planners headed by Leo Pasvolsky wanted to have anything to do with the resolutions the ILO had adopted in New York. They would have preferred to use the Philadelphia Conference to restrain the ILO to the core activities of the pre-war period.

As the Conference drew closer, the problem of the Soviet attitude to the ILO became virulent again. If Philadelphia was going to be an occasion to work on plans for reconstruction, and if the ILO was to assume a role in the post-war order, it would be a major handicap if the Soviet Union was not included. Accordingly, the British and US governments made serious efforts to get the Soviet Union to come to the table. Roosevelt attempted to convince Stalin personally to send a delegation, and he even secured the consent of the AFL to abandon its resistance to the participation of Soviet Workers' representatives. In the end, however, all efforts were in vain. One likely reason for the Soviets' intransigence was their ongoing attempt to establish a unified trade union international, which would become either a counterweight to the ILO in the emerging UN system or, ideally, replace the ILO altogether.[330]

Philadelphia, 1944

Unperturbed by these diplomatic manoeuvres, the ILO staff in Montreal spent the first months of 1944 preparing a long memorandum on the "Future Policy, Programme and Status of the International Labour Organisation".[331] Building on the resolutions of the New York Conference, the memorandum repeated the ILO's calls for a broad social (and economic) mandate. It listed a wide range of fields that the ILO considered to be its rightful future area of influence and positioned itself at the very centre of the future international system and all its branches. This might have seemed like risky gamble, given the precarious situation the ILO had found itself in for most of the two and a half years that has passed since the gathering in New York. However, from a different perspective, the ILO had little to lose.

329 Quoted in van Goethem, "Phelan's War", 329.

330 Ibid., 331.

331 ILO, *Record of Proceedings*, "Future Policy, Programme and Status of the International Labour Organisation", International Labour Conference, 26th Session 1944 (Montreal: ILO, 1944).

The Conference would prove that the ILO leadership had made the right decision. In light of the circumstances, the meeting turned out to be an unqualified success. Once again, an impressive number of delegations made their way to Philadelphia. Except for the Soviet Union and a handful of other countries, almost all of the future UN Member States were present at the Conference, which provided the ILO with the legitimacy it needed for its recommendations. Most of the delegates supported the ILO's claim for a broadened social mandate. An important factor was that labour put its weight fully behind the Organization's claims. At the Conference, the British labour leader Joseph Hallsworth confirmed labour's continuous support for the ILO and the expectations of the Workers' group stating that "this Organisation cannot live, and, I predict that no other organisation that can be set up now can live, which denies the right of the workers to be in at the start of any measures which are designed to encompass this policy of peace and prosperity".[332]

Indeed, as the ILO leadership had hoped for, the Conference quickly assumed the character of a "first meeting of the Peace Conference". This also meant that the solemn Declaration which the ILO adopted at the end of the meeting was regarded as a social preamble of the future peace negotiations. In Philadelphia, the ILC adopted altogether 23 resolutions and seven Recommendations, with the first resolution dealing with the "social provisions in the peace settlement", including recommendations to the United Nations for present and post-war social policies.[333]

The main outcome of the Conference was the now famous Declaration of Philadelphia – a "Declaration Concerning the Aims and Purposes of the International Labour Organisation" – that was later incorporated in the ILO's Constitution.[334] It was hardly surprising that the first paragraph of the Declaration of Philadelphia confirmed and reinforced the basic social liberal statements of the ILO's Constitution from 1919 – "labour is not a commodity" and "freedom of association and of expression are essential to sustained progress".[335]

Next, "poverty anywhere constitutes a danger to prosperity everywhere" was a statement that insisted on the global vision necessary for the formulation of

332 ILC, 26th Session (1944), *Record of Proceedings*, 52.

333 ILO, *Resolutions Adopted by the Twenty-sixth Session of the International Labour Conference (Philadelphia, April–May, 1944)* (Montreal: ILO, 1944).

334 The Declaration concerning the aims and purposes of the International Labour Organisation (1944) in ILO, 26th Session (1944), *Record of Proceedings*, App. XIII, 621–623; Eddy Lee, "The Declaration of Philadelphia: Retrospect and Prospect", *International Labour Review* 133, no. 4 (1994): 467–84.

335 ILO, Declaration of Philadelphia.

economic and social policies and emphasized the objective of a fair economic order. It anticipated, by pointing out worldwide economic interdependence, an international discourse about the problem of development, which would emerge in the decades to come. Finally, the Declaration reconfirmed the ILO's commitment to tripartism and democratic decision making as the method of choice to fight the "war against want".

Section II of the Declaration contained the passages that marked a real and radical new beginning. It stated that all policies, both on the domestic and the international levels, "in particular those of an economic and financial character", should be scrutinized in the light of an overriding social objective. This claim found its justification in the idea of universal human rights, which appeared in an international document for the first time:

> All human beings, irrespective of race, creed or sex, have the right to pursue both their material well-being and their spiritual development in conditions of freedom and dignity, of economic security and equal opportunity.[336]

The Declaration of Philadelphia elevated the establishment of conditions in which these rights could be realized to a "central aim of national and international policy", stating that it was the ILO's duty "to examine and consider all international financial and economic policies and measures in the light of this fundamental objective". This was a direct reference to the resolution passed at the New York Conference, and the idea of universal human rights added significant strength to this claim.[337]

Obviously, the human rights language of the Declaration of Philadelphia did not come out of nowhere. The ILO did not act in isolation, but rather as part of a broader movement. The Four Freedoms speech and the Atlantic Charter, which had already featured prominently at the New York Conference, continued to be important reference points, as their repeated quotations by Conference participants and the American press coverage of Philadelphia confirmed.[338] In the years between New York and Philadelphia conferences, the ILO had actively helped to promote human rights as the foundation, both ideological and legal, of the post-war order. One of the main authors of the Declaration was the ILO's Legal Adviser, Wilfred Jenks. He had close connections to the American Law Institute, a private organization of lawyers, which, at President Roosevelt's suggestion, had been working since 1942 on the draft of a universal charter of human rights. Jenks

336 Ibid.
337 Ibid.
338 Jensen, "From Geneva to the Americas", 231–232.

also kept in touch with Latin American law experts working in a similar direction, championing socio-economic rights, in particular. Philadelphia offered one of the first opportunities to seal these ideas in an international document.[339]

Section III listed what the ILO regarded as its future areas of activity. As in Phelan's 1941 report on "The ILO and Reconstruction", full employment and standards of living came first, followed by vocational training and wage policies. Another sub-section was dedicated to the recognition of the right of collective bargaining. It promoted the cooperation of management and labour in increasing productivity and the participation of both in implementing social and economic measures. This was followed by social security, occupational health and safety, protective measures targeting children and mothers, nutrition, housing, facilities for recreation and culture, and, finally, the "assurance of equality of educational and vocational opportunity". Thus, the section not only referred to the improvement of working conditions and the promotion of labour rights as the traditional area of ILO activity but, at the same time, largely represented the Organization's new, more expansive understanding of the close link between social and economic policies.[340]

Sections IV and Section V also signalled a new beginning by focusing on the less industrialized countries as well as on the part of the world's population that was still under colonial rule. The ILO now considered it its task to "promote the economic and social advancement of the less developed regions of the world" at both the national level and, more importantly, the international level. To this end, the Organization committed itself to collaborating with all international institutions working towards the same goals in areas such as world trade, health policy, and education. The Latin American countries, in particular, were gratified to see their demands reflected in this objective.[341]

Few were the voices that spoke out at the Conference against the broadening of the ILO's mandate. The US Workers' delegate Robert Watt was among the few who warned that the ILO should refrain from "making everyone's business" its concern.[342] The Belgian Workers' delegate and future Deputy Director-General of the ILO, Jef Rens, by contrast, confronted the opposition from some employers by pleading for a bold new mission of the Organization. "The role of the International Labour Organisation," he proclaimed, "is now to formulate the rights of the masses of the workers, to make them prevail over the privileges, whatever those

339 Hanne Hagtvedt Vik, "Taming the States: The American Law Institute and the 'Statement of Essential Human Rights'", *Journal of Global History* 7, no. 3 (2012): 461–482.
340 ILO, Declaration of Philadelphia.
341 Ibid.
342 ILC, 26th Session (1944), *Record of Proceedings*, 39.

privileges may be, of the minority, and to have them inscribed in the laws of the States Members.”[343]

Rens might well have felt that the momentum was on his side when it came to the discussion of future national policies. However, debates about possible international action in support of full employment policies showed very clearly that much of what was listed in Section IV was primarily not more than a joint declaration of intent. As part of the “Resolution Concerning Social Provisions in the Peace Settlement”, the Australian government had suggested the adoption of an international agreement that would have obliged all countries to coordinate their national policies with those of other countries, with the intent of seeking global full employment. An agreement of this nature would have established, above all, mechanisms to protect the efforts of developing countries to both industrialize and build their own systems of social security; it would have affected mainly the domestic employment and the economic and trade policies of industrialized countries. This proposal had the support of many Latin American states and some Commonwealth countries, such as South Africa. The US government delegation, however, was in the forefront of those who opposed such an agreement, which eventually failed to gain the necessary votes.[344]

Against the background of the Philadelphia Declaration’s emphasis on the importance of a “high and steady volume of international trade” and the “great contribution that the international exchange of goods and services can make to higher living standards and to high levels of employment”, the failure of Australia’s proposal was symbolic. Many of the Conference participants did not necessarily see a contradiction between free trade and international regulation. The failure of the employment initiative, however, did put an early brake on the ILO’s ambitions of becoming the social guardian of international economic and trade policies.

A Declaration for “All Human Beings”?

The tensions between the universalistic approach of the Declaration and the immediate political practices and goals of the ILO’s members could be observed in other fields, too, but they became even more visible when it came to the status of the colonial territories. Section V, the final part of the Declaration, was dedi-

343 Ibid., 117.

344 The Australian government wanted “to see the I.L.O. play a much greater role in the future in international economic collaboration, and, in particular, in maintaining high levels of employment and consumption”, ibid., 30–34.

cated entirely to colonial populations. It stated that the human rights principles of the Declaration should be "fully applicable to all peoples everywhere", but it simultaneously made "the manner of their application" dependent on the "stage of social and economic development reached by each people". The gradual application of the Declaration's provisions in the colonial territories was proclaimed to be a "matter of concern to the whole civilized world" (thus elevating the international community, represented by the ILO, to the role of a "social policy development trustee" in the colonies).[345] But the fact remained that the universality of the Declaration of Philadelphia was, with regard to the colonies, implemented only gradually, which compromised the application of its human rights claims. The ambivalence of the ILO's approach to colonial social policy was visible in other places, too. In what Edward Phelan termed "a parallel action" to the Philadelphia programme, the ILO adopted a Recommendation under the programmatic heading of "Social Policy in Dependent Territories"[346] (which would eventually inspire a series of Conventions in 1947–1948).

Most of the underlying principles (such as the overriding social objective, the active role of the state, freedom of association, and the demand for an expansion of the ILO's competencies) reflected the main sections of the Philadelphia Declaration. The colonial reforms announced in Philadelphia were, in this sense, a real breakthrough. They elevated the colonies for the first time from the inferior position in the native labour code to a sphere in which universal social policy norms applied.

At the same time, the very fact that the colonial territories were once again the subject of their own specific norms showed that it was mainly their political status and less their socio-economic stage of development that excluded them from the full application of ILO standards. The colonial powers recognized that concessions on social matters might keep the demands for political reform at bay. Gentle pressure from the colonial powers' American allies and the Workers' group also played a part in convincing many of the colonial government representatives of the propaganda value of the reforms. However, the following years would prove on more than one occasion that the conflict surrounding the validity and application of the Philadelphia principles in the colonial territories was far from over.[347]

Philadelphia brought visible changes in the treatment of women's work, too. The principle of equal rights was strengthened in the second article of the

345 ILO, Declaration of Philadelphia.

346 Social Policy in Dependent Territories Recommendation, 1944 (No. 70).

347 Maul, *Human Rights, Development, and Decolonization the International Labour Organization, 1940–70*, 152–184.

Declaration, which, from its human rights perspective, emphasized equal rights “irrespective of race, creed or sex”. In the run-up to the meeting and during the Conference itself, the women’s movement had pleaded for a departure from the predominantly “protective approach” of the pre-war period. The massive involvement of women in wartime production in many countries, even greater than during the First World War, had created a momentum for this demand and played a major part in its success. However, the tension between the protective and the equality approach remained a defining feature of the ILO’s treatment of women’s work for years to come. This was illustrated, in particular, by the ILC debates in 1950 and 1951 concerning the Equal Remuneration Convention (No. 100), which was perfectly in line with the equality and anti-discrimination mandate of the Philadelphia Declaration.[348]

Eventually, steps were taken for the establishment of “Industrial Committees” – in order to create a new international framework for bipartite or tripartite discussion within leading industries (textile, building, metal works, etc.).[349] The idea of Industrial Committees was essentially born out of the demands, partly in response to the war, of certain sectoral trade unions, which wanted the ILO to establish offices for specific branches of production. There was a general agreement that these offices would help the ILO to become even more deeply connected with its constituents. The Philadelphia Conference formally initiated the creation of tripartite Industrial Committees, but left it to the Governing Body to decide about their exact form, role, and scope.[350]

In retrospect, the war years turned out to be a phase of expansion for the ILO. The new human rights basis on which the work of the Organization was placed at the Philadelphia Conference changed both the ideological foundation and the scope of its activities. From another perspective, Philadelphia also marked the continuation of a transformation that had begun on many levels in the 1930s. The ILO turned from an organization whose primary focus was on the problems of labour and the conditions of work to an agency concerned with social life and policy in a much broader sense. Social security replaced social insurance as the central theme of social policy, as it covered ever-increasing areas in the lives of

348 Silke Neunsinger, “The Unobtainable Magic of Numbers: Equal Remuneration, the ILO and the International Trade Union Movement, 1950s–1980s”, in *Women’s ILO,* ed. Boris, Hoehtker, and Zimmermann, 121–148.

349 The decision to create Industrial Committees had already been taken by the Governing Body at the New York Conference three years earlier, but since the Philadelphia Conference was the first regular ILC during the war, they came into existence only at that time.

350 Edward Weisband and Edward Singleton “ILO Industrial Committees and Sectoral Activities: An Institutional History”, Working Paper SAP 2.53/WP.100 (ILO: Geneva, 1996).

working people. All this was pointing out to a new vision which was debated and eventually codified by the International Labour Conference in Philadelphia. What emerged from Philadelphia was a consensus based on the understanding of an intrinsic relationship of social and economic policies and an agreement on the ultimate primacy of a social objective for all policies.

Equipped with a strong mandate, the ILO now turned its attention to the economically less advanced regions. Even colonial territories were, at least in principle, elevated from a sphere in which different rights applied and were included in the universal social policy framework of the Declaration of Philadelphia. Although these developments were still a work-in-progress, Philadelphia laid the foundations that gave the ILO the image of a truly global organization – both geographically and in terms of its work programme. Before it could get to this point, however, the ILO would have to manage the difficult transition to the post-war order. The participation of the Soviet Union continued to be a major hurdle. One direct effect of the Soviet Union's absence from Philadelphia was that the Conference was essentially a meeting of liberal democracies. Compared to the Charter of the United Nations or the Universal Declaration of Human Rights, the clear language of the Declaration was much less subject to the "competing universalisms" of the age.[351] Thus, the Declaration of Philadelphia was, in some respects, more of a maximum consensus than a minimum compromise.

Just a few weeks after Philadelphia, the Allies landed in Normandy and the war entered its final, decisive phase. In August 1944, representatives of the Allied powers met at Dumbarton Oaks to discuss the design of the new United Nations Organization. As in the aftermath of the New York Conference, the ILO had to realize that its role in these negotiations, if it had one at all, would be very limited. Only months after the boost that Philadelphia had given to the ILO, it found itself once again with its back against the wall.

---

351 Sunil Amrith and Glenda Sluga, "New Histories of the United Nations". *Journal of World History* 19, no. 3 (2008): 251–274.

4 A Place in the New Order

When the transition to the new world order began, the International Labour Organization (ILO) found itself once again relegated to a back seat. Before the Organization could eventually join the United Nations in 1946, it was more than once confronted with its precarious position within the new power constellation that had been established at the end of the Second World War. The open hostility of the Soviet Union towards the ILO and the Organization's reliance on the Western bloc turned out to be both a liability and an asset, depending on the development of the relationship between the wartime allies. Against this backdrop, the beginning of the first wave of decolonization, marked by India's independence in 1947, likewise was both a challenge and an opportunity to the Organization. On the one hand, decolonization resulted in new conflicts for the ILO inasmuch as it carried the potential to clash with both its focus on European reconstruction and its reliance on the support of the major colonial powers. On the other hand, by responding to the growing demands to shift its focus from Europe to the developing world, the ILO won new elbow room. Under the leadership of the new Director-General David Morse, it kept and even sharpened its profile as a frontline organization of the Western camp in the looming Cold War, while starting a whole new set of activities.

Joining the UN Family

As the war drew to an end, the planning for the post-war architecture of international organization became more concrete by the day. At all levels, governmental and non-governmental groups continued to work on evermore detailed plans for a stable peace order following the Allied victory. If the ILO increasingly took but a back seat in the midst of these buzzing activities, it was due, above all, to the growing consensus among the Allies that collective security would have to become the top priority for the future world organization at the heart of the new international system. If the peace was to last, the key to its success lay in the degree to which the interests of the two "superpowers" emerging from the war – the United States and the Soviet Union – could be accommodated to form the pillars of the new post-war order.[352]

---

352 Daniel Plesch, *America, Hitler and the UN: How the Allies Won World War II and a Forged Peace* (London: I. B. Tauris, 2010); Paul M. Kennedy, *The Parliament of Man: The Past, Present, and Future of the United Nations* (New York: Random House, 2006).

https://doi.org/10.1515/9783110650723-006

This naturally put the ILO in a difficult position. Even if the euphoria of Philadelphia had quickly given way to more sober assessments of the Organization's prospects, few were prepared for the setbacks it suffered at two crucial meetings in the summer of 1944. The first blow came in July, when the Allies met in the tranquil atmosphere of the mountain resort of Bretton Woods in New Hampshire to discuss the financial and economic aspects of the post-war order. The only representative the ILO was able to send – and only in the role of an observer – was its Acting Director, Edward Phelan, who was not in the position to have any significant impact. While the ILO managed to be present when the heads of the British and American delegation, John Maynard Keynes and Harry Dexter White, and the delegates of 44 Allied nations thrashed out the foundations of the post-war financial and economic order, it had no allies. The Bretton Woods agreement paved the way for the creation of the International Monetary Fund (IMF) and the International Bank for Reconstruction and Development (IBRD), which later became part of the World Bank Group, but there was no mention whatsoever of any overarching social objective or of international labour standards, let alone of any significant role for the ILO.[353]

The ILO faced a similar situation in August 1944 at Dumbarton Oaks in Washington, D.C., where the negotiations on the structure of the future world organization took place. It was more than alarming that the Allies decided on the establishment of an Economic and Social Council (ECOSOC), which would be given the task of coordinating all future sub-agencies of the United Nations. The existing agency, the ILO, was not even mentioned in the official minutes of the Dumbarton Oaks Conference. This outcome was due in large part to the influence of the Soviet Union, and neither the British nor the US representatives were prepared to confront their wartime ally on the ILO's behalf. Their main priority was to see the Soviet Union involved in a future system of collective security.[354]

Even then, the ILO's lowest point had not been reached. It came in San Francisco in the spring of 1945, when the United Nations was eventually founded. During the entire year that had passed since the Philadelphia Conference, the situation of the ILO had constantly deteriorated. At Yalta, in February 1945, the Allied powers had straightened out last issues relating to their respective spheres of influence. The way was now clear for the founding of a new world organization, and a meeting was called for the following April in San Francisco. When it opened with the participation of 46 nations, the ILO found itself entirely shut out

353 Eric Helleiner, *Forgotten Foundations of Bretton Woods: International Development and the Making of the Postwar Order* (Ithaca, NY: Cornell University Press, 2014).

354 Georg Schild, *Bretton Woods and Dumberton Oaks. American Economic and Political Post-war Planning in the Summer of 1944* (New York: St.Martin's Press, 1995).

of the proceedings. Phelan had sought, with growing desperation, to obtain an invitation to the gathering, but the closer the opening date approached, the more obvious it became that the US State Department did not wish the ILO to participate directly, mainly out of consideration for the Soviet Union. Moreover, the news of Roosevelt's death two weeks before the start of the Conference came as a real shock to the ILO. The transition from Roosevelt to Harry S. Truman, who had had no prior relationship whatsoever to the Organization, added to the uncertainty.

The ILO could not, at this stage, count on the support of the international trade union movement either. Following the founding of the unified World Federation of Trade Unions (WFTU) in February 1945, which counted among its members the British TUC and most of the other European and Latin American trade unions that had previously belonged to the IFTU, the deep rift among the trade unions in the West had become obvious. The AFL bitterly resented the demise of the IFTU and the merger with the Soviet trade unions – particularly because it meant that the AFL's rival trade union federation, the Congress of Industrial Organizations (CIO), would be represented in the WFTU. Consequently, the AFL attempted to thwart, with some success, the participation of the WFTU in San Francisco. Given these divisions and the political and ideological difficulties within the new unified trade union international to find a common position on the future role of the ILO, no immediate help could be expected from this direction.[355]

It was only due to the intervention of a handful of countries, most prominently among them Great Britain and certain Latin American states, that the ILO was at least allowed to send an unofficial five-person delegation to the San Francisco Conference for the purpose of informal consultation.[356] As it turned out, Phelan himself could not join the delegation, as one of the Soviet Union's last attempts to prevent the ILO from participating focused on his Irish nationality. Since Ireland had remained neutral throughout the war and was, therefore, not a member of the United Nations, Moscow insisted that Phelan could not attend. The rest of the ILO delegation's journey to San Francisco was far from smooth, either, as the delegates were accommodated in a hotel located miles from the Conference site. Up to the last minute, it was not clear whether they would get

---

355 Van Goethem, "Labor's Second Front", 670–680. For a broader context, see Anthony Carew, *American Labour's Cold War Abroad: From Deep Freeze to Detente, 1945–1970* (Edmonton, AB: Athabasca University Press, 2018), 9–28; Oliver Pohrt, *Die Internationale Gewerkschaftsbewegung zwischen Einheitswunsch und Kaltem Krieg. Der Weltgewerkschaftsbund (WGB) von der Gründungsphase bis zu seiner Spaltung (1941–1949)* (Regensburg: S. Roderer, 2000).

356 The participants for the ILO were next to John Carter Goodrich, Assistant Director Lindsay Rodgers, Wilfred Jenks, chief of the ILO's Legal section at the time, and the British and Dutch labour leaders Joseph Hallsworth and Jacobus Oldenbroek.

invitations to the Conference at all, and they were not invited to official receptions or to the formal closing session.[357] During the session, the British delegation made a modest attempt to add to the Dumbarton Oaks proposals an amendment that would have placed the ILO in a special relationship with the United Nations, but this was immediately opposed by both the United States and the Soviet Union. The future of the ILO thus remained subject to further negotiations. As the war came to an end both in Europe and Asia, and the pillars of the new international order were being erected, the Organization faced the threat of falling victim to this very order. In the worst case, it would suffer the fate of the League of Nations, which was in the process of being wound up. Paradoxically, the ILO was again facing the threat of oblivion when, at the same time, many European governments were about to translate the principles of Philadelphia into concrete policies in their efforts to establish the foundations of the post-war welfare state.

What brought the ILO back from the sidelines into the centre of the debate and made the desired relationship with the United Nations possible was the rapid deterioration of the relationship between the wartime allies after San Francisco. The fissures in the relationship between the Western powers and the Soviet Union now became ever more apparent. At the Potsdam Conference in July and early August 1945, Truman, Churchill, and Stalin clearly diverged in their views on the Polish borders and a general approach to the occupation of Germany. Truman's decision to employ a nuclear bomb at Hiroshima and Nagasaki, taken at Potsdam and executed two weeks later, was intended to pave the way for a quick victory and the occupation of Japan without Soviet participation. It was yet another sign of discord. After Potsdam, the writing was on the wall: the alliance between the West and the Soviet Union was giving way to a new antagonism.

It was in this context that the first ILC on European territory since 1939 took place in Paris in the autumn of 1945. In Phelan's words, it was the first international gathering in the "atomic age", while for the ILO it constituted "the end of the war period and the beginning of the post-war period".[358] Despite all the difficulties the ILO faced with regard to the transition into the new world order, the general tone at the Conference was cautiously optimistic. Frances Perkins transmitted to the gathering President Truman's intention "to make clear to you beyond the possibility of doubt that the United States of America intends to continue whole-hearted participation in the work of the Organization". Therefore, Perkins continued, it was desirable from the point of view of the US government

---

357 Alcock, *History of the International Labor Organization*, 189.

358 ILO, *Record* of Proceedings, International Labour Conference, 27th Session 1945 (Geneva: ILO, 1946), 34, 182.

that the ILO entered into a "mutually satisfactory relationship with the United Nations Organization".[359] This was an important signal for many of the governments present in Paris. It implied that, in cooperation with the United Nations, the maximum autonomy for the ILO was desirable. This position was also taken by a large number of European and Latin American delegations.[360] As a result, Phelan considered the Organization strong enough to counter any proposals that would have degraded the ILO to a mere executive body of ECOSOC.[361]

During the first General Assembly meeting of the United Nations in London in January 1946, the Soviet Union made one final bid for a direct formal association of the WFTU with the United Nations. However, the proposal was turned down by a vast majority in ECOSOC. Instead, a general framework was created in which non-governmental organizations (NGOs) could become formally associated with the work of the United Nations without being granted voting rights or any other form of direct influence. In the same session, ECOSOC decided to enter into direct negotiations with the ILO's Governing Body, with the result that, a few months later, an agreement was signed that made the ILO a "specialized agency" of the United Nations.[362] The ILO, by force of this agreement, would lose the quasi-independent status it had enjoyed vis-à-vis the League of Nations but kept a far-reaching financial autonomy. ECOSOC and the ILO granted each other the right to be invited and to speak on issues within the respective organization's sphere of interest. This might have seemed a modest outcome if measured by the claims of the Philadelphia Declaration that the ILO was to become the central international agency for all social matters in the post-war order. To most observers in 1946, however, this outcome was entirely satisfactory. The ILO had survived and found its place in the new world order, even with a significant degree of independence. As many ILO supporters clearly realized, this was more – even much more – than could have been expected during most of the two years that had passed since the heady days of Philadelphia.

To a large degree, it had been the looming Cold War that had prevented the ILO from falling victim to the new post-war order. Yet, for this very reason, its position continued to be an uneasy one as the ILO was not spared the effects of

359 ILC, 27th Session (1945), *Record of Proceedings*, 136–137.

360 Ibid., 71–86.

361 ILC, 27th Session (1945), *Record of Proceedings*, 182.

362 The ILO became the first of five specialized agencies to sign an agreement with the United Nations Economic and Social Council in that year: the United Nations Food and Agriculture Organization (FAO), the United Nations Educational, Scientific and Cultural Organization (UNESCO), the International Bank for Reconstruction and Development (IBRD), and the International Monetary Fund (IMF).

the conflict between East and West that kept on creeping into its debates. On the one hand, and although the Soviet Union remained outside the Organization for the time being, Poland and Czechoslovakia continued their membership, even after they had joined the Communist camp. On the other hand, the ILO – which had relied on the support of the Western allies for its survival – had, if anything, become more dependent on the continued good will of its major sponsor, the US government. In the context of the Cold War, as will be shown in the third section of this chapter, this pushed the Organization quite naturally into becoming a frontline organization of the Western camp.

Indian Independence and the First "Decolonization" of the ILO

The exposed position of the ILO and its dependence on the Western allies also influenced the way the ILO dealt with the onset of decolonization in Asia. In August 1947, India's independence became the prelude to a movement that saw Ceylon (Sri Lanka) and Burma (Myanmar) following the Indian model. Elsewhere, in Indonesia, Malaya, and Indochina – but also in countries outside of Asia, such as Algeria – in the 1940s and 1950s the colonial powers waged bloody wars to counter what they saw as a domino effect of uncontrolled anti-colonial nationalism. Before long, the UN system became one of the main arenas of the ideological conflicts accompanying the decolonization process in which countries from the global South fought to establish "an entirely new conception of world order – one premised on the breakup of empire rather than its continuation".[363]

The ILO initially remained relatively unaffected by these developments. Since the Soviet Union had left the ILO in 1940, it could not use the Organization for the anti-colonial rhetoric that it was increasingly employing at the international level. This, in turn, allowed the colonial powers greater leeway in their attempts to shield themselves from what they saw as an undue "internationalization" of their imperial affairs.[364] In 1947, the ILC adopted a Convention on "social policy in non-metropolitan territories" that brought the colonial work begun in Philadelphia to a conclusion.[365] Their commitment to the establishment of what were essentially colonial welfare states, with all policies "primarily directed to the well-being and development of the peoples" in the colonial territories, was

363 Mazower, *No Enchanted Palace*, 185.
364 Maul, *Human Rights, Development, and Decolonization*, 86–99.
365 Social Policy (Non-Metropolitan Territories) Convention, 1947 (No. 82).

understood by the colonial powers as a licence to fend off any demands for more far-reaching political concessions.

After 1947 and until the end of the 1950s, colonial affairs within the ILO were handled exclusively by a "Committee of Experts on Social Policy in Non-Metropolitan Territories". The Committee met for a total of five sessions from 1950 to 1957 and treated a wide range of social and labour policy issues. By and large, its findings were very much in line with the general development discourse of the time. As had been the case for its predecessor in the 1920s – the Committee of Experts on Native Labour – the composition of the panel ensured that any topics touching upon politically controversial issues concerning official colonial policy were kept in the background. Until it was eventually dissolved, the Committee remained a gathering of predominantly white men, most of them colonial administrators and scholars from the colonial metropolises.[366]

The ILO was also eager not to be too closely involved with the colonial work of the United Nations. For instance, the Organization was initially very hesitant to respond positively to requests for collaboration with the United Nations' Trusteeship Council and the new colonial commissions established by ECOSOC, because of concerns that the highly "politicized" debates in these bodies might easily spill over to the ILO. Thus, when colonial issues finally entered the ILO's discussion during the early post-war years, it was due to the influence of those new Asian member States – above all India – that had just cut the ties of colonial rule. India's position within the ILO was exceptional in more than one regard. As the only "colonial" member State, it had already gained solid first-hand experience of the ILO's policies during the interwar years. Indian representatives to the ILC had long argued for a shift of the Organization's focus from its Eurocentrism and its bias towards the problems of industrialized nations of the West to the problems and needs of Asian countries.[367] The size and the economic potential of the country lent credibility to these claims. In financial terms, even before independence, India was the ILO's third-largest contributor, after the United States and Great Britain, providing 8% of the Organization's budget.[368] With Japan under US military administration and China torn apart by civil war, India naturally assumed the leadership role for the region. What was more, its government showed a firm willingness to act not only as the voice of Asia but also as the

366 Maul, *Human Rights, Development and Decolonization*, 173–183.
367 Rodgers, "India, the ILO and the Quest for Social Justice"; L. N. Birla and P. P. Pillai, *India and the ILO* (Oxford: Oxford University Press, 1946).
368 Rodgers, "India, the ILO and the Quest for Social Justice".

spearhead of anti-colonialism in the international sphere. India's declared aim was to "decolonize" international organizations.[369]

Before long, the ILO became one of the major venues for this struggle. A necessary first step in this direction from an Indian perspective was seen in the further regionalization of the Organization. After the war, India and China had called repeatedly on the ILO to strengthen its "local" structures. During the inter-war years, the ILO had entertained two contact bureaus in East Asia, in Delhi and in Nanjing. Beyond these small outposts, a few visits by ILO officials were the only means of direct contact with East Asia. A first step in devoting more attention to the problems of the Asian continent was to convene an Asian Regional Conference according to the model of the American Regional Conferences in Santiago de Chile (1936) and Havana (1939). While this idea had already been raised during the tenure of Harold Butler in the 1930s, the outbreak of the Second World War had prevented it from being carried out. However, the ILO started to prepare for such a meeting as early as 1942. After a preparatory meeting in Delhi in late 1947, the first official Asian Regional Conference took place in Nuwara Eliya (Ceylon) in late December 1949 and early January 1950.

A corresponding effort to reform the ILO's organizational structures proved to be a much more difficult undertaking. First attempts to make the Governing Body reflect more accurately the geographical composition of the Organization's membership were not successful. It maintained its predominantly Western and industrialized bias, with 12 out of 32 seats occupied by European representatives, and additional seats reserved for 11 North and South American countries. Asia, which represented about half of the world's working population, was given only five seats. Africa, still mainly under colonial rule, had no representation other than that of the white-dominated South Africa. For the time being, the industrialized countries remained dominant. In comparison, attempts to push the International Labour Office towards a geographically more balanced recruitment policy were slightly more successful.[370]

Indian representatives had long criticized what, in their view, were glaring geographical asymmetries in the composition of the ILO's staff, in particular in the higher echelons. The problem was deep-rooted, indeed. During the entire period between the wars, only one representative of a non-Western nation – Japan – had reached a senior post in any of the subdivisions of the League of Nations system. Even in the lower ranks of the ILO, a staff of about 200 people only included a maximum of four Indians. In addition to demanding that this

369 Mazower, *No Enchanted Palace*, 185–187.
370 Maul, *Human Rights, Development, and Decolonization*, 111–118.

number be increased significantly at all levels, China and India had together begun, during the war, to insist that the symbolically charged post of the Assistant Director-General be filled by an official from Asia. But it would take almost four years after Phelan had first sounded out the Asian representatives at the Philadelphia Conference before the Indian staff member Raghunath Rao could take up this position in March 1948. In the years preceding his appointment, the matter had been deferred repeatedly, largely because of British resistance, which was based on misgivings about an Assistant Director-General with potentially anti-colonial leanings. Change came slowly, and it took the accelerating momentum of decolonization during the 1950s before a more balanced geographical representation at all levels of the administration gained hold in the ILO.[371]

The most significant contribution India and the first wave of decolonization rendered to the ILO's programme and structure lay in an entirely different field. At the first "preparatory" Asian Regional Conference in Delhi in 1947, Asian states argued for more than just better representation in the Organization. What countries like India or Burma, which had just freed themselves from colonial domination, demanded was, above all, assistance in overcoming their state of underdevelopment. As the Indian Prime Minister Jawaharlal Nehru stated in his opening address to the Delhi Conference, he wanted the ILO to become a broker of knowledge and expertise for the developing countries, an institution that would organize the transfer and re-distribution of resources from the Western industrialized countries to the South. The appeals by Nehru and others who spoke in the same vein were founded both on moral and practical arguments. The ILO should, in their minds, help the developing countries to overcome their colonial past and, at the same time, respond to the growing interdependence in the new post-colonial world economy. In practical terms, this would imply for the ILO to shift its attention to building up the poorer countries' national economies, supporting their efforts towards industrialization and rural development, and providing technical expertise in order to raise productivity and develop a modern labour force. The voices from Asia were echoed in Latin America, where Regional Conferences in Mexico City (1946) and Montevideo (1949) took up on the demands for international economic security and socio-economic rights that had been expressed during the pre-war period and taken up by the Philadelphia Declaration. Those appeals were reinforced by calls for a more practical outlook in the Organization's work, which originated from an entirely different angle.[372]

371 Ibid.
372 Asian Regional Conference I (1947), *Record of Proceedings*, Rep X, 1–6.

From Reconstruction to Development

While the ILO broadened its horizon beyond Europe and the Americas, it took the first steps to establish itself as an operational agency through an expansion of its technical assistance work. As previous chapters have shown, the ILO had already, during the interwar years, built expertise and sent out technical assistance missions to Latin America, South-Eastern Europe, and, in some cases, even to Asia and Northern Africa. As a recent study on the League of Nations has pointed out, a "vision of development as an interventionist project of systematic socio-economic transformation" had already taken hold, which was also true for the ILO. What the post-war era experienced, then, was less of the "birth of development" but rather the "re-actualisation of global development policy as it had been formulated and practised in the prior decades".[373] If anything, the war had helped to strengthen the ILO's commitment to position itself as an unique source of technical knowledge. The Philadelphia Declaration had mandated the ILO to lend its services both to the post-war reconstruction effort in Europe and to "promote the economic and social advancement of the less developed regions of the world".[374] Both parts of this mandate implicitly called for the expansion of the Organization's practical activities.

Yet, it was only the particular historical context of the immediate post-war period that helped to translate this mandate into action. Pressure on the ILO to expand its operational activities – even when this meant downplaying the significance of the Organization's "classical" standard-setting activities – came from various sources. In addition to the growing demands from Asian and Latin American countries, a significant impulse derived from shifts in the domestic and foreign policy of the United States, where a Republican-dominated Congress began to roll back on New Deal policies. In the ILO, the changing climate was felt through the increasingly critical attitude of US officials towards standard-setting, not to speak about the openly hostile tone which representatives of US business adopted towards the ILO at the end of the 1940s.[375]

---

373 Frey, Kunkel, and Unger, "Introduction: International Organizations, Global Development, and the Making of the Contemporary World", 7.

374 ILO, Declaration of Philadelphia.

375 Discussions on the Freedom of Association Convention, 1948 (No. 87) were a case in point. At the same time that the Convention was adopted by the ILC, the Taft-Hartley Act curtailed trade union rights in the US. See Nelson Lichtenstein, *State of the Union: A Century of American Labor. Politics and Society in Twentieth-Century America* (Princeton, NJ: Princeton University Press, 2002), 115–122.

At the same time, the beginning aid under the American Marshall Plan – officially the European Recovery Programme (ERP) – gave a positive boost to the expansion of the technical assistance functions of the ILO. In June 1947, Washington offered its European allies (including those governments in the Soviet zone of influence) support for reconstruction through a broad-based ERP. The Soviet refusal, and that of its allied countries like Czechoslovakia and Poland, led to the foundation of the Organization for European Economic Cooperation (OEEC), which was given the task of administering US aid. The United States urged the ILO to make its technical expertise in vocational training and its knowledge of statistical data on labour deficits and surpluses available to the newly created organization. It became clear soon afterwards that, from now on, any ILO participation in European reconstruction would be conditional on its cooperation with the OEEC.[376]

It was against this backdrop that a long-anticipated change at the helm of the ILO took place. In June 1948, the Governing Body elected the 40-year-old acting US Secretary of Labour, David Abner Morse, as the new Director-General of the International Labour Office. Before his transfer to Geneva, Morse had devoted almost the whole of his professional life to issues related to labour and social policy, first on a national and then on an international level. His work for New Deal agencies that were engaged with the wider field of labour law during the 1930s qualified him for assignments during the Second World War. During those years, Morse, as head of various US military departments occupied with labour affairs, was the main official responsible for drafting plans for the re-democratization of labour relations, and in particular the re-building of free trade unions in Italy and Germany. Like those of many other liberal New Dealers, Morse's domestic and wartime experiences informed his later activities in the international arena. Upon his return to the United States in 1946, Morse was appointed (the first) Assistant Secretary of Labor for International Affairs by President Truman. In this capacity, Morse built on his wartime experience and became instrumental in turning the Department of Labour into an instrument of American foreign policy. In 1947, one of his main tasks had been to secure the support of the AFL and CIO, as well as their European allies, for the implementation of the Marshall Plan. Morse had also been an early advocate of extending the policies behind the Marshall Plan beyond Europe. He was thus involved in the debates preceding the announcement of Truman's Point IV Program in January 1949, in which this idea would become clearer. The main reason why the American government pushed for Morse's appointment

376 On the OEEC, see in particular Mathieu Leimgruber and Matthias Schmelzer, eds., *The OECD and the International Political Economy since 1948* (Basingstoke: Palgrave Macmillan, 2017).

was undoubtedly the hope that he would be able to use his position to generate support for the Marshall Plan and early international development policies, both of which implied a massive expansion of the ILO's technical services.[377]

It was in the tense atmosphere of growing Cold War animosities that Morse started his first months in office. The new Director-General, during his first term in office, did indeed stay in close touch with the State Department on a whole range of issues. A key element of the discussions was the way in which Morse could best make use of his position to overcome scepticism towards the Marshall Plan and fears of US dominance that it generated. According to his own recollection, one of Morse's first official actions was to organize, together with the US Secretary of Commerce, Averell Harriman, a meeting with Leon Jouhaux and the French Minister of Finances, Paul Ramadier. In this meeting, Morse and Harriman explained to their French counterparts the significance of the Marshall Plan, from the American perspective, as a measure to counter communist advances in Europe.[378]

In late 1948, Morse gave his first programmatic speech to the Governing Body, in which he called for measures to first consolidate and then systematically expand all ILO technical activities related to "manpower". His move was coordinated with the OEEC, which, at its founding conference earlier in the year, had suggested a role for the ILO in European reconstruction precisely in this area, as well as in the international coordination of labour migration.[379] By the time Morse addressed the Governing Body, the debate on technical assistance had already began to significantly widen beyond the European context. Shortly afterwards, in January 1949, in the inauguration speech of his second term in office, also known as the Four Points Speech, President Truman made the case for an expansion of the Marshall Plan to the non-European world. Under Point IV he pledged to provide the underdeveloped regions of the world with technological resources and expert know-how to help them increase their productivity. As in the Marshall Plan, the goal of increased productivity was at the centre of the programme,

377 All biographical information is based on my own research in the David A. Morse Papers (DAMP), MC097, Public Policy Papers, Department of Rare Books and Special Collections (RBSC), Princeton University Library, and the ILO Archives in Geneva (ILOA). See also Daniel Maul, 'Morse, David Abner' in *IO-BIO, Biographical Dictionary of Secretaries-General of International Organizations*, ed. Reinalda, Kille, and Eisenberg, www.ru.nl/fm/iobio.

378 The OHIM collection is kept in the Archives of the Harry S. Truman Presidential Library & Museum, NARA, Independence, MO. Three different interviews were recorded with Morse in 1977: on July 25, July 30, and August 3. Concerning the meeting with Jouhaux and Ramadier, see OHIM, 30 July, 1977, 110. Transcripts of these interviews are available online: https://www.trumanlibrary.org/oralhist/morse.htm.

379 Alcock, *History of the International Labor Organization*, 210.

and this provided an angle for the ILO to become directly attached to it.[380] In his speech, Truman had expressly proposed the UN system as the channel to provide such technical support, as this would allow the financial burden to be shared and avoid the kind of political criticism in the recipient countries that could be expected when funds came directly from the United States.[381]

In the wake of Truman's speech, Morse had made sure that the US government was aware of the ILO's readiness to play an active part in the implementation of the Point IV Program. As early as November 1948, on the eve of Morse's trip to India for the Asian Regional Conference, he received the assurance of Secretary of State George Marshall that the US government rated very highly the possible contribution of the ILO for "aggressive social and economic action" in the struggle against communism.[382] Shortly afterwards, the State Department supplied Morse with a memorandum confirming that the ILO and its so-called "Manpower Programme" were, from an American point of view, the best suited agency to provide technical assistance.[383] Finally, in January 1949, after Truman's speech, Morse contacted the new Secretary of State, Dean Acheson, to remind him that the ILO could make a real contribution to the defensive battle against communism by providing help to underdeveloped regions of the world. As he pointed out, the ILO's project of a programme of technical assistance for European reconstruction fitted "completely into the policy laid down by the president", and he assured Acheson that the Organization was "available for maximum cooperation".[384]

It was agreed that the ILO should initially receive one million US dollars from the Economic Cooperation Administration (ECA), which was the body responsible for the distribution of funds under the Marshall Plan, for a model project in the field of vocational training. This procedure caused some uneasiness, both among representatives of the trade unions and among European governments. For example, Leon Jouhaux, chairman of the Workers' group in the Governing Body, expressed concern that the Technical Assistance Programme (TAP) could

380 Charles Maier, "The Politics of Productivity: Foundations of American International Economic Policy after World War II", *International Organization* 31, no. 4 (1977): 607–633.

381 Robert A. Packenham, *Liberal America and the Third World: Political Development Ideas in Foreign Aid and Social Science* (Princeton, NJ: Princeton University Press, 1973), 43–49.

382 Marshall to Morse 24 November 1948, quoted in Maul, *Human Rights, Development, and Decolonization*, 126.

383 The internal memorandum anticipated the Point IV Program and emphasized the fundamental importance of the role that international organizations would play in it. The ILO was deemed to be the furthest ahead of all the international organizations in terms of technical assistance, together with FAO and WHO.

384 David Morse to Dean Acheson 31 January 1949 quoted in Maul, *Human Rights, Development, and Decolonization*, 127.

cause the ILO to fall under the control of the United States.[385] In addition, at that stage, the representatives of many European trade union organizations still feared that this policy would further advance the disintegration of the WFTU, which, virtually from the beginning, had experienced a bitter controversy among its members about the Marshall Plan.[386]

By 1949, however, the WFTU started to unravel. In October 1949, the bulk of the non-communist trade unions broke with the WFTU and set up the International Confederation of Free Trade Unions (ICFTU). The US trade unions participated in the new international, which duly gained a similar qualified majority – or monopoly – position in the ILO's Workers group as the one the IFTU had before the war. For David Morse, this meant that the turbulence in the Workers' group during the interlude of the WFTU from 1945 to 1949 was finally over.[387]

The early history of the TAP was thus in more than one way closely embedded in a Cold War context. There can be hardly a doubt that Morse did intend using technical assistance to turn the ILO into a more effective instrument for the Western camp and to put the Organization's activities on the front line of the conflict with the Soviet Union. It was no coincidence that one of the first countries outside of the ERP framework that would profit from the Manpower Programme was Tito's Yugoslavia, which had just broken with Stalin and become a dissident within the Eastern bloc.[388]

The looming Cold War provided the background for the discussions in a second area where the ILO aimed to contribute to European reconstruction: the regulation of international migration. Migration, obviously, was not a new field for the ILO. During the interwar years, the Organization had been occupied first with the social integration of refugees and later with promoting the international coordination of labour migration as a means to counter the effects of the Great Depression. After 1945, the issue had returned to the agenda with renewed urgency. The demobilization of millions of soldiers aggravated existing labour surpluses built up in many countries during the war, and their re-integration in the labour market posed a significant challenge. In addition, millions of so-called displaced persons, who were often unable or unwilling to return to their countries of origin, were stuck in places where they could not find work. At the same time,

385 OHIM, 30 July 1977, 109.

386 Anthony Carew, "A False Dawn: The World Federation of Trade Unions (1945–1949)", in *The International Confederation of Free Trade Unions*, ed. Carew et al., 165–187. With regard to the broader context of the AFL's position in the early Cold War and towards the Marshall Plan, see Carew, *American Labour's Cold War Abroad*, 58–64.

387 Ibid.

388 OHIM, 3 August 1977, 145.

there was massive demand for skilled labour in Latin America and in countries like Australia, which underwent processes of economic expansion and industrialization. In this context, Morse renewed the ILO's interwar claim to become the central international agency for both the study and regulation of migration.[389] Unlike before the war, in 1948, there were several organizations that took an interest in the migration issue. Next to the ILO, the United Nations, UNESCO, the WHO, the FAO and the World Bank participated in the debate. There was, however, no coordination of the efforts of these organizations, and none of them had the ILO's prior experience. Morse, accordingly, took the initiative, and the ILO began to set up field missions in potential emigration countries such as Italy, Germany, and Austria and send pilot missions to two potential recipient countries in Latin America (Ecuador and Bolivia).[390]

In the end, however, all these initiatives came to almost nothing. At the time, as today, migration turned out to be a highly politicized, if not toxic, issue. Some European nations – in particular those with a long tradition of overseas emigration, such as Italy – appreciated the role that "planned and organised emigration" could play as a "safety valve" to avoid large-scale unemployment, and they welcomed the ILO's endeavours. A majority of governments, however, opposed the idea of an international body interfering with their own domestic immigration policies, for political as well as for economic reasons. The concern that migration from poor countries would lower the standards at home was common also among trade unions.[391]

With regard to refugees and displaced persons, apprehensions were particularly strong from the government side. The situation was in a way quite paradoxical. Even though most participants in the discussion – governments, employers, and trade unions – agreed that the coordination of international migration was a crucial factor in the reconstruction of the world economy, very few were prepared to compromise their national prerogatives and transfer responsibility and decision-making power to an international body. While few questioned the technical competence of the ILO in the field, the political considerations, exacerbated by the deepening divide between East and West, eventually outweighed this aspect. At the International Migration Conference in Naples in 1951, it was particularly the lack of support from the United States that eventually brought the project down. At the height of McCarthyism, fears of communist infiltration loomed large and prevented American officials to enter into any binding agree-

389 Alcock, *History of the International Labor Organization*, 220–234.

390 Ibid.

391 ILO, *Record of Proceedings*, International Labour Conference, 33rd Session 1950 (Geneva: ILO, 1951), 261.

ments with international organizations whose membership included communist countries (in the case of the ILO, these were Poland and Czechoslovakia). In the end, a provisional Migration Administration with restricted competences was installed at Naples, and the ILO ended up with the minor task of providing technical assistance in the field of vocational training. In hindsight, it was the last nail in the coffin of the ILO's high-flying ambitions in this field. What remained from the ILO's engagement with international migration was a Convention (The Migration for Employment Convention, No. 97), and a Recommendation (No. 86) with the same title, adopted by the ILC in 1949. In the end, both dealt predominantly with technical matters related to migration and the treatment of migrants with regard to salaries, hours of work, and training, but the ILO's involvement was devoid of any aspects of international regulation of labour migration.[392]

Viewed from a different angle and against the backdrop of the impending Cold War, the failed claim to become an international agency for international migration provided the ILO with yet another reason to redirect its attention from the European scene towards the developing countries. However, the Cold War only provided one part of the story. Equally important was the fact that the ILO's leadership decided to respond to a genuine demand and a growing number of voices from member States asking the Organization to pay attention to the problems of the non-European world. Discussions with various ILO correspondents and representatives of Latin American and Asian countries, in particular, had given the new Director-General an idea of both the existing need and the huge potential for success of technical assistance activities tailored to the requisites of the less developed regions of the world. The conflict between East and West also added a sense of urgency to these considerations, in particular in China after the Communist Party, in 1949, had emerged victorious from the protracted Chinese civil war and given the fact that a similar conflict was looming on the Korean peninsula.

This was the setting in which Morse proposed to the ILC in 1949 to transform the ILO into an agency serving the specific needs of "underdeveloped nations". The Office, he declared, favoured the change because it sought "to continue to persist in ensuring that its work is of the utmost practical value to all State Members and not merely to certain groups among them". This statement, of course, directly addressed the sense of neglect that wide regions of the world had felt about the work of the ILO in the past. Morse declared that the Organization had understood that there was an enormous demand for industrialization, increased production, and improved living standards for wide swathes of the world's population. He

392 The sole opposition to the Conventions came from the communist countries.

offered support and assistance in implementing vocational training, increasing the productivity of labour, introducing modern methods of labour protection, and organizing labour relations. Morse's promises were received with enthusiasm by a great number of Asian and Latin American representatives at the Conference.[393]

In his report to the Asian Regional Conference in Nuwara Eliya at the end of 1949, Morse declared Asia to be the new focus of ILO activities. He later assured the meeting that the "cry of misery that rises from the throats of the millions of people of Asia" had been heard in Geneva.[394] In a greeting message to the Conference, Nehru praised the ILO for following up on the promises of the Declaration through concrete action, and a Ceylonese Workers' representative echoed the general mood, when he applauded the fact that the "ILO has at last realized its duties to this so far neglected continent".[395] The Cold War aspect of the ILO's transformation was not ignored by the participants, but while those who were leaning towards the Western camp in any case welcomed the TAP as a means of containing the advance of Communism in Asia, other countries – such as India, Burma, and Indonesia –which took a neutral stand, remained largely silent on the issue. A Philippine representative deliberately called upon the industrialized nations of the West to "pour their resources into this part of their world", thus establishing a security that "no force of arms can conquer".[396] In this way, the potential recipients used the programme's anti-communist thrust to intensify their demands on the prospective donor countries.

It was against this background that the ILO, at the turn from 1949 to 1950, officially became an agency for development.[397] In this, it did not of course act in isolation, as plans for a coordinated approach to development by the entire UN system had existed in the General Assembly and in ECOSOC even before Truman's initiative. In 1948, an ECOSOC resolution had created a number of regional commissions devoted to the economic and social problems of developing countries. In March 1949, ECOSOC passed another resolution calling upon the Secretary General to come up with a coordinated programme for the provision of technical assistance to underdeveloped nations.[398] Negotiations within the United Nations

393 ILO, *Record of Proceedings*, Rep. I: Report of the Director General, International Labour Conference, 32nd Session 1949 (Geneva: ILO, 1949), 3.

394 See, in particular, the section "The ILO and Asia" in Asian Regional Conference II (1950), *Record of Proceedings*, Rep. I: Report of the Director-General, 137–153.

395 Asian Regional Conference II (1950), *Record of Proceedings*, 81.

396 Ibid., 115.

397 ILO, Minutes of the Governing Body, 109th Session, Geneva 1949, 60–64.

398 The first of these institutions, created at the beginning of 1947, was the Economic Commission for Asia and the Far East (ECAFE, today known as ESCAP). It was followed just over a year

Figure 8: ILO Director-General David Morse with Indian Prime Minister Jawaharlal Nehru at the Fourth Asian Regional Conference, New Delhi, India, 1957.

on the design of such a programme, which included the ILO, were carried on through all of 1949. In 1950, the ILO became one of the executive organs of the new UN Expanded Programme of Technical Assistance (EPTA), which subsequently financed the majority of TAP projects. Morse and the heads of the other institutions involved in EPTA (FAO, WHO, and six other UN specialized agencies)

later by the Economic Commission for Latin America (ECLA, today known as ECLAC). ECOSOC Resolution 180 (VIII), 3 Apr. 1949, Technical Assistance for Economic Development.

now met on the Technical Assistance Board (TAB) to discuss the allocation of funds. The TAP was thus part of the broader framework of UN development activities. From the ILO's point of view, this had the advantage that it removed (or at least obscured) the strong external connection to US foreign policy aims that the initial turn towards technical assistance had implied. It helped to soften concerns within and outside the ILO that technical assistance would be synonymous with increased US influence on the Organization's policies.

Part III **Between Decolonization and the Cold War: 1949–1976**

During the long era of David Morse (1948–1970), the International Labour Organization (ILO) underwent a profound transformation. The Cold War and decolonization were the two main drivers behind this process, which changed the ILO's face and its internal power balance and left hardly any area of its work untouched. The year 1954 proved to be an important milestone in this regard. One year after Stalin's death, the Soviet Union took up its membership again. As a result, the ILO no longer occupied the status of a quasi-front organization in the Western camp.[399] While this change "normalized" the ILO's position within the UN system, fundamental controversies now reappeared directly on the agenda, including the question of the ILO's tripartite composition. The confrontation with the alternative social model of the communist bloc forced the ILO to continuously examine its foundations and search for a workable balance between the quest for universalism and conflicting ideas of social organization.[400]

At the same time, during the "Morse era", the ILO underwent another transformation that was at least as drastic. As a result of the accelerated dissolution of the European colonial empires in Asia and Africa, it gained more than twice the number of member States within a period of two decades – from 55 countries in 1948 to 121 in 1970. This growth in membership was almost exclusively accounted for by former colonies.[401] From the 1960s onwards, "developing countries" formed a majority of the ILO's member States. This was a strong incentive for the Organization to adapt its profile, policies, and programmes to the needs and demands of these countries. It pushed the ILO to further expand its technical functions and to place an evermore pronounced emphasis on development. On another level, decolonization contributed to the further "politicization" of the ILO's meetings. The struggle of the new nations against the last remnants of colonial rule and racist regimes in Southern Africa hit the Organization during the 1950s and the 1960s with full force.

The dynamics that drove the ILO during this period resulted to a large degree from the entanglement and overlap of Cold War and decolonization debates. This became most apparent in the area of standard-setting, where human rights

399 Together with the Soviet Union, the Soviet Republics of Ukraine and Byelorussia were admitted as independent members in accordance with the UN formula in place, which strengthened the position of the Eastern bloc. Morse's negotiations with the Soviet leaders are recorded in ILOA MF Z 5/1/64/1, Re-admission USSR, 1954, 1961. See also Cox, "ILO–Limited Monarchy", 105–106.

400 Daniel Roger Maul, "The 'Morse Years': The ILO 1948–1970", in *ILO Histories*, ed. Van Daele et al., 365–400.

401 Ghébali, *The International Labour Organization*, 119–120

https://doi.org/10.1515/9783110650723-partIII

issues assumed a prominent role particularly during the 1950s. In the discussions about the adoption and implementation of standards on freedom of association, forced labour, and discrimination, initial controversies along the East–West divide increasingly developed into parallel debates along the conflict line between the industrial nations of the West and an emerging group of countries from the global South.

5 The Development Turn

With the expansion of its technical assistance, the massive changes that the ILO underwent as a result of decolonization became very tangible. After moderate beginnings in the 1950s, the area that became known as "technical cooperation" outgrew during the 1960s and 1970s all other areas by far. At the same time, the ILO's move from limited technical assistance to large-scale technical cooperation affected virtually all the ILO's fields of action. By turning into an agency of technical cooperation, the ILO eventually lost its European bias. The Organization took on a much more global face, and its operational efforts became more and more directed towards the needs of less industrialized countries.

To be sure, the ILO did not pursue this transition in isolation. Just like other international agencies at the time, it acted as a part of the United Nations' growing development machinery.[402] At the same time, driven by strategic considerations, by its constituents and by inter-agency competition, the ILO sought to develop its own profile. Two major programmes serve to illustrate this point: the Andean Indian Programme (AIP) of the 1950s and 1960s, and the World Employment Programme (WEP) launched on the occasion of the ILO's 50th anniversary in 1969. Both programmes reflected general trends in development thinking at the time. Through the WEP, in particular, the ILO took a lead in this discussion and was instrumental for a short-lived – but nevertheless major – turn in development thinking towards poverty-centred approaches during the 1970s.

Help Them Move the ILO Way – Technical Assistance in the 1950s

When the ILO's technical assistance activities began to take off in the early 1950s, they essentially consisted of building labour force capacities by means of vocational training or projects aimed at raising workers' productivity. During the 1950s, the working area of "human resources" accordingly occupied around 75% of all Tech-

402 Corinna R. Unger, *International Development. A Post-War History* (London: Bloomsbury Academic Publishing, 2018); Frey, Kunkel, and Unger, "Introduction: International Organizations, Global Development, and the Making of the Contemporary World"; Richard Jolly et al., *UN Contributions to Development Thinking and Practice*, United Nations Intellectual History Project (Bloomington, IN: Indiana University Press, 2004).

https://doi.org/10.1515/9783110650723-007

nical Assistance Programmes (TAP).[403] Vocational training schemes alone, with a clear direction to support developing countries' efforts towards industrialization, accounted for around half of the ILO's technical assistance activities in this period.[404] Even in the 1960s, when the ILO's programmes underwent a substantial reform, and services stretched more widely to include agriculture and fields like workers' education and management training, the development of "human resources", with vocational training at its core, remained at the heart of technical cooperation.[405]

The early TAP's heavy industrial bias can easily be explained by the general context of its beginnings. Originally the departure into technical assistance had been an extension of the 1948 Manpower Programme, tailored to the needs of war-torn Europe and focused on industrial training.[406] The relative insignificance of rural development, in turn, had to do with the fact that agricultural training was the prerogative of the FAO, which was also funded through the United Nations' EPTA. In general, however, the industrial focus simply reflected the prevailing view of development policy. Within the "dualistic" approach of a first generation of development economists like W. Arthur Lewis, the central dynamic of development was a movement of underdeveloped societies from the traditional to the modern, or industrial, sector. Only the latter could lead to productivity and growth and thus to an improvement in the standard of living.[407] The task of development agencies, both national and international, was to support and accelerate such a modernization process. The TAP's focus on "manpower" fits perfectly with the dualistic vision. The general opinion was that through training workers the ILO contributed significantly to industrialization and increased productivity.[408]

The new programmatic orientation was accompanied by substantial changes on the level of the International Labour Office, where staff became more diverse, both in terms of expertise and geographical distribution. Recruitment strategies had already started to change under Harold Butler in the 1930s, and this change accelerated as a

403 The other areas were "living conditions" and "social institutions". The latter included also the ILO's activities in the field of cooperatives. On the evolution of the ILO's Technical Assistance Programme, see Ghébali, *The International Labour Organisation*, 242–267.

404 ILO, "The Role of the ILO in the Promotion of Economic Expansion and Social Progress in Developing Countries" (Geneva: ILO, 1961); ILO, *A Great Adventure of our Time. International Co-operation and the ILO* (Geneva: ILO, 1962), 36.

405 The Governing Body confirmed in 1965 that all the ILO's technical activities would fall under the three main headings of (1) human resources, (2) development of social institutions, and (3) improvement of working and living conditions.

406 See, e.g.: "The I.L.O. Manpower Programme", *International Labour Review*, 59, no. 4 (April 1949): 367–393.

407 Unger, *International Development*, 109.

408 Ibid., 70–71.

result of the extended economic mandate the ILO had received in Philadelphia: economists and social scientists started to represent a much larger proportion of the ILO's staff. The sheer quantity of operations in the 1950s drove another change. While the technical assistance missions of the interwar period had been conducted mostly by ILO officials, the Organization now relied to a much greater degree on the services of external experts. Between 1950 and 1965, the ILO sent almost 2,000 experts from a total of 78 nations on 3,000 expert missions to around 100 countries.[409]

Moreover, the geographical composition of the International Labour Office underwent significant change. Under Morse, senior posts were filled with nationals from Asian and African countries. One prominent example was Abbas Amar, a former Egyptian Minister of Education and of Social Affairs. He was recruited by Morse and occupied the post of Assistant Director-General from 1959 to 1974. Albert Tévoédjrè, a former Minister of Information from Dahomey (Benin), would follow in 1965 as the first member in the Director-General's Office from sub-Saharan Africa.[410] On another level, technical assistance also contributed to the further geographical decentralization of the ILO. Between 1949 and 1952, field offices were set up in Asia (Bangalore), Latin America (Sao Paulo), and, for the Middle East, Istanbul. In sub-Saharan Africa, which was still under colonial rule, the establishment of ILO regional representation took longer. Fears among colonial officials that such an office would turn into a centre of "agitation" and open the door for an "internationalization" of colonial affairs prevented the ILO for a long time from gaining a foothold on the African continent. Only in 1959, on the eve of the independence of numerous African countries, was the Organization able to open its first African field office in Lagos, Nigeria.[411] The main task of the field offices was to facilitate the coordination of technical assistance in their respective regions. This process of dispersal continued into the 1960s, with further decentralization of the ILO. Between 1965 and 1968, the field offices became area offices, which were in turn placed under newly founded Regional Offices, assuming responsibility for all the ILO technical cooperation programmes and projects in a particular region.[412]

Finally, the new activities also affected the ILO's budget. While the initial fears that technical assistance might become the gateway for American domina-

409 Ghébali, *The International Labour Organisation*, 256.

410 Oral History Interview with David Morse, Oral History Research Office, Columbia University 1981, conducted by Peter Jessup, Columbia University, in Washington, D.C., July 1980–March 1981, 122–123.

411 Maul, Puddu, and Tijani, "The International Labour Organization". For a general overview, see also Nicholas Alexander Bernards, "Actors and Entanglements in Global Governance: The ILO in Sub-Saharan Africa" (PhD diss., McMaster University, Hamilton, ON, 2016).

412 Ghébali, *The International Labour Organisation*, 162; Alcock, *History of the International Labor Organization*, 239, 240.

tion of the ILO soon dissipated, new dependencies arose in other areas. Through the EPTA and the so-called Special Fund – another UN source of funding set up in 1958 for the purpose of facilitating larger projects – the ILO now had access to extra-budgetary sources. At the same time, it increased the ILO's reliance on the United Nations, notably on ECOSOC, which managed these funds. This dependency became even more pronounced when the United Nations Development Programme (UNDP) was established in 1965. Under the EPTA, the funds available in the 1950s had generally fallen short of enabling the ILO to meet all the requests it received for technical assistance.[413] With the establishment of the UNDP, this changed; funds could now be obtained for longer-term development programmes, which opened up entirely new opportunities for projects that could not be financed through the ILO's regular budget. At the same time, however, the ILO lost a considerable degree of independence, as an increasing proportion of ILO work eluded the financial oversight of the Governing Body, which had few opportunities to influence the UNDP's criteria for awarding funds.[414]

Dependence on UN development policy premises was a weighty, if not the sole, reason why the ILO was keen from the outset to put its own recognizable signature to its technical activities. The TAP rested on a series of basic principles and ILO-specific assumptions that also determined its form. For the architects of the TAP, it was above all necessary to counter concerns that the new field of development policy would push the "classical" standard-setting activities into the background and thus to dilute the ILO's core identity. To dispel these widespread concerns, David Morse started as early as 1949 to promote an ILO-specific integrated approach to development. Technical assistance and ILO standards were not seen as opposing principles but as concepts that had a catalytic and mutually beneficial effect.[415] The operational activities on which the ILO was about to embark were, with regard to standard-setting, "the other half of the same coin", as the new Director-General told the ILC in 1949. Their purpose was, according to Morse, to trigger and sustain a process of development in line with the aims of the ILO Constitution.[416]

---

413 Among the different recipients of the funds of the United Nations' technical assistance programme, the ILO was only fourth in line, receiving only 11% of the EPTA budget and trailing organizations such as UNESCO, WHO, and FAO. In absolute numbers, the ILO was given just over US$25 million between 1950 and 1960 under the EPTA, while the FAO received US$68 million, the WHO US$45 million, and UNESCO US$35 million. ILO, *The Role of the ILO in the Promotion of Economic Growth* (Geneva: ILO, 1961), 7.

414 Hugo Stokke, "Decent Work. Principles, Policies and Programmes of the International Labour Organisation" (PhD diss., University of Bergen, 2015), 136–144.

415 See Alcock, *History of the International Labor Organization*, 219.

416 Ibid., 259.

Such assurances were also meant to dilute more general concerns that the ILO, through the TAP, might turn further into an organization primarily following an economic rationale. Morse's emphasis on "productivity" initially fuelled these concerns.[417] Wedded as the concept of productivity was to American ideas of economic progress, it met a fair degree of suspicion, in particular from the trade unions. In 1952, Morse explained that, from his point of view, raising productivity in all economic sectors was the only practicable route to development. But he underlined that the ILO's approach to productivity differed from that of other development agencies by recognizing that increased productivity alone did not guarantee social progress. Morse promoted a three-pronged approach that took into account "the educational, the social and the technical sides" of the issue. He pledged that, for the ILO, promoting increased productivity would lead rapidly to improvements in economic and social welfare for the community in general. Governments, he affirmed, would consider good industrial relations and satisfactory wages and employment policies not merely as accessory measures but as "integral parts of programmes to raise productivity".[418]

Underlying the TAP was the basic assumption of modernization theory that the developing world had to repeat, in accelerated form, the development of industrialized countries.[419] "There [is] nothing peculiar to this region", Morse told a press conference on the occasion of the Asian Regional Conference in Delhi in 1957: "Asia and India [are] going through a process of economic expansion and development that Western countries [were going] through long ago." The challenges that they faced as a result of this process were "new in Asia, but old problems in other countries".[420] In this sense, the ILO's international labour standards, its Constitution, and the principles of the Declaration of Philadelphia featured as tools for democratic modernization in the global South. These standards and values were interpreted and promoted in practice as a set of lessons which the liberal democracies of Europe and North America had learned from past political and economic crises, which were linked to the development of their

417 For the debate and Morse's reply, see ILC (1949), *Record of Proceedings*, 25–254, 255–264.
418 Memorandum by Morse, "Memorandum on the Report of the Director-General to the 34th Session of the International Labour Conference", quoted in Maul, *Human Rights, Development and Decolonization*, 135.
419 On the political implications of modernization theory, see Michael E. Latham, *Modernization as Ideology: American Social Science and "Nation Building" in the Kennedy Era* (Chapel Hill, NC: University of North Carolina Press, 2000); Nils Gilman, *Mandarins of the Future: Modernization Theory in Cold War America* (Baltimore, MD: Johns Hopkins University Press, 2003).
420 Minutes of a press conference held by Morse in New Delhi, 12 November 1957, quoted in Maul, *Human Rights, Development and Decolonization*, 138.

own capitalist order in the nineteenth and twentieth centuries. The historic role of the Organization in this endeavour was described by Morse in quasi-religious terms: "If it does this the ILO will light a beacon which will guide men and women through the uncertain times which lie ahead and give to those whose hearts and minds are troubled, confused and afraid a positive faith by which they can work and live and a belief in themselves and in their future which will be proof against attacks from any quarter."[421]

It was thus clear that entering the field of development was by no means a politically neutral undertaking. It gave the ILO a key role on one of the major front lines of the Cold War which were expanding rapidly beyond Europe to the developing world. "Change and revolution are sweeping the world today", Morse wrote in 1950, and the ILO was caught up in a "struggle for the hearts and minds of men and women the world over".[422] Social unrest and instability caused by rapid modernization, Morse argued, were breeding grounds for communist agitation. To Morse, the core values of the Declaration of Philadelphia – which combined the subordination of all national and international policies to the higher aim of social justice for everybody with a "fundamental view of society, of morality and of the freedom and dignity of the individual" – were the tools to counter this challenge.[423] The Cold War undertones of technical assistance were thus part and parcel of its very beginnings. After the Soviet Union resumed its membership in the ILO in 1954, the statements accompanying technical assistance became less confrontational. Yet, what remained unchanged was the persistent claim that the ILO represented a particular "integrated" model of development that was of liberal-democratic nature at its core.

During the 1950s, ILO officials went out to promote this approach with almost missionary zeal. On his return from Egypt in 1953, Deputy Director-General Jef Rens maintained that the changes taking place there and in other countries in transition should spur the ILO on to assert its approach in the rapidly advancing process of economic development: "This part of the world and similar areas are moving – that's certain", Rens stated. "Let's not miss the chance to help them move the ILO way."[424]

The ways in which the Office went about promoting the "ILO way" of development remained nevertheless – not least due to a lack of funding – fairly

421 Memorandum by Morse, "Memorandum on the Report of the Director-General to the 34th Session of the International Labour Conference", quoted in Maul, *Human Rights, Development and Decolonization*, 139.
422 Ibid.
423 Ibid.
424 Quoted in Maul, *Human Rights, Development and Decolonization*, 139.

small-scale and indirect. The Organization provided information, advice, and practical support, for instance, on how to set up a vocational training centre in a specific area, and how to educate local trainers and supervise the creation of vocational training institutions in the recipient countries. ILO experts gave advice on occupational health and safety as well as on the establishment of "healthy" labour relations, and they provided manuals teaching how to write standard employment contracts or formulate reasonable wage policies.[425] ILO projects tended to be small, isolated, selective, and short-term. In Indonesia, in 1956, an ILO expert was assigned to carrying out a study to determine various aspects of the workforce for the Ministry of Labour. In Pakistan, ILO experts were supporting staff at the ministry to conduct enquiries on employment and potential future demand. The ILO was assisting the establishment of vocational training centres in countries like (South) Vietnam, Burma, Libya, Egypt, and Nepal.[426]

The experts who were deployed to provide assistance naturally played an important role in the implementation of the programme. Short introductory seminars before their departure familiarized them with the objectives and principles of the ILO, but it is difficult to determine to which extent these experts really internalized the integrated approach to development and put it into practice. The same can be said of the other method of knowledge transfer used in the early stages of the TAP, which was based on education. The ILO awarded study grants and arranged for a large number of people from developing countries – ranging from skilled workers to future employees in labour administrations – to visit industrialized countries for on-the-job training or further education. All these projects relied on the assumption that industrial development would create the workplaces where the newly acquired skills and knowledge would be used.

With the growing scale of activities, a great majority of experts sent to the field were not ILO staff but recruited from outside the Organization on the basis of an earlier career in the required field. This raised a plethora of new and sometimes politically explosive issues: from the use of former colonial officials to charges of

425 The limited funding available to the ILO in the 1950s necessarily impacted on the efficacy of the Organization's campaign. A typical example was a project in Libya, where the ILO set up a vocational education centre; in Iran where the ILO built a specialized vocational training centre for the building trade; or India where several small-scale projects aimed at raising productivity in selected enterprises of the textile and engineering industry. See ILO, *The Role of the ILO in the Promotion of Economic Growth*.

426 ILO, *The ILO and Asia* (Geneva: ILO,1962); ILO, *The ILO and Africa* (Geneva: ILO, 1960).

favouring Western experts over those from Eastern communist countries to recurring issues of geographical balance.[427]

An important step on the institutional level in this regard was the founding of the International Institute for Labour Studies (IILS) in 1960,[428] an autonomous body within the Office for research and training that would focus on the socio-political problems faced by the developing world. In particular, it wanted to establish a working environment in which controversial topics such as industrial relations could be discussed apart from the politically charged atmosphere of the ILC. Its main purpose, next to research, was "educational action". IILS courses were directed at "potential leaders" from the developing countries' social sector, as Robert Cox, one of the Institute's first directors, explained. The courses on offer covered a wide range of areas, from employment issues to industrial relations. According to the Institute's vision, however, it served a broader purpose: the world's future policy makers would go to Geneva, encounter the methods and principles of the ILO, and take them back to their home countries.[429]

In 1964, the ILO set up an International Centre for Advanced Technical and Vocational Training in Turin, thus increasing its range of services on the institutional level.[430] The courses offered at the Centre were directed first and foremost at skilled workers, vocational trainers, and management personnel from developing countries. The new Centre thus institutionalized an existing area of work, but, once again, with the added advantage that its visitors could be given a thorough grounding in the goals of the ILO.[431] "In the last analysis", Morse wrote in this regard as early as 1959, "the most and perhaps only effective answer to communism and other antidemocratic forms lies in the success of social and economic development complemented with education and training in all of its aspects".[432] Viewed from another perspective, the establishment of the IILS and the Turin Centre were part of a broader trend towards professionalization, driven by the per-

427 For the general debate about the colonial legacy of developmental expertise, see Joseph Morgan Hodge, *The Triumph of the Expert. Agrarian Doctrines of Development and the Legacies of British Colonialism* (Athens, OH: Ohio University Press, 2007).

428 Maryse Gaudier, "The International Institute for Labour Studies: Its Research Function, Activities and Publications 1960–2001," Geneva: ILO, 2001.

429 Memorandum by Robert Cox, "Aims and Purposes of the IILS", 15 July 1965, quoted in Maul, *Human Rights, Development and Decolonization*, 256; See also a more comprehensive analysis of the IILS functions Robert Cox, "Education for Development", *International Organization* 23, no. 1 (1968): 310–331.

430 The opening was made possible by a grant from the Italian government, which offered the premises of the Italia 61 exhibition built on the occasion of the centenary of Italian unity in 1961.

431 Ghébali, *The International Labour Organisation*, 258.

432 Quoted in Maul, *Human Rights, Development and Decolonization*, 223.

Figure 9: Training course in car mechanics, International Training Centre of the ILO, Turin, 1960s.

ception that "more scientific" approaches were necessary to gain credibility, both with the public and vis-à-vis other organizations carrying out similar functions.[433]

Indigenous Labour and the Andean Indian Programme

While much of the ILO's technical work way until the 1960s was of rather limited scope due to the lack of funding, the new working area of "indigenous labour" paved the way to a broader vision of modernization beyond development. Here, an entirely new field opened up for the ILO after 1945, including both technical

433 Unger, *International Development*, 74–75.

assistance and standard-setting. While the "Andean Indian Program" (1953–1962) provided the framework for one of the ILO's largest development aid project of all times, two Conventions on indigenous populations (1957) and on indigenous peoples (1989) were pioneering instruments that made indigenous peoples and their rights, for the first time, a subject of international law.[434]

The original interest of the ILO for the concerns of indigenous peoples resulted from the opening of the Organization towards Latin America in the late 1930s. Until then, the term "indigenous labour" (or native labour) had almost exclusively been used with colonial connotations. The living conditions of indigenous peoples as culturally identifiable groups within independent states had not yet caught the attention of the ILO. At the ILO's first two American Regional Conferences in Santiago de Chile (1936) and Havana (1939), ILO officials came into contact with the continent-wide political and academic movement of "*indigenismo*", which promoted the "uplifting" and ultimately assimilation of indigenous populations with their respective national societies. In Santiago, the ILO had already been urged to pay special attention to the economic and social problems of indigenous populations. Through its subsequent collaboration with indigenist institutions such as the *Instituto Indigenista Interamericano* in Mexico City, the ILO soon gained a reputation of being the "International Indigenist Organization". Thus, the "Indian problem" had already become an integral part of the ILO agenda well before the Second World War. After 1945, it turned into a priority of the ILO's regional work in Latin America.[435]

Equipped with new opportunities for socio-economic and development action after 1945, the ILO received a mandate from the American Regional Conferences in Mexico City (1946) and Montevideo (1949) to set up an Indigenous Labour Programme. Deputy Director-General Jef Rens, who oversaw the ILO's technical assistance activities at the Office level, and the Argentine economist and anthropologist David Efron became the main persons responsible for the move of the ILO into the area of indigenous labour. The establishment of a Committee of Experts on Indigenous Labour, chaired by renowned New Zealand anthropologist Ernest Beaglehole, initiated the practical phase of the indigenous labour programme in 1950. A report entitled "Indigenous Peoples: Living and Working Conditions of Aboriginal Population in Independent Countries" was the most important outcome of the Committee's two meetings in La Paz (1951) and Geneva

434 Indigenous and Tribal Populations Convention, 1957 (No. 107) and the Indigenous and Tribal Peoples Convention, 1989 (No. 169). Luis Rodríguez-Piñero, *Indigenous Peoples*; Hanne Hagtvedt Vik, "Indigenous Internationalism", in *Internationalisms: A Twentieth Century History*, ed. Sluga and Clavin, 315–339. Cambridge: Cambridge University Press, 2017. Jason Guthrie, "The ILO and the International Technocratic Class, 1944–1966", in *Globalizing Social Rights*, ed. Kott and Droux, 115–136.
435 Rodríguez-Piñero, *Indigenous Peoples*, 53–112.

(1954). It included a set of guidelines for the gradual integration of indigenous groups into "modern" society under a broad development policy premise, as well as measures to attenuate this process from an anthropological point of view.[436]

The undisputed centrepiece of all activities was the Andean Programme (also known as the Andean Indian Programme, AIP), which was officially launched in 1953. After becoming part of the EPTA, the ILO was given the lead by the ECOSOC to prepare the ground – together with WHO, UNESCO, FAO, and the Organization of American States (OAS) – for a tailor-made development project in the three Andean countries of Bolivia, Ecuador, and Peru, which had a high proportion of indigenous populations.[437] The AIP consisted of three phases. During the first phase, so-called action bases were set up in selected locations in all three countries that would serve as pilot projects for the expansion of the programme in the second phase. During the third and final phase, the programmes were to be transferred to the respective national governments, while, at the same time, the AIP was to be extended to other countries in the region.

Figure 10: Jef Rens, Deputy Director-General of the ILO, visiting the cooperative in Huana Pasto Grande, Ecuador, in the framework of the Andean Indian programme (AIP).

436 For the report, see ILO, *Indigenous Peoples: Living and Working Conditions of Aboriginal Populations in Independent Countries*, Studies and Reports, New Series, No. 35 (Geneva: ILO, 1953).
437 Martin Breuer, "Exploring the Technical Assistance Activities of the International Labor Organization in the Field of Indigenous Peoples: Development and Human Rights in the Andean Indian Program (1954–1968)", *Forum for Inter-American Research* 11, no. 3 (2018): 110–123.

Under the leadership of the ILO, the AIP became a laboratory for the "international technocratic class", which had set itself the task of leading "backward" and "underdeveloped societies" into the modern age by using methods of social engineering.[438] The broad design of the programme, which included questions of nutrition, health, and education, in addition to employment creation and vocational training, reflected not only the specific competencies of the participating international institutions but also the overriding, integrated modernization approach. The bases for action included the installation of ILO projects, such as vocational training centres and productivity programmes, a WHO medical clinic, a UNESCO-run agricultural school, and an agricultural research station led by the FAO. The same integrated approach reappeared in the 1957 Convention, which in its various aspects extended well beyond indigenous labour and included socio-medical, educational, and other aspects of comprehensive modernization.[439] All action for indigenous populations was, in line with the indigenist spirit of the time, aimed at the integration and ultimately full assimilation of indigenous groups, per se defined as backward and underdeveloped. The treatment of the "indigenous question" reflected the perceived roles of international organizations as "global civilizers" that shaped the first development policy initiatives of the UN system at large.[440] There was no room for the recognition of cultural diversity or the autonomy of indigenous peoples. Such an understanding would emerge only gradually during the 1970s in the wake of a growing movement towards "indigenous internationalism". ILO discussions reflected this changing approach. It eventually found its expression in the Indigenous and Tribal Peoples Convention (No. 169) of 1989, which removed all the integrationist undertones of the 1957 standard. At the same time, this Convention for the first time introduced the notion of "indigenous people" as a legal term in an international instrument.[441]

The balance for the AIP was mixed, with success and failure about equally distributed. The programme received much praise during its initial phase and, as of 1957, was extended to Argentina, Venezuela, Colombia, and Chile. Around the same time, however, it already began to lose its dynamics. With the progress of decolonization speeding up in Asia and Africa in the late 1950s and early 1960s, the main focus of UN development work gradually shifted to these

---

438 Guthrie, "The ILO and the International Technocratic Class, 1944–1966", 115.
439 Indigenous and Tribal Populations Convention, 1957 (No. 107).
440 Dykmann, "Only with the Best Intentions: International Organizations as Global Civilizers".
441 Hagtvedt Vik, "Indigenous Internationalism".

regions. In addition, the intended handover of the AIP to the national governments proved difficult. The regionally integrated aspect of the programme was frequently not easy to maintain in the face of economic and political instability, financial problems, and diverging governmental priorities. These factors explain why, although the AIP was one of the most ambitious projects of technical cooperation that the ILO has ever embarked on, it eventually fell into oblivion.[442]

At a different level, however, the AIP had far-reaching implications for the ILO. It consolidated the ILO's reputation in the field of indigenous labour more generally and prepared the ground for its reputation to be one of the leading international institutions in the field to the present day. In retrospect, the AIP, as well as the resulting normative work on indigenous labour, was significant in an even broader sense. It helped to consolidate the position of the ILO as a development agency and reaffirmed the self-perception among the "development politicians" in the Organization, who saw their mandate not limited to the field of vocational training. The way in which the ILO defined its scope of action during the AIP, reaching beyond the ILO's traditional areas of competence into the broader social field, prepared the direction its development work would take during the 1960s.

The World Employment Programme

When the ILO started to rethink its contribution to development in the early 1960s, it did so in an environment where international debates on the economic progress of the global South had already taken on an increasingly critical tone. The assumptions of early developmental theorists like W. Arthur Lewis that the growth of the "modern" economic sector would be sufficient to create employment and thus absorb labour from the "traditional sector" had proven erroneous. Even in countries where governments were reporting high levels of economic growth, the results were not enough to increase the standard of living by any significant degree for the majority of the population. Projections of unchecked population growth – and of the misery and despair it would create in growing urban conglomerates in Latin America, Asia, and Africa and in the drained rural communities alike – added to the crisis scenario.[443]

442 Breuer, "Exploring the Technical Assistance Activities of the International Labor Organization in the Field of Indigenous Peoples".
443 Unger, *International Development. A Post-War History*.

Starting from these observations the ILO began to view its activities in developing countries under a new heading. From the early 1960s onwards, it promoted the creation of "productive employment" as the best way out of the developmental impasse. The World Employment Programme (WEP), launched in 1969 on the occasion of the ILO's 50th anniversary, would become the first culmination of these activities.[444]

In 1961, the ILO published a report on its role in the promotion of economic growth and social progress in developing countries, which was meant to define its contribution to what soon would be announced as the United Nations' first "development decade".[445] Its key idea was that the social aspects of development, thus far largely ignored, had to take centre stage, in order to save the concept of development itself from being discredited. From the perspective of the ILO, the single most important step was the creation of "productive employment" in developing countries and the inclusion of employment goals as a key element in national development plans. From then onwards, the topic remained constantly on the agenda. A Convention and a Recommendation on employment policy, both adopted in 1964, provided the normative framework for the debate on the shape of a future technical programme. Both standards defined the basic principles and aims of active employment policies, and they were in large parts tailored to the situation in the developing world.[446] Subsequently, this debate was taken to the regional level, with the so-called Ottawa Plan, emanating from the American Regional Conference of 1966 in the Canadian capital, as the first in a series of regional employment programmes that were intended to form the pillars of a

444 I am very grateful to Michele Sollai, Camille Bolivar, Véronique Plata-Stenger, and Dorothea Hoehtker, who shared with me their rich and not yet published research on the World Employment Programme: Dorothea Hoehtker and Veronique Plata-Stenger, "The Future of Work and Technological Change – the ILO Debate between 1919 and the Early 1980s", unpublished working paper (Geneva: ILO, 2018); Michele Sollai, "Humanizing Development. The International Labour Organisation and the Making of the World Employment Programme (1969–1976)", unpublished working paper for the ILO Century Project (Geneva: ILO, 2018); Camille Bolivar, "La genèse du World Employment Programme et le projet pilote en Colombie: Un réseau d'experts hétérodoxes pour un gouvernement réformiste", Master's thesis, Université de Genève, 2017.
445 ILO, *The Role of the ILO in the Promotion of Economic Expansion and Social Progress in Developing Countries* (Geneva: ILO, 1961).
446 Employment Policy Convention, 1964 (No. 122); Employment Policy Recommendation, 1964 (No. 122). They contained measures to be taken on both the national and international levels and covered areas ranging from investment and income policy, through special methods for creating industrial and agricultural employment, to the implementation of demographic studies. They also reflected the developing countries' view that international agreements on raw materials prices were a precondition for the success of employment policies.

future worldwide ILO programme.[447] One year later, Morse presented his plan for a World Employment Programme to the ILC, to be launched on the occasion of the ILO's 50th anniversary in 1969.[448]

The focus on employment as a means of development had several advantages. Employment policies had been a key topic in the ILO from the beginning, especially at the time of the world economic crisis. They had been high on the agenda at Philadelphia. In addition, they could be easily connected to some of the ILO's previous technical activities, for example the so-called manpower programmes after the war. Despite the fact that employment and manpower policies had so far been mostly associated with industrialized countries, they had also occupied a prominent position with regard to Latin America and influenced parts of the Andean Indian Programme.

It was even more important, however, that the focus on "productive employment" in the global South offered the ILO a way out of an increasingly uneasy position in which it had found itself during the development debates of the early 1960s. Against the backdrop of a widening gap between industrialized and developing countries, some economists started to shift their attention to the biased and "neo-colonial" nature of the world economy, which put the developing countries deliberately and structurally at a disadvantage and made them dependent on others. In the analysis of dependency theorists like Hans Singer and Raul Prebisch, both high-ranking UN officials at the time, the international division of labour and the shifting terms of trade between primary producers and industrialized countries were continuously playing out against the developing countries. At the beginning of the 1960s, their arguments gained increasing currency among developing countries, which soon began to act as a bloc – in particular through the "Group of 77", founded at the first United Nations Conference on Trade and Development (UNCTAD) in Geneva in 1964 – and voiced their demands now more forcefully in all available international fora. As a result, the ILO soon faced com-

447 Under the Ottawa Plan, all the American members agreed to take concerted steps to create more productive employment. The plan's authors saw this as a positive alternative to other measures, such as birth control or forced restrictions on the mobility of the population, which – for political, religious, or administrative reasons – would be difficult to enforce or would take longer to have an impact. Two years later, the Asian Regional Conference in Tokyo launched the Asian Manpower Plan, an adaptation of the Ottawa Plan. At its meeting in Dakar in 1967, the African Advisory Committee also laid the foundations for an African Jobs and Skills Programme, which was finally launched at the third African Regional Conference in Accra in 1969. Alcock, *History of the International Labor Organization*, 354–360.

448 ILO, *Record of Proceedings*, International Labour Conference, 51st Session 1967 (Geneva: ILO, 1967), 422–423.

petitors, such as the recently founded United Nations Industrial Development Organization (UNIDO), which threatened to move into some of its core areas of competence.[449]

The ILO also saw its hands tied with regard to any action that would concern the rules and structures of world trade. Resolutions by African and Asian Regional Conferences, which called on the ILO to broker international agreements guaranteeing price stability for raw materials on the world market,[450] were met with little sympathy by governments, trade unions, and employers of the industrialized Western countries. Placing the focus on employment, therefore, also served the ILO in initially directing the attention of developing countries away from world trade and to the competences which the ILO potentially had in remedying internal factors of underdevelopment.

The proposal to focus on the creation of "productive employment" has to be seen also in the context of the entanglement between the development debate and the population discourse, which took on an increasingly alarmist overtone during the 1960s. Catastrophic projections of population growth and predictions of the misery that it would entail became bestsellers – such as *The Population Bomb* by American biologist Paul Ehrlich.[451] Employment creation was seen as an answer to the threat of uncontrolled urban growth and rural poverty alike, beyond neo-Malthusian prescriptions, such as birth control programmes.[452] This resonated well with member States with a strong Catholic influence, especially in Latin America. Accordingly, the Ottawa Plan had put special emphasis on this aspect.[453]

Last but not least, the WEP cannot be seen in isolation from a general trend towards large global campaigns, which almost all parts of the UN system followed in the 1960s. These campaigns were encouraged by new sources of development funding available through the UNDP, which gave a strong incentive to

---

449 Alcock, *History of the International Labor Organization*, 343–346.

450 Resolution concerning the Stability of World Commodity Markets and Their Influence on Levels of Living and Employment, African Regional Conference (AFRC) I (1960), *Record of Proceedings*, Appendix VI: Resolutions and Conclusions Adopted by the Conference, 280–281; Resolution concerning Measures to Promote Stable Prices of Basic Commodities in World Markets and other Measures for the Effective Utilisation of Resources and the Improvement of Living Standards, Asian Regional Conference V (1962), *Record of Proceedings*, Appendix VII, Resolutions and Observations Adopted by the Conference.

451 Paul R. Ehrlich, *The Population Bomb* (New York: Ballantine Books, 1968).

452 Thomas Robertson, *The Malthusian Moment: Global Population Growth and the Birth of American Environmentalism*, Studies in Modern Science, Technology, and the Environment (New Brunswick, NJ: Rutgers University Press, 2012).

453 For an overview, see Alison Bashford, "Population, Geopolitics, and International Organizations in the Mid-Twentieth Century", *Journal of World History* 19, no. 3 (2008): 327–348.

Figure 11: ILO Director-General David Morse arriving to the First African Regional Conference, Lagos, Nigeria, 1960.

international agencies to both launch large size programmes and get involved more directly in the developing countries' planning processes. Campaign-style programmes were also in line with new techniques tested by international agencies to reach out to a broader international public through cooperation with NGOs and academic partners. The WEP has to be seen in the context of a whole series of similar campaigns taking off from within the United Nations system during the 1960s and 1970s. Examples are the FAO's Freedom from Hunger Campaign (launched in 1960), UNESCO's Experimental World Literacy Programme (1967), and the WHO's Global Eradication of Smallpox Programme (1967).[454]

Once the WEP had started with developing regional employment plans, the actual programme was supposed to consist of a research and an implementation phase. In 1969, Morse put his Egyptian Deputy Director Abbas Ammar in charge of the programme. He then entrusted the operational planning to Hans Singer, who had just ended his latest United Nations assignment as Director of Research at UNIDO, and to Walter Galenson, an American labour economist who, since 1968, had counselled the Director-General on the economic aspects of the WEP. For the research work, the ILO obtained the cooperation of the leading developmental economists in those years, including W. Arthur Lewis and Jan Tinbergen. The key part, however, fell to the Sussex-based Institute for Development Studies (IDS) and its head, Dudley Seers. Their role in the context of the WEP was significant, as it had been Seers and his colleagues who in the 1960s had formulated the most coherent counter-position to the growth-centred orthodoxy of Lewis and the first generation of developmental economists. The IDS, under Seers, went beyond the aim of economic growth and shifted the focus instead to poverty as the main obstacle of economic progress. The Institute argued in favour of social policy measures and redistributive action as a way to put economic development back on track. These positions became prominent through research conducted by the WEP, but, even more importantly, they had an impact through the participation of Seers and other IDS scholars in highly publicized pilot country missions that would form the heart of the WEP's initial phase.[455]

The first of the pilot missions, led by Seers to Colombia in 1970, already set the tone for the expansive approach the WEP would take. Its final report, *Towards Full Employment: A Programme for Colombia*,[456] was regarded a "major breakthrough in development thinking" because of the "complete look at the problem of employment" in relation to a whole set of other economic and social factors like land tenure, income distribution, and international trade.[457] The report argued that income inequality should be treated as a cause, and not as an effect,

---

454 Frey, Kunkel, and Unger, "Introduction: International Organizations, Global Development, and the Making of the Contemporary World"; Kevin O'Sullivan, "A Global Nervous System: The Rise and Rise of European Humanitarian NGOs", in *International Organizations and Development*, ed. Frey, Kunkel, and Unger, 196–219.

455 For a summary of the research output, see Hans Singer, *Research of the World Employment Programme: Future Priorities and Selective Assessment* (Geneva: ILO, 1992).

456 *Towards Full Employment: A Programme for Colombia Prepared by an Inter-Agency Team Organised by the ILO* (Geneva: ILO, 1970).

457 Sollai, "Humanizing Development", 13.

of unemployment. To overcome it, a comprehensive set of measures was needed. These included land reform, the redistribution of wealth through taxation, and a foreign exchange policy that favoured the growth of export-oriented industries. The reduction of poverty, attention to the rural sector, and the implementation of redistributive measures were seen by the report as the main ways to create employment.[458]

The Colombia report received wide acknowledgement within the United Nations, and this paved the way for all the future WEP missions. Of the three missions that followed – to Sri Lanka, Iran, and Kenya – the last one, in particular, contributed to the WEP's legacy. The Kenya mission of 1972 was conducted by Hans Singer together with a number of his IDS colleagues, who were accompanied by the new head of the WEP, the Dutch economist Louis Emmerij. It was carried out with the same broad conceptual approach as the Colombia mission, and it, too, focused on the problem of poverty as the single most important obstacle to development.[459]

The lasting legacy of the Kenya mission was mainly due to the establishment of two central terms in Singer's report, which was published under the programmatic title *Employment, Incomes, and Equality*.[460] It called for a "redistribution from growth" to fund investments in order to improve productivity and raise the incomes of the poorest sections of the population. At the same time, Singer emphasized the strategic importance of the so-called informal sector of the economy. His report elevated the informal sector, in its many different facets, from its status as a simple marker for underdevelopment and stagnation to the central role of a dynamic – if not the most dynamic – element of developing economies.[461]

Together with the research conducted by the WEP in the first half of the 1970s, the Columbia, Kenya, and Sri Lanka reports helped to establish a new focus in development thinking that, for the first time, centred on the problem of poverty. The innovative approach and the easy-to-understand central postulates of the reports helped to calm whatever criticisms there was of the WEP's increas-

458 Bolivar, "La genèse du World Employment Programme", 10–15.

459 Sollai, "Humanizing Development", 15–20.

460 ILO, *Employment, Incomes, and Equality: A Strategy for Increasing Productive Employment in Kenya* (Geneva: ILO, 1972).

461 The term "informal sector" was originally introduced at the IDS by the anthropologist Keith Hart in 1971, but it was first used in a publication by Hans Singer. See Aaron Benanav, "The Origins of Informality: The ILO at the Limit of the Concept of Unemployment", *Journal of Global History* 14, no. 1 (2019): 107–125. For an overview, see Paul E. Bangasser, *The ILO and the Informal Sector: An Institutional History*, ILO Employment Paper 2000/9 (Geneva: ILO, 2000).

ingly expansive drive. The success of the pilot missions cast a favourable light on the WEP. It also helped to distract from the fact that, in almost all of its aspects, the programme had distanced itself from its originally planned set-up. The WEP had been conceived as a cross-departmental undertaking that would engage all sections of the International Labour Office. As it developed, it was instead run by a small group of staff within the ILO, with only a slight connection to the ILO's daily work, and a group of outside consultants, most of which were affiliated with the IDS. While the ILO's Regional Offices were supposed to play a key part in the implementation of the programme, the WEP had quickly turned into a highly centralized undertaking managed from the Geneva headquarters.

The same was true for the intended cooperation with other UN agencies, which never materialized on the ground. And finally, while it had always been a declared aim to include in the programme all social aspects related to the overarching goal of creating "productive employment", the ILO assurances to other UN agencies that it would not intrude in their core areas of competence became obsolete after the publication of the first mission reports. The WEP existed mainly outside of the ILO's regular structures, and it was financed mostly through the contributions of single governments like Denmark, the Netherlands and Sweden.[462]

The WEP drew criticism from many quarters. Some of the officials at the International Labour Office felt that the programme was too detached from the rest of the Organization's work, and many of the ILO's constituents shared those views. Trade unions resented the fact that the WEP escaped oversight by tripartite bodies, which the programme itself did not set up on the ground. The Employers' and Workers' groups were also generally critical of the focus on the informal economy. They were alarmed, especially after the first pilot country mission to Colombia had left them out of the projected activities.[463] The employers and some governments, particularly the United States, were not too keen on the priority that the WEP gave to economic planning and state-directed redistribution strategies. The same was true for some of the recipient countries, whose political leadership all too often showed little sympathy for forceful calls for redistribution and land reform. Colombia, which had hosted the first pilot project, was an exception in this regard, since its President, Carlos Lleras Restrepo, had invited the WEP mission for the express purpose of winning external support and legitimacy for his plans for comprehensive land reform.[464] In Kenya, by contrast, the government quickly shelved the proposals of the Singer mission.[465] The elite-centred

462 Sollai, "Humanizing Development", 21.
463 Ibid.
464 Bolivar, "La genèse du World Employment Programme".
465 Ibid.

approach of the WEP and a certain *naiveté* (or even arrogance) regarding the role of post-colonial elites as willing executors of the programme proposals – which the missions and the reports took for granted – led to a different kind of criticism of the WEP from the political left.[466]

Despite or even because of these circumstances, the WEP was (and could still be seen as) a success story for the ILO. This had less to do with the actual impact of the WEP on the employment situation in the developing countries, which would have been hard to measure in any case. What the WEP achieved, however, was to contribute significantly to a shift in the development discourse of the 1970s. Its concern with poverty as a prime obstacle to development also served as an inspiration to the UN system in general. As an alternative to the traditional insistence on economic growth and the gross national product (GNP) as the prime yardstick of development in the global South,[467] it offered the possibility of a fresh start under a new paradigm. Through the WEP, however short-lived its heyday would prove to be, the ILO took a decisive step towards gaining recognition as an international development agency. The WEP encouraged an impressive body of research by highly renowned scholars such as Amartya Sen. It left a rich research legacy in fields ranging from population growth, rural development, to urbanization, trade, education, automation, migration, the environment, and the use of "appropriate technology".[468]

The World Employment Conference in 1976 and its final report on "Employment, Growth, and Basic Needs: A One World Problem" was the high point of the WEP.[469] What its authors, Louis Emmerij, and his successor as Director of the WEP Research Section, the Kenyan Dharam Ghai, proposed was the creation of employment by a combination of poverty reduction and redistributive measures, such as taxation or land reform. "Basic needs", the key term of the report, included aspects of food security, housing, essential services in health care, sanitation, education, and public transport. These were seen as an essential precondition of employment policies. Its authors did not invent the notion of "basic needs", but they greatly helped to popularize the term. Over the following

466 Chris Gerry, "The Theoretical Basis of the World Employment Programme: A Note on Pragmatism, Social Democracy and Ideology", *Manpower and Employment Research* 10, no. 2 (1977): 25–31.
467 For a discussion on the GNP and growth-centred paradigm in a broader perspective, see Matthias Schmelzer, *The Hegemony of Growth: The OECD and the Making of the Economic Growth Paradigm* (Cambridge: Cambridge University Press, 2016).
468 Bangasser, *The ILO and the Informal Sector*.
469 ILO, "Employment, Growth and Basic Needs: A one-World Problem". Report by the Director-General of the International Labour Office. Tripartite World Conference on Employment, Income Distribution, and Social Progress and the International Division of Labour (Geneva: ILO, 1976).

years, the United Nations, the World Bank, and several other international and national agencies, such as the United States Agency for International Development (USAID), adopted the concept for a short while.[470]

However, the World Employment Conference not only marked the take-off of the basic needs concept. It also was the WEP's swan song and the beginning of its slow decline. The oil crises of the 1970s, which hit the majority of developing countries much harder than the industrialized West, had by then already shattered the hopes for the realization of the programme's most ambitious goals. At the same time, many developing countries had all along been critical of calls for a "dethronement of the GNP"[471] and the emphasis on basic needs. Against the background of discussions on the New International Economic Order (NIEO), proclaimed by the UN General Assembly in 1974, they feared that the WEP was steering the debate away from the most fundamental issue, the unfair global trade order. Many leaders of countries in the global South also were hesitant, to say the least, to fully embrace the redistributive aspects of the WEP for internal political reasons.[472]

In any case, when basic needs caught on in the World Bank under its President, Robert McNamara, and elsewhere in the UN system, a new paradigm shift in development thinking was already on the horizon. Despite all discussions on the NIEO, little had happened. Many countries, on the contrary, faced massive debt crises. Thus, the tide gradually began to turn, and international institutions became part of this development. During the 1980s, under the influence of an all-out attack on Keynesian economics – which seemingly had not been able to provide solutions for the economic crises – poverty-centred approaches to devel-

---

470 The term "basic needs" had been first used in the 1940s by the renowned psychologist Abraham Maslow and had been picked up by the Bariloche Foundation in 1975.

471 Obviously, the WEP was not inimical to growth as such; according to Louis Emmerij, a 6% growth was the target. See Guy Standing, "The ILO: An Agency for Globalization?", *Development and Change* 39, no. 3 (2008): 355–384, esp. 362. Morse had used the expression "dethronement of the GNP" upon leaving the post as Director-General 1970 to pinpoint the shift of emphasis. The citation of the Morse article is taken from: David A. Morse, "The Employment Problem in Developing Countries", in *Prospects for Employment Opportunities in the Nineteen Seventies. Papers and Impressions of the Seventh Cambridge Conference on Development Problems 13th to 24th September 1970 at Jesus College, Cambridge*, ed. Ronald Robinson and Peter Johnston, 5–13 (Foreign and Commonwealth Office, Overseas Development Administration, Cambridge University Overseas Studies Committee, London, HMSO).

472 The discussions on the NIEO are covered in a broader context by Christopher R. W. Dietrich, *Oil Revolution: Sovereign Rights and the Economic Culture of Decolonization, 1945 to 1979*, Global and International History (Cambridge: Cambridge University Press, 2017).

opment gave way to structural adjustment programmes that reversed much of the preceding decade's emphasis on social development.[473]

For the World Bank, which had from the start downplayed the role of "redistribution from growth" in its version of basic needs, it was only a small step toward using the concept as an alternative to redistributive measures, both at the local and global levels.[474] Rather than a means to lift up the poor, basic needs became a mere modicum of structural adjustment and an excuse for not addressing the structural causes of increasing inequality. Under the neoliberal paradigm, the informal economy turned from a springboard for the creation of productive employment to a pool of entrepreneurial energies.[475] Against this backdrop, the WEP, once promoted as the carrier of a new concept of "development with a human face",[476] slowly fell into oblivion and faded out on the institutional level until it was wrapped up in the mid-1990s.[477]

473 An overview and critical assessment of the Washington Consensus and structural adjustment after two decades is provided in Narcís Serra and Joseph E. Stiglitz, *The Washington Consensus Reconsidered: Towards a New Global Governance*, The Initiative for Policy Dialogue Series (Oxford: Oxford University Press, 2008).
474 Rob Konkel, "The Monetization of Global Poverty: The Concept of Poverty in World Bank History, 1944–90", *Journal of Global History* 9 (2014): 276–300.
475 John Toye, *Dilemmas of Development: Reflections on the Counter-Revolution in Development Economics*, 2nd ed. (Cambridge, MA: Blackwell, 1993).
476 Santosh Mehrotra and Richard Jolly, eds., *Development with a Human Face: Experiences in Social Achievement and Economic Growth* (Oxford: Oxford University Press, 1998).
477 Research continued throughout the 1980s, as did regional programmes, such as the Regional Employment Programme for Latin America and the Caribbean (PREALC), the Jobs and Skills Programme for Africa (JASPA), the Asian regional team for Employment Promotion (ARTEP). See Gerry Rodgers, ed., *The Poverty Agenda and the ILO. Issues for Research and Action* (Geneva: International Institute for Labour Studies, 1995).

6 The Human Rights Decade

When, in 1949, David Morse spoke about standard-setting as the "other half of the same coin" in relation to the International Labour Organization's (ILO) new activities in the field of technical cooperation, he was not talking about the whole International Labour Code set out in the ILO standards. What he had in mind were rather the basic principles of the ILO's Constitution which had received a new human rights foundation with the Declaration of Philadelphia. The period between 1948 and 1958 became a decade when the ILO's human rights principles were set out in international labour standards. During these ten years, the ILO adopted most of what today are regarded to be the Organization's fundamental Conventions. The ILO was a major inspiration for the international human rights regime, which was canonized four years after Philadelphia in the UN's Universal Declaration of Human Rights (UDHR). At the same time, these principles were immediately put to a test within the ILO itself.

The debates on human rights standards led to a veritable battle for the soul of the ILO. This took place in a shifting international environment conditioned first by the Cold War and soon thereafter the rapidly accelerating decolonization. In this arena, alternative visions of human rights clashed: between East and West, between North and South, and in many cases across these divides. Apart from sometimes unpredictable outcomes, what the human rights debates brought to the fore more than anything else was the tension between the ILO's universal approach to standard-setting and the desires of an increasingly universal membership, which, at the same time, had become more diverse.[478]

The ILO and Human Rights after 1945

The ILO was both insider and outsider to the international human rights regime emerging after the Second World War. While the Declaration of Philadelphia had inspired the UN Charter (1945) and the UDHR (1948), the ILO still did not fit easily into the new UN human rights framework. The relationship of the ILO's labour standards, in particular, to the human rights norms enshrined in the UDHR and,

---

478 For an overview on the ILO and human rights and a discussion in the larger in context, see: Janelle Diller, "Social Justice, Rights and Labour" in *The Oxford Handbook of International Human Rights Law*, ed. Dinah Shelton (Oxford: Oxford University Press 2013); Maul, "The International Labour Organization and the Globalization of Human Rights, 1944–1970"; Wobbe, "Das Globalwerden der Menschenrechte in der ILO".

https://doi.org/10.1515/9783110650723-008

later, in the two international Covenants on Civil and Political Rights and Economic, Social and Cultural Rights (1966) has never been clearly defined.[479]

There can be no doubt that the ILO's labour standards have been part and parcel of the history of both the emergence and the gradual recognition of the concept of social and economic rights. The supervisory mechanism of the ILO's standards is, furthermore, the closest that one could get to enforcing those rights.[480] At the same time, there has been an element of tension in the ILO's human rights work from the very beginning. ILO standard-setting had not been framed in the language of individual rights before the Philadelphia Conference. And even though the Declaration of Philadelphia claimed the unity and mutual interdependence of political, social and economic rights, the ILO has, ever since 1944, walked a thin line when it has come to defining its exact position in international human rights debates.

The ILO has navigated between a more comprehensive approach, according to which *all* of its standards form part of its work for human rights, and a more restricted approach, which focuses on those Conventions that the ILO adopted explicitly under human rights auspices during the post-war period. Those Conventions, by and large, reflected the basic principles of the Declaration of Philadelphia and were later included in the fundamental Conventions defined by the 1998 Declaration on Fundamental Principles and Rights at Work. They claim political and civil freedoms that represent preconditions or "enabling" rights for the realization of social and economic rights: freedom of association, the abolition of forced labour, and the elimination of discrimination in the work place. In contrast to these Conventions, the vast majority of international labour standards adopted after the Second World War, including the ones on social security (such as Convention No. 102 from 1952), did not contain references to human rights. The notable exception was the Employment Policy Convention (No. 122) of 1964, which explicitly referred to the UDHR in its preamble.[481]

Finally, the way the ILO treated human rights has to be seen also from a more functional point of view. It was in very particular historical contexts – in the era

479 Roger Normand and Sahra Zaidi, *Human Rights at the UN: The Political History of Universal Justice* (Bloomington, IN: Indiana University Press, 2008); Johannes Morsink, *The Universal Declaration of Human Rights: Origins, Drafting, and Intent* (Philadelphia, PA: University of Pennsylvania Press, 1999).

480 On the relationship of labour and human rights and the ILO's human rights beginnings, see Diller, "Social Justice, Rights and Labour"; Wobbe, "Das Globalwerden der Menschenrechte in der ILO".

481 "Considering that the Universal Declaration of Human Rights provides that 'everyone has the right to work, to free choice of employment, to just and favourable conditions of work and to protection against unemployment' ...". Employment Policy Convention 1964 (No. 122).

during and after the Second World War and (as will be shown later on) in the post–Cold War period of the 1990s – that the Organization jumped on the bandwagon of human rights in order to assert its role in the international debate on the topic.

Beyond these general considerations, the outcome of the debates and the form of the conventions adopted in the ILO's "human rights decade" between 1948 and 1958 were highly contingent on the specific political environment in which these debates took place. Particularly during the early years, the ILO's situation was complicated by its position within the Cold War constellation. An important problem was the strained relationship with ECOSOC, which generated a good number of the initiatives for human rights action in the ILO. The Soviet Union, which was not a member of the ILO at the time, tried to use ECOSOC and its commissions to restrict the ILO's activities wherever it could. These tensions eased when the Soviet Union was readmitted to the ILO in 1954, but the ILO itself now became more exposed to the Cold War tensions. Yet, in practice, the positions of the Soviet Union and its allies tended to vary. During ILO debates, Soviet delegations were on the defensive on such human rights topics as forced labour and freedom of association, but they were keen on issues that allowed them to promote their own concept of economic and social rights. This was particularly true with regard to racial discrimination and women's rights, where the socialist countries could denounce Western democracies and benefit from allying themselves with countries from the global South.[482]

Viewed from the other side of the East-West divide, discussions inside the ILO were shaped by the attitude of the US government, which, for various reasons, became more cautious with regard to human rights debates. During the war, the United States of President Roosevelt had been instrumental in creating a new human rights basis for the ILO's work.[483] At the same time, Washington had always put the brakes on efforts to codify economic and social rights beyond mere declarations of intent.[484] In the wake of the conservative turn in US domestic

482 Jennifer Amos, "Embracing and Contesting: The Soviet Union and the Universal Declaration of Human Rights, 1948–1958", in *Human Rights in the Twentieth Century*, ed. Hoffmann, 147–165; Mark B. Smith, "Social Rights in the Soviet Dictatorship: The Constitutional Right to Welfare from Stalin to Brezhnev", *Humanity* 3, no. 3 (2012): 385–406.

483 On US human rights policy and the United Nations in general, see Rowland Brucken, *A Most Uncertain Crusade: The United States, the United Nations, and Human Rights, 1941–1953* (DeKalb, IL: Northern Illinois University Press, 2013); Mark Philip Bradley, *The World Reimagined. Americans and Human Rights in the Twentieth Century* (Cambridge: Cambridge University Press 2016.)

484 Daniel J. Whelan and Matthew Donnelly, "The West, Economic and Social Rights, and the Global Human Rights Regime: Setting the Record Straight", *Human Rights Quarterly* 29, no. 4

politics after the end of the war, the United States further hardened its traditional position to avoid international obligations that encroached on national jurisdiction.[485] In addition, the experience of being attacked by the newly established bloc of communist countries on issues like racial discrimination in its Southern states made the United States lose much of its remaining interest in the ILO's human rights work in the 1950s.[486]

While the Cold War influenced the debates on human rights within the ILO, it reflected the diplomatic struggles accompanying the dissolution of the European colonial empires in a similar way. In this arena, too, human rights language was used liberally by nationalist movements and new ILO member States that emerged from colonial rule. This latter group brought their own perspectives and aspirations to the human rights debates. Countries such as India or Egypt used international institutions primarily as fora to promote the right to self-determination and the struggle against such racist regimes as the apartheid state of South Africa. National liberation movements like the Algerian *Front de libération nationale* (FLN) sought legitimacy and recognition for their fight from the margins, sometimes with considerable success.[487] Like other international organizations, the ILO inevitably became an arena for these struggles.

One aspect of human rights policies is often ignored: in this early period, human rights discourses originating from countries in the global South were not exclusively about the right to self-determination. Many of these countries took a keen interest in social and economic rights from the start. Their position was shaped by perceptions of the nature of colonialism, which they attacked as a system that denied both political and social rights to its subjects. These voices added to those from the Latin American countries, which were the most outspoken proponents of the inclusion of social and economic rights in the UN's human rights instruments during the war. However, the concept of social and economic

(2007). With regard to the discussions on social and economic rights within the drafting committee of the UDHR, see Kathryn Sikkink, *Mixed Signals: U.S. Human Rights Policy and Latin America* (Ithaca, N.Y.; London: Cornell University Press, 2004).

485 On the debates regarding the constitutional hurdles to American human rights policy, see Hanne Hagtvedt Vik, "How Constitutional Concerns Framed the US Contribution to the International Human Rights Regime from Its Inception, 1947–1953", *International History Review* 34, no. 4 (2012): 908–949.

486 Carol Anderson, *Eyes Off the Prize: The United Nations and the African American Struggle for Human Rights, 1944–1955* (Cambridge: Cambridge University Press, 2003).

487 Matthew James Connelly, *A Diplomatic Revolution: Algeria's Fight for Independence and the Origins of the Post-Cold War Era* (Oxford: Oxford University Press, 2002); Fabian Klose, *Human Rights in the Shadow of Colonial Violence: The Wars of Independence in Kenya and Algeria*, Pennsylvania Studies in Human Rights (Philadelphia, PA: University of Pennsylvania Press, 2013).

rights as *individual* human rights, promoted, among others, by Hernan Santa Cruz, the Chilean member of the human rights commission preparing the UDHR, was tied to the idea of international economic security that had been prominently discussed at the ILO's American Regional Conferences before the war.[488] In other words: the realization of those rights depended on the willingness of the rich countries to enter into international agreements to re-organize the world economy in a way that would first enable poorer countries to create the conditions for welfare programmes for their own populations. In the post-war era, this discourse was easily translatable into demands on the industrialized countries to help post-colonial nations to build up their economies. It was in this sense that development and human rights discourses were intertwined from the start. Social rights, other than in the debates of recent decades, were initially understood and promoted as rights of the individual, rather than those of the state.[489]

The use of human rights language by different actors with widely varying agendas created an environment full of tensions for debates in the ILO. The politically explosive nature of these discussions raised the question of how far the Organization could proceed under the human rights banner. But governments, employers, and trade unions alike were not content with somehow neutralizing the ILO on these issues. In addition, the ILO itself had good reasons to embrace the human rights concept. The claim for a comprehensive social mandate of the Declaration of Philadelphia was based on human rights principles. Both the ILO's involvement in economic policies and the expansion into the field of development ultimately drew their ideological legitimacy from their connection to the human rights project. More importantly, and more practically, this gave the ILO a much needed tool to bridge the growing diversity among its membership. Both with regard to the Cold War and decolonization, human rights offered a way out of an impasse in which the ILO, with its standard-setting activities, seemed to have gotten stuck in the early 1950s. There was growing concern that the type of labour standards the ILO had adopted thus far appealed to a shrinking part of its membership and constituents. This was true not only for the group of developing countries and the socialist states. Even among the Western democracies, standard-setting was met with varying degrees of enthusiasm. The 1952 Social Security Convention (No. 102) was a case in point. Intended as a kind of codifica-

488 Roland Burke, "Some Rights Are More Equal Than Others: The Third World and the Transformation of Economic and Social Rights", *Humanity* 3, no. 3 (2012): 427–448.

489 Roland Burke, *Decolonization and the Evolution of International Human Rights*, Pennsylvania Studies in Human Rights (Philadelphia, PA: University of Pennsylvania Press, 2010); Jan Eckel, "Human Rights and Decolonization: New Perspectives and Open Questions", *Humanity* 1, no. 1 (2010): 111–135 .

tion of various post-war projects to create welfare states, the Convention included a complete list of all different aspects of social security, defining minimum standards with regard to medical care, sickness, unemployment, old age, maternity, and several other items. While it made no specific recommendations about the mode of financing social security schemes (through contributions or taxation), the Convention still contained a commitment to universal coverage. This was one of the reasons why it drew bitter antagonism from the Employers, who all voted against it, with the US representatives agitating vehemently against "socialized medicine".[490] Most Government and the Workers' representatives, on the contrary, supported the Convention, including those from developing countries, who were offered a set of options and flexibility clauses that would allow them to adopt it as an ideal for future implementation. The debates, however, showed little enthusiasm for the Convention, and ratifications were coming in very slowly.[491]

For David Morse, the debates served as a further confirmation that the ILO had to shift its attention away from its normative functions, in particular when it came to its approach regarding the developing world. Next, the orientation towards technical cooperation seemed to draw more legitimacy from the principles and general objectives stated in the Declaration of Philadelphia under human rights auspices than from the provisions of ILO standards in their entirety. Morse promoted a "fundamental view of society, of morality and of the freedom and dignity of the individual", based on the principles enshrined in the Declaration of Philadelphia. At the same time, he made it implicitly clear that the body of standards adopted by the ILO did not have the same universal scope. The subtext was that the ILO's principal aim with regard to developing countries was no longer the ratification of labour standards but the promotion of principles which could guide those countries on their path towards modernization.[492]

Freedom of Association

It was no coincidence that the Freedom of Association Convention (No. 87) of 1948 and the Right to Organise and Collective Bargaining Convention (No. 98) of 1949 became the first international labour standards that were explicitly debated under human rights auspices. They occupied a special position within the spectrum of ILO standards because of their dual nature. There was an understanding

490 ILO, *Record of Proceedings*, International Labour Conference, 35th Session 1952 (Geneva: ILO, 1953), 409.
491 For example, by the Netherlands and Chile. See ILC (1952), *Record of Proceedings*, 308, 317.
492 Morse quoted in Maul, *Human Rights, Development and Decolonization*, 136.

that they enshrined, above all, the rights of trade unions. They were also seen as individually enabling rights, meaning as an essential precondition for the realization of workers' social and economic rights in open market economies. For this very reason, they had a more general meaning – as basic principles on which the ILO rested, and which represented the essentially liberal democratic character of the Organization. This partly explained why the question of freedom of association and its implications for the ILO's tripartite structure would unleash a particularly bitter struggle along the East-West divide. In the same sense, it became one of the main fields of controversy in the process of decolonization, in which the ILO promoted freedom of association as a means to secure democratic participation and a key principle to facilitate sound economic and social development.[493]

The debate itself, however, was much older, because freedom of association had been among the founding principles of the International Labour Organization. The ILO Constitution of 1919 had declared freedom of association "for all lawful purposes" an essential means of improving the situation of workers everywhere and thus securing "universal and lasting peace". In the 1920s the International Labour Office conducted a broad inquiry on freedom of association. Its results were published between 1927 and 1930 and thereby left a legacy to build upon.[494] Even a first Convention on the topic was adopted in 1921, which granted rural workers the "same rights of association and combination as to industrial workers".[495] However, there was no further legal action during the interwar years. The Workers' group, which had initially fought for a Convention, stopped pushing for it when it realized that there was not sufficient support, against the opposition of employers and most governments, for an instrument that would include the "right to strike". The political climate of the 1930s and the rise of authoritarian regimes eliminated the prospects of such an initiative.[496]

The Second World War gave a fresh impetus to the debate. Within the Allied countries, trade unions gained wider recognition for their participation in the war effort. As early as 1941, at the ILO's first wartime Conference in New York, the question of freedom of association was taken up again, and the path was cleared for the introduction of a convention.[497] The Declaration of Philadelphia confirmed

493 Rodgers et al., *The ILO and the Quest for Social Justice*, 45–50.

494 ILO, *Freedom of Association*, 5 vols. (Geneva: ILO, Studies and Reports, Series A, 28–32, 1927–1930).

495 Right of Association (Agriculture) Convention, 1921 (No. 11).

496 ILO, *Freedom of Association*.

497 A committee on collaboration between public authorities, employers' and workers' organizations had been established by the Conference. The Conference adopted a resolution submitted by Latin American workers, which declared that "real collaboration is possible only within the

freedom of association as a key element of the "war against want" within democratic societies. Not restricting it to advanced industrial societies, the Declaration further proclaimed the principle to be of universal value and fully applicable to developing societies, inasmuch as "freedom of expression and of association are essential to sustained progress".[498]

Redefined as both a human right and a precondition for the realization of social rights more generally, freedom of association seemed to be predestined to become subject to an early convention after World War II. The Cold War complicated the discussion, as the Soviet Union and the communist-leaning unions of the World Federation of Trade Unions (WFTU) first attempted to place the question on the agenda of ECOSOC. Their major argument against leaving the issue to the ILO was that, as a tripartite organization, it would give employers a say in the definition of what should be framed as a question of trade union rights. At this point, the WFTU was a unitary federation of both Eastern and Western trade unions, but contradictory views on the Marshall Plan had already rendered it inoperative. The American Federation of Labor (AFL) vigorously opposed the WFTU. Since the AFL, like the WFTU, had a consultative status with ECOSOC, it issued a counterproposal, which asked ECOSOC to mandate the ILO with producing a survey on the legal situation with regard to freedom of association as a basis for a future ILO Convention. The AFL's move was not only supported by the US government but was, in fact, coordinated with Washington. In turn, the Truman administration ensured that the ILO would place the issue of freedom of association on the agenda of the ILC in 1947. The Conference Committee that drew up a resolution outlining a new Convention on freedom of association was headed by the then US Assistant Secretary of Labor, David Morse.[499]

In the ensuing debate, the main line of conflict concerned the question of the right to join (or not to join) a trade union and the question of explicitly recognizing the right to strike. The workers succeeded in removing from the final version of the Convention a paragraph that would have included "the right not to join a union", an issue for which the employers had long fought tooth and nail. Conversely,

framework of democratic political institutions which guarantee the freedom of association of workers and employers". It affirmed that "the application of the principle of collaboration requires that in law and in fact (a) the right of industrial organisations to represent workers and employers should be recognised by the State; (b) the workers' and employers' organisations should recognise each other's right to represent workers and employers respectively". Conference of the ILO, New York and Washington D.C. (1941), *Record of Proceedings*, 166.

498 ILO, Declaration of Philadelphia, art I (b), (d).

499 The non-Communist trade unions, which would soon leave the WFTU supported this move. Alcock, *History of the International Labor Organization*, 252–255.

the right to strike was not explicitly mentioned either, but, from the context, it was clear that this was regarded as a natural expression of trade union rights. The Convention stipulated the right of workers' and employers' organizations to "organize their administration and activities and to formulate their programmes" (Article 3), and acknowledges the aims of such organization as "furthering and defending the interests of workers or of employers" (Article 10).[500] The Convention guaranteed freedom of association without mentioning any more "for all lawful purposes", a passage from the Constitution that had given governments much leeway for effectively restricting trade union rights. An initiative pushed by Eastern European countries and some members of the WFTU to exclude the employers from the Convention was equally rejected. This rejection, carried by a majority of the Workers' representatives, was a strong statement and underpinned both the Western orientation and the tripartite character of the ILO. It also stood in stark contrast to the Universal Declaration of Human Rights, drafted at the same time as the ILO Convention, which did not mention employers' organizations and spoke exclusively about a "right to form and to join trade unions" for the protection of interests.[501]

The two Conventions adopted in 1948 and 1949 were seen to be mutually complementary. While the Freedom of Association Convention (No. 87) was first and foremost intended for the protection of workers' and employers' organizations from state interference, the Right to Organise and Collective Bargaining Convention (No. 98) defined the rights of workers vis-à-vis their employers. The central importance given to the principle of freedom of association was further emphasized in 1950, when a special mechanism was put in place to oversee compliance with this principle, supplementing the regular supervisory procedures linked to the ratification of Conventions No. 87 and No. 98. In 1951, an ILO tripartite Committee on Freedom of Association (CFA) was created, whose task has been ever since to investigate allegations received by the UN or the ILO regarding the violation of trade union rights, whether or not the country concerned has ratified the two Conventions.[502]

Contrary to all other ILO "human rights Conventions", the most controversial debates regarding freedom of association would take place *after* the Conventions had been adopted. The re-entry of the Soviet Union into the ILO in 1954, which was accompanied by the admission of Byelorussia and Ukraine and thus increased the votes of the communist group, once again raised questions about

500 See Bernard Gernigon, Alberto Odero, and Horacio Guido, "ILO Principles concerning the Right to Strike", *International Labour Review* 137, no. 4 (1998):441–481.
501 UN General Assembly, Universal Declaration of Human Rights, art. 23 (4) (Paris, 1948).
502 Alcock, *History of the International Labor Organization*, 268–270.

the meaning of the principle and its implications for the tripartite structure of the ILO. The communist state, according to the official doctrine, embodied the interests of the workers, and at the same time was the only employer. Thus, state socialism left no room neither for employers' nor for workers' associations that were independent of the state, nor did it provide the possibility for an individual to freely join such an organization. Trade unions existed mainly as institutions that administered significant parts of the socialist welfare state, secured social stability, and implemented party directives with regard to production. Freedom of association as defined by the ILO did not exist in the Soviet Union and its satellite states. They effectively sent four Government delegates to the ILC, as Western delegations complained over and over again.[503]

It was not the first occasion on which credentials of Workers' representatives had been challenged in the ILO. Fascist Italy had been the main target during the interwar years. In the late 1940s, the legitimacy of Argentinian Workers' delegates was seriously questioned. With memories of Italian fascism still alive, labour organizations under the Peronist regime seemed to many a legacy of fascist corporatism. The Soviet case differed primarily because, after the re-admission of the Soviet Union and before the acceleration of decolonization, the Eastern bloc accounted for nearly one third of the ILO's membership and thus seriously challenged the very hegemony of the liberal democratic principles on which the ILO had long rested. The debate boiled down to a fundamental question: should the ILO stick to its tripartite principle regardless of the cost, or was universalism of membership and the full inclusion of the socialist states – or, for that matter, all states irrespective of their political system – the more important goal? As a first step to contain the question on a politically less contagious level, the Governing Body, in 1955, commissioned an independent Committee on Freedom of Employers' and Workers' Organizations, headed by the renowned British international lawyer Lord Arnold McNair, to investigate the independence from government control of workers' and employers' organizations worldwide.[504] In the views of some observers, the 1956 report of the McNair Committee came close

503 The ICFTU, although divided on the matter, protested in 1954 against the credentials of Soviet Workers and filed a complaint with the CFA regarding the independence of Soviet trade unions. The Soviet Employers' credentials were equally challenged by the Employers' group, but the ILC decided in the end not to follow up on the objections in either case. However, the questions stayed on the agenda for many years. See Valticos, *International Labour Law*, 31–34; Alcock, *History of the International Labor Organization*, 290–292.

504 McNair had been the president of the International Court of Justice and was a longstanding member of the CEACR. His two colleagues on this particular committee were the Mexican expert on international law and former Mexican Government representative Pedro de Alba and A.R. Cornelius, Judge of the Pakistan Federal Court.

to redefining the tripartite principle, which, the report argued, was actually not confined to only one particular economic and social system. When it came to the relationship between the state, workers' and employers' organizations, the report even observed a certain convergence of the Eastern and Western socioeconomic systems. The massive increase in state involvement in the economy and the continuous expansion of the public sector that had taken place in Western countries after the war had changed the role of employers' and workers' organizations even in the West. For example, trade unions often got deeply involved in politics to raise productivity. Against this background and despite great differences in the degree of independence, the actual functions fulfilled by trade unions and employers' organizations in socialist states and free market democracies were seen as becoming increasingly similar. Therefore, the report saw no valid reasons to exclude the Workers' and Employers' representatives of the Eastern bloc countries from the ILO's sessions.[505]

When the report was discussed by the ILC in 1956, emotions ran high, and Western employers, in particular, were bitterly opposed to its conclusions. Eventually, however, while the conflict lingered on for another decade, a majority of the ILO's members had no interest in an open break with the East and silently conceded the participation of Workers' and Employers' representatives from the Soviet bloc. At this point, it was also hard to ignore that the international context was about to affect the practice of tripartism and the very principle of freedom of association. Both had been prominently affirmed in the Philadelphia Declaration (Article 1) and now became part of an essentially global debate on the role of trade unions in state-led processes of social and economic development.

Against the background of decolonization, freedom of association and tripartism came to occupy a central position in the discussions with the newly independent states of Asia and Africa on the role of ILO standards in the development process. Here, colonialism had often left a difficult legacy. The "colonial clause" and the parallel existence of a weaker "colonial" Convention that governed the right to freedom of association "in dependent territories" (Convention No. 84 of 1947) allowed late colonial regimes to maintain a double standard with regard to trade union rights, and this often until the very eve of independence. The colonial Conventions differed from the regular standards in one essential way: They contained different provisions concerning the political role of trade unions – a case in which the colonial Conventions put tight restrictions on trade unions' activi-

505 For the McNair report, see also Alcock, *History of the International Labor Organization*, 300–303; Ghébali, *The International Labour Organisation*, 127–131.

ties. While their policies differed, colonial powers shared a basic ambiguity about granting trade union freedoms within their territories. On the one hand, and at least with regard to Britain and France, promoting the establishment of trade unions as part of post-war "welfare colonialism" was seen as a means of building reliable partners whose support would be key in the realization of colonial development projects. On the other hand, and with "regular" political activities limited, these organizations were not easily confined to the kind of "apolitical" work that the colonial authorities had intended for them. Even before independence, trade unions and their leaders had often become involved in projects of anti-colonial emancipation. As a result, the reality on the ground often directly contradicted one of the basic ideas underlying both the "regular" and the colonial Conventions, which both regarded free and democratic labour relations a precondition for social and economic development. Instead, the colonial legacy entailed a different, essentially authoritarian, concept of modernization, in which governments and political elites saw unrestricted labour relations as an obstacle to productivity and growth. They featured, if at all, as a distant target that was secondary to economic considerations.[506]

It was quite easy to draw a line from here to the findings of the McNair report. Viewed from this perspective, the Soviet Union represented just another authoritarian model of modernization – and an attractive one at that – to many countries of the global South.[507] As a matter of fact, the McNair report confirmed this trend also with regard to the post-colonial situation in Asia. Here, it found widespread "restrictions and limitations" in the legislation regulating trade union freedoms for political and economic reasons. Governments generally saw the concept of freedom of association in the way it was anchored in the ILO standards as irreconcilable with the demands of national development. Trade union activities were, therefore, subjected to tight state control. The state authorities wanted to have the last say in the organization of industrial relations, and this made the right to collective bargaining, in particular, unpopular and suspect among developing countries. As India's Prime Minister Nehru pointed out in 1957, the good of the nation had to take precedence over certain workers' rights, and he thought it "quite absurd when we are talking about increasing production [...] to waste our energy in industrial conflict".[508]

506 Maul, *Human Rights, Development and Decolonization*, 108–111.
507 During the debate on freedom of association, governments such as South African had proposed to extend the "colonial clause" to parts of the population of independent countries that was not yet "mature" enough to benefit from a freedom of association Convention.
508 Asian Regional Conference IV (1957), *Record of Proceedings*, 8.

The idea that the trade union movement needed to be subordinate to national (economic) development interests recurred over the following years. It further gained strength during the 1960s, when many African countries attained independence. Freedom of association then became one of the prime areas in which the consequences of the ILO's geographical and political expansion became tangible. The Organization reacted with a further strengthening of its technical functions. With regard to standard-setting, the experience of the debates on freedom of association and tripartism drove the development of a new "promotional" or "educational" approach introduced by David Morse in his human rights report of 1958 (on the occasion of the ten year anniversary of both the UDHR and the Freedom of Association Convention). A first consequence of this approach was the launching technical assistance programmes in the area of labour relations, followed by workers' education and management training schemes. All these programmes were directed almost exclusively at developing countries and were intended to encourage democratic models of modernization and industrial relations. The latter were strongly influenced by US experts as this new field of activity began to emerge in the 1960s.[509]

Freedom of association and the right to collective bargaining have remained on the agenda of the ILO ever since, and they have continued to be – because of their intrinsic link to the tripartite principle – in the very centre of the battles about the ILO's identity. The function and position of trade unions in the development process is still a controversial issue (and has become even more so with the growing weight of China). Meanwhile, new dimensions have been added to the debate in the context of globalization, where trade union rights have to be defended against the power of multinational enterprises, in extra-territorial special economic zones, and within complex, and largely non-transparent, global supply chains.[510]

---

509 Workers' education had been a key element within the ILO's programme from the early 1950s onwards and a way to frame the question of trade union rights in a technical and "apolitical" way inspired mainly by US models. There is hardly any research on this key field of action. For the general background and the implementation in Latin America, see Gabriela Scodeller, "Educar in derechos laborales: politicas y acciones desplegadas por la OIT en América Latina durante los anos 1950–1970", in *Una historia regional de la OIT*, ed. Caruso and Stagnaro, 213–254.

510 See for a discussion of freedom of association and the position of trade unions against the background of a globalizing economy the contributions in Yossi Dahan, Hanna Lerner, and Faina Milman-Sivan, eds., *Global Justice and International Labour Rights* (Cambridge: Cambridge University Press, 2016).

Equal Remuneration for Men and Women

Two years after the instruments on freedom of association were adopted, the ILO passed in 1951 another Convention on a topic – related to the work of women – that had been on the Organization's larger agenda from the very beginning. The Equal Remuneration Convention (No. 100), for the first time, moved beyond the protective approach that had so far characterized the ILO's policies. Legal equality feminists saw the Convention as a confirmation that the pendulum was about to swing in their direction.[511] However, both the debate and its result reflected ongoing tensions about women's position in the world of work.

The roots of the Equal Remuneration Convention can be traced back to the 1919 Constitution, and especially the debate of the 1930s.[512] By that time, legal equality had not only gained some ground among women's organizations but also made inroads into the thinking of the ILO. Against the backdrop of the war economy's demand on women, as well as their mobilization for reconstruction, this trend gathered momentum. In 1939, the ILO's Second American Regional Conference in Havana had passed resolutions that proclaimed women's right to representation, their right to equal pay, and the right of married women to work. Five years later, the Philadelphia Declaration had elevated the question of equal treatment of both men and women to the level of a human rights issue.[513]

A major reason why it took another seven years for a Convention to be adopted was the circumstance that the question of gender equality, too, became entangled in Cold War controversies. For the Soviet Union and its allies, the question of equal pay was intrinsically linked to the broader question of equal social and economic rights for women and men as a precondition for the realization of political rights. Western countries, on the contrary, tried to restrict the debate to the extension of individual rights to women. Because of the antagonism of the Eastern bloc countries towards the ILO, the Organization found itself in an awkward position. In 1946, the United Nations had established a Commission on the Status of Women (CSW) under ECOSOC. While the Commission focused on political and civil rights, it clearly considered that women's economic rights were also part of its mandate. During the early post-war years, the ILO had reason to be wary of competition by the CSW. From the Commission's ranks, the ILO received criticism for not fully renouncing its protective labour standards. As a consequence, the

511 About the different aspects of the debate on women's labour, see the contributions in Boris, Hoehtker, and Zimmermann, eds., *Women's ILO.*

512 See the sub-chapter on "Women", Part I, Chapter 1.

513 Eileen Boris, "Equality's Cold War: The ILO and the Un Commission on the Status of Women, 1946–1970s", in *Women's ILO,* ed. Boris, Hoehtker, and Zimmermann, 97–120.

Figure 12: Worker members of the Committee on Equal Remuneration: Adrian Vermeulen (Netherlands), Beatrice Ann Godwin and Florence Hancock (both from the United Kingdom) at the 33rd Session of the ILC, 1950.

WFTU, Poland, and the Soviet Union, tried to move in 1949 the question of equal pay from the mandate of the ILO to that of ECOSOC. This attempt reflected the unsuccessful effort some years earlier to transfer freedom of association issues to ECOSOC.[514]

Western women's activists, such as Frieda S. Miller of the United States,[515] played an important role in convincing governments to aim for an ILO Convention on equal pay. She served as reporter for the Drafting Committee of the Equal Remuneration Convention in 1951. Many Western governments, like the US administration, agreed to normative action. They did not want to be criticized for standing in the way of women's rights. In addition, they sought to lend their support to the ILO and did not want to see its portfolio reduced vis-à-vis the United Nations. Despite all the progress made, however, and notwithstanding the far-reaching agreement on the principle, the adoption of a Convention was by no means an easy task. In

514 Neunsinger, "The Unobtainable Magic of Numbers", in ibid., 121–148.
515 Jensen, "US New Deal Policy Experts and the ILO, 1948–1954", 172–189.

addition to the Employers' group, the United States and Great Britain were among the many governments that would have preferred a mere Recommendation to a Convention. The different opinions clearly came to the fore in the report prepared for the 1950 ILC. While socialist countries were in favour of a strong Convention, some Western countries voiced their reservation regarding such an instrument, drawing on a mix of cultural and practical arguments. The United Kingdom and the Netherlands pointed out that the "higher costs of production connected with the natural characteristics of women cannot be entirely ignored". The Swiss government bluntly stated, that the "structure of the country, its way of thinking and the conditions peculiar to it are opposed to the principle of remuneration for men and women for work of equal value". It questioned whether such an instrument was "really in the best interests of women", as it would ultimately reduce their employment opportunities.[516] Finland and Sweden, which had strong collective bargaining mechanisms in place, initially also argued against a Convention. They regarded equal pay essentially as a part of the larger complex of wage policy, and the state was not supposed to interfere in negotiations between trade unions and employers.[517] Beyond economic arguments, claims of the higher costs of production of women's work (due to maternity, etc.) were most common among the opponents of equal pay. Some countries from the global South had their own concerns. India, for instance, preferred a Recommendation, pointing to the practical problems arising from the lack of a proper wage fixing machinery that was based on job contents in major parts of its economy. Consequently, this would make it near impossible to implement the principle of equal pay.[518]

In the second ILC debate in 1951, the front lines remained largely unchanged. Socialist countries like Poland and Czechoslovakia argued for a strong Convention with clear provisions for legal implementation. By contrast, a majority of Workers' delegates and some governments – among them Germany, France, the Latin American countries – now favoured the combination of a Convention containing general principles and a practical Recommendation along the lines of the draft documents which the Office had prepared for the Conference. Employers and other governments, among them the United Kingdom, Italy, Australia, India, South Africa and the Scandinavian countries, favoured a recommendation and

516 ILO, *Record of Proceedings*, Report V (2): Summary of positions in countries who answered the 1949 general survey, International Labour Conference, 33rd Session 1950 (Geneva: ILO, 1951), 6, 61.

517 ILC 33 (1950) Rep. V (2), 69.

518 It also pleaded for gradual application of any type of regulation in the matter, asking for exemptions for "family undertakings, domestic work, unorganised industries, and employments where the output of women was as a rule less than that of men". Ibid., 32.

abstained from the final vote on the Convention. The United States, although leaning towards a Convention, finally voted for a dual instrument. In the end, the Convention was adopted by a vote of 105 to 33 (mostly employers voted against it), with 40 abstentions.[519] This was a relatively small margin, in particular if compared to other human rights standards of the ILO. The apprehensions were clearly reflected by the rather complex formulation of Article 2 of the Convention, which asks all members "by means appropriate to the methods in operation for determining rates of remuneration" to promote and, "in so far as is consistent with such methods", to ensure the application "to all workers of the principle of equal remuneration for men and women workers for work of equal value".[520]

Even with the new Convention, gender equality in the workplace remained more of a distant goal.[521] The Equal Remuneration Convention, while regarded as a major step forward by legal equality activists in the West, did not spell an end to the debate on women's place in the world of work. Yet, its impact was felt in the coming years, when it provided a yardstick for discussions on the national level. Within the Organization, the debate continued. The pendulum on the international level had swung decisively to the side of legal equality, but in the ILO, a set of women-only protective standards continued to coexist alongside the new Convention.[522] From the 1950s onward, the debate gradually shifted from the situation in the industrialized world to the situation of women in developing countries. The latter had initially been treated as a separate issue. Technical cooperation programmes directed at women in the non-industrialized parts of the world had sought by default to integrate women in the general development process of their respective countries. By doing so, they had often unintentionally concealed the particularly precarious status of women in many countries of the global South. Women were carrying the burden of "reproduction" by taking care of the family, and sustaining the household; they were also at the heart of the rural subsistence agriculture and what would later come to be called the "informal economy". During the 1970s, women's organizations from the global South increasingly challenged the modernization paradigm, but they were also critical of the blind spots within Western feminist activism. When the ILO "discovered" the informal

519 ILO, *Record of Proceedings*, International Labour Conference, 34th Session 1951 (Geneva: ILO, 1952), 447–448.

520 Equal Remuneration Convention, 1951 (No. 100), Art. 2.

521 A more detailed account of the debates on Convention No. 100 and the role of international women's organizations will be provided in Eileen Boris, *Making the Woman Worker: Precarious Labor and the Fight for Global Standards, 1919–2019* (Oxford: Oxford University Press, 2019).

522 Eloisa Betti, "Unexpected Alliances: Italian Women's Struggles for Equal Pay, 1940s–1960s", in *Women's ILO,* ed. Boris, Hoehtker, and Zimmermann, 276–299.

economy in the 1970s, some of the research conducted under the auspices of the World Employment Programme took account of the pivotal position that women occupied in rural development.[523] In its technical cooperation programmes, the ILO began to put more emphasis on women in developing countries. However, it would take another twenty to thirty years before discussions started to focus on the additional strain that globalization put on women in the global South. This eventually led to new standards, which, also gender neutral in design, addressed more specifically the situation of women working in the informal economy, such as Convention No. 177 of 1996, which dealt with home based workers and the Domestic Workers' Convention No. 189 of 2011. They both expressed a heightened awareness for the plight of women, who often were at a double disadvantage in a globalizing world.[524]

The Total Abolition of Forced Labour

The debate on forced labour took off in the ILO in parallel to the discussions on freedom of association and equal pay, but it developed a different dynamic. As in the case of freedom of association, the topic had been discussed during the interwar years. In contrast, to the former, however, the abolition of forced labour had been subject to international labour standards directed primarily at colonial territories, with the Forced Labour Convention of 1930 (No. 29) as its centerpiece.[525] When the topic was put back on the ILO agenda immediately after the end of World War II, the traditional colonial aspects were overshadowed by fresh memories of the Nazi regime's massive use of forced labour as a tool of economic exploitation, political punishment, and means of extermination. From there, attention immediately turned to the system of labour camps established in the Soviet Union to deal with perceived political opponents. Against this backdrop, the problem was reframed as a human rights issue, and the debate shifted to the forms of forced labour employed in the Gulags for both political and economic purposes. The debate thus started from anti-totalitarian premises, but it quickly became a battlefield of the East-West-Conflict, with the Socialist countries ending

523 Sollai, "Humanizing Development", 26; Singer, *Research of the World Employment Programme*.
524 Boris, Hoehtker, and Zimmermann, "Introduction", *Women's ILO*, 1–23.
525 Daughton, "ILO Expertise and Colonial Violence"; Rodríguez-Piñero, *Indigenous Peoples, Postcolonialism, and International Law*; Daniel Maul, "The International Labour Organization and the Struggle against Forced Labour from 1919 to the Present", *Labor History* 48 no. 4 (2007): 477–550.

up on the defensive. However, the new Abolition of Forced Labour Convention (No. 105), adopted in 1957, reflected a much broader understanding of the problem than originally intended by the Western initiators of the new instrument.[526]

In November 1947, the American Federation of Labor (AFL) called upon ECOSOC to commission the ILO with a comprehensive study of new-style forced labour systems in UN member States. The AFL's petition had been composed and submitted with the support and approval of the US government, and it was directly aimed at the Soviet Union and its Eastern European satellites. After heated debates in the UN, where the Soviets tried without success to block the topic from being transferred to the ILO, the Governing Body voted in 1949 to set up a joint UN-ILO committee to investigate forced labour. The communist countries reacted to their defeat by changing strategy. They launched counterattacks by highlighting the forms of labour coercion resulting from the capitalist economy in the West and, at the same time, attempting to redirect the attention to the persisting forms of colonial forced labour.[527]

This, then, was the point of departure, when, in 1951, the UN and the ILO created a committee of three internationally renowned human rights advocates under the leadership of the Indian diplomat and international lawyer Ramaswami Mudaliar. Mudaliar personified a degree of continuity with the forced labour debate of the 1920s, since he had been a member of the Conference Committee in charge of drafting Convention No. 29. The Committee's original mandate largely reflected the efforts of the Western countries to restrict the inquiry to forms of coercion prevalent in the Eastern bloc countries. It was specifically called to examine the existence of "systems of forced or 'corrective' labour, which are employed as a means of political coercion or punishment for holding or expressing political views, and which are on such a scale as to constitute an important element in the economy of a given country".[528] The Committee's work was supported by a wealth of primary source material and testimonies provided by private pressure groups, such as the American-based International League for the Rights of Man and the originally French *Commission contre le régime*

---

526 Sandrine Kott, "The Forced Labor Issue between Human and Social Rights, 1947–1957", *Humanity* 3, no. 3 (2012): 321–335.

527 The American initiatives were initially not welcomed by the colonial powers, because they feared being exposed to criticism for some of their own practices. France, in particular, rejected the proposal until the very end. The State Department complained as late as 1951 that the French envoy in ECOSOC was "making every effort to undermine US position on forced labor". Quoted in Maul, *Human Rights, Development, and Decolonization*, 205.

528 Maul, "The ILO and the Struggle against Forced Labour", 485–486. On the work of the Mudaliar Committee, see also Kott, "The Forced Labor Issue", 326–327.

concentrationnaire, the latter representing the survivors of Nazi and Stalinist camps.[529] The Mudaliar Committee, however, partly ignored the restrictions and expanded its mandate beyond the limits that were politically *and* economically motivated. Instead, it looked also into cases where only one of the two criteria was fulfilled, which allowed for a more complete picture of the forced labour situation. In its final report in 1953, the Committee found systems of forced labour that were simultaneously politically and economically motivated in all Eastern bloc countries. Among the countries where politically or economically motivated systems existed, South Africa came out on top, but two colonial powers, Portugal and Belgium, were also listed.[530]

On the basis of the Mudaliar report, the Governing Body gave the go-ahead for a new Convention in 1954, and a new committee, this time without UN participation, was set up under Paul Ruegger, the Swiss president of the International Committee of the Red Cross. Its final report, delivered in 1955, basically confirmed the findings of its predecessor. The Ruegger report found indications that systems of forced labour with a political and/or economic background existed in thirteen states, including all ten socialist members of the ILO, the People's Republic of China,[531] the Portuguese Overseas Territories and the Union of South Africa.[532]

On the basis of the Ruegger report, the ILO drafted a new Convention aimed at bringing about the complete abolition of forced labour. The new standard banned forced labour as (a) a means of political coercion and political education and (b) a method of mobilizing and using labour for purposes of economic development. On the initiative of the Workers' group, the Convention was eventually extended to include a ban on forced and compulsory labour as a means of labour discipline, of punishment for participation in strikes, or as a means of racial, social, national, or religious discrimination. The latter point was also a reference to the discussions on a Convention against discrimination, which took place at the same time (see below).[533] The discussion was overshadowed by a last-minute attempt of the Soviet Union to turn the tables on the Western powers. The Eastern bloc countries signalled for the first time their support for a Convention, but, at

529 The International League for the Rights of Man was founded in 1942 by Roger Baldwin and European emigrants like the French physiologist Henri Laugier, who later became Assistant Secretary-General of the UN. Kott, "The Forced Labour Issue", 327.
530 Maul, "The ILO and the Struggle against Forced Labour", 486–487.
531 On this particular subject, a wealth of incriminating material was provided by the Nationalist government of Taiwan, which then occupied the seat of China in the ILO.
532 Maul, "The ILO and the Struggle against Forced Labour", 487, n. 46.
533 See, *Record of Proceedings*, Report VI: Forced Labour, International Labour Conference, 39th Session 1956 (Geneva: ILO, 1956), 721–726.

the same time, they invited the ILC delegates to make the debate on forced labour into a tribunal against colonialism. However, this manoeuvre, in the end, fell flat, as only a few countries were ready to let Moscow win a propaganda battle, only a few months after the Soviet crushing of the 1956 Hungarian uprising. At the same time, it did not go unnoticed that the position of the Western powers was weakened by the attitude of the US government, which had announced just before the start of the Conference that it would not ratify the future Convention. Although this position was in line with the general US attitude towards the ratification of ILO standards, few had imagined that the US government would actually go so far as to state up front its disavowal of a Convention that it had significantly helped to bring about in the first place.[534]

By the time the Abolition of Forced Labour Convention (No.105) was finally adopted, the global situation had started to change. With de-Stalinization, Soviet camps were less in the focus of the debate which started to centre more on other places, where forced labour for political and economic purposes existed. The Mudaliar Committee had found that the modern phenomenon of using forced labour as a means of economic development was a general trend independent of political systems.

Although the report was not primarily targeted at developing countries, it is easy to draw a line to the situation in many newly independent states. In Asia and Africa, in the early 1960s, voices grew in strength that wanted to make the acceptance of ILO Conventions conditional. They should not the superior goal of national development. In this context, the use of coercive measures for developmental purposes became one of the prime fields of controversy.

In a telling way, in 1962, a conflict emerged when the ILO published a report of its Committee of Experts on the Application of Conventions and Recommendations (CEACR) on the situation regarding the application of the Forced Labour Convention of 1957. The report contained an outright attack on a group of mainly sub-Saharan African countries, where, according to the report, some forms of forced and compulsory labour had survived the transition to independence.[535] Some governments had even set up new forms of coercive labour for purposes of development. The report singled out in particular so-called "youth labour ser-

---

534 Maul, "The ILO and the Struggle against Forced Labour", 487–489.

535 According to the Committee's report, forms of forced labour were to be found all over the world, in independent countries and colonial territories alike. Labour services under the auspices of the military were particularly frequent in West and East Africa. See ILO, *Record of Proceedings*, Report III (Part IV): Report of the Committee of Experts on the Application of Conventions and Recommendations, International Labour Conference, 46th Session 1962 (Geneva: ILO, 1962).

vices", where the "recruits" generally worked on public infrastructure projects.[536] The states concerned reacted with deep indignation to the findings. Part of the bitterness of the reactions could be explained by the fact that African countries now stood accused of a "classically colonial crime". This was further aggravated when Portugal, which itself had been accused of using wide-scale forced labour in its African territories in a complaint lodged in 1961, was largely acquitted of those accusations by an ILO Commission of Inquiry.[537]

In the debates, however, countries that had emerged from colonial rule also made a more general point. They emphasized the basic vocational training that youth services provided and stressed the absolute necessity of the work carried out under its auspices. In their defence, they argued that their present state of underdevelopment constituted an emergency situation, comparable to a state of war. This justified the mobilization of all forces for a common goal. As a government representative from the Ivory Coast put it, the developing countries were involved in a battle for economic independence that was just as serious as any military struggle. The young people prepared to shed blood for their country had to be given a chance "to defend the real independence of the country, by which I mean its economic independence".[538]

In this highly politically charged context, the debate on the African youth labour services lingered on until the beginning of the 1970s, when a new Recommendation on youth services and training was adopted, containing a compromise formula that settled the matter in a way that calmed down the debate.[539]

536 The model for these youth labour services, as the CEACR collectively termed them, was an institution that had been established at the beginning of the 1950s in Israel; indeed, the help of Israeli experts had been enlisted in setting up most of the labour services in Africa.

537 As an immediate reaction, Portugal filed a forced labour complaint only a few months later against Liberia, which was found guilty by an ILO Commission of Inquiry in 1962 of violating both Forced Labour Conventions it had ratified in 1931 and 1962. The Portuguese case is well covered by José Pedro Monteiro, " 'One of Those Too-Rare Examples': The International Labour Organization, the Colonial Question and Forced Labour (1961–1963)", in *Internationalism, Imperialism and the Formation of the Contemporary World. The Past of the Present*, ed. Miguel Bandeira Jerónimo and Pedro José Monteiro (Basingstoke: Palgrave Macmillan, 2018), 221–251.

538 Quoted from Maul, *Human Rights, Development and Decolonization*, 265.

539 Special Youth Schemes Recommendation, 1970 (No. 136).

Discrimination in Employment and Occupation

Decolonization and the Cold War also provided the background for a Convention to ban discrimination in employment and occupation (No. 111), adopted in 1958. Although other forms of discrimination (for instance, based on sex and religion) came also under scrutiny, the abolishment of unequal treatment because of race was at the centre of the discussions.[540] The dynamics of the debate differed significantly from those previously held on freedom of association and forced labour. Apart from the highly symbolic value that African and Asian countries attached to the issue, it initially provided the Eastern bloc countries also with an opportunity to disparage the West because of the domestic situation in some Western countries and in European colonial territories. It is noteworthy that the struggle against racial discrimination forced the international trade union movement to take a stand across the dividing lines of the Cold War. The ensuing debate ultimately led to the adoption of one of the most coherent and concise international human rights instruments, which became an important step leading a decade later to the UN's International Convention on the Elimination of all Forms of Racial Discrimination (1969).[541]

As with forced labour and freedom of association, the problem was by no means a new one. The unsuccessful Japanese attempts to establish racial equality as a founding principle of the League of Nations had been the first in a series of efforts to eradicate discrimination on grounds of ethnicity and skin colour in both national and international law. As was the case with forced labour during the Second World War, the atrocities committed in the name of racist ideologies fuelled the debates after 1945. To eradicate racism was also the declared aim of countries that had emerged from colonial rule. In the United Nations, newly independent India led an early attack in 1947 on the South African government's policies of racial discrimination.[542] The previous year, the General Assembly, at its very first session, had already passed a resolution condemning discrimination on racial and religious grounds and calling upon the new UN family to fight against it in all its forms. During the immediate post-war period, in particular, UNESCO spearheaded international efforts to counter the continuing legitimacy of racial discrimination and segregation.[543]

540 Sex and religion were also among the categories that the authors of the 1958 Convention would list among the areas in which discriminatory practices should be abolished.

541 Paul Gordon Lauren, *Power and Prejudice: The Politics and Diplomacy of Racial Discrimination* (Boulder, CO: Westview, 1988).

542 Ibid.

543 Amrith and Sluga, "New Histories of the United Nations", 257–260.

The voices calling for action against racial discrimination became louder at the ILCs after 1945, too, but the ILO was comparatively slow to react. The Declaration of Philadelphia had predictably been unambiguous about racial discrimination, speaking in its rights part about "all human beings, irrespective of race, creed or sex". The reasons why it took the ILO more than a decade to get a Convention on its way was due mainly to the politically controversial nature of the question itself. During much of the period in question, the countries that had to fear most from a debate on the issue were those which largely dominated the ILO.

This was clearly the case for the United States, where the African-American population in many Southern states still lived with discriminatory "Jim Crow" legislation. It had become a diplomatic embarrassment, which the Soviet Union early on sought to exploit in all international fora.[544] It was equally true for such countries as South Africa, which became the preferred target of anti-racist activities in the UN, in particular after 1948, when the election of the Nationalist Party marked the official onset of the apartheid era. The majority of the colonial powers was not eager to see their discriminatory policies scrutinized. Many of them still permitted the existence of "colour bars" that were anchored in law and administrative practice and denied particular groups access to education, certain professions, promotion, equal pay, or equal social services. In fact, a considerable number of countries had reason to be concerned about a debate on this issue. Immigration policies that excluded groups of people of colour were at the heart of government policies in Australia, New Zealand, and Canada, and indigenous populations were subject to discrimination here as well as in a range of Latin American countries.[545]

In the light of the resistance from many of the ILO's original members and supporters to whom the Organization owed its very survival during the post-war years, it remained wary of taking the initiative on the issue of discrimination. It was only in 1954, with the Soviet Union re-joining the Organization, that the discussion gained momentum. In the same year, the debates surrounding the Convention concerning the Abolition of Penal Sanctions for Breaches of Contract of Employment by Indigenous Workers (No. 104), eventually adopted in 1955, put a spotlight on existing forms of discrimination under colonial rule. The Penal Sanctions Convention was the last standard directed at indigenous workers in colonial territories. In essence, the debate centred on the question whether breaches of employment contracts by an employee (e.g. the refusal to work or unilateral termination), which, in most independent countries, were dealt with in

544 Anderson, *Eyes Off the Prize*.
545 Lauren, *Power and Prejudice*, 169–171.

the civil courts, could be punished by penal sanctions in the colonies. As early as 1939, the ILC had already adopted a Convention calling for the "progressive abolition" of such sanctions, and the Social Policy in Non-Metropolitan Territories Convention of 1947 had again called for putting an end to them. However, a report of the ILO's Expert Committee on Social Policy in Non-Metropolitan Territories, published in 1951 revealed that penal sanctions continued to be used excessively throughout colonial Africa by most colonial powers and by the South African apartheid regime.[546] In 1954, when the matter was brought up by the ILC, the Belgian government representative William Van Remoortel declared that penal sanctions were an indispensable part of the "educational work" provided by the colonial powers to "native populations". They were a means to help them to overcome their "primitive conditions" by "putting them to constructive work".[547] The ensuing debate showed that this attitude no longer represented the views of a majority of ILO members. The discussion quickly turned into a symbolic struggle against racial discrimination, and the original plan for a Recommendation was replaced by much more far-reaching proposals. In the end, a new Convention that aimed for the complete and immediate abolition of penal sanctions was adopted by an overwhelming majority of 169 votes to one (that of South Africa).[548]

This set the stage for further action. In the same year, ECOSOC called upon the ILO to examine in detail the various forms of discrimination that existed in "employment and occupation" and to investigate the possibility of introducing new means to tackle them. The pressure on the Western nations to give up their opposition to the ILO handling the issue was mounting, and eventually it was agreed that discrimination would be addressed by means of a new Convention. The discussions preceding the adoption of a new standard put the dynamics of the human rights discourse on full display. It also brought about coalitions that, at least to some extent, transcended the dividing lines of the Cold War.

A first draft Convention, which the Office had prepared for the ILC in 1957, mainly called for "educational" action to tackle racial discrimination at the workplace. It took account of the resistance of many Western states to anything that would commit them to taking concrete policy measures. This attitude, however, was soon overtaken by events. African and Asian Member states, increasingly numerous and by then energized by the Bandung Conference of African-Asian solidarity in 1955, had taken an uncompromising stand on the issue of racial dis-

---

546 In the Belgian Congo, for instance, there had been around 40,000 criminal convictions for breaches of employment contracts or breaches of discipline at work in 1949 alone, but penal sanctions were in use also in Portuguese and British territories in Africa.

547 Quoted in Maul, *Human Rights, Development and Decolonization,* 196.

548 Ibid., 192–196.

crimination.[549] As the debate proceeded, this new "non-aligned" force gained the support of not only the Socialist bloc but also the great majority of the Workers' group. For the ICFTU, the issue provided an opportunity to demonstrate its credibility to Workers' representatives from the global South.[550] In the drafting committee, the workers pushed for an inclusion of a set of political and legal steps to enforce the principles of the Convention. The final draft took account of most of the demands made by the advocates of a strong Convention.

When the ILC convened in 1958, the US government was fighting a losing battle. It drew angry criticism when it announced that it would abstain from voting the final Convention. The colonial powers were subject to a historical defeat on the issue. Government representatives of Czechoslovakia and the Workers' group separately proposed an amendment that would oblige the signatories to extend without reservations the provisions of the Convention to their colonial territories. In opposing the amendment, the colonial powers argued that it would be incompatible with Article 35 of the ILO Constitution, which covered the separate application of Conventions in non-metropolitan territories. Alas, this contention only served to put an even brighter spotlight on the untenable position of the colonial powers. By invoking the infamous "colonial clause", they were challenging the very human rights nature of the question. The outcome was a clear victory for both the Afro-Asian and the Eastern bloc delegations, which unanimously supported the amendment. The Convention prohibited discrimination "on the basis of race, colour, sex, religion, political opinion, national extraction or social origin" and was, according to its wording, fully applicable to the colonies.[551] It was indeed a triumph for the Afro-Asian countries. Unlike the issues of forced labour and freedom of association, the topic of racial discrimination gained even further impetus in the coming decades. Next to the right to self-determination, it was by far the most important human rights question for the growing group of newly independent countries.

If the movement did not lose momentum, it was also due to its finding a focus in the South African apartheid regime which, at the beginning of the 1960s, seemed determined to consolidate and even expand its racist policies. Events like the Sharpeville massacre in March 1960, when the police opened fire on a crowd of unarmed black demonstrators, and mass imprisonments of African opposition

549 On South-South solidarity and the Non-Aligned Movement as new forces in international politics, see Jürgen Dinkel, *The Non-Aligned Movement: Genesis, Organization and Politics (1927–1992)* (Leiden: Brill, 2019).

550 Anthony Carew, "Conflict within the ICFTU. Anti-Communism and Anti-Colonialism in the 1950s", *International Review of Social History* 41, no. 2 (1996): 147–181.

551 Discrimination (Employment and Occupation) Convention, 1958 (No. 111).

leaders further cemented the regime's status as the stronghold of institutionalized racism. The Afro-Asian countries used their growing numerical strength in the UN to condemn South Africa, and they called for excluding it from all international organizations, including the ILO.

The ILO became a special target, which is easily explained by the fact that a highly racialized labour regime was at the core of apartheid. This became even more obvious at the beginning of the 1960s with the creation of 'homelands', territories set aside for various black ethnic groups and primarily intended to provide South Africa's industry with cheap black labour. Even on earlier occasions, ILO bodies like the Mudaliar Committee on Forced Labour, the Committee on Freedom of Association, and the CEACR had repeatedly condemned the social practices of the apartheid regime.[552] In 1960, a new level of conflict was reached, when the Nigerian Labour Minister Joseph Modupe Johnson, as the spokesperson of a group of African and Asian countries, submitted a resolution to the ILC which called upon South Africa to voluntarily leave the ILO.[553] South Africa's Western allies, the United States and the United Kingdom among them, initially resisted this move for economic and also geopolitical reasons. In their perspective, the regime in Pretoria was an anti-communist bulwark in Southern Africa.

In 1963, the newly strengthened group of African nations resumed their fight to remove South Africa from the ILO. The ILO was put to a test of strength, when they tried, albeit unsuccessfully, to deny the South African Employers' delegate the right to speak. They then organized a walk-out, which was supported by the Eastern bloc and many Asian and Latin American delegations. This put the ILO in an extremely difficult position, and, for a moment, even the future of the Organization itself seemed to hang in the balance. As a Liberian government delegate stated, "We have a rat in the house", and he asked rhetorically: "Shall we burn the house in order to get rid of the rat"?[554] In an improvised and highly emotional speech, David Morse condemned racial discrimination as the "enemy of the civilized world community" and "a challenge to world peace", but he still appealed to the African nations to stick to the Constitution of the ILO and "fight this enemy

552 Summarized in Ghébali, *The International Labour Organization*, 83–84.
553 The resolution also called upon the Governing Body to advise South Africa to leave the Organization. See the Resolution Calling for the Withdrawal of the Union of South Africa from Membership of the ILO, on the Grounds of the "Apartheid" (Racial Discrimination) Policy Practised by the Union Government, in ILO, *Record of Proceedings*, Appendix IV: Report of the Resolutions Committee, International Labour Conference, 45th Session 1961 (Geneva: ILO, 1961), 696–697.
554 Maul, *Human Rights, Development and Decolonization*, 239.

[…] with methods which strengthen the foundations of world order".[555] He eventually succeeded in bringing all delegations back to the Conference.

South Africa could not be expelled, as the ILO Constitution had no provision for it. In the end, South Africa itself announced that it would put on hold its membership, thus effectively ending its cooperation with the Organization, undoubtedly in the hope that this would, to a certain extent, leave the country in peace. But soon afterwards, the ILO started to take additional steps against apartheid. In 1964, the ILC adopted a "Declaration Concerning the Policy of Apartheid of the Republic of South Africa", accompanied by a "Programme of Action for the Elimination of Apartheid in the Field of Labour". The Declaration denounced the South African government in human rights terms, declaring that its violation of ILO principles could no longer be considered an internal affair of the country. It also recommended amending the Constitution of the ILO to allow members that had been condemned by the United Nations for policies of racial discrimination to be barred from all ILO bodies except the Conference. When the Governing Body approved this plan by a large majority, South Africa declared that it was leaving the ILO. Pretoria's departure was greeted mostly with relief, and it gave the ILC an opportunity in the years to come to sharpen the anti-discriminatory profile of the ILO by regularly denouncing in the strongest possible terms South Africa's "degrading, criminal and inhuman policies". In 1965, the Director-General began to submit special annual reports to the Conference detailing whatever progress had been made in the struggle against apartheid. Over the years, the ILO continuously stepped up its anti-apartheid activities, including the set-up of a special technical assistance programme for liberation movements, which mainly benefitted the Southern African groups in exile. The reports on both, progress made and assistance to liberation movements, were discussed regularly by a special committee of the Conference. This continued until the first democratic elections were held in South Africa in 1994 and, as a result, the country returned to the ILO.[556]

The late 1960s offered the opportunity to draw a balance of the ILO's record as a human rights agency. In 1968, the Organization published a report on "The ILO and Human Rights", as part of the UN's commemorations of 20 years of the Universal Declaration and a contribution to the UN's International Year of Human Rights. In 1969, the ILO celebrated its 50th anniversary and the 25 years of the Declaration of Philadelphia, which had added the human rights dimension to its work. In the same year, the ILO was awarded the Nobel Peace Prize. On this occa-

---

555 ILO, *Record of Proceedings*, International Labour Conference, 47th Session 1963 (Geneva: ILO, 1963), 168–172.

556 On the ILO's participation in the international struggle against apartheid, see Rodgers et al., *The ILO and the Quest for Social Justice*, 50–57.

sion the Norwegian Nobel Committee paid tribute to the Organization's achievements. In his own Nobel lecture Morse referred explicitly to the ILO's work for "basic human rights".[557]

Despite these accolades, there was no way of concealing the fact that tensions lingered on during the ILO's "human rights decade". Earlier conflicts about tripartite representation had lost much of their vitriol, at least in Europe, where the Cold War had moved in the second half of the 1960s towards détente and a phase of East-West dialogue. But the discontent felt by some – and in particular by the trade unions of the United States – about the coexistence and accommodations that had been developing, was thinly veiled and would soon erupt again.

The contradictory views on how to achieve an adequate balance between political and social rights that had marked the post-colonial debates on freedom of association and forced labour continued to be played out within the ILO's meeting halls. In international fora, the "Third World", now acting as the Group of 77 (G77), as it was referred to since the first UNCTAD Conference in 1964, was increasingly weighing in on human rights debates.[558] The struggle for self-determination and the fight against racial discrimination were permanent rallying points under human rights premises for countries from the global South, with the continued practice of apartheid and Portugal's die-hard colonialism as prime targets. Additionally, from 1967 onwards, Israel's occupation of the West Bank and Gaza in the wake of the Six-Day War became another rallying point for human rights mobilization for countries of the global South.

At the same time, a discourse in which developing countries promoted the primacy of social and economic over political and civil rights was gaining ever more strength. At an international human rights conference convened by the UN in Teheran in 1968, the trend became very clear. Asian and African countries, which frequently pursued the modernization of their societies by authoritarian means, collided head-on with the Western conceptions of individual human rights.[559] The increasingly worsening economic situation of post-colonial states was marked by underdevelopment and structural disadvantages. According to these countries, this "state of emergency" warranted the subordination of individual freedoms to the common goal of development. While, in this rhetoric, social and economic rights took precedence over political rights, the promotion of

557 International Labour Organization, Nobel lecture, "ILO and the Social Infrastructure of Peace", Nobel Peace Prize appreciation, 1969.

558 Steven L. B. Jensen, *The Making of International Human Rights: The 1960s, Decolonization, and the Reconstruction of Global Values*, Human Rights in History (New York: Cambridge University Press, 2017).

559 Burke, *Decolonization and the Evolution of International Human Rights*, 92–111.

the former came with a re-interpretation of those rights concerning the question of who was entitled to them. Social and economic rights were now increasingly promoted as being first and foremost the rights of states, and not of individual citizens.[560] Within this paternalistic vision of modernization, those rights became part of the quest for a "right to development", to be attained and granted not through national legislation, but rather on the international level, in the fight for what would soon be called the New International Economic Order (NIEO).[561]

These discussions had a direct consequence for the human rights policy of the ILO. The claims of the developing countries could not be ignored, not only because of the shifting majorities within the ILC but also because frictions about the role of ILO standards for development ran right through the International Labour Office. In 1963, the Director-General had convened a working group to discuss the ways in which the ILO's forced labour standards could be made more compatible with the demands of economic and social development. The ensuing discussion quickly went beyond the field of forced labour and resulted in a much more general debate, which saw a "labour standards faction" within the Office set against a "development faction". While the former believed that the ILO, as the only development agency in the UN system concerned with social affairs, could not subordinate its standard work to economic considerations, the latter sought to make the implementation of standards dependant on economic factors such as productivity. They supported, therefore, a gradual implementation, even of human rights standards, where necessary. The underlying conflict was if authoritarian models of development could be acceptable as long as the ultimate goal remained a social one, or whether ILO standards were just one of the means rather than the goal of the development process.[562]

The conflicts resonated in David Morse's report to the ILC in 1968, in which he defended the integrated approach to development, where human rights standards were not only ideals to be reached but means to an end. Morse reaffirmed the universal value of the four basic principles of the Declaration of Philadelphia – freedom, equality, economic security, and dignity. At the same time, he acknowledged that, "while certain rights, such as the right to work, the right to conditions of work and life compatible with human dignity or the right or equality of

560 For alternative views, see Vijay Prashad, *The Darker Nations: A People's History of the Third World*, A New Press People's History (New York: New Press, 2007); Jensen, *The Making of International Human Rights*.

561 On the NIEO, see Dietrich, *Oil Revolution*.

562 During the 1970s and against the backdrop of the debate on forced labour, the Office produced various memoranda on the African Youth Labour Services. Maul, *Human Rights, Development and Decolonization*, 268–272.

opportunity are essentially goals to be reached, others like freedom of association or the right to collective bargaining are not only objectives but represent means of action that can render great service to the cause of all the rights and freedoms that concern us".[563] Twenty-five years after the Declaration of Philadelphia had first introduced them into the orbit of the ILO, some basic insecurity clearly still existed about whether, and to what degree, the ILO was actually "doing human rights".

563 ILO, *Record of Proceedings*, Report of the Director General (Part I): Thee I.L.O and Human Rights, International Labour Conference, 52nd Session 1968 (Geneva: ILO, 1968), 13.

Part IV On Shifting Ground: 1970–1998

When David Morse left the International Labour Organization (ILO) after 22 years as Director-General in May 1970, an era that had transformed the Organization ended. The two men who succeeded him in office, Wilfred Jenks and Francis Blanchard, were different in temperament and leadership style, but both, in their own specific ways, embodied continuity. When the Englishman Jenks became Director-General in 1970, he looked back on four decades of experience in the ILO. He had joined the Organization in 1931. From the 1940s onwards, he had occupied high-ranking posts, as Legal Adviser during the war period; as Assistant Director-General; and, finally, as Morse's Principal Deputy. From an early point in his career, he had been well connected to the broader field of international organizations. He had been part of the ILO delegation at the Bretton Woods Conference and present at the foundation of the United Nations. Joining the ILO as a student of the eminent law scholar Hersch Lauterpacht at Cambridge University, Jenks gained a reputation outside of the ILO through his many publications in the field of international law. He played a key part in drafting the Declaration of Philadelphia and worked on international commissions in the run-up to the UDHR of 1948. A staunch believer in the steady progress of international law, Jenks, more than any other leading official in the ILO's history, stood for the idea that the ILO's social mandate rested on a human rights foundation.[564] However, Jenks did not have an opportunity to make a lasting imprint as Director-General, since he died suddenly after only three years in office.[565]

Jenks' French successor, Francis Blanchard, came into office with nearly a quarter of a century of experience in the ILO. He had joined the Office in 1951, at the age of 35, and had moved up quickly to become Assistant Director-General in 1956 and Deputy Director–General in 1968. While Blanchard might have had less of Jenks' intellectual ambition and idealism, he, too, represented the ILO's traditions, but from a different angle. His perspective was shaped primarily by the technocratic orientation, which the ILO had taken under David Morse's directorship. Like Jenks a lawyer by education, Blanchard had worked for the International Refugee Organization (IRO) immediately after the Second World War before becoming a member of the ILO's Manpower Division, which he headed from 1956 onwards. He had been heavily involved in the Organization's transformation into

564 Jaci Leigh Eisenberg, "Jenks, Clarence Wilfred", in *IO Bio: Biographical Dictionary of Secretaries-General of International Organizations*, ed. Reinalda, Kille, and Eisenberg, www.ru.nl/fm/iobio; Jaci Leigh Eisenberg, "Butler, Harold Beresford", in ibid.

565 Blanchard had been Jenks' competitor for the post of Director-General in 1970, after Morse's departure. Jenks carried the day by only two votes, in the narrowest of competitions in the ILO's history of Director-General elections. But he had little time to prove his capacity to navigate the ILO through what would turn out to be a difficult period of transformation.

https://doi.org/10.1515/9783110650723-partIV

a development agency, and was responsible for technical cooperation and the ILO's field services.[566]

Blanchard's term lasted from 1973 to 1989, and it would turn out to be a period of many different, often countervailing tendencies for which the ILO served as a sounding board and a litmus test. It was a period in which the Cold War progressed into détente, disarmament, and some degree of cooperation. The Final Act of the Conference on Security and Cooperation in Europe, in Helsinki in July 1975, constituted the centrepiece of an apparently stabilized and pacified bipolar order in Europe. At the same time, for the ILO, the 1970s became a time of serious institutional turmoil, triggered by the brief withdrawal of the United States from the Organization from 1977 to 1981.

The period was rich with political changes in many parts of the world: While the Israeli-Palestinian conflict intensified, democratic governments were toppled in Latin America, where military dictatorships seized power in the 1970s. In other regions, democratic transition processes got under way, as in Southern Europe, where longstanding authoritarian regimes collapsed. In Eastern Europe, the demise of state socialism eventually culminated in the fall of the Berlin Wall and the dissolution of the Soviet Union between 1989 and 1991. Around the same time, the last remnants of colonial rule in Africa ended with the fall of the apartheid regime in South Africa. From Spain and Portugal to Chile and Argentina, from South Africa to Poland, the ILO was taking part in these transition processes. Against this background, new human rights discourses that accompanied these developments found their way into the ILO, where they put to the test some of the standards and mechanisms the Organization had established during its "human rights decade" in the immediate post–Second World War era.

Economically, the 1970s were a period of crisis and reorientation as well. Blanchard took over from Jenks in the context of the first oil crisis of 1973, which, in hindsight, was the beginning of the end of the "golden age" of post-war growth and prosperity. In the wake of the economic downturn and the rise of unemployment, the ILO felt the repercussions of the paradigm change in economic thinking. When Keynesianism lost its decades-long supremacy in economic discourse to supply-side economics, this change deeply affected the ILO. It eventually impacted also the ILO's development policies. While it seemed to be on top of the debate during the mid-1970s – with the World Employment Conference of 1976 launching the basic needs concept – it faced marginalization only a decade

566 There is no biography of Blanchard. For further information, see his memoirs: Francis Blanchard, *L'Organisation internationale du Travail: De la guerre froide à un nouvel ordre mondial* (Paris: Seuil, 2004). A concise account of Blanchard's time at the ILO is contained in Carol Riegelmann Lubin's unpublished manuscript, "Book on ILO", (2002), 165–201.

later, when structural adjustment was imposed by the international financial institutions to address the debt crises in which many developing countries found themselves.

Against this highly volatile backdrop, the ILO was still able to launch new initiatives with regard to one of its traditional field of activity, the improvement of conditions at work. The early 1970s saw the beginning of a debate on the "humanization of labour" which was institutionalized by the ILO in the International Programme for the Improvement of Working Conditions and Environment (PIACT) starting in 1976. It opened a space for new topics on the ILO's agenda, including environmental issues, and integrated for the first time the informal economy, in parallel to the discussions of the World Employment Programme. Its innovative set-up and its broad scope, which included industrialized and developing countries, gave new impulses to the debate on working conditions worldwide that went beyond the programme as such and the difficulties it faced at a time of serious financial constraints resulting from the US withdrawal from the ILO.

7 New Insecurities

New Questions of Universality – The US Withdrawal

In May 1970, after only three weeks in office, Jenks announced that he would appoint a representative of the Belorussian Soviet Republic, Pavel Astapenko, as Assistant Director-General. Thus, for the first time, a national from an Eastern bloc country became a member of the Director-General's senior management team. The main weight that this appointment carried was symbolic. While it seemed a long overdue step in the eyes of one of the two superpowers, the Soviet Union, it contributed to the withdrawal of the other world power, the United States, in 1977.

Although a key factor leading to the American exit, Jenks' decision to nominate a Soviet national for a top position in the ILO was part of a longer and more complex story. To a certain degree, it was the expression of a "normalization" of the participation of the Eastern bloc in the ILO at this time. On a technical level, such normalization had already taken place at an earlier stage.[567] In the fields of development collaboration and knowledge transfer, in particular, cooperation between the two ideological camps had become rather commonplace. On the political level, however, this process was somewhat slower. David Morse remained convinced that the underlying aim of the Soviet Union was to sabotage and ultimately split the United Nations system.[568] When the Soviet Union had first expressed its wish for a senior post in the ILO in 1960, he had accordingly refused to comply and successfully managed to fend off all further attempts until the end of his last term in office. With the spirit of détente increasingly shaping international politics in Europe in the 1970s, the situation began to ease. From then onwards, the Soviet demands played a secondary role compared to the growing estrangement of the major US labour union, the AFL-CIO,[569] which was opposed to the slightest concession to the Eastern bloc. This, more than anything else, complicated matters for Morse. Furthermore, this alienation was part of an even longer story of the often complicated relationship between the ILO and the United States during the Morse years.[570] It was witnessed by the increasingly hostile attitude the US Employers' representatives displayed from the 1950s on towards the Organization, which they denounced as socialist. This became also visible in the human rights discussions of the 1950s. For this very reason, Morse always placed

567 For a longer-term perspective, see Kott, "OIT, justice sociale et mondes communistes".
568 On Morse and the Cold War tensions of this era see, Maul, "David Morse", 2–3.
569 The AFL and its former rival CIO had merged in 1955 to form the AFL-CIO.
570 Maul, "David Morse", 3.

https://doi.org/10.1515/9783110650723-009

great emphasis on ILO-US relations and tried to strengthen them through the ILO's recruitment policy and its Washington office.[571] During the initial part of his tenure, he could count on the constant and reliable support of the AFL-CIO. This changed, however, in the early 1960s, when the AFL-CIO leadership under its president, George Meany, became increasingly critical of Morse. In the eyes of Meany, a staunch and uncompromising anti-communist, Morse was "soft on communism".[572] This impression, which was based on Morse's position in the bitter struggles over Soviet representation in the framework of the ILO's tripartite structure at the end of the 1950s, was confirmed by Morse's handling of the first Soviet demands for a high-ranking position in 1960. Morse had tied his refusal to comply with the Soviet request with the announcement that he would not stand again for re-election as Director-General in 1962. When Morse changed his mind shortly afterwards, the circumstances of his "retreat from retreat" were the last straw for the AFL-CIO, which had already committed its support to Morse's deputy, Jef Rens, and now felt sidelined.[573]

During the late 1960s, when many Western European trade unions displayed more openness for some degree of cooperation with the East, the AFL-CIO's position was hardening even more. In 1966, the US Workers' delegation walked out from the ILC after a Polish Government representative had been elected President of the Conference. In the same year, the Workers' group elected into the Governing Body for the first time the Soviet Workers' delegate.[574] A growing alienation between the AFL-CIO and the Europeans ultimately led to the American trade unions' withdrawal from the ICFTU in 1968.[575] Their increasing isolation, lack of faith in the ILO as an ally in the Cold War during the last years of Morse's mandate, and the failed expectation that Jenks, elected as Director-General in 1970, would bring the ILO "back on track" characterized the situation in which events unfolded. The United States perceived Jenk's nomination of Pavel Astapenko as a betrayal, in particular, since they had supported Jenks against Blanchard for the very reason that they believed him to be less likely to give in to Soviet pressure.[576]

---

571 Eisenberg, "Butler, Harold Beresford". On the US-ILO relationship in the post-war era, particularly for the early period, see Jensen, "US New Deal Policy Experts and the ILO, 1948–1954". On labour standards, see Lorenz, *Defining Global Justice*.

572 See Maul, "David Morse".

573 Morse took the decision to stay on after an intervention from the administration of President John F. Kennedy and Secretary of Labor Arthur Goldberg; DAMP.

574 Carew, *American Labour's Cold War Abroad*, 268–269, n. 104.

575 Carew, "Conflict within the ICFTU". The AFL-CIO returned to the ICFTU in 1982, after Meany's death.

576 Francis Maupain, "A Former Legal Adviser as ILO Executive Head: The 'Immanent Force of Law', Its Role and Vicissitudes in the Context of a Changing International System", unpublished article.

Not only the Americans were taken by surprise by Astapenko's nomination, and Jenks' motives remain to some degree unclear. What is certain – according to people close to Jenks at the time – is that his almost religious belief in the mission of international organizations and in "due process" would have left him with no doubt that he was perfectly entitled to appoint whomever he wished to appoint to senior positions in the ILO. He also might have underestimated the political repercussions and might have lacked – as many claimed – the diplomatic skills necessary to handle this highly delicate issue. But whatever motivated Jenks, he was not the only one who thought that the Eastern bloc countries were underrepresented in senior positions at the ILO, and their claims for representation and inclusion were to some extent justified.[577]

During the late 1960s, some Western European governments had already tried to accommodate Soviet claims in this regard. During the ensuing years, more attempts would follow.[578] The changing attitudes had worried many in the United States who felt that their country might be losing ground on the international level. The lost war in Vietnam and the inglorious end of the Nixon administration contributed to a growing perception that the American ability to exert control or, seen from a more critical perspective, some kind of "hegemony"[579] over international organizations was eroding, which, in turn, translated into increasing discontent. In this situation, it took little to tip the balance in favour of those who argued for an American exit from international agencies. In hindsight, this move has to be interpreted less as a sign of strength than an expression of a growing feeling of weakness and isolation.

The ultimate pretext to leave the ILO, however, came from a different side. For years, the US government had taken issue with what it perceived as the growing politicization of the ILO (and even more so of other institutions like UNESCO), carried out by a more and more assertive group of countries from the global South.[580] At the centre of their concerns was the conflict over the Israeli occupation of the West Bank, East Jerusalem, and the Gaza Strip after the 1967 Arab-Israeli war. Arab states supported by Eastern bloc countries and a majority of the

---

577 Eisenberg, "Jenks, Clarence Wilfred".

578 In 1973, a Soviet national was designated for the chairmanship of the Governing Body for the first time. Both the AFL-CIO and the American government protested. Instead, with the support of the majority of both workers and employers but against the vote of most West European governments, they secured the election of a Mexican government representative. Lubin, "Book on ILO", 158.

579 Cox, "Labor and Hegemony".

580 Mark F. Imber, *The USA, ILO, UNESCO and IAEA: Politicization and Withdrawal in the Specialized Agencies* (New York: St. Martin's Press, 1989).

G77 increasingly used their majority in international organizations to put Israel in the dock on every possible occasion. In 1973, a resolution that condemned Israel for its treatment of Arab workers in the occupied territories failed by only a slim margin. Seeking to secure due process – and also to send a political signal to Washington – Jenks criticized the draft resolution of the Arab states for demanding the condemnation of Israel even before an official ILO inquiry had taken place on the ground.[581]

The following year, the Arab countries were more successful. Against the nearly unanimous resistance of Western governments, Employers and a good part of the Workers' group, a resolution condemning the "Policy of Discrimination, Racism and Violation of Trade Union Freedoms and Rights Practised by the Israeli Authorities in Palestine and the other occupied Arab territories" was adopted by the ILC.[582] In 1975, when the Palestinian Liberation Organization (PLO) achieved observer status in the ILO, some Western delegations, including those of the United States and West Germany left the conference hall in protest. Immediately after the end of the 1975 ILC, the AFL-CIO asked the US government to announce its intention to withdraw from ILO membership. In November 1975, Secretary of State Henry Kissinger sent a letter to the ILO in which he proclaimed the US intention to withdraw within the regular two-years-time period. He gave four reasons for this step: (1) The erosion of the tripartite principle and the presence of a growing bloc of Workers' and Employers' delegates "wholly under the domination of government"; (2) the "appallingly selective concern" in the pursuance of human rights in the ILO; (3) the "utter disregard" which the ILC had repeatedly shown for "due process" when it came to the passing of resolutions against Israel without a prior inquiry having taken place; and (4) undue politicization of the ILO inasmuch as it had become "increasingly and excessively involved in political issues which are quite beyond the competent mandate of the Organization". There was a glimmer of hope in the letter from the ILO's point of view, however, since it contained an announcement to work out proposals for changes in the Organization's conduct, which would allow the United States to stay on as a member.[583]

The following two years passed with intense lobbying of the ILO and the major Western powers to keep the United States within the Organization. Representa-

581 Maupain, "A Former Legal Adviser as ILO Executive Head".

582 ILO, *Record of Proceedings*, International Labour Conference, 59th Session 1974 (Geneva: ILO, 1975), 808.

583 Imber, *The USA, ILO, UNESCO and IAEA*. Yves Beigbeder, "The United States' Withdrawal from the International Labor Organization", *Relations industrielles/Industrial Relations* 34, no. 2 (1979): 223–240 (Kissinger notice summarized on pp. 228–229).

tives of the European Community, the IOE, and the ICFTU all tried to convince the Americans that their voice and influence was needed in order to tackle the problems listed in Kissinger's notice. Even the Pope sought to convince Meany (a devout Catholic) and the incoming President, Jimmy Carter.[584] In the end, none of these efforts paid off. On 1 November 1977, Carter announced that, in light of the fact that the course corrections requested by the United States had not been implemented in sufficient measure, US membership in the ILO would be terminated. Still Carter and his Secretary of Labour, Ray Marshall, who were personally sceptical about the step taken, left a door open by stating that the United States remained "ready to return whenever the ILO is again true to its proper principles and procedures".[585]

It is hard to see how the ILO could have satisfied the American demands to a degree that would have allowed the United States to stay. All three of the American core demands posed dilemmas that could hardly be solved, as they were part of a broader debate between widely diverging and yet legitimate interests. The questions of freedom of association and forced labour were difficult to tackle in the way suggested by the Americans without endangering the hard-won balance between universalism (of membership) and adherence to ILO principles – all the more so as these principles had come under even greater pressure in the course of decolonization. The same was true for the "selectiveness" in the application of human rights principles and the accusations of growing politicization, since much of it simply reflected the shifting balances and priorities within the ILO's growing and changing membership.

At least with regard to Occupied Palestinian Territory (OPT), Director-General Blanchard succeeded in defusing the political tensions in the ILC from 1975 onwards. He established a mechanism according to which missions would be sent regularly to the occupied territories, and their findings became a fixed part of the Director-General's annual report to the Conference. Another element of the mechanism was to provide technical assistance to the OPT.[586] Blanchard undertook in 1979 a two week's mission to Syria, Jordan, Iraq, Qatar, and Kuwait. He succeeded in convincing the representatives of governments, trade unions, and employers in these countries to avoid escalation of the issue and thus help preserve the interest of the ILO in the resumption of US membership by accepting the report mechanism, which put the spotlight on the issue during the ILCs but

584 This followed a tradition; Morse had asked Pope John XXIII to convince Meany to accept Soviet representation.

585 Quoted in Lubin, "Book on ILO", 170.

586 See the account of former Assistant Director-General responsible for the Arab states (with a preface by Guy Ryder), Shukri Z. Al-Dajani, *Encounters with Fate and Destiny: A Life in International Politics* (London: I.B. Tauris, 2018).

had very little impact on the ground.[587] From another perspective, the US argument that the ILO was providing a forum mainly for human rights accusations against Western allies lost in strength in the course of the 1970s. Growing human rights activism in the wake of the Conference on Security and Co-operation in Europe (CSCE) from the mid-1970 onwards gave new grounds also in the ILO for placing a spotlight on human rights violations in the East.

The years of the United States' factual absence (1977–1981) would put the ILO to a stress test. As early as 1970, as a reaction to the nomination of a Soviet Assistant Director-General, the United States Congress decided to withhold the American contributions to the ILO budget, a measure that was renewed throughout each of the following years. The consequences for the ILO were severe: even though many of the ILO's programmes, like the WEP, were funded from external sources, the ILO lost around 25% of its regular budget. It forced Blanchard to make deep cuts with regard to both operational activities and staff. The political consequences in contrast were less dramatic. In the American absence, the leadership within the Western camp was shared among the United Kingdom, Canada, the Nordic countries, and others, which set up the Industrialized Market Economy Countries Group (IMEC) for policy coordination. Meanwhile, a rapprochement between the ILO and the United States got under way almost immediately after the American withdrawal. As early as 1978, the State Department commissioned a report on possible future relationships between the ILO and the United States, which read like a straight recommendation for re-entry. The bottom line was that the United States was far better off inside the Organization, where it was able to make its influence felt. The report also attested to the ILO's efforts made to accommodate the American demands. In early 1980, President Carter issued a statement concluding that:

> [A] majority of ILO members – governments, workers, and employers – have successfully joined together to return the ILO to its original purposes. Through their efforts, steps have been taken to strengthen the independence of employer and worker delegates, undertake investigation of human rights violations in a number of countries, including the Soviet Union, reinforce the principle of due process, and generally reduce the level of politicization in the ILO.[588]

Viewed from a bird eye's view, the American absence created a paradox, inasmuch as it compromised the ILO's universality at the very moment when this

587 Ibid.

588 "International Labor Organization: Statement on the U.S. Decision to Rejoin the Organization, February 13, 1980", *Public Papers of the Presidents of the United States: Jimmy Carter, 1980–81*, 3 Books (Washington, DC: U.S. Government Printing Office, 1981–1982), Book 1, 306.

universalism made steady progress. In the 1970s, the ILO admitted another group of new members, such as the former Portuguese colonies that gained independence after 1974 and Bangladesh, which split from Pakistan in 1973. The long conflict in Rhodesia ended with the membership of an independent Zimbabwe in 1980. Most importantly, the People's Republic of China was recognized as the official representative of China, replacing Taiwan. The Governing Body's decision was based on that of the United Nations in 1971 to restore the rights of the People's Republic to the seat of China. But China had not been approached directly by the ILO and was not familiar with the Organization. As a result, its status remained non-active for several years. Blanchard visited China three times in the early eighties, and, in 1983, after the first signs of opening under the leadership of Deng Xiaoping, China sent a full ILC delegation for the first time.[589] It was only in 1986–87, that China actually began to play a more assertive role in the ILO.[590]

From Spain to South Africa: The ILO and the New Human Rights Activism

In parallel to the political struggles surrounding the temporary American exit, the ILO became a medium of the new human rights universalism for which the 1970s have been described as the "breakthrough" decade.[591] It was only then, the argument goes, that human rights really took off as a moral language in international politics and a "last utopia"[592] that allowed an ideologically disillusioned left to challenge their own governments and political elites while transcending the Cold War framework. The grassroots human rights activism of Amnesty International (founded in 1961) and other groups was directed primarily at authoritarian regimes that could be regarded as allies of the West. Their focus shifted from the dictatorships in Spain, Portugal, and Greece to the military juntas in Latin America[593] and eventually to South Africa, where the consolidation of the white

589 As a gesture of good will, based on a request of the Governing Body, the ILO cancelled China's membership debts that had accrued since 1971. On China's entry, see; Ghébali, *The International Labour Organisation*, 116–125.

590 See Ann Kent, *Beyond Compliance: China, International Organizations, and Global Security* (Palo Alto, CA: Stanford University Press, 2007), 186–189.

591 Jan Eckel and Samuel Moyn, *The Breakthrough: Human Rights in the 1970s*, Pennsylvania Studies in Human Rights (Philadelphia, PA: University of Pennsylvania Press, 2014).

592 Samuel Moyn, *The Last Utopia: Human Rights in History* (Cambridge, MA: The Belknap Press of Harvard University Press, 2010).

593 Patrick William Kelly, *Sovereign Emergencies: Latin America and the Making of Global Human Rights Politics*, Human Rights in History (Cambridge: Cambridge University Press, 2018).

apartheid regime had galvanized a growing transnational campaign in Western countries.[594] At the same time, an increasing number of governments from the Scandinavian countries, the Netherlands, Canada and notably the US administration under Jimmy Carter (1977–1981) declared human rights to be part of their foreign policy.[595]

In the mid-1970s, the new human rights discourse spilled over to the Eastern bloc. A first entry was provided by the CSCE, a meeting of 35 European countries from the East and the West as well as the United States and Canada. It took place in the Finnish capital of Helsinki in the summer of 1975. Promoted as a step to reduce Cold War tensions, the final document, known as the Helsinki Final Act, contained principles that were intended to guarantee peaceful co-existence between the two power blocs in Europe. Although the Conference was first seen primarily as a diplomatic success for the Soviet Union, the provisions under point VII on "respect for human rights and fundamental freedoms", mainly ignored by the public at the time, would cause unexpected consequences. The monitoring mechanism spurred by the Helsinki accords established a network of national committees, loosely united across the East-West divide in an international federation. The Helsinki process encouraged the creation of a new Western human rights organization – Human Rights Watch – which started to attack the communist countries for human rights violations with regard to the provisions of the Final Act. Even more importantly, it provided the basis for the foundation of Helsinki groups in Moscow and other Eastern European countries, such as the Czechoslovak Charter 77 movement. These groups, for their part, started to hold their governments accountable for their commitments and used human rights as an instrument to challenge Communist party rule.[596]

All of these discussions invariably found their way into the ILO's meeting halls, where they took on specific forms. Due to the framework provided by the ILO's tripartite structure and the monitoring mechanisms established for the observance of international labour standards, in particular with regard to freedom of association, these debates focused mainly on trade union rights. This was the case for

594 Håkan Thörn, *Anti-Apartheid and the Emergence of a Global Civil Society* (Basingstoke: Palgrave Macmillan, 2006).

595 On human rights policies in Scandinavia, see Thorsten Borring Olesen, Helge O. Pharo, and Kristian Paaskesen, *Saints and Sinners: Official Development Aid and Its Dynamics in a Historical and Comparative Perspective*, Issues in Contemporary History (Oslo: Akademika Publishing, 2013).

596 Daniel C. Thomas, *The Helsinki Effect: International Norms, Human Rights, and the Demise of Communism* (Princeton, N.J.: Princeton University Press, 2001); Sarah B. Snyder, *Human Rights Activism and the End of the Cold War: A Transnational History of the Helsinki Network*, Human Rights in History (New York: Cambridge University Press, 2011).

Southern Europe and Latin America, and it shaped the ILO's involvement with Poland in the 1980s. While the ILO's established mechanisms, especially concerning the monitoring of freedom of association, and provided unique opportunities to effectively pursue labour rights violations, this approach also came with certain limitations, as the Latin American situation would demonstrate.

One of the regions in which the new turn towards human rights activism influenced the ILO's attitude was Southern Europe, and in particular Spain. For a short period after the war, the regime of General Francisco Franco, which ruled the country from the end of the Civil War in 1939 until the *Caudillo's* death in 1975, had been an international outcast. The suppression of trade union rights which drove the biggest independent trade union of the country, the *Unión General de Trabajadores* (UGT) into exile for 36 years, was a core feature of the regime. Even after Spain's readmission to the United Nations and the ILO in 1955 (against the background of the Cold War, in which Spain became part of the Western alliance), relations remained distant. While the Office under David Morse initiated a process of rapprochement during the 1960s, the international trade union movement rallied with an increasingly vocal human rights campaign against the dictatorship. At the Conference, in the Governing Body, and particularly through the Committee on Freedom of Association (CFA), the Workers' representatives did not tire attacking the Franco regime for its suppression of trade union rights.[597]

Around the end of the decade, the debate intensified. After passing new trade union laws in 1967, which confirmed the corporatist character of labour relations, the regime intensified its repression against any kind of trade union activism outside the narrowly defined boundaries of the law. As a result, numerous complaints were filed with the ILO against the Spanish government for the violation of the principle of freedom of association (it had not ratified at the time the corresponding Conventions), and the Governing Body decided in 1967 to appoint a study group to investigate the labour and trade union situation in Spain. Within the Organization, serious differences of opinion existed about how to treat the Spanish dictatorship. Morse's first visit to Spain in 1965 had caused a fierce altercation with the Workers' group in the Governing Body, since Morse had addressed the country as "a great nation among the members of the free world".[598] In 1969, the Spanish government declared a state of emergency and suspended basic

597 ILO, Interview with Manuel Simon, ILO Century Project, unpublished transcript, Geneva, 2014.

598 See Jean-Michel Servais, *International Labour Organization (ILO)* (Alphen aan den Rijn: Kluwer Law International, 2005), 30; Sébastian Farré, "Trois experts, une visite, un rapport. L'Organisation international du travail et la liberté syndicale en Espagne franquiste", in *L'Organisation internationale du travail*, ed. Lespinet-Moret and Viet, 121–130.

individual freedoms. Both the ILO and the ICFTU condemned this action in no uncertain terms. Notwithstanding the ICFTU's doubt about the effectiveness of the study group previously appointed by the Governing Body, the group decided to visit Spain for two weeks. It was composed of high-ranking experts, among them Paul Ruegger of Switzerland, a member of the Permanent Court of Arbitration at The Hague and of the ILO's CEACR, also the main author of an ILO report on forced labour in the mid-1950s; another expert was P.P. Spinelli of Italy, the former director of the UN Office in Geneva. The group talked to over 100 people, including ministers, judicial and church authorities, members of the provincial councils of workers and employers, and academics. It conferred with representatives of management and workers' councils and visited industrial and agricultural enterprises as well as social services. It also asked to talk to 12 imprisoned unionists. The report of the study group stated that, in Spain, trade union rights where not respected and trade unionists were imprisoned and tortured. It concluded that the social uprisings, which had led the government to proclaim the state of emergency and allowed trade union repression, had their origins in the universities.[599] The Spanish government published a distorted version of the report and drafted a trade union bill, ignoring the ILO's criticism and declaring independent trade unions and strikes illegal. Thereafter, the situation reached a stalemate, which continued until Franco's death and the subsequent demise of the dictatorship in 1975. In the meantime, the international trade union movement stepped up its campaign and used the CFA and other fora extensively to attack the Spanish government. In the following years Spanish workers' protest at home and from trade unionists in exile grew as well, encouraged by the ILO's condemnation of government policies, and especially of the imprisonment of trade unionists, which further undermined the legitimacy of the Franco regime.[600]

Somewhat similar processes took place in Portugal, where the "Carnation Revolution" of 1974 ended more than 60 years of authoritarian rule, and in Greece, which had been ruled by a junta of colonels from 1967 to 1974. Both countries were repeatedly targeted by the CFA for their violation of trade union rights, although with limited impact on actual policies. In all these cases – and in the absence of means that would have forced the respective regimes to make any concessions – the role of the ILO was restricted to lending moral support and serving as an outside reference to trade unionists, especially those in exile, and other opposition groups. The meaning those groups attached to the ILO's role is

---

599 Pilar Ortuño Anaya, *European Socialists and Spain: The Transition to Democracy, 1959–77* (Basingstoke: Palgrave Macmillan, 2002).
600 Ibid., 61–69.

highlighted, for instance, by the fact that the Spanish transition government ratified both the Freedom of Association Convention and the Right to Organize and Collective Bargaining Convention in 1977.[601]

While, in Southern Europe, the remnants of authoritarian rule fell around the middle of the 1970s, Latin America was moving in the opposite direction. In Chile, a military coup against the government of the Socialist president Salvador Allende in 1973 was accompanied by a massive repression of the Chilean labour movement. A state of emergency was declared almost immediately, social rights were curtailed, most trade unions were immediately outlawed, and their members were persecuted. Together with other groups, labelled indiscriminately as "Marxist-Leninists", many trade unionists were tortured and killed. Others were tried by military courts or driven into exile. News about the atrocities committed against anyone suspected to be an opponent of the new regime under General Augusto Pinochet generated an international outcry. A broad coalition of human rights activists in the West rallied against the Chilean dictatorship.[602]

Here, too, the ILO's focus was from the beginning on the violations of freedom of association, which led to a series of complaints on which the CFA could act. Chile had not ratified Conventions Nos. 87 and 98 at the time. On the basis of two reports submitted to the Governing Body in 1974, the ILO decided to appoint a Fact-Finding and Conciliation Commission. It visited Chile in November–December 1974 and was the only group of international observers formally allowed into the country during the dictatorship. In its report, the Commission squarely denounced the violations of human rights in general, and trade union rights in particular, and condemned the incarceration, torture, and murder of trade unionists. It concluded that the Pinochet regime had violated the right of freedom of association and issued a number of recommendations that focused primarily on the restoration of civil and political rights.[603]

The regime responded with a mix of denial and dilatory statements. It made some smaller concessions but extended the state of emergency, and otherwise remained largely indifferent to the constant appeals and accusations. In the course of the 1970s, in the face of growing international isolation, the Pinochet Regime relaxed some of its oppressive measures and implemented new labour

---

601 See the interviews with the Spanish trade unionists Nicolas Redondo Urbieta and Marcelino Camacho in N.N., "Voices for Freedom of Association", *Labour Education* 112, no. 3 (1998): 37–41.
602 Kim Christiaens, Idesbald Goddeeris, and Magaly Rodríguez García, *European Solidarity with Chile, 1970s–1980s* (Frankfurt am Main: Campus, 2014).
603 César F. Rosado Marzán, "The Limits of Human Rights for Labour Rights. A Retrospective Look at the Case of Chile", in *The ILO from Geneva to the Pacific Rim*, ed. Jensen and Lichtenstein, 206–230.

legislation that – while reinstalling some space for legal trade union activities – still fell short of the ILO's demands. In 1979, the dictatorship eased some of its most radical measures and lifted the ban on collective bargaining, but only at the enterprise level. Designed in accordance with a radical free market reform project which was implemented by Pinochet´s neoliberal economic advisors, his so-called "Chicago boys", labour rights were limited to the individual rights of the worker. The reform was stripped of any notion of collective rights, and it put very strict limits on the right to strike. The reforms helped the regime, however, to reduce international pressure by appeasing some of the critics from the Carter administration and the American labour movement, which were satisfied by the restoration of some basic individual human freedoms. Most of these limited reforms survived the return to democracy in 1990, and they have been repeatedly criticized by the ILO. According to a 2009 decision of the CFA, they still violated Conventions No. 87 and 98, which Chile had finally ratified in 1999.[604]

In 1976, the discussion extended to neighbouring Argentina, where a military junta had overthrown the government of Isabel Peron. As in Chile, from day one the new regime was bent on destroying the workers' movement, arguably the strongest and best organized on the continent and a stronghold of Peronism. The biggest Argentinian trade union, the *Confederación General del Trabajo* (CGT), had joined the ICFTU in 1975. The military regime massively curbed trade union rights and, similar to the Chilean case, thousands of trade unionists, together with other targeted groups (including refugees from neighbouring countries and Catholic priests), were tortured, murdered or "disappeared". As early as 1976, the CFA condemned the regime and demanded a return to normality and adherence to ILO standards. Throughout the coming years, the ICFTU, WFTU, and the World Confederation of Labour (WCL)[605] all helped to relentlessly keep up the pressure on the regime within the ILO. They joined forces with a broad spectrum of national, especially Western European, and international human rights organizations, such as Amnesty International, which made the violation of human rights under the Chilean and Argentine military dictatorships a major focus of their activities.[606]

---

604 Wehrli, "ILO and Latin America", 26.

605 The World Confederation of Labour (WCL) was the successor of the International Federation of Christian Trade Unions (IFCTU), which from the 1950s onwards, also organized Buddhist and Muslim workers on Asia and Africa, and which propagated a third way between capitalism and communism.

606 David Weissbrodt and Maria Luisa Bartolomei, "The Effectiveness of International Human Rights Pressures: The Case of Argentina, 1976–1983", *Minnesota Law Review* 75 (1991): 1009–1035.

While there were striking similarities between the two countries, the Argentine case differed from the Chilean in a couple of aspects. In contrast to the Pinochet regime, the junta in Buenos Aires was eager to show its willingness to cooperate with international organizations. It denied violating Conventions No. 87 and 98, which Argentina had ratified in 1960 and 1956, respectively, received ILO missions of inquiry openly and tried to display a pluralistic face to the visitors. At the same time, it kept a strong presence in Geneva and, with a few exceptions, sent complete delegations to the ILC. This strategy, however, was not accompanied by any substantive changes – neither with regard to the restoration of trade union freedoms, nor concerning the general human rights situation. While the regime claimed that the restrictions were temporary and denied the disappearances of trade unionists, both continued essentially uncompromised.[607]

The situation in the ILO was somewhat ambiguous: while the CFA regularly condemned the situation in Argentina in harsh terms, the missions of enquiry sent to the country came sometimes close to whitewashing the practices of the regime. A mission led by Antonio Malintoppi, an Italian professor of law and personal envoy of Director-General Blanchard, in August 1978 emphasized in its report the cooperation of the authorities. From this report, the Governing Body concluded that the situation was evolving positively. In 1979, a long-promised new law regulating trade union activities was eventually passed. It still contained various loopholes for violations of freedom of association, which led to new complaints to the CFA. In its report of March 1980, the Committee reiterated most of the criticism made by the international trade union federations and Argentinian workers' organizations. A second mission by Malintoppi in December 1980 and the release of several trade union leaders prompted the delegation once again to highlight in its report the progress made towards the normalization of labour relations. But as late as May–June 1983, while the military regime was reeling after its defeat in the Falkland/Malvinas War in early 1982, the CFA was still calling for the harmonization of trade union legislation with ILO standards and the release of imprisoned trade union leaders.[608]

The ILO's record with regard to the Latin American dictatorships (which also included those in Brazil and Uruguay, which drew less attention) was somewhat mixed. The Organization was acting as a sounding board for human rights accusations against the military regimes and remained one of the very few international forums open to dissident voices. Its capacity to influence policy on the ground,

607 Victoria Basualdo, "The ILO and the Argentine Dictatorship (1976–1983)", in *ILO Histories*, ed. Van Daele et al., 401–422.
608 Ibid.

however, remained strictly limited. While the Chilean and Argentine cases differed with regard to the attitudes which the respective regimes showed towards the international community, the outcomes in terms of respect for ILO standards and basic human rights were essentially the same. It has even been argued that the Argentine junta's decision to cooperate with the ILO, without making any substantive concessions, paid out for the regime inasmuch as it added a degree of legitimacy to its repressive policies.[609] The Chilean case, in turn, demonstrated some of the weaknesses in the ILO's human rights activism in a more general sense. It showed, in particular, that labour rights and human rights "do not always sit comfortably next to each other".[610] When the Chilean regime stopped its worst human rights abuses, the international pressure by the human rights community diminished significantly. While the ILO continued to admonish the violation of freedom of association and the right to collective bargaining as a precondition for the full realization of workers' rights, the attention of international human rights organizations shifted to other places. It was a pattern that was to repeat itself on future occasions.

The ILO, nevertheless, was able to offer help in the transition process after the demise of the respective regimes. When the Argentine junta eventually fell in 1983, the ILO instantly offered its help to the government of Raul Alfonsin to reinstall democratic labour legislation.[611] In Chile, the ILO played a part through technical assistance in the drafting of a new Labour Code in 2001, which would remove some of the most severe restrictions of the Pinochet years.

While the CSCE process helped to turn human rights into a new language of dissidence in many countries of the Eastern bloc, it was only in Poland that it grew into a mass movement. And in contrast to other countries, the ILO would become heavily involved because of another peculiarity of the Polish situation: it was only here that the fight for political freedoms would become closely tied to the struggle for labour rights.[612]

---

609 Basualdo, "The ILO and the Argentine Dictatorship (1976–1983)".

610 Rosado Marzán, "The Limits of Human Rights for Labour Rights", 225.

611 The ILO dispatched a technical mission advising the government in May 1984, and, in 1985, Blanchard paid a visit to the country. Victoria Basualdo, however, is rather critical of the role of the ILO technical mission in the preparation of post-junta labour legislation, because, in her view, it supported those who had occupied positions of power during the military rule against interference by the state. Victoria Basualdo, "La OIT entre la dictadura y la democracia en la Argentina: aportes sobre el papel de organizaciones internacionales en la reconfiguración de las relaciones laborales en la primera mitad de los años 80", *Anuario del Instituto de Historia Argentina* 17, no. 1 (2017): 1–18.

612 Idesbald Goddeeris, "The Limits of Lobbying: ILO and Solidarnosc", in *ILO Histories*, ed. Van Daele et al., 423–442.

In the summer of 1980, strikes broke out in several sea ports of the Baltic Sea, most prominently at the Lenin shipyards of Gdansk. After weeks of turmoil, the Polish government signed an agreement that granted workers the right to form independent unions. As a result, *Solidarnosc* (Solidarity) was born, which soon grew into a large movement for labour and civil rights with a membership of up to ten million people, more than one third of Poland's working-age population. With tensions steadily growing, the communist government under General Wojciech Jaruzelski eventually declared martial law in December 1981 and started to crack down on *Solidarnosc*. The trade union was declared illegal and several thousand of its members, including the leadership around Lech Wałęsa, were arrested and detained. In reaction to the events, an international alliance, including the Catholic Church and its Polish Pope John Paul II, Western governments, and civil society groups came out in support of *Solidarnosc*.

Against this background, the ILO became a major outlet for *Solidarnosc's* struggle for recognition. The ICFTU, the European Trade Union Confederation (ETUC), and the WCL, as *Solidarnosc's* main allies on the international scene, made sure that the topic would not be put to rest. They helped the exiled leaders to set up an office to coordinate their international efforts, and their insistence made sure, that the topic remained on the international agenda, even when over time the attention of some of the groups supporting *Solidarnosc* began to shift away from Poland. The ILO itself, from the late 1970s onwards, had examined – and sent delegations to investigate – complaints filed by the ICFTU and the WCL regarding the violation of freedom of association and the corresponding ILO Conventions, both of which Poland had ratified in 1957.

With the banning of *Solidarnosc*, the ILO actively came out in support of the movement, and Blanchard personally travelled to Poland to convince the government to let Lech Wałęsa take part in the 1981 ILC as a Polish Worker's representative. In January 1982, the ICFTU handed over to the ILO a list of almost 700 union leaders imprisoned in Poland. The CFA then examined the situation, and the Governing Body, based on the CFA's report, openly condemned the Polish government, sent a fact-finding mission to Poland, and demanded the liberation of imprisoned *Solidarnosc* leaders.[613]

At the 68th Session of the ILC in 1982, to which Pope John Paul II was invited, Polish authorities were accused by Workers' delegates of violating ILO Conventions Nos. 87 and 98. However, efforts to pass a resolution that would have condemned Poland failed because of resistance from the Eastern bloc countries, which were supported by a majority of the G77, in particular the Arab states

---

613 Goddeeris, "The Limits of Lobbying".

Figure 13: Lech Wałęsa at the 67th Session of the ILC, 1981.

(which, in return, received the backing for another resolution denouncing Israel). In March 1983, however, the Governing Body decided to establish a Commission of Inquiry, which found that there was no legal basis for the ban of *Solidarnosc*. The Polish government, supported by other socialist countries reacted with great indignation to the Commission's report which was submitted to the Governing Body in June 1984. In November of the same year, Poland submitted a notice announcing its intention to withdraw from the ILO within the regular two-year period. At this point, and despite continuing protests from the Workers' group, the ILO softened its approach towards Poland in order to keep the door for membership open. Martial law restrictions were progressively relaxed, and Solidarnosc could legally function again in 1986. Poland postponed its withdrawal and then actually never left.[614] By that time, the pace for changes in the region was set by the policy of *perestroika* under the new Soviet leader Mikhail Gorbachev. As one of the consequences of this change, the Workers' representatives of the formerly monolithic communist bloc were no longer obliged to vote in accordance with

614 In 1986, it extended the notice, but in 1987, it officially retracted it. Ghébali, *The International Labour Organisation*, 112–113.

their governments' policies in the ILO. When Poland, in 1989, became the first country in the Eastern bloc to end the political monopoly of the Communist party and *Solidarnosc* won the first free elections held since 1945, the discussions had already lost much of their political explosiveness. The symbolical end to the discussion came in 1990, when the democratically elected Prime Minister Tadeusz Mazowiecki spoke to the Conference. He was accompanied by Lech Wałęsa, who soon became the first President of post-communist Poland.

Around the same time, another conflict in which the ILO had been involved from a very early point in time, came to its end: In February 1990, Nelson Mandela was released from prison after 27 years of confinement by the South African apartheid regime. This was the first step in a period of transition, which ended with the abolishment of all features of apartheid. Mandela was elected President in the first free elections for all South Africans in 1994.

The transition marked an end point for the ILO's long confrontation with the South African apartheid regime. Anti-apartheid action had started in earnest almost 30 years earlier with the adoption in 1964 of a "Programme for the elimination of apartheid in labour matters in the Republic of South Africa" as well as a "Declaration concerning the Policy of Apartheid".[615] From this point onwards, the Director-General submitted annual special reports to the ILC on this matter. Action against apartheid was constantly stepped up during the next decades. It included calls for boycotts and the international isolation of the regime, as well as the material and political support for both internal opposition groups and South African and Nambian national liberation movements working in exile.[616]

ILO action against apartheid was unique in more than one aspect. It was the only time the Organization actively took sides in an ongoing internal political conflict. It was even more remarkable, since, until way into the 1980s, South Africa was not without international allies and support. For geopolitical and economic reasons, the United States and the United Kingdom maintained a certain degree of support for the regime in Pretoria, as did a number of other Western governments. If the ILO was able to act as it did, it was due to the high symbolic value attached to the struggle against apartheid as the major manifestation of institutionalized racial discrimination. The ILO's policies were made possible largely because of the Workers' group's close alliance with the international anti-apartheid movement.[617]

---

615 See Part III, Chapter 6 ("The Human Rights Decade"), above.

616 In the broader UN context, see United Nations, *The United Nations and Apartheid 1948–1994* (New York: United Nations, Dept. of Public Information, 1994).

617 Rodgers et al., *The ILO and the Quest for Social Justice*, 50–57.

Eventually, the ILO also played a role in the South African reconciliation process following the official end of apartheid. In 1991, an ILO Fact-Finding and Conciliation Commission visited South Africa, undertaking a broad inquiry into labour law and relations under apartheid.[618] When South Africa rejoined the ILO in 1994, after the election of the first government headed by the African National Congress (ANC), the report of the Commission provided the basis for technical cooperation and training programmes.[619]

The Humanization of Work – New Perspectives on Working Conditions

Not all thinking during the 1970s went into employment policies, human rights promotion, or the management of the "American crisis". At the beginning of the decade, the ILO also breathed new life into its activities on the improvement of working conditions, a topic that long had been dormant in the Organization. In 1975, Director-General Blanchard used his annual report to the Conference – under the programmatic title of "Making Work More Human" – to place the issue at the centre of the debate. Simultaneously, the ILO launched its International Programme for the Improvement of Working Conditions and the Environment (PIACT).[620] The new focus on working conditions also offered an opportunity to take a broader view on the manifold ways work shapes human life and on the widely differing meanings people attach to it. So far, ILO activities in this field had been preoccupied with industrial work. Blanchard now tried to introduce a global approach that included working conditions in developing countries and the "informal sector". In this respect, PIACT was seen as complementary to the WEP. At the same time, the ILO saw the topic of humanizing work as a means to

618 Its original mandate was derived from a complaint directed in 1988, still under the apartheid system, by the Confederation of South African Trade Unions (COSATU) against the regime because of violations of trade union rights. When the ILO Fact-Finding Commission eventually took up its work, it did so on the invitation of the post-apartheid transitional government. This allowed for the extension of the ILO's mandate into a comprehensive study of labour relations under apartheid as part of the overall reconciliation process.

619 In 1996, South Africa, in a symbolic gesture, ratified both Freedom of Association Conventions, Nos. 87 and 98.

620 The acronym PIACT referred to its French title, *Programme international pour l'amélioration des conditions et du milieu de travail.* Jean de Givry, a long-serving French official with a specialization in labour relations and social institutions since the 1950s, had been one of the major brains behind it. See Jean de Givry, "The ILO and the Quality of Working Life. A New International Programme: PIACT", *International Labour Review* 117, no. 3 (1978): 261–271.

raise first questions about the link between the working environment and the environment in general, and to respond to post-materialist trends within Western societies.[621]

With its emphasis on the "humanization of labour", the ILO responded to a trend detectable in many Western societies that was marked by a growing feeling of discontent directed at the "over-rationalized" and inhumane nature of modern industrial production and its monotonous and fragmented character. Signs were everywhere, that the "Fordist compromise" – a compromise between management and organized labour based on the assumption that growing productivity and technological progress would ultimately lead to rising wages and improved working and living conditions for workers – was about to reach its limits. While rationalization and automation, in particular, had also caused anxieties and even resistance on the part of the workers in earlier periods, these concerns were now fuelled by a broader societal movement that was critical of the blind trust in technological progress and showed a growing awareness of its negative effects on the natural environment.[622] When the ILO took up the issue of the humanization of labour, it built on discussions that had occupied the major industrial countries throughout the 1960s and early 1970s – starting in the United States, but quickly spilling over to European countries like France, Great Britain, and Germany.[623]

Blanchard's report on "Making Work More Human" took account of these debates and called for a more holistic approach to the conditions of work, including workers' participation, fair wages, and human rights. His focus, however, was on three aspects: safety and health, working time, and the organization as well as the content of work. The report suggested an approach that would help to realize "human aspirations" at work everywhere and correspond to the needs of workers

---

621 So far, there is very little research about this programme. See Dorothea Hoehtker, "Die Internationale Arbeitsorganisation (ILO) – Versuch einer 'systemimmanenten' Humanisierung", unpublished conference paper for the conference "Humanisierung der Arbeit" – Aufbrüche und Konflikte in der Arbeitswelt des 20. Jahrhunderts, organized by the Friedrich-Ebert-Foundation and the Heinrich-Heine-University, 16/17 October 2017, Düsseldorf.
622 Hoehtker and Plata-Stenger, "The Future of Work and Technological Change".
623 In 1972, for example, the US Department of Health, Education and Welfare published a landmark report on "Work in America" that carried the idea of "humanization of labour" to an official level. United States Department of Health Education, and Welfare, *Work in America. Report of a Special Task Force to the Secretary of Health, Education, and Welfare. Prepared under the Auspices of the W. E. Upjohn Institute for Employment Research* (December 1972). For a broad overview of the debate in a long term perspective, see Nina Kleinöder, Stefan Müller, and Karsten Uhl, eds., *Humanisierung der Arbeit. Aufbrüche und Konflikte in der rationalisierten Arbeitswelt des 20. Jahrhunderts* (Bielefeld: Transcript Verlag, 2019).

in industrialized and developing countries alike.[624] Moreover, the report constituted an important juncture in the Organization's history, because it connected these problems with environmental issues. Blanchard, however, was not the first ILO head to raise this point. Wilfred Jenks' report to the ILC on "Technology for Freedom. Man in his Environment" of 1972 – which drew attention to the impact of technological change on the world of work – had already concluded that "on a global scale, present patterns of technological change are having a potentially disastrous effect on the relationship between man and his natural environment".[625] The references in both reports must be seen as first reactions to the rising concerns in the international community about the pollution and destruction of the natural environment and the limits of growth, as had become evident at the first UN Conference on the Human Environment in Stockholm in 1972.[626]

With regard to developing countries, the discussion of working conditions had a different point of departure. Where formal employment was the exception rather than the rule, international labour standards in areas like occupational safety and health, wages, and social security were of little direct relevance. To extend the concept of humanization of labour to countries where large parts of the population worked in the (mostly rural) informal economy, with little or no access to welfare, created very different challenges, to which PIACT was supposed to provide answers. While the WEP's emphasis had been on employment creation and poverty reduction, PIACT was, from the beginning, a programme dealing with the quality of employment.

The programme struggled from the outset with significant difficulties. It was an integrated programme that contained elements of technical cooperation, research, and standard-setting. At its heart, it offered interested countries, with the help of so-called "regional mobile operational teams", the possibility of defining targets to improve working conditions. It sought especially to reduce the rising numbers of work accidents, as a quantifiable result, and to help countries reach the targets that had been set. It also undertook substantial research on selected topics. In parallel, it promoted the ratification of existing ILO standards, especially

---

624 ILO, *Record of Proceedings*, Report of the Director-General: Making work more human, International Labour Conference, 60th Session 1975 (Geneva: ILO, 1975), 57.

625 ILO, *Record of Proceedings*, Report of the Director-General: Technology for Freedom. Man in his Environment, International Labour Conference, 57th Session 1972 (Geneva: ILO, 1972), 4. See also Yves Delamotte and Kenneth F. Walker, "Humanization of Work and the Quality of Working Life – Trends and Issues", *International Journal of Sociology* 6, no. 1 (1976): 8–40.

626 There is hardly any research on the ILO's dealing with environmental issues. In the context of the PIACT environmental concerns were mostly related with the workplace. The ILO significantly expanded its activities in this area following the Brundtland Report in 1987 and the new focus on sustainable development.

on safety and health, and was involved in the development of three new Conventions.[627] The ILO's high ambitions for the programme were frustrated, however, by a lack of funding and political support as well as an increasingly "unpromising international environment".[628] When PIACT was started, substantial support came from the Scandinavian countries, which, like other Western European countries, showed a keen interest in new, more participatory forms of work organization in order to increase productivity and satisfaction at work. But these new concepts were not entirely without its critics. Trade unions often were suspicious, as they feared that the improvements could turn out to be just new tools to raise productivity, bypass the unions, and increase pressure on workers.[629]

The main interest of developing countries focused much more on securing ILO support for the concrete improvement of working conditions, which presented major health risks as a result of rapid industrialization. Information and training were bitterly needed, especially for small enterprises. PIACT was born out of "the economic optimism which made possible the emergence of working conditions and environment as a major policy issue",[630] but as it progressed, it came under increasing financial pressure, especially with the loss of US funding. The programme was launched in the context of the 1970s oil crises and the resulting economic downturn with the return of larger scale unemployment to Western Europe. Therefore, the programme also lost traction, because priorities began to drift away from the "humanization of work" agenda, following the logic of a trade-off between work quality and employment creation, which has always been a major challenge for the ILO. A period of growth and expansion had come to an end in the industrialized countries, while many nations of the global South were still engaged in basic struggles of creating jobs, regardless of their quality. In this respect, the ILO was caught in the dilemma of navigating between two different sets of expectations concerning the creation of productive employment on one hand, and improving its quality on the other hand.

What was left of PIACT during the 1980s came under ever-growing pressure as a result of the neo-liberal turn in economic policies. In industrialized countries, calls for the deregulation of labour markets and growing demands on workers

---

627 Working Environment (Air Pollution, Noise and Vibration) Convention, 1977 (No. 148); Occupational Safety and Health (Dock Work) Convention, 1979 (No. 152); and Occupational Safety and Health Convention, 1981 (No. 155).

628 Rodgers et al., *The ILO and the Quest for Social Justice*, 100.

629 Delamotte and Walker, "Humanization of Work", 30.

630 ILO, *Record of Proceedings*, Report VII: Evaluation of the International Programme for the Improvement of Working Conditions and Environment, International Labour Conference, 70th Session 1984 (Geneva: ILO, 1984), 12.

for greater flexibility undermined the very foundations on which the case for the humanization of labour rested. In developing countries, structural adjustment programmes imposed by the international financial institutions forced countries to reduce social costs instead of building new structures for improved working conditions. Evaluations of PIACT in the mid-1980s already showed that, with regard to its major aims, the programme was mostly unsuccessful. Ratifications of corresponding international labour standards stayed low and the country programmes launched in developing countries could do little with the scarce resources at the programme's command. The one area where PIACT produced tangible results until it was phased out in 1998–1999, was occupational safety and health. In a context of a worldwide economic slowdown, this formed the lowest common denominator among the ILO's tripartite constituents. Occupational safety and health was an objective that was shared across the North/South divide and the divergent conditions in which the concept of "humanizing work" was experienced in industrialized and developing countries.[631]

631 Hoehtker, "Die Internationale Arbeitsorganisation (ILO) – Versuch einer 'systemimmanenten' Humanisierung".

8 The End of the "Philadelphia Consensus"?

When Lech Wałęsa and Nelson Mandela addressed the ILC in 1990, it might have seemed to some that the ILO was entering a bright new future. With the Cold War at its end and the liberal model prevailing, the ILO could see itself on the right side of history. Yet, even in this solemn moment, few within the ILO felt that way. On the contrary, many foresaw that the political sea changes taking place could mark a pyrrhic victory for the Organization. In fact, as early as the 1980s, there were signs everywhere that the ILO was constantly losing ground in the international arena. It saw itself widely excluded from the debates on the newly emerging international economic governance structures which led to the founding of the World Trade Organization (WTO) in 1995. At the heart of these debates, which were dominated by the quest for economic liberalization under the new buzzword of "globalization", was the accelerating disentanglement of economic and social questions, with the latter pushed to an ever more subordinate role.

Against this background, the ILO faced mounting pressure to reassert its position. Under the leadership of a new Director-General, Michel Hansenne, it tried to make its voice heard in the international debate on the social dimension of globalization that got under way. Hansenne's main legacy, and the tangible result of his strategy to position the ILO as a "social voice" within the post–Cold War world, would be the Declaration on Fundamental Principles and Rights at Work (1998). It defined for the first time a number of core labour standards promoted as a minimum set of common values that were applicable to all of the ILO's members.

Writings on the Wall

During the 1970s, the architecture of the international trading system underwent substantial changes. In 1971, US President Richard Nixon's decision to cancel the US dollar's international convertibility to gold laid the axe to the Bretton Woods system established in 1944. Within a couple of years, a system based on fixed exchange rates gave way to one in which currencies could float freely. In parallel, most Western governments lifted the restrictions on capital flows across national borders. Both steps jointly worked as a major boost for the internationalization of financial markets and the extension of foreign direct investment, which fuelled much of the processes that are summarized today under the heading of "globalization".[632]

632 Catherine R. Schenk, *International Economic Relations since 1945* (London: Routledge, 2011).

https://doi.org/10.1515/9783110650723-010

Figure 14: Nelson Mandela at the 77th Session of the ILC, 1990.

While unleashing an ever-increasing flow of goods and capital on an unprecedented scale and opening opportunities for businesses to expand, globalization has, at the same time, restricted the capacity of countries to control the economic forces working within their own national borders. As a consequence, governments – some more voluntarily than others – have abdicated some of their means to pursue social and employment goals, under the impression of presumably irrefutable demands of globalization. For the ILO, these developments and the debates accompanying them, spelled immediate dangers. Already during the late 1970s and 1980s some of the certainties – and indeed the foundations and premises on which the ILO's work had rested ever since the Second World War – began to erode. If national governments and national trade union federations were losing part of their capacity to steer economic and social policies on the state level, the ILO would necessarily lose part of its influence, too.

The first time that some of the phenomena associated with globalization were debated in the ILO was with regard to multinational enterprises (MNEs). While not an entirely new phenomenon at the time, the power of such transnational corporations, which controlled increasingly complex structures transcending national borders and creating new international divisions of labour, was greatly strengthened by the liberalization of world trade after the demise of the Bretton

Woods system. Incidents such as the active participation of US-based MNEs in the Chilean putsch against President Salvador Allende in 1973 put a spotlight on the most problematic aspects of their growing influence. Flexible and mobile, they were hard to control by national jurisdictions and capable of wielding immense power, in particular in developing countries.[633] The UN reacted with the creation of the United Nations Centre on Transnational Corporations (UNCTC). Between 1975 and 1992, it tried to develop a code of conduct, torn between the demand of developing and socialist countries for a binding instrument and the insistence of Western market economies on a voluntary code of principles, asserting the importance of MNEs for development and growth. MNEs posed a serious problem also for the ILO, because their multinational nature allowed them to easily escape the reach of internationally adopted but nationally applied labour standards. In 1974, in his first report to the ILC, Blanchard addressed the need to regulate multinational enterprises more effectively as one of the most pressing problems of the time. Early on in the debate, it turned out that a possible convention dealing with MNEs would not gain enough support within the ILO, especially not from the Employers' group. At the World Employment Conference in 1976 the Workers and the G77 wanted a convention. The Employers however were in favour of a tripartite declaration of principles which would have voluntary character.[634]

Therefore, in 1977, the Governing Body issued a "Tripartite Declaration of Principles concerning Multinational Enterprises and Social Policy", which provided international guidelines for such entities on a broad range of issues – from training to recruitment, from wage policies to trade union rights – often in direct relationship to the ILOs existing labour standards.[635] The attempt to build a broad consensus around the Declaration became visible in the first paragraphs, which emphasized the positive contribution MNEs could make with regard to "satisfaction of basic needs", the improvement of living conditions and welfare, and, in particular, the creation of employment. On the other hand, the Declaration

---

633 On MNEs, see Christine Kaufmann, *Globalisation and Labour Rights. The Conflict between Core Labour Rights and International Economic Law* (Oxford: Hart Publishing, 2007), 155–169; Marieke Louis, "La diplomatie sociale des multinationales", *La vie des idées*, 9 October 2018, https://laviedesidees.fr/La-diplomatie-sociale-des-multinationales.html.

634 Roger Blanpain, Michelle Collucci, eds., *The Globalization of Labour Standards: The Soft Law Track* (The Hague: Kluwer Law International, 2004), 21; Chloé Maurel, "OIT et responsabilité sociale des sociétés transnationales depuis 1970", in *L'Organisation internationale du travail*, ed. Lespinet-Moret and Viet, 179–192; For an overview of the contemporary debate, see Kari Tapiola, "Die 'Multis': Ein Thema für die Vereinten Nationen", *Vereinte Nationen* 5 (1978): 151–154.

635 The ILO Declaration built on a similar Declaration of the Organisation for Economic Co-operation and Development (OECD), including a follow-up mechanism which involved a trade union advisory committee (1976).

also provided a clear rationale for some kind of international regulation of the activities of MNEs. The "abuse of concentrations of economic power", MNEs' potential to interfere with national policies, and their capacity to escape national jurisdiction were named as cases in point why this regulation was in the public interest.[636]

Important as the Declaration was as a step forward to put MNEs on the international agenda and to get them involved in the debate, the effects were somewhat limited. While it established a procedure to address disagreements regarding the interpretation and application of the Declaration's single paragraphs, it excluded conflicts on freedom of association (which remained the domain of the CFA). Given that it was exactly this kind of conflicts that accounted for the bulk of complaints raised from the trade unions' side against multinationals in the years to come, this omission arguably reduced the impact of the Declaration.[637]

Towards the end of the 1970s, the debates about the globalizing economy and its implications entered a new phase. The background was provided by increasing signs of economic crisis. In Western Europe, an almost thirty-year era of economic growth and nearly full employment slowly came to an end. While Western European governments were now struggling with rising unemployment and inflation, they were ever more anxious to fence off increasing demands from developing countries for a reorganization of world trade. One tangible result was the first meeting of the so-called G6, the governments of the richest market economies at the time (United States, Great Britain, West Germany, France, Italy, and Japan; later the G7 by the addition of Canada) in Rambouillet, France, in November 1975.[638] Within international institutions, these countries tried to streamline their efforts to revive growth as Industrial Market Economy Countries (IMEC) and to counter demands from the global South for a New International Economic Order (NIEO), intended to strengthen the bargaining position of the primary producing countries. However, the latter's hopes to repeat the success of the oil producing countries and to use

636 ILO, *Tripartite Declaration of Principles concerning Multinational Enterprises and Social Policy* (Geneva: ILO, 1977).
637 This became apparent, in particular, in comparison with the OECD, whose 1976 Guidelines for Multinational Enterprises preceded the ILO's MNE Declaration. Other than the ILO, the OECD's Trade Union Advisory Committee, chaired by the Finnish trade unionist and later ILO Deputy Director-General Kari Tapiola, collected, documented, and commented regularly on cases of violation of trade union's rights by multinationals. See Kari Tapiola, *The Teeth of the ILO. The Impact of the ILO Declaration on Fundamental Principles and Rights at Work* (Geneva: ILO, 2018), 10–11.
638 The meeting's primary purpose was to find a common answer to the perceived threat from the developing countries. See for a concise summary Harold James, *Rambouillet, 15. November 1975. Die Globalisierung der Wirtschaft* (Munich: Deutscher Taschenbuch Verlag, 1997).

strategic market power would soon prove to be illusory. Differences between, on the one hand, the successful oil producers and the export-oriented Asian countries ("Asian tigers") such as the Republic of Korea, which became development models, and, on the other hand, the bulk of developing countries with varying economic bases turned out to be impossible to overcome.[639]

It was against this generally gloomy backdrop that the "Philadelphia consensus", based on an understanding of an intrinsic relationship of social and economic policies and the ultimate primacy of a social objective of all policies, began to crumble. In Western Europe and across the North Atlantic, calls for liberalization and deregulation of labour markets replaced the decades-long conviction that growth, high levels of employment, and income security through welfare spending would mutually reinforce each other. The ILO was affected by the crisis of Keynesianism, which now came under attack by neo-classical, monetarist, and supply-side-oriented economists. Their ideas, based on a narrative of auto-regulated free markets as a solution to the crisis, were first put into practice in Chile by the Pinochet regime, and then entered the bigger stage with the election of Margaret Thatcher in the United Kingdom and Ronald Reagan in the United States.[640] Meanwhile, the international financial institutions, namely the IMF and the World Bank, supported by some of the UN's regional commissions prescribed a set of ten neoliberal economic policy principles, known in the 1990s as the "Washington Consensus", as a reform package to crisis-ridden developing countries.[641]

Before long, there were writings on the wall that the tide was turning, and the ILO felt the consequences. Pressure mounted from the outside, but also from within, given the strong inclination of employers to embrace the neoliberal doctrine. With regard to Western Europe, from the mid-1970s to the mid-1980, the ILO was gradually losing its momentum. Increasingly, it was also losing the capacity of making its voice heard in debates on how to overcome the economic crisis, which conventional Keynesian economic tools did not seem able to control. On the international as well as on the national level, the political initiative was seized increasingly by those who blamed the economic downturn on structural and institutional "rigidities" of the labour market, which in their view reduced the international competitiveness of European enterprises. It was in this context that the ILO was partially replaced by the Organisation for Economic

639 Dietrich, *Oil Revolution*.

640 For an intellectual history of neoliberalism, its proponents, and historical context, see Quinn Slobodian, *Globalists: The End of Empire and the Birth of Neoliberalism* (Cambridge, MA: Harvard University Press, 2018).

641 On the history of structural adjustment programmes, see Unger, *International Development. A Post-War History*, 127–152.

Co-operation and Development (OECD), which began to argue ever more forcefully for economic liberalization and a flexibilization of labour markets as a way out of the crisis.[642]

While last restrictions on capital flows were abolished during the late 1980s as part of the European economic integration process in the run-up to the Maastricht Treaty, some governments started to implement labour market reforms.These reforms allowed employers to expand or reduce the workforce and to employ workers on a part-time or temporary basis more easily. They also allowed more flexibility with regard to working time and payment.[643] In reaction to all this, the ILO remained largely in a defensive and observant position. The approach the Organization took towards labour market reforms under the auspices of "labour market flexibility" was essentially a pragmatic one, due, most probably, to a mix of realism and resignation.

By and large, the ILO played a secondary role also in the process of European integration that led to the Maastricht Treaty and the creation of the European Union (EU) in 1992. However, the Organization could consider it at least a partial success that it had helped to successfully introduce the concept of "social dialogue" into the debate on the social dimension of the European single market. When, in 1985, Jacques Delors, then the president of the European Commission, met with high-ranking European trade union and employer representatives at a summit on social dialogue, the trade unions, in particular, regarded it as an important step. To them, it was a sign that their concerns regarding the social impact of the European market were taken seriously.[644]

The trend towards supply-side economics was even more pronounced with regard to the international development debate. At the beginning of the 1980s,

642 Matthieu Leimgruber, "The Embattled Standard-bearer of Social Insurance and Its Challenger: The ILO, the OECD and the 'Crisis of the Welfare State', 1975–1985", in *Globalizing Social Rights*, ed. Kott and Droux, 115–136.

643 See a summary of the debates in Tiziano Treu, "Labour Flexibility in Europe", *International Labour Review* 131, no. 4–5 (1992): 497–512. For the debate on working time flexibility, see Dietmar Süss, "Der Sieg der grauen Herren? Flexibilisierung und Kampf um Zeit in den 1970er und 1980er Jahren", in *Die Vorgeschichte der Gegenwart. Dimensionen des Strukturbruchs nach dem Boom*, ed. Anselm Döring-Manteuffel, Lutz Raphael, and Thomas Schlemmer (Munich: Beck, 2016), 109–127.

644 See Jean Lapeyre, *Le dialogue social européen. Histoire d'une innovation sociale (1985–2003)* (Brussels: European Trade Union Institute, 2017), 35–43. For a longer-term perspective on the role of the ILO in shaping the social dimension of European integration, see Lorenzo Mechi, "Du BIT à la politique sociale européenne: l'origine d'un modèle", *Mouvement social* 244, no. 3 (2013): 17–30; Mechi, "Economic Regionalism and Social Stabilization"; Guinand, *Die Internationale Arbeitsorganisation (ILO) und die soziale Sicherheit in Europa (1942–1969).*

countries in Sub-Saharan Africa and Latin America, in particular, were struggling with huge foreign debts, restricting their room for manoeuvre both domestically and internationally. Poverty-centred and redistributive development strategies, which had been at the heart of the WEP, gave way to "stabilization policies" or, more concretely, programmes of "structural adjustment" applied by the IMF. They imposed the deregulation of labour markets, privatization of major industries, and cuts in public spending, often triggering unemployment in parallel to the scaling down of social programmes. Here, too, the ILO struggled to find an answer. As other institutions, such as the United Nations Children's Fund (UNICEF), it tried to push the IMF to make certain exceptions and to take employment effects into consideration. In 1987, Blanchard called a "High Level Meeting on Structural Adjustment and Employment" to which he invited representatives of the international financial and economic institutions, including the IMF, the World Bank, UNCTAD and the GATT, as well as the OECD, to sit down with an ILO tripartite delegation.[645] The objective was to discuss the social costs of neoliberal policies in developing countries and to bring the ILO back into the picture. Blanchard's efforts resulted in some concessions regarding the conditionality of IMF loans, but beyond this, the impact of the meeting was very limited. The message was clear enough: liberalization and deregulation were the answer, while social considerations, if not completely disregarded, had to be treated separately and were ultimately relegated to a subordinate position.[646]

The political sea change of 1989/1990 worked as yet another catalyst for the new thinking. When the Soviet Union dissolved, and state socialism came to an end in Eastern and Central Europe, the post-communist world became an El Dorado for the advocates of market liberalism with no social strings attached. "Big Bang" economics that were applied to countries which after decades of planned economies were already in severe crisis. This triggered radical and often chaotic transition processes to market economies. The shock therapy prescribed by international financial institutions and "Chicago boys" style market radicals included the privatization of state enterprises and a far-reaching and abrupt liberalization of labour markets. In the course of this process, the economies collapsed amidst high unemployment rates, and state Socialist welfare systems were dismantled without proper replacement policies. As a result, poverty rose, education and health levels declined, and inequalities increased dramatically, with traumatizing effects and long-term political consequences. Some countries of the Common-

645 Peter J. Richards, "Preserving Jobs under Economic Stabilisation Programmes: Can there be an Employment Target?" *International Labour Review* 125, no. 4, (1986): 423–433.
646 Rodgers et al., *The ILO and the Quest for Social Justice*, 214–215.

wealth of Independent States (CIS), which succeeded the Soviet Union after its end in 1991, suffered from civil war, and most of them did not manage the transition to democratic systems as did the Eastern European states.[647] Initially, the ILO was hardly more than a bystander in this process, although its experts and advisors became active in the transitioning countries from Eastern Europe to the Caucasus. The major problem was that attempts to install (tripartite) collective bargaining mechanisms or to help in the creation of social security systems ran up against different concepts promoted by the international financial institutions, which commanded much bigger resources than the ILO. The ILO was fighting a losing battle everywhere, and it was rarely able or willing to speak up against the general trend. According to critical observers, the ILO's self-imposed restraint was due to a (surely justified) concern over losing access to the sources of funding for its own technical assistance programmes, for which the World Bank and the IMF functioned as gate keepers.[648]

An example for the ILO's shrinking capacity to shape the discourse even in fields that comprised its core competence was the discussion on pension privatization, a key component of the neoliberal project. In the early 1990s, a "transnational coalition" including the World Bank, the OECD, and USAID promoted the transition to pension systems based on individual capitalization, with the objective of complementing or even substituting contributory pension schemes run by the state or such long-established social institutions as trade unions. The ILO, which had long been the standard bearer of the latter model, now found itself on shifting ground, as the World Bank and the OECD used their superior resources successfully to promote pension reforms along the privatization paradigm in Western and Eastern Europe, the successor states of the Soviet Union, and in Latin America. The ILO could warn and suggest corrections, but it was not in a position to stem the tide.[649]

Towards the 1998 Declaration

Half a year before the fall of the Berlin Wall marked the beginning of a new era, in March 1989, Michel Hansenne, a former Belgian Minister of Employment and

---

647 See as an example Mitchell Orenstein, "Transitional Social Policy in the Czech Republic and Poland", *Czech Sociological Review* 3, no. 2 (1995): 179–196.
648 Guy Standing, "The ILO: An Agency for Globalization?" *Development and Change* 39, no. 3 (2008): 355-384, here 364.
649 Mitchell A. Orenstein, "Pension Privatization: The Transnational Campaign", in *Globalizing Social Rights*, ed. Kott and Droux, 280–292.

Labour, took over as the eighth Director-General of the ILO. Unlike his predecessors, Jenks and Blanchard, Hansenne brought an outsider's perspective to the Office. His prior experience with the ILO was restricted to the years when he had served as the Belgian Government delegate to the ILC. At a time of rapid change, he took some time to accustom himself to the functioning of the Organization. However, once he had ended his "apprenticeship year", he was ready to reform it.[650]

Hansenne came from a Christian Democratic political background. Economically more liberal than his predecessors, he was a believer in the benefits of free trade. As a Minister of Employment and Labour, he had favoured a moderate flexibilization of the labour market. As Director-General, he considered it his task to bring the ILO more in line with what he perceived as the requirements of the global economy. He felt that the Organization was ill-prepared for making its voice heard in the context of the new emerging order of international economic governance, which would eventually lead to the establishment of the WTO in 1995. More than anything else, Hansenne saw the ILO in danger of being bypassed and ultimately becoming irrelevant. In his view, the ILO did too much, while lacking a clear focus. In his recollections, written immediately after leaving office in 1999, he likened the ILO to a clockwork that, despite moving regularly, failed to give "the right time".[651]

This somewhat hidden dysfunctionality was particularly pronounced in the area of standard-setting. Many of the standards seemed outdated and of little value, particularly for developing countries. Previous criticism had led as early as 1974 to the creation of a working party to review and update the standards system. In 1987, it had proposed a classification of ILO standards in order to identify the instruments whose ratification and application should be promoted on a priority basis.[652] After 1990, and in line with the prevailing anti-regulatory mood, governments generally were less inclined to ratify international labour standards, and employers were more committed than ever to go against the ILO's standard-setting ambitions.[653] Hansenne's strategy to save the ILO from falling into irrelevance was to focus instead on a few basic principles. Starting from this idea, the ground work for a "Declaration on Fundamental Principles and Rights at Work",

650 Marieke Louis, "Hansenne, Michel", in *IO Bio: Biographical Dictionary*, ed. Reinalda, Kille, and Eisenberg, www.ru.nl/fm/iobio.

651 Michel Hansenne, *Un garde-fou pour la mondialisation. Le BIT dans l'après-guerre froide* (Chêne-Bourg: Editions ZOE, 1999), 21.

652 Report of the Working Party on International Labour Standards, paragraph 14: ILO, Minutes of the Governing Body, 235th Session, Geneva 1987.

653 Ulf Edström, "International Labour Standards after the End of the Cold War", unpublished working paper for the ILO Century Project (Geneva: ILO, 2015).

eventually adopted by the ILC in 1998, would become Hansenne's major project and his legacy as Director-General. Inspiration came also from post–Cold War human rights discourses, which emphasized liberal rights of the individual over social and economic rights to support political democratization and the rule of law.

At the 1993 Conference on Human Rights in Vienna, this new mood was all too visible. While most Western countries treated social and economic rights as non-justiciable objectives, developing countries more than ever conceived of those rights as enuring to the state rather than to individuals. The result was a trade-off between the two groups in which the developing countries accepted the universality of political and civil rights in return for the West's vague commitment to a "right to development", which included social and economic rights.[654] De facto, the Vienna conference confirmed the view that only political and civil rights constituted "real" human rights.[655] Translated into the ILO's work, this could be – and in fact was – seen as a further encouragement to focus on basic principles rather than on international labour standards in their entirety. There was arguably less room than ever for a comprehensive approach to human rights that would include a strong social component. In contrast, a momentum seemed to be building up for the promotion of the basic principles and "enabling rights" that were necessary for the realization of social rights, such as freedom of association, legal equality/non-discrimination, and freedom of labour/the abolition of coercive forms of labour.

In 1994, the ILO celebrated its 75th anniversary and half a century since the adoption of the Declaration of Philadelphia. That year, already fraught with historic significance, would become a turning point for the ILO. At the ILC, Hansenne opened a discussion on the Organization's future role, which led to the installation by the Governing Body of a "Working Party on the Social Dimensions of the Liberalization of International Trade". This Working Party, open to all members, was given the task of reviewing national policies, liaising with other international institutions, and serving as a sounding board for all ideas on the ILO's potential contribution to the globalization debate. In this regard, it also became an important element in the run-up to the 1998 Declaration.

The initial idea of "fundamental labour rights", however, had not been Hansenne's but came from the trade union side. For the Workers' group, freedom of association and the right to collective bargaining were by far the most impor-

654 Burke, "Some Rights Are More Equal Than Others".

655 Stefan-Ludwig Hoffmann, "Human Rights and History", *Past & Present* 232, no. 1 (2016): 279–310.

tant issues at stake. The inclusion of forced labour and discrimination in the list of fundamental rights was partly due to the fact that these were rather "appealing" rights from a political point of view, allowing for a fairly close connection to general human rights discourses. This was even more the case with child labour, which made it to the list some time later.

In parallel to the discussions of the Vienna Conference and the preparations for the 1994 celebrations, the Workers' group launched an initiative for a "world charter of workers' rights", which listed freedom of association, absence of discrimination (this included the right to equal pay), and forced labour. In a resolution, the ILC confirmed the Conventions which expressed these rights, namely Conventions Nos. 87, 98, 100, 29 and 105, and 111 (supplemented later by Convention No. 138 on minimum age as a reference to child labour).[656] The list was presented as the necessary basis from which workers could "negotiate freely, both individually and collectively, their conditions of work" in the context of an ever more rapidly progressing liberalization of international trade.[657]

From there the road was open for the 1998 Declaration. The process that led to its adoption, however, was far from straightforward.. The Declaration was in fact one of a number of possible outcomes arising out of a quite volatile context. Three main factors led to its ultimate adoption: First, the establishment of the WTO and the preparations for the UN's Social Summit in Copenhagen, both in 1995, provided the general background against which the ILO was forced to define its position. Secondly, the debate on the so-called social clause – tying trade agreements to compliance with ILO standards (see below) – and emerging business initiatives advocating self-regulatory mechanisms represented alternative visions of the social regulation of globalization and provided further incentives to pursue the promotion of fundamental labour rights. Third, the field of child labour proved a testing ground for key features of the Declaration.

The UN World Summit for Social Development (Social Summit), which took place in Copenhagen in March 1995, served as an important stepping stone on the road towards a declaration on fundamental labour rights. More than anything, the Social Summit was an expression of the uneasiness and disillusion with the results of the liberalization of trade under the new neoliberal paradigm. The emergence of global supply chains, which marked a new phase in

656 Freedom of Association and Protection of the Right to Organise Convention, 1948 (No. 87); Right to Organise and Collective Bargaining Convention, 1949 (No. 98); Equal Remuneration Convention, 1957 (No. 100); Discrimination (Employment and Occupation) Convention, 1958 (No. 111); Forced Labour Convention, 1930 (No. 29); Abolition of Forced Labour Convention, 1957 (No. 105); and Minimum Age Convention, 1973 (No. 138).
657 Reynaud, *The International Labour Organization and Globalization*, 4.

the international division of work and production – together with the often dire consequences of deregulation, structural adjustment programmes, and the shock therapy prescribed to the former Eastern bloc countries – raised the awareness of the high cost of unfettered economic "hyper-globalization". While it did not yet question the prevailing free-market paradigm, the need to deal with the social dimension of globalization was increasingly acknowledged. The initiative for a world meeting to deal with the entire range of social issues came from the UN's ECOSOC, and particularly from its chairman, the Chilean representative to the United Nations, Juan Somavía, who had been given the task of organizing the Social Summit. Initially, the ILO's participation in the preparation of the summit took off rather slowly. Hansenne, according to an insider's recollection, had to be pushed from the Workers' and Employers' sides to grab the opportunity offered by the UN's initiative. Resolutions adopted by the ILC both in 1993 and 1994 pushed the Organization to play an assertive role in the preparation of the Social Summit, in particular in the fields of poverty reduction and employment.[658]

When the summit eventually took place, it helped to galvanize the ILO's constituents around the idea of fundamental labour rights. Roughly twenty thousand people participated, among them 117 heads of state. The Social Summit produced a final declaration that could well be read as a wake-up call: it called, among other things, for poverty eradication, full employment, social integration based on the respect of all human rights, including equality between men and women and universal access to education, and the need for structural adjustment programmes to contain social development goals.[659] In a way, the connection it made between economic and social policies only highlighted the deep imbalance in the treatment of both areas. The very fact that the Social Summit took place practically in parallel to the foundation of the WTO underpinned the latter's superior position: in the same year that the WTO implemented one of the toughest sanction regimes on the international level, the Social Summit produced mere declarations of intent, without any direct consequences or clear follow-up mechanisms. All the power in the realm of global governance remained with the international economic and financial institutions.

658 Tapiola, *The Teeth of the ILO*, 23.

659 The summit, in its final agreement contained an endorsement of full, productive, and freely chosen employment that was based on the wording of Employment Policy Convention, 1964 (No. 122). It also confirmed the central role of employment in the reduction of poverty. See United Nations, *Report on the World Summit for Social Development*, 19 April 1995, A/CONF.166/9, Chapter 1, Annex 1, "Copenhagen Declaration on Social Development.

For the ILO, however, the Social Summit was an important step forward. While it received credit, above all, for its comprehensive *World Employment Report* produced for the summit,[660] it also put its official seal on the concept of "fundamental workers' rights". The "Copenhagen Declaration on Social Development", the summit's final document, related directly to the resolutions of the 1994 ILC. It asked governments to enhance the quality of work and employment by safeguarding and promoting respect for "basic workers' rights, including the prohibition of forced labour and child labour, freedom of association and the right to organize and bargain collectively, equal remuneration for men and women for work of equal value, and non-discrimination in employment". The Declaration also called on governments to fully implement the respective ILO Conventions and to take into account "the principles embodied in those Conventions", as a means to "achieve truly sustained economic growth and sustainable development".[661]

The last and unquestionably most important argument for the Declaration, however, emanated from the heated debate of the 1990s on the so-called "social clause". Its proponents intended to create a direct link between trade agreements and adherence to certain ILO standards. In the early 1990s, the discussion on the social clause intensified in view of the new order of international economic governance centred around the WTO.

The idea of a social clause itself goes back to the immediate post–Second World War period and the debates on the rebuilding of world trade. Some countries had pushed for a connection between international agreements on employment policies (which never materialized) and labour standards in the wake of the Philadelphia Conference. Similar considerations had also accompanied the discussions surrounding the Havana Charter of 1948 and the attempts, ultimately unsuccessful, to create an International Trade Organization (ITO).[662] In the context of the GATT, which "provisionally" took the place of the ITO (before the founding of the WTO in 1995), there was no follow-up on the idea. In the 1960s, the ICFTU had submitted the idea of a social clause to the first conference of UNCTAD as its contribution to the first UN "development decade". However, it

660 ILO, *World Employment 1995. An ILO Report* (Geneva: ILO, 1995).

661 UN, *Report on the World Summit for Social Development*, "Copenhagen Declaration", which confirmed the ILO's 1994 list in paragraph 54(b) of its action programme. Chapter III, C of the Declaration covered the issue of "enhanced quality of work and employment" in a comprehensive way.

662 Jill Jensen, "Negotiating a World Trade and Employment Charter: The United States, the ILO and the Collapse of the ITO Ideal", in *The ILO from Geneva to the Pacific Rim*, ed. Jensen and Lichtenstein, 83-109.

had met with significant resentment from developing countries, who saw it as a protectionist tool imposed by the industrialized countries.[663]

After lying somewhat dormant, the idea re-emerged when the first great push for a liberalization of trade and capital flows took place in the 1970s. While the paradigm shift towards full-scale liberalization was on its way, Western industrial countries felt a growing need to protect their own companies and workers from the adverse effects of global competition. At a time when developing countries increasingly were told that liberalization and "adjustment" of their economies to the requirements of the global market were the answers to their problems, the industrial countries supported the erection of new barriers. When the US government, the OECD, and Western trade unions increasingly argued for social clauses as a way to tackle "unfair competition", their main targets were the "Asian tigers", whose export-oriented development models rested on authoritarian premises, cheap labour, and low social standards. But their calls sounded shallow to developing countries across the board, and they were viewed as just another attempt to perpetuate unequal economic power relations. This conflict was exacerbated by the debt crisis and "structural adjustment" constraints in the global South. During the 1980s and the beginning of the 1990s, the social clause repeatedly appeared in the ILO debates, where the United States and other OECD and EU countries, as well as the ICFTU, ran up against a nearly united front of developing countries (often including their Workers' representatives) and Employers, who were traditionally opposed to any measures suspected to interfere with free trade.[664]

The ILO was put in a difficult situation, since after all, the dividing lines ran through the Organization itself. At the beginning of the GATT's so-called Uruguay Round in 1986, when the United States, in particular, pushed for the inclusion of a social clause, Blanchard initiated a debate on the question with Arthur Dunkel, Secretary-General of the GATT, but failed to achieve any results. The discussion then continued into Hansenne's term. In 1994, a group of Asian countries promoted a Conference resolution "calling upon the ILO to resist the introduction of the social clause in international trade".[665] While it failed to get enough votes,

---

663 An overview in Tapiola, *Teeth of the ILO*, 12; Tony Royle, "The ILO's Shift to Promotional Principles and the 'Privatization' of Labour Rights: An Analysis of Labour Standards, Voluntary Self-Regulation and Social Clauses", *Journal of Comparative Labour Law and Industrial Relations* 26, no. 3 (2010): 249–271.

664 George Tsogas, "Labour Standards in International Trade Agreements: An Assessment of the Arguments", *The International Journal of Human Resource Management* 10, no. 2 (1999): 351–375.

665 ILO, *Record of Proceedings*, Resolution Calling upon the ILO to Resist the Introduction of the Social Clause in International Trade and to Review ILO Standards, Submitted by the Government

the discussion reflected the irreconcilable positions on the question. The fact that the strongest resistance to the social clause was led by South-East Asian countries like Malaysia and Singapore revealed the connection of this debate to the ongoing controversies on human rights, as the same countries were heading the opposition – invoking "Asian values" – to what they considered neo-colonial Western conceptions of human rights.[666]

In the run-up to the GATT meeting in Marrakesh in April 1994, which was to end the Uruguay Round and decide on the foundation of the WTO, industrial countries and Western trade unions once again pushed for an inclusion of a social clause in the WTO's charter. However, when the WTO eventually took up its work on the first day of 1995, developing countries could see with satisfaction that their efforts to keep the social clause off the agenda of the new organization had been successful. The First WTO Ministerial Conference in Singapore in December 1996 put a seal on the question. Developing countries won their first victory, when they made sure that the ILO Director-General's invitation to the Singapore meeting was withdrawn. The meeting's final communiqué mentioned "core labour standards" and credited the ILO as the competent agency to pursue their realization. At the same time, the Singapore conference plainly rejected the idea of social clauses as a form of protectionism. International labour standards would help to secure social progress only if disconnected from international trade policies. The best way to realize social standards, the final communiqué proclaimed, was "economic growth and development fostered by increased trade and further liberalization". If there had been any illusions as to a new institutionalized role for the ILO within the emerging economic order, they were shattered by the meeting. Any dreams that parts of the "Philadelphia consensus" could be transposed to the new age clearly had to be buried. From Hansenne's perspective, however, the WTO episode, sobering as it was, provided the final incentive for focusing on the preparation of a legal instrument that would define and promote core labour standards.[667]

If, for the international trade union movement, the social clause was the preferred way of tackling the social consequences of globalization, a different vision came from the opposite end of the ILO's meeting rooms in the form of Corporate Social Responsibility (CSR). Driven by brand-oriented consumer and human rights

---

Delegation of Indonesia, Malaysia Philippines, Singapore and Thailand, International Labour Conference, 81st Session 1994 (Geneva: ILO, 1994).

666 There were notable exceptions on both sides. While the United Kingdom, for instance, objected to the social clause, some countries from the global South, like South Africa and Brazil, were not entirely opposed. See Tapiola, *The Teeth of the ILO*, 20–21.

667 Reynaud, *The International Labour Organization and Globalization*, 5–6.

activists who were scandalized by the use of child labour, inhumane working conditions, and the suppression of workers' rights at the producing end of the global supply chains, some multinational corporations (like Nike, Nestlé, and Walmart) pledged adherence to self-imposed "codes of conduct". Starting from the early 1990s (the first codes of conducts were from the 1970s), more and more MNEs and brand-name businesses subscribed to self-regulation through CSR, with the latter becoming a regular part of companies' public relations departments. As the system has been refined, CSR has created its own "tripartite" set-up: while brands usually design and administer their own codes of conduct and apply them to the manufacturers producing their goods, the third party involved consists of human rights organizations, which monitor the application of CSR codes, sometimes in direct cooperation with the brands.[668]

For the ILO, CSR has always posed a conundrum. On the one hand, codes of conduct were one possible way to strengthen the acceptance of international labour standards by presenting them as a yardstick for the governance of working conditions, trade union rights, or minimum age regulations within global supply chains. From a pragmatic point of view, CSR codes seemed to provide an additional tool, given the difficulties of regulation through national legislations. On the other hand, CSR aroused little enthusiasm within the ILO outside the Employers' group. The promotion of CSR codes could hardly be separated from the employers' increasingly hostile attitude towards ILO standard-setting, which had generally stiffened in the 1990s. Moreover, the IOE made it very clear that it would oppose anything that could compromise the completely voluntary character of CSR. Any initiatives of human rights activists to push the ILO to develop a more binding instrument – such as a convention or a recommendation defining minimum standards for CSR on such issues as freedom of association or equal pay – met with strong resistance from the Employers.[669] The Workers' group, in turn, had its own reasons to be sceptical of the concept: as much as its representatives welcomed human rights activism in the field of working conditions (since it supported their own aims), they never perceived CSR as an end in itself but only as a poor substitute for the achievement of workers' rights through binding laws.[670]

668 Archie B. Carroll, "A History of Corporate Social Responsibility: Concepts and Practices", in *The Oxford Handbook of Corporate Social Responsibility*, ed. Andrew Crane et al. (Oxford: Oxford University Press, 2008), 19–46.

669 Louis, "Building a Transnational Business Community", 20.

670 On the ILO discussion, see Nelson Lichtenstein, "The ILO and the Corporate Social Responsibility Regime in East and South Asia", in *The ILO from Geneva to the Pacific Rim*, ed. Jensen and Lichtenstein, 277–296; Royle, "The ILO's Shift to Promotional Principles and the 'Privatization' of Labour Rights".

For all these reasons, the ILO reacted hesitantly to the calls that it should become more assertive in its embrace of CSR. Hansenne's idea of creating an ILO-governed "social label", in the hope of reviving the debate on MNEs, was nipped in the bud by the resistance of the Employers and many emerging countries from the global South.[671] The International Labour Office, nevertheless, tried to embrace the concept of CSR in its own work from the latter part of the 1990s onwards. For instance, it created a help desk to advise companies on how to bring codes of conduct in line with ILO standards. In 2001, the Organization launched the "Better Factories Cambodia" programme, which can be seen as an attempt to create a model CSR environment, because it was repeated in other countries. By contrast, the ILO's impact on the broader debate has remained marginal, in particular when it comes to MNEs.[672] However, in the mid-1990s the CSR debate contributed to the dedication of Hansenne and many others in the ILO to develop a promotional approach, focusing on specific ILO standards as the primary tool to regulate globalization "the ILO way".

An early opportunity to test this new approach arose in the field of child labour, where an old topic received new attention as it emerged as one of the major negative social consequences of economic globalization which triggered growing consumer activism. In the early 1970s, the topic had already returned to the agenda of the ILO, when a Minimum Age Convention, 1973 (No. 138), had created a new framework for the existing minimum age instruments. While the aim of this Convention was "the total abolition of child labour" in all its forms, the debate was also shaped by the parallel discussions on development and the NIEO. The new Convention reflected these discussions inasmuch as it allowed developing countries to apply a gradual approach and to exclude certain sectors of the economy where work was not dangerous to the children's health.[673] In 1979, when the ILO examined the (low) impact of Convention No. 138, it further took account of the situation in the global South, where poverty created an environment that made it impossible, and in some cases also undesirable, to instantly abolish all forms of child labour. The approach would have to be to fight first against those forms of child labour that were highly exploitative and that exceeded the mental and physical abilities of children of a certain age and endangered their educational advancement.[674] The UN Convention on the Rights of the Child (1989) gave

671 Louis, "Hansenne, Michel", 4.

672 Lichtenstein, "The ILO and the Corporate Social Responsibility Regime in East and South Asia".

673 G.K. Lieten, "The ILO Setting the Terms in the Child Labour Debate", in *ILO Histories*, ed. Van Daele et al., 443–460.

674 Ibid., 448.

further support to this approach when it put the emphasis on children's protection from economic exploitation and "from performing any work that is likely to be hazardous or to interfere with the child's education, or to be harmful to the child's health or physical, mental, spiritual, moral or social development".[675]

In the beginning of the 1990s, when there was a tailwind for the fight against child labour as a general human rights issue, the limits of the ILO's standard-setting approach focussing on minimum age regulations seemed all too obvious. This was the point of departure for a new strategy. It took greater account of the concerns of developing countries, in particular, and would ultimately result in the 1999 Convention on the Worst Forms of Child Labour (No. 182). The new Convention was built on a broad consensus on what should be regarded as the most unacceptable forms of child labour: the trafficking of children, child prostitution, children's use as soldiers and for such illicit activities such as drug dealing, and generally work that was likely to cause grave harm to the health, safety, or morals of a child.[676]

The groundwork for the nearly complete consensus that carried the new Convention had been laid already in the beginning of the 1990s with the launching of the International Programme on the Elimination of Child Labour (IPEC), in which standard-setting was only one part of a broader strategy. In 1992, Hansenne received significant support from the German government, which provided fifty million Deutschmarks to get IPEC under way. The new programme rested on two main pillars – technical assistance and the mobilization of public opinion. It lent technical support to countries in their activities against child labour and reached out to other humanitarian and human rights agencies working in the field, such as UNICEF or Save the Children, to rally public opinion around the issue. Initially, IPEC was met with some apprehension by the developing countries and also the Workers' group. The former feared that new action on the issue might put a spotlight on the problem in their export-oriented industries, which, in turn, could lead to economically harmful sanctions. Their fears were fanned by the fact that the start of IPEC coincided with the debates on the social clause and with calls for boycotts of products made by children. Trade unions, for their part, were anxious lest the programme would turn out to be yet another attempt to

---

675 UN General Assembly, Convention on the Rights of the Child, art. 32 (1) (New York, 1989).

676 How strong the consensus was on this issue could be seen from the fact that the Convention was unanimously adopted by the ILC in 1999 and instantly received ratifications from member States. Before long, the Worst Forms of Child Labour Convention, 1999 (No. 182) turned into one of the most widely accepted among all the ILO's international labour standards. In 2019, 186 countries had ratified Convention No. 182. Lieten, "The ILO Setting the Terms in the Child Labour Debate".

devalue international labour standards. Some workers and governments were also generally opposed to what they saw as a watering down of the ILO's goal of a complete elimination of child labour, enshrined in the minimum age concept. They feared that too close a cooperation with organizations like Save the Children or UNICEF might compromise the clarity of the ILO's message, given that both of them favoured a more general child welfare approach that did not prioritize the abolition of child labour as such.[677]

Ultimately, most of the fears were alleviated by the relative success of IPEC, by which the ILO gained considerable attention and the sustained support of major donors like the US government. However, there were two aspects that probably helped most to reconcile the programme's critics with IPEC: it clearly paved the ground for the Worst Forms of Child Labour Convention (No. 182); and it helped to boost ratification of the 1973 Minimum Age Convention, which had stood at about fifty in 1990 and has since then risen to 172 (2019).[678] Child labour helped to connect the ILO directly to the international human rights discourse concerning children and to forge alliances with groups outside the Organization's core constituency: for instance, the "Global March against Child Labour" network, which brought together a broad coalition of children's rights organizations, trade unions, and UN agencies; or the "Red Card to Child Labour" campaign, launched in 1998 on the occasion of the football world cup, which involved cooperation with the international football federation, FIFA. In this sense, fighting against child labour has proved its value as a door opener for the ILO. At the same time, however, it failed to entirely silence the critics – even more so, since the success of child labour campaigns was not to be repeated easily with regard to other fundamental principles. This was true, in particular, for issues like freedom of association or discrimination, which did not draw the same degree of across-the-board support as the highly emotionalized topic of child labour.[679] In the meantime, IPEC contributed significantly to creating a momentum for fundamental labour rights. This connection became plainly visible when hundreds of children from all over the world who were among the thousands of participants in the Global March against Child Labour that convened in Geneva in early June 1998 mounted the stage during the opening of the 86th Session of the ILC that would later adopt the Declaration on Fundamental Principles and Rights at Work.

677 Lieten, "The ILO Setting the Terms in the Child Labour Debate".
678 Minimum Age Convention No. 138 (1973).
679 Tapiola, *The Teeth of the ILO*, 17–18.

Figure 15: The Global March against Child Labour is welcomed by ILO Director-General Michel Hansenne at the opening session of the 1998 ILC in Geneva.

The Declaration and Its Critics

The Declaration on Fundamental Principles and Rights at Work referred to a set of specific rights and obligations that were expressed in "Conventions recognized as fundamental".[680] It stipulated that all ILO member States, by the very fact of their membership in the Organization, were obliged to adhere to and promote the principles relating to the "fundamental rights" that were expressed in these Conventions, regardless of whether or not they had ratified them. The four categories of fundamental rights were: (a) freedom of association and the effective recognition of the right to collective bargaining; (b) the elimination of all forms of forced and compulsory labour; (c) the effective abolition of child labour; and (d) the elimination of discrimination in respect of employment and occupation. The Declaration introduced a follow-up mechanism that included an annual review report and global reports, which would cover all four principles of fundamental rights within a four-year cycle. The ILO also received a new mandate to assist its member states by means of technical cooperation, which triggered a reorientation

680 See the list in fn. 656.

of the ILO's programmatic work towards an integrated approach, with the promotion of "fundamental standards" at its core.

In the end, the Declaration was carried by a fairly broad consensus. The fact that it did not contain any new obligations for the members was not only an explanation but a precondition for this outcome. Member States were asked for their acceptance of principles only, without a direct obligation to ratify or implement the fundamental Conventions. Yet, when a vote was eventually taken (on the initiative of the Egyptian government), instead of adopting the Declaration by mere acclamation, it reached the necessary quorum only by nine votes.[681] More than anything, this result reflected the developing countries' continuing apprehensions about accepting any interference with their policies when labour rights potentially conflicted with trade issues or the "right to development". Without the explicit statement in the Declaration that labour standards "should not be used for protectionist trade purposes" and the pledge that "the comparative advantage of any country should in no way be called into question by this Declaration and its follow-up",[682] it is highly doubtful that it would have been adopted at all.

Still, from the ILO's point of view, the adoption of the Declaration was a major success. At a minimum, it provided a reorientation of the ILO that almost all in the ILO could agree to. Certain early indications that justified a positive assessment. Throughout the following years, the ratification rates for ILO standards increased significantly, and some of the fundamental Conventions – above all, the Worst Form of Child Labour Convention (No. 182) and the Equal Remuneration Convention (No. 100) – were at least in theory available as a legal reference in almost all countries of the world. Fundamental labour standards have undoubtedly increased the ILO's visibility. They found their way into trade agreements and entrepreneurial codes of conduct and built a new point of reference in the public debate which was also used by other international organizations. In addition, the promotional campaigns built around the follow-up mechanism earned the Organization new resources from member States such as the United States. The campaigns helped the ILO to expand its public outreach, and its initiatives against child labour, forced labour and discrimination in employment and occupation helped it to widen its network of connections with a range of civil society groups around the world.

The Declaration, however, was not welcomed by all and drew sharp criticism from some quarters. Most of the critics took issue with the fact that the Declara-

681 There were 273 votes in favour and 43 abstentions, which meant the quorum was only just reached by 9 votes.

682 ILO, The Declaration on Fundamental Principles and Rights at Work, adopted by the International Labour Conference at its 86th Session, 18 June 1998, art. 5.

tion implicitly created a hierarchy of standards. In their judgement, standards dealing with working conditions, the right to a safe and healthy work place, fair wages and a limitation of working hours, income security through health care, pensions, unemployment insurance, and other protections had lost in weight. Often, these critics made a connection between the Declaration and certain neoliberal tendencies in other aspects of the ILO's work. The adoption of the Private Employment Agencies Convention of 1997 (No. 181) was a case in point. It compromised the almost eighty-year-old principle, enshrined in the Unemployment Convention of 1919, that public employment services were the sole legitimate institutions in the field. Some of the critics regarded this step as an unforgivable mistake in the face of what they saw as an all-out neoliberal assault. An unsuccessful parallel attempt to create a Convention regulating contract labour provided additional grist to the mill for these critics.[683]

Inasmuch as the ILO and the supporters of the Declaration argued that all four fundamental principles constituted "enabling rights", the critics pointed to the heavy imbalance among them. And indeed, while the fight against forced and child labour has found very high if not almost unanimous acceptance among the ILO's constituents, freedom of association and the right to collective bargaining – arguably the "enabling rights" par excellence – have enjoyed much less support. Less than half of the world's population is covered by Conventions Nos. 87 and 98, and the countries that have not ratified one or both of them include major economic players such as China, India, Mexico, Brazil or the United States. The same goes for the resources that the ILO has been able to generate for its promotional campaigns. While "popular" rights on the list have attracted huge resources – child labour alone accounted for more than three quarters of the total in extrabudgetary contributions from state donors during the period from 2000 to 2011 – freedom of association has always ended up with a significantly smaller share. The reasons have been manifold, but it is clear enough that the political character of freedom of association makes it much less attractive to state donors. The publicity value of promoting trade unions is negligible in contrast to a campaign for the eradication of child labour.[684]

Another point of contention concerned the monitoring of the core labour standards. There was criticism that the promotional and non-confrontational mechanisms the ILO had put in place with the Declaration further weakened the ILO's already small power of sanctions. Some have attributed this outcome to the

---

683 Standing, "The ILO: An Agency for Globalization?" 365–369; Royle, "The ILO's Shift to Promotional Principles and the 'Privatization' of Labour Rights", 258–261.
684 Reynaud, *The International Labour Organization and Globalization*, 10.

influence particularly of the United States and have thus characterized the Declaration in general as a major victory for the US government. For the human rights law scholar Philip Alston, the Declaration offered an "ideal route" for the United States to escape from the dilemma of having itself ratified only two fundamental Conventions, on the worst forms of child labour and on forced labour (Convention No. 182 and Convention No. 105), while applying sanctions in its domestic legislation – and seeking them at WTO level –to other countries violating core labour standards.[685] Against this background, the more radical critics see the Declaration as an expression of the ILO's ultimate complicity in the establishment of an international neoliberal order and the acceptance of its own subordinate role with regard to the prevailing Washington Consensus.[686]

In response to these criticisms, the defenders of the Declaration placed most of their emphasis on the new procedural possibilities that its follow-up mechanisms offered to the ILO with regard to monitoring the evolution of principles and rights and providing technical assistance to help their promotion. They argued that the additional opportunities provided by these mechanisms, namely to reach out to groups beyond the ILO's classical constituencies, were the best hope for the ILO to revitalize its standard-setting activities through the mobilization of people directly affected on the national and transnational levels.[687] The dynamics in connection with IPEC and, to a certain extent, the mobilization for the adoption of the Domestic Workers Convention (No. 189) of 2011 seemed to prove the point.[688] Moreover, one of the main authors of the Declaration as the ILO's Legal Adviser, Francis Maupain, refused to accept the widespread criticism that the ILO had replaced "hard" labour standards with "soft" law principles. For Maupain, this contention was based on an overly simplistic view about the ILO's presumed "golden age" of standard-setting after the Second World War, which, on closer scrutiny, would display a much more complex picture, considering that the ideological confrontation of the Cold War had led to the adoption of rather sectoral standards that earned only few ratifications.[689] There is, indeed, much to say in support of this argument. David Morse's focus in the 1950s on the principles of

685 Philip Alston, "'Core Labour Standards' and the Transformation of the International Labour Rights Regime", *European Journal of International Law* 15, no. 3 (2004): 457–521.

686 Royle speaks about an "acceptance of the neo-liberal agenda", Royle, "The ILO's Shift to Promotional Principles and the 'Privatization' of Labour Rights", 270.

687 For a summary of the positions, see Reynaud, *The International Labour Organization and Globalization*, 8–9.

688 On domestic work, see the Epilogue.

689 Francis Maupain, *The Future of the International Labour Organization in the Global Economy* (Oxford: Hart Publishing, 2013).

the Declaration of Philadelphia and a few human rights standards was already driven by the observation that ILO standard-setting was losing its universality in the face of an ever more diverse membership as a result of decolonization and the Cold War. Given the currency which human rights enjoyed in international discussions of all kinds in the 1990s, it must have seemed obvious for Hansenne to deploy a similar strategy in reframing the ILO as a human rights agency.[690]

To the critics of the ILO's "neoliberal turn" the answer is less straightforward. Whatever Hansenne's primary intentions in steering the process in the direction of the Declaration might have been, and how far his inclinations towards free trade and labour market flexibility might have carried his actions, remains subject to interpretation. In hindsight, though, and with a view of the bigger picture, it seems both unfair, and, to a certain degree, also ahistorical, to judge the Declaration with a view to its content alone. In the early to mid-1990s, taking a firmer and more principled stand on standard-setting was probably not a realistic option for the ILO. Against the background of the superior position which the WTO, the OECD, and the international financial institutions had acquired both with regard to their material means and the dominant discourse, the alternative might well have been the further marginalization of the Organization. In this view, Hansenne's move to bring the ILO back into the debate on the social dimension of globalization by focusing on a limited number of core labour standards was possibly the only way to secure the ILO's continuing relevance. While this is no small accomplishment from an organizational point of view, it still leaves open the question whether the ILO had the capacity – in the given historical context – to make an impact on the globalization debate, let alone to claim a new "social mandate" for itself. At least, with the 1998 Declaration, the ILO has shown its capacity to make its voice heard. It may not have been the renewal of a social mandate for the global age, but it was surely a small step towards the restoration of the Philadelphia consensus and the acknowledgement that, ultimately, all policies have to be evaluated with reference to an overarching social objective.

690 Normand and Zaidi, *Human Rights at the UN*, 316–341.

Epilogue

Decent Work and the Social Dimension of Globalization

In early 1999, the International Labour Organization (ILO) took another turn when the Chilean diplomat Juan Somavía became its ninth Director-General. Somavía was the first Director-General from the global South, and he brought a fresh perspective to the ILO's work. Yet Somavía's views were probably shaped less by his origins than by the many years he had spent at the United Nations, where he had been particularly involved with social and economic affairs. He was the Permanent Representative of Chile to the UN from 1990 to 1999; had served as the Chairman of the UN's Third Committee on Social, Humanitarian and Cultural Affairs; and had twice been the President of ECOSOC.[691] His closest interaction with the ILO before he took office was as Chairman of the Preparatory Committee for the Copenhagen Social Summit in 1995. As Director-General, he wanted to move the ILO closer to the centre of global debates, which meant a closer relationship with the United Nations and a renewed emphasis on development and the social consequences of an accelerated globalization. While Somavía acknowledged Hansenne's accomplishments, and in particular the recognition the ILO had gained with the Declaration on Fundamental Principles and Rights at Work, he felt that the ILO still needed more focus and visibility. The tool which was designed to reorient and reintegrate the ILO's activities, was the concept of "decent work". This became the central and all-embracing framework of Somavía's 13 years in office, and it has remained so under his successor, Guy Ryder.[692]

Somavía introduced the decent work concept in his very first speech to the Governing Body in March 1999 as a guiding principle, defining four strategic objectives to refocus the ILO's activities. According to Somavía, these objectives were the essence of the ILO's work: realizing fundamental principles and rights at work; creating greater opportunities for men and women to secure decent employment and income; enhancing and extending social protection for all; and strengthening tripartism and social dialogue.[693] In the same speech, Somavía

691 Somavía's biographical data can be found on the ILO's official website.

692 Leah Vosko, "Decent Work: The Shifting Role of the ILO and the Struggle for Global Social Justice", *Global Social Policy* 2, no. 1 (2002): 19–46.

693 "I believe that the central purpose of the ILO today, is to promote opportunities of decent work for all. The four strategic objectives must converge on this overarching goal. If the ILO's values are to be translated into action, rather than just a reaffirmation of belief, then the four strategic objectives must be mutually supportive." Statement by Mr. Juan Somavía, Director-

https://doi.org/10.1515/9783110650723-011

felt that the ILO's activities had not sufficiently embraced the increasingly heterogeneous realities of working life across the globe, including the large and growing informal economy. The decent work concept was designed as a means to overcome this weakness, firstly, by reclaiming a strengthened role for the ILO in the field of development and, secondly, by reaching out more effectively to all working people. Starting from Somavía's observation that "Almost everyone works, but not everyone is employed", decent work reaffirmed the ILO's moral obligation and mandate to improve conditions for *all* working people, regardless of their employment status. Consequently, it has also functioned as a basis for and a gateway to new initiatives.

During Somavía's first term in office, the ILO worked intensively to implement the decent work concept on the ground, for example through specific Decent Work Country Programmes, and in parallel to promote it within the Organization as well as in the international community. A first opportunity opened up at the WTO Ministerial Conference in Seattle in 1999.[694] The massive and violent protests against the meeting, which drew the attention of the international public to the growing counter-globalization movement, provided a dramatic backdrop that lent additional weight to Somavía's message. He used the opportunity to present the decent work concept as a response to the inequality and unfairness globalization had produced – and was continuing to produce – for too many people in the world.[695]

The next step was to establish the decent work concept in the general global policy debates at the United Nations that were taking place around the turn of the millennium. In 2002, the ILO set up a World Commission that was tasked with producing a comprehensive report, published in 2004 with the title *A Fair Globalization: Creating Opportunities for All.* Its real value lay less in its content – which was described by some observers as a "list of good intentions" – than in the consolidation of the decent work approach at the highest intergovernmental level.[696] In 2007, decent work was included in the renewed Millennium Development Goals (MDGs) of the United Nations, which

General of the International Labour Office, upon taking his Oath of Office, Geneva, 22 March 1999, https://bit.ly/2IgT6F1.

694 Somavía decided to attend the meeting on the basis of a general invitation to all organizations (originally without the right to speak). It was the first time that an ILO Director-General took part in a WTO meeting, after Hansenne had been invited to the Singapore WTO Ministerial Conference in 1996 and then disinvited.

695 Reynaud, *The International Labour Organization and Globalization*, 12–13.

696 "Decent Work for all should be made a global goal and be pursued through coherent policies within the multilateral system. This would respond to a major political demand in all countries and demonstrate the capacity of the multilateral system to find creative solutions to this critical

listed "full and productive employment and decent work for all, including women and young people" as a target under Goal No. 1 (Eradicate extreme poverty and hunger).[697] Finally, in the context of the 2008 global financial and economic crisis, Somavía was once again able to push the ILO towards the core of international policy-making, when the Organization was asked to prepare a report on the impact of the crisis on jobs for the G20 Summit in September 2009 in Pittsburgh.[698]

An important codification of the decent work agenda was the Declaration on Social Justice for a Fair Globalization, adopted by the 97th Session of the ILC in 2008.[699] The intention of this Declaration was twofold. It proclaimed the universality of the decent work approach, based on its four strategic objectives: employment, social protection, social dialogue, and fundamental principles and rights at work.[700] In addition, it formulated "the contemporary vision of the ILO's mandate in the era of globalization",[701] thus inscribing the decent work concept in an important ILO instrument – together with references to the ILO's Constitution of 1919, the Declaration of Philadelphia of 1944, and the 1998 Declaration on Fundamental Principles and Rights at Work.[702] Written on the eve of the financial crisis of 2008 (which broke out only three months after its adoption), the Social Justice Declaration addresses both the problems in a "world of growing interdependence and complexity" and defines the ILO's approach to reducing the social cost of these developments.

If anything, the Social Justice Declaration reflects a minimum consensus among the ILO's constituents. Nevertheless, it established a scheme of "recurrent discussions" by the ILC, covering each of the four strategic objectives in turn. So far they have paved the way for several new Recommendations and a Protocol.[703]

---

problem." World Commission on the Social Dimension of Globalization, *A Fair Globalization: Creating Opportunities for All* (Geneva: ILO, 2004), xiii.

697 Reynaud, *The International Labour Organization and Globalization*, 14–15.

698 Marieke Louis, "The ILO, Social Partners and the G20: New Prospects for Social Dialogue at the Global Level", *Global Social Policy* 16, no. 3 (2016): 235–252.

699 ILO Declaration on Social Justice for a Fair Globalization, adopted by the International Labour Conference at its Ninety-Seventh Session, Geneva, 10 June 2008.

700 Ibid., 2, 9, 10.

701 Ibid., 1.

702 In his Preface, Somavía defined the Social Justice Declaration with explicit reference to these documents as "the third major statement of principles and policies adopted by the Intenational Labour Conference since the ILO's Constitution of 1919". Ibid.

703 The Social Protection Floors Recommendation, 2012 (No. 202) with regard to minimum social protection; the Transition from the Informal to the Formal Economy Recommendation,

In October 2012, Guy Ryder,[704] a British national and former general secretary of the ITUC, succeeded Somavía. As Director-General he has continued to promote decent work in the UN system. At the early stages of Ryder's mandate, decent work coupled with economic growth became Goal 8 of the 17 Sustainable Development Goals (SDGs) of the United Nations' 2030 Agenda for Sustainable Development, adopted in 2015.[705]

The decent work concept has received an almost equal share of praise and criticism. Together with its proven value in (re-)connecting the ILO to the rest of the "international community", it was lauded by its supporters as a timely reaction to the realities in the world of work under the conditions of globalization. In their view, decent work means a more inclusive approach to improving the conditions of working people worldwide.[706] From this perspective, the concept represents a certain historical continuity, starting in the 1930s with the ILO's participation in the broader economic debate on unemployment, and continuing after the war with the broadened mandate of the Declaration of Philadelphia, the employment-centred approach of the WEP, and the efforts under the PIACT to improve working conditions in both the industrialized and developing countries.

On the other hand, the concept of decent work has also encountered strong criticism. Some of its critics have taken issue with the "vagueness" of the concept, in particular with regard to the term "decent". For Guy Standing, one of Somavía's collaborators at the beginning of his first term, this vagueness and the initial reluctance to create measurable indicators for decent work were intentional.[707] Standing's assessment continues to echo with other critical voices, mostly from the political left, who see the deliberately non-ideological or non-political

---

2015 (No. 204); and, in 2014, the Supplementary Protocol to the Forced Labour Convention, 1930 (No. 29) and the Forced Labour (Supplementary Measures) Recommendation (No. 203).

704 Ryder combines a trade union background with prior experience in the ILO (from 1998 to 2002 and again from 2010 to 2012 as the Executive Director responsible for international labour standards and fundamental principles and rights at work). He had been appointed General Secretary of the ICFTU in 2002, managing its transition into the new unified International Trade Union Confederation (ITUC) in 2006.

705 According to UNResolution A/RES/70/1, 25 September 2015, Goal 8 which usually appears under the heading of "Decent Work and Economic Growth", aims to "promote sustained, inclusive and sustainable economic growth, full and productive employment and decent work for all".

706 Or a "metaphor", as in Vosko, "Decent Work. The Shifting Role of the ILO."

707 Standing, "The ILO: An Agency for Globalization?". In September 2008, the ILO convened an international Tripartite Meeting of Experts on the Measurement of Decent Work, and adopted a framework of Decent Work Indicators that was endorsed by the 18th International Conference of Labour Statisticians in December 2008.

character of the concept as a way to conceal its compatibility or even complicity with the hegemonic neoliberal agenda. In their view, the ILO has once again (after the 1998 Declaration) failed to adopt a "counter-hegemonic" position, one which would have tackled the root causes of inhumane working conditions.[708] Whether the ILO would have been able to launch and defend such an unequivocal strategy given the realities of its tripartite structure, and an overall unfavourable context, is, however, open to question.

Social Justice for a New Century

What lessons can be learned from 100 years of ILO history? The questions posed at the start of this book – whose organization is the ILO, what defines it as an international organization, and what could or should be its contribution to the quest for social justice – seem to be as valid today as they were in 1919 in Paris or 1944 in Philadelphia.

In the summer of 2011 the International Labour Conference produced some unusually colourful images of grassroots activists representing household workers from many different countries urging delegates to the ILC adopt a "Convention concerning decent work for domestic workers"[709] Their presence, their songs, chants, and slogans written on t-shirts and banderoles communicated in a very immediate way the importance they attached to a Convention that for the first time extended to domestic workers labour protections with regard to wages, regulation of working time, weekly rest, and overall working conditions.[710]

Domestic work is a recent area of ILO activities, but it has a historical continuity with the constant expansion of the ILO's mandate to integrate new forms of work and address the needs of new groups of workers. In the case of domestic work, roughly 53 million people (as of 2010) worldwide are now in the orbit of ILO standard-setting. Together with less well-known labour standards, Convention No. 189 is an attempt to tackle the problems of the "informal" economy, which has long been regarded as difficult to regulate. These standards are part of the

708 For a summary of the discussion, see Felix Hauf, "The Paradoxes of Decent Work in Context: A Cultural Political Economy Perspective", *Global Labour Journal* 6, no. 2 (2015): 138–155.
709 Convention on Decent Work for Domestic Workers, 2011 (No. 189).
710 Chris Bonner, Pat Horn, and Renana Jhabvala, "Informal Women Workers Open ILO Doors through Transnational Organizing, 1980s to 2010s", in *Women's ILO,* ed. Boris, Hoehtker, and Zimmermann, 176–202; Eileen Boris and Jennifer N. Fish, "'Slaves No More': Making Global Labor Standards for Domestic Workers", *Feminist Studies* 40, no. 2 (2014): 411–443.

Figure 16: Representatives of domestic worker organizations celebrating the adoption of the Domestic Worker Convention (No. 189) with ILO Director-General Juan Somavía at the 2011 ILC.

ILO's long history of engagement with informality, which started in the 1970s with the World Employment Programme.[711]

From yet a different point of view, domestic work is also part of the equally long history of struggles for representation and participation within the ILO's tripartite framework. On the one hand the adoption of the Domestic Workers Convention can be attributed to the creative strategies pursued by a transnational advocacy network and the "strategies of affect" applied by "real" domestic workers present as visible and audible defenders of their cause in the ILO's meeting rooms.[712] On the other hand, the reason why these networks could get their concerns on the ILC agenda was the result of alliances built with Workers' and Government groups and the connections made between domestic work and the ILO's focus areas of "fair globalization" and "decent work".[713] Something

---

711 Other standards which are addressing the informal economy are e.g. the Home Work Convention, 1996 (No. 177); the Home Work Recommendation, 1996 (No. 184); the Domestic Workers Recommendation, 2011 (No. 201); and the Transition from the Informal to the Formal Economy Recommendation, 2015 (No. 204).

712 Boris and Fish, " 'Slaves No More': Making Global Labor Standards for Domestic Workers", 437.

713 What ultimately secured the success of the Convention and helped to overcome significant resistance in particular from the Employers' side and on the part of some national governments,

similar had already happened with indigenous peoples' representatives in 1989 and NGO activists against child labour in 1999, when Conventions on their rights were negotiated and adopted.

This particular case indicates the capacity of the tripartite structure, despite resistance, to incorporate and accommodate new demands. In a broader sense it presents tripartism as a predictable mode of operation which allows a certain degree of flexibility to better adapt to changing historical circumstances, political constellations, structural and technological change. As the book has shown at various points, the tripartism that the ILO had developed during the inter-war years survived the authoritarian challenges of the 1930s as well as the ideological battles of the Cold War and the decolonization era without losing the core of its democratic impetus.

Tripartism, as this book has shown, has worked as an asset for the ILO at the national level as well, where it had to be adapted to the specific context and the situation of local employers' organization and trade unions. However, cooperation with extended networks beyond the tripartite framework was a decisive part of the International Labour Office's strategy from the beginning. Without ever questioning the institutional tripartite representation, the ILO has established close working relationships with a broad set of actors ranging from the cooperative movement to scientific institutions such as the International Management Institute (IMI) of the interwar period, to social security institutions, to the Catholic Church and, in the more immediate past, to children's and human rights NGOs.

At the same time, questions of representation and participation have continued to give rise to conflict and debate. The inclusion of colonial or indigenous workers into delegations and the ILO standard-setting process had initially been met with resistance. The same is true for feminists and women activists who were claiming not only equal rights and better conditions for women workers, but also better representation. Some of these struggles belong to the past, others continue to this day. Given the expansion of the informal economy and the explosion of precarious work even in countries where formal and protected employment has been the rule for decades, the question of how

---

was owed to the support of trade unions and accordingly domestic workers organizations' adaptation to the formal trade union criteria. The International Domestic Workers Network (IDWN), a global network of domestic workers' organizations that was launched during the 98th Session of the ILC in 2009, was integrated as a semi-autonomous entity into the structure of the International Union of Food Workers, which provided it with the necessary recognition and legitimacy and established contact with key people in the International Labour Office and in the trade unions.

to organize workers and support their fight for jobs, rights, and better working conditions is as urgent as it was in the first decades of the ILO. In terms of direct membership, both the Workers' group in the ILO as well as the IOE[714] represent a limited and mostly shrinking proportion of the world of work. Unionization rates have been on the decline during the last decades. Trade unions find themselves under continous pressure from calls for labour market flexibility. As recent debates on the right to strike have highlighted, this pressure is increasingly felt within the Organization, too.[715] Trade unions see many good reasons to resist any calls to modify the principle of tripartism that could recognize other bodies as mandated representatives of workers within the Organization, a move that would only further weaken their capacity to represent their members' interests and conclude agreements on their behalf. From the trade union's point of view (shared in principle by the Employers) this capacity depends on their ability to avoid further fragmentation.[716] Also, their argument that the fluid world of NGOs lacks transparency, accountability and proper representation cannot easily be dismissed as an expression of vested interests.

Last but not least, domestic work opens a window to present debates on social justice. Both in itself and as part of the wider issue of international labour migration, domestic work has global dimensions which connect poor, middle-income, and rich countries with each other. It is an indicator of global inequalities but also of gender imbalances – in the light of the fact that the overwhelming majority of domestic workers are women.

The world today is different compared to 1919, but many of the ILO's founding principles have lost nothing of their relevance. This is certainly true for the constitutional maxim, "labour is not a commodity". It encapsulates the social liberal consensus that has carried the ILO for a century. At its core rests the insight that the survival of open market economies ultimately depends on a decommodification

---

714 Louis, "Building a Transnational Business Community", 19–21. While the United States Council for International Business (USCIB)represents corporate giants like Google, IBM, Nestlé, DuPont and Coca Cola in the IOE, some powerful MNEs like Amazon are not IOE members.
715 At the 2012 Session of the ILC, the Employers' group broke with an almost seventy-year-old unwritten agreement, according to which the CEACR deals with infringements on the right to strike as violations of the freedom of association and right to collective bargaining Conventions No. 87 and 98 – even though this right is not explicitly mentioned in the respective Conventions. Observers see this as part of a broader strategy by the employers of gaining a "freer hand" to push for further deregulation of international labour law and for a reform of the ILO's supervisory system. Hauf, "The Paradoxes of Decent Work in Context".
716 Ibid.

of labour, as far as possible and feasible – through living wages and social policies that safeguard workers and their families from falling into poverty. Modern welfare states have been built on this premise, and the ILO's labour standards both testify and add substance to this project. The maxim that "labour is not a commodity" has never reflected the reality of labour markets, where labour has de facto always been treated as a commodity. If anything, globalization and the imperatives it sets for working people – both real and alleged –, have exacerbated this. "Labour is not a commodity" in this sense stands for the conviction that its human and social dimension distinguishes labour from other commodities and implies a call for governments and business alike to respect and act upon it.

ILO activities in the field of human trafficking are a recent case in point. The debates surrounding the adoption of the 2014 Forced Labour Protocol targeting various forms of modern slavery underscored the dimensions of the most brutal forms of commodification of labour, with approximately 40 million people suffering under inhumane conditions in private households, agriculture, on construction sites, or as victims of sexual exploitation.[717] Incidents such as the collapse of the Rana Plaza factory in Dhaka, Bangladesh, in 2013, remind us that even when labour is formally free, at the dark end of global supply chains workers can be trapped in hazardous working conditions that resemble in many ways those that existed in the ILO's early days.

Similar points can be made about one of the core messages of the Philadelphia Declaration of 1944, which holds that "Poverty anywhere constitutes a danger to prosperity everywhere". This statement builds on the ILO's constitutional assumption that "the failure of any nation to adopt humane conditions of labour is an obstacle in the way of other nations which desire to improve the conditions in their own countries".[718] Together, these assertions make the case for international labour standards as a means to manage the potentially hazardous effects of international economic competition. To live up to these ambitious goals, the ILO has moved far beyond standard-setting. From its early technical assistance missions to the World Employment Programme, the large-scale technical cooperation programmes starting in the 1990s, and the Social Justice Declaration, the ILO has taken an active part in the discussion of the international dimension of social justice and addressed it through assistance and development activities on the ground. "Poverty anywhere constitutes a danger to prosperity everywhere" in this sense could well be read as a timely commentary on another

717 ILO and Walk Free Foundation, *Global Estimates of Modern Slavery: Forced Labour and Forced Marriage* (Geneva: ILO, 2017), 5.
718 Preamble to the ILO's Constitution.

issue which has become more closely connected to the problem of poverty: international migration. The ILO's contribution to the Global Compact on Migration of 2018 explicitly emphasizes this connection explicitly.[719] This area has been complicated and aggravated by the global refugee crisis that has unfolded since 2011, and the ILO is encountering the same problems that have inhibited the work for refugees and migrant workers since its inception. With regard to labour migration, the ILO faces one of the contradictions in today's global economy – between receiving countries' claims for border control and immigration restriction on the one side, and their obvious demand for flexible and mobile labour forces on the other.[720] In the current political climate, to organize a global discussion on the social dimension of migration and migration policies, or to address the question of how best to integrate migrants and refugees into the labour markets of their host countries, has become more difficult than ever.

Finally, social justice appears in a central message of the ILO Constitution: "Whereas universal and lasting peace can be established only if it is based on social justice".[721] For the Constitution's authors, who drafted the document with fresh memories of the horrors of the First World War, it must have seemed only natural to give this message a prominent position. This seemed even more true in 1944 in Philadelphia, when many thought that the failure of liberal democracies to address the social consequences of the Great Depression had facilitated the rise of fascism that had led to the war. Most of the political leaders, trade unionists, and employers gathering in Philadelphia subscribed to one lesson of the past: that social justice was a precondition not only for peace but also for the stability of democratic government. The rise of neo-nationalist and right-wing populist movements in recent years, due in part to the very real experience of social inequalities both globally and within societies, bears echoes of the past that still resonate today.

Against this background, the major question for the ILO in its Centenary year is not whether it is still relevant, but rather how much momentum it can retain and gain back in a world that has– despite the recent return to neo-protectionist rhetoric – for the last decades been dominated by a widespread belief in the primacy of markets and the calls for deregulation and flexibilization that accom-

719 ILO, "UN Secretary-General's report on the global compact for safe, orderly and regular migration. Inputs of the International Labour Organization" (Geneva: ILO), 6 November 2017.
720 This contradiction is pointed out by Antoine Pécoud, "What Do We Know about the International Organization for Migration?" *Journal of Ethnic and Migration Studies* 44, no. 10 (2018): 1621–1638.
721 ILO Constitution.

pany it. The dominant discourse that sees globalization as a quasi-natural force leaves limited space for an organization which has always relied on the capacity and willingness of states to intervene on behalf of their own citizens in order to limit the destructive potential of open market economies. The future success of the ILO depends largely on the degree to which it will be able to facilitate a renewed "Philadelphia consensus" in the context of globalization and to gain support for its vision that the objective of social cohesion and justice should guide all policies. A first step would be to recognize that the concept of social progress itself has changed significantly since Philadelphia. It is no longer just about a fair distribution of the fruits of economic growth, but increasingly also about a redefinition – from a social justice perspective – of what progress could mean in the face of the vast ecological challenges in the present and future

After decades in which international discourse on human rights has been largely dominated by the primacy of liberal freedoms, recent debates show a new awareness and sense of urgency for the inclusion of and emphasis on social rights.[722] The ILO seems better equipped than any other organization to respond to these new calls to reconcile social justice with human rights, both between and within nations.

Climate change and environmental destruction, global migration, the digital revolution, and the persisting growth of the informal economy are among the forces which will continue to have a major impact on the world of work. It is changing more rapidly than ever before, although by far not in the same way and at the same speed for all workers. In addition, in rich and poor, industrialized and non-industrialized countries, outrageously inhumane working conditions continue to exist. These developments come with new questions of social justice as well as challenges to traditional notions of the term itself..

Various initiatives launched for the Centenary by Director-General Ryder, especially the Future of Work initiative and the Global Commission on the Future of Work, which submitted its report in early 2019, have addressed many of these problems. In June 2019 the ILC adopted a Centenary Declaration and the Violence and Harrassment Convention (No. 190). Whether the ILO will be able to meaningfully contribute to the practice of social justice in the 21st century, however, is not in the hands of the Organization alone. There has to be a political climate that favours multilateralism, and trade unions and employers' organizations must have enough political support to render a significant contribution. States cannot

722 Samuel Moyn, *Not Enough: Human Rights in an Unequal World* (Cambridge, MA: The Belknap Press of Harvard University Press, 2018).

be satisfied by relegating the ILO to being a mere passive social conscience of the world. Despite all setbacks and limitations, the last 100 years have proven one point – the ILO has always been an organization for difficult times. For the ILO to be able to act, however, its constituents have to be both willing and able to use the tools provided by the Organization to shape global social policy, as they have done on so many occasions before.

List of Abbreviations

AFL	American Federation of Labor
AFL-CIO	The American Federation of Labor and Congress of Industrial Organizations
AIP	Andean Indian Programme
CEACR	Committee of Experts on the Application of Conventions and Recommendations
CFA	Committee on Freedom of Association
CIO	Congress of Industrial Organizations
CITI	*Confédération internationale des travailleurs intellectuels*
CSR	corporate social responsibility
DAF	*Deutsche Arbeitsfront*
DAMP	David A. Morse Papers, Seely G. Mudd Rare Manuscript Library, Princeton University
ECOSOC	Economic and Social Council
EPTA	Expanded Programme of Technical Assistance
ETUC	European Trade Union Confederation
ERP	European Recovery Programme
FAO	Food and Agriculture Organization of the United Nations
GATT	General Agreement on Tariffs and Trade
IACP	International Association for Child Protection
IALL	International Association for Labour Legislation
IASP	International Association for Social Progress
ICFTU	International Confederation of Free Trade Unions
ICIC	International Committee on Intellectual Cooperation
IDS	Institute for Development Studies (Sussex, UK)
IFTU	International Federation of Trade Unions
IIA	International Institute of Agriculture
IILS	International Institute for Labour Studies
ILC	International Labour Conference
ILO	International Labour Organization/International Labour Office
ILOA	ILO Archives
IMEC	Industrialized Market Economy Countries
IMI	International Management Institute
IMF	International Monetary Fund
IOE	International Organisation of Employers
IPEC	International Programme on the Elimination of Child Labour
IPR	Institute for Pacific Relations
ITO	International Trade Organization
LNHO	League of Nations Health Organization
LNU	League of Nations Union
MDG(s)	Millennium Development Goals(s)
MNE(s)	multinational enterprise(s)
NGO	Non-governmental organization
NIEO	New International Economic Order

https://doi.org/10.1515/9783110650723-012

OECD	Organisation for Economic Co-operation and Development
OEEC	Organization for European Economic Cooperation
OHIM	Oral History Interview David A. Morse, Harry S. Truman Library
OPT	Occupied Palestinian Territories
PIACT	International Programme for the Improvement of Working Conditions and Environment
PMC	Permanent Mandate Commission of the League of Nations
SCIU	Save the Children International Union
SDG(s)	Sustainable Development Goal(s)
TAB	Technical Assistance Board
TAP	Technical Assistance Programme
TUC	Trades Union Congress
UIASDN	*Union internationale des associations pour la Societé des Nations*
UNCTAD	United Nations Conference on Trade and Development
UNDP	United Nations Development Programme
UNESCO	United Nations Educational, Scientific and Cultural Organization
UNICEF	United Nations Children's Fund
UNIDO	United Nations Industrial Development Organization
USAID	United States Agency for International Development
WCL	World Conference of Labour
WEP	World Employment Programme
WFTU	World Federation of Trade Unions
WHO	World Health Organization
WTO	World Trade Organization

Bibliography

Al-Dajani, Shukri Z. *Encounters with Fate and Destiny: A Life in International Politics*. London: I.B. Tauris, 2018.

Alcock, Antony. *History of the International Labor Organization*. New York: Octagon Books, 1971.

Alston, Philip. "'Core Labour Standards' and the Transformation of the International Labour Rights Regime." *European Journal of International Law* 15, no. 3 (2004): 457–521.

Amos, Jennifer. "Embracing and Contesting: The Soviet Union and the Universal Declaration of Human Rights, 1948–1958." In *Human Rights in the Twentieth Century*, edited by Stefan-Ludwig Hoffmann, 147–165. Cambridge: Cambridge University Press, 2010.

Amrith, Sunil, and Glenda Sluga. "New Histories of the United Nations." *Journal of World History* 19, no. 3 (2008): 251–274.

Anderson, Carol. *Eyes Off the Prize: The United Nations and the African American Struggle for Human Rights, 1944–1955*. Cambridge: Cambridge University Press, 2003.

Azara, Liliosa. "The Holy See and the International Labour Organization: The Origins of a Special Relationship." In *Christian Democrat Internationalism: Its Action in Europe and Worldwide from post-World War II until the 1990s. Volume II: The Development (1945–1979). The Role of Parties, Movements, People*, edited by Jean-Dominique Durand, 42–56. Brussels: Peter Lang, 2013.

Bangasser, Paul E. *The ILO and the Informal Sector: An Institutional History*. ILO Employment Paper 2000/9. Geneva: ILO, 2000.

Bashford, Alison. "Population, Geopolitics, and International Organizations in the Mid-Twentieth Century." *Journal of World History* 19, no. 3 (2008): 327–348.

Basualdo, Victoria. "The ILO and the Argentine Dictatorship (1976–1983)." In *ILO Histories*, edited by Van Daele et al., 401–422.

Basualdo, Victoria. "La OIT entre la dictadura y la democracia en la Argentina: aportes sobre el papel de organizaciones internacionales en la reconfiguración de las relaciones laborales en la primera mitad de los años 80," *Anuario del Instituto de Historia Argentina* 17, no. 1 (2017): 1–18.

Benanav, Aaron. "The Origins of Informality: The ILO at the Limit of the Concept of Unemployment," *Journal of Global History* 14, no. 1 (2019): 107–125.

Benson, Wilfrid. "A People's Peace in the Colonies." *International Labour Review* 47, no. 2 (1943): 141–168.

Bernards, Nicholas Alexander. "Actors and Entanglements in Global Governance: The ILO in Sub-Saharan Africa." PhD diss., McMaster University, 2016.

Betti, Eloisa. "Unexpected Alliances: Italian Women's Struggles for Equal Pay, 1940s–1960s." In *Women's ILO*, edited by Boris, Hoehtker, and Zimmermann, 276–299.

Beveridge, William. "Social Insurance and Allied Services." London: HMSO, 1942; reprinted in *Bulletin of the World Health Organization* 78, no. 6 (2000): 847–855.

Birla, L.N., and P. P. Pillai, *India and the ILO*. Oxford: Oxford University Press, 1946.

Blanchard, Francis. *L'Organisation internationale du Travail: De la guerre froide à un nouvel ordre mondial*. Paris: Seuil, 2004.

Böhning, W.R. "The ILO and Contemporary International Economic Migration." *International Migration Review* 10, no. 2 (1976): 147–156.

Bolivar, Camille. "La genèse du World Employment Programme et le projet pilote en Colombie: Un réseau d'experts hétérodoxes pour un gouvernement réformiste." Master's thesis, Université de Genève, 2017.

https://doi.org/10.1515/9783110650723-013

Bonner, Chris, Pat Horn, and Renana Jhabvala. "Informal Women Workers Open ILO Doors through Transnational Organizing, 1980s to 2010s." In *Women's ILO*, edited by Boris, Hoehtker, and Zimmermann, 176–202.

Bonvin, Jean-Michel. *L'Organisation internationale du Travail: Etude sur une agence productrice de normes*. Paris: Presses Universitaires de France, 1998.

Boockmann, Bernhard. "The Ratification of ILO Conventions: A Failure Times Analysis." In ZEW Discussion Papers, edited by ZEW – Zentrum für Europäische Wirtschaftsforschung, 2000.

Borgwardt, Elizabeth. *A New Deal for the World: America's Vision for Human Rights*. Cambridge: Cambridge University Press, 2005.

Boris, Eileen. "Equality's Cold War: The ILO and the UN Commission on the Status of Women, 1946–1970s." In *Women's ILO*, edited by Boris, Hoehtker, and Zimmermann, 97–120.

Boris, Eileen. *Making the Woman Worker: Precarious Labor and the Fight for Global Standards, 1919–2019*. Oxford: Oxford University Press, 2019.

Boris, Eileen, and Jennifer N. Fish. "'Slaves No More': Making Global Labor Standards for Domestic Workers." *Feminist Studies* 40, no. 2 (2014): 411–443.

Boris, Eileen, Dorothea Hoehtker, and Susan Zimmermann, eds. *Women's ILO: Transnational Networks, Global Labour Standards and Gender Equality, 1919 to the Present*. Studies in Global Social History. Leiden: Brill; Geneva: ILO, 2018.

Boutros-Ghali, Boutros. *The United Nations and Apartheid 1948–1994*. New York: United Nations, 1994.

Bradley, Mark Philip. *The World Reimagined. Americans and Human Rights in the Twentieth Century*. Cambridge: Cambridge University Press, 2016.

Brégain, Gildas. "Un problème national, interallié ou international? La difficile gestion transnationale des mutilés de guerre (1917–1923)." *Revue d'histoire de la protection sociale* 9, no. 1 (2016): 110–132.

Breuer, Martin. "Exploring the Technical Assistance Activities of the International Labor Organization in the Field of Indigenous Peoples: Development and Human Rights in the Andean Indian Program (1954–1968)." *Forum for Inter-American Research* 11, no. 3 (2018): 110–123.

Brucken, Rowland. *A Most Uncertain Crusade: The United States, the United Nations, and Human Rights, 1941–1953*. DeKalb, IL: Northern Illinois University Press, 2013.

Burke, Roland. *Decolonization and the Evolution of International Human Rights*. Pennsylvania Studies in Human Rights. Philadelphia, PA: University of Pennsylvania Press, 2010.

Burke, Roland. "Some Rights Are More Equal than Others: The Third World and the Transformation of Economic and Social Rights." *Humanity* 3, no. 3 (2012): 427–448.

Burkman, Thomas W. *Japan and the League of Nations: Empire and World Order, 1914–1938*. Honolulu: University of Hawai'i Press, 2008.

Butler, H. B. *Confident Morning*. London: Faber and Faber, 1950.

Cabanes, Bruno. *The Great War and the Origins of Humanitarianism, 1918–1924*. Studies in the Social and Cultural History of Modern Warfare. Cambridge: Cambridge University Press, 2014.

Carew, Anthony. *American Labour's Cold War Abroad: From Deep Freeze to Détente, 1945–1970*. Edmonton, AB: Athabasca University Press, 2018.

Carew, Anthony. "Conflict within the ICFTU. Anti-Communism and Anti-Colonialism in the 1950s." *International Review of Social History* 41, no.2 (1996): 147–181.

Carew, Anthony. "A False Dawn: The World Federation of Trade Unions (1945–1949)." In *The International Confederation of Free Trade Unions*, edited by Anthony Carew, Michel

Dreyfus, Geert Van Goethem, Rebecca Gumbrell-McCormick, and Marcel van der Linden, 165–187. Bern: Peter Lang, 2000.
Carew, Anthony, Michel Dreyfus, Geert Van Goethem, Rebecca Gumbrell-McCormick, and Marcel van der Linden, eds. *The International Confederation of Free Trade Unions*. Bern: Peter Lang, 2000.
Carroll, Archie B. "A History of Corporate Social Responsibility: Concepts and Practices." In *The Oxford Handbook of Corporate Social Responsibility*, edited by Andrew Crane, Dirk Matten, Abagail McWilliams, Jeremy Moon, and Donald S. Siegel, 19–46. Oxford: Oxford University Press, 2008.
Caruso, Laura, and Andrés Stagnaro. *Una historia regional de la OIT: Aportes sobre regulación y legislación del trabajo latinoamericano*. La Plata: Universidad Nacional de La Plata. Facultad de Humanidades y Ciencias de la Educación, 2017.
Cayet, Thomas. "The ILO and the IMI: A Strategy of Influence on the Edges of the League of Nations, 1925–1934." In *ILO Histories*, edited by Van Daele et al., 251–270.
Cayet, Thomas, Marie Thébaud-Sorger, and Paul-André Rosental. "How International Organisations Compete: Occupational Safety and Health at the ILO, a Diplomacy of Expertise." *Journal of Modern European History* 7, no. 2 (2009): 174–196.
Christiaens, Kim, Idesbald Goddeeris, and Magaly Rodríguez García, eds. *European Solidarity with Chile, 1970s–1980s*. Studies in Political Transition. Frankfurt am Main: Campus Verlag, 2014.
Clavin, Patricia. *Securing the World Economy: The Reinvention of the League of Nations, 1920–1946*. Oxford: Oxford University Press, 2013.
Clavin, Patricia. "What's in a Living Standard? Bringing Society and Economy Together in the ILO and the League of Nations Depression Delegation, 1938–1945." In *Globalizing Social Rights*, edited by Kott and Droux, 233–248.
Cobble, Dorothy Sue. "Japan and the 1919 ILO Debates over Rights, Representations and Global Labour Standards." In *The ILO from Geneva to the Pacific Rim*, edited by Jensen and Lichtenstein, 55–79.
Cobble, Dorothy Sue. "The Other ILO Founders: 1919 and Its Legacies." In *Women's ILO*, edited by Boris, Hoehtker, and Zimmermann, 27–49.
Connelly, Matthew James. *A Diplomatic Revolution: Algeria's Fight for Independence and the Origins of the Post-Cold War Era*. Oxford: Oxford University Press, 2002.
Conrad, Sebastian, and Dominic Sachsenmaier, eds. *Competing Visions of World Order: Global Moments and Movements, 1880–1930*. New York: Palgrave Macmillan, 2007.
Cooper, Frederick. *Decolonization and African Society: The Labor Question in French and British Africa*. Cambridge, MA: Harvard University Press, 1996.
Cox, Robert W. "Education for Development." *International Organization* 23, no. 1 (1968): 310–331.
Cox, Robert W. "ILO–Limited Monarchy." In *The Anatomy of Influence. Decision Making in International Organizations*, edited by Robert W. Cox and Harold K. Jacobson, 102–138. New Haven, CT: Yale University Press, 1973.
Cox, Robert W. "Labor and Hegemony." *International Organization* 31, no. 3 (1977): 385–424.
Cross, Gary. "Les Trois Huits: Labor Movements, International Reform, and the Origins of the Eight-Hour Day, 1919–1924." *French Historical Studies* 14, no. 2 (1985): 240–268.
Dahan, Yossi, Hanna Lerner, and Faina Milman-Sivan, eds. *Global Justice and International Labour Rights*. Cambridge: Cambridge University Press, 2016.
Daughton, J.P. "ILO Expertise and Colonial Violence in the Interwar Years." In *Globalizing Social Rights*, edited by Kott and Droux, 85–97.

De Givry, Jean. "The ILO and the Quality of Working Life. A New International Programme: PIACT," *International Labour Review* 117, no. 3 (1978): 261–271.
De Grazia, Victoria. *Irresistible Empire: America's Advance through Twentieth-Century Europe*. Cambridge, MA: Belknap Press of Harvard University Press, 2005.
Delamotte, Yves, and Kenneth F. Walker. "Humanization of Work and the Quality of Working Life – Trends and Issues." *International Journal of Sociology* 6, no. 1 (1976): 8–40.
Delpal, Bernard. "Le refuge américain de l'OIT (1940–1946). De l'esprit de Genève a l'esprit de Philadelphie, place du syndicalisme dans la strategie de reconstruction." In *L'Organisation internationale du travail*, edited by Lespinet-Moret and Viet, 107–120.
Dhermy-Mairal, Marine. "L'Unification du mouvement coopératif au Bureau international du travail: La 'revolution silencieuse' d'Albert Thomas (1919–1932)." *Le Mouvement Social* 263 (January 2018): 15–29.
Dietrich, Christopher R. W. *Oil Revolution: Sovereign Rights and the Economic Culture of Decolonization, 1945 to 1979*. Global and International History. Cambridge: Cambridge University Press, 2017.
Diller, Janelle M. "Social Justice, Rights, and Labour." In *The Oxford Handbook of International Human Rights Law*, edited by Dinah Shelton, 295–324. Oxford: Oxford University Press, 2013.
Dinkel, Jürgen. *The Non-Aligned Movement: Genesis, Organization and Politics (1927–1992)*. Leiden: Brill, 2019.
Dreyfus, Michel. "The Emergence of an International Trade Union Organization (1902–1919)." In *The International Confederation of Free Trade Unions*, edited by Carew et al., 25–73.
Droux, Joëlle. "From Inter-Agency Competition to Transnational Cooperation: The ILO Contribution to Child Welfare Issues During the Inter-War Years." In *Globalizing Social Rights*, edited by Kott and Droux, 262–279.
Dykmann, Klaas. "Only with the Best Intentions: International Organizations as Global Civilizers." *Comparativ* 23, no. 4/5 (2014): 21–46.
Eckel, Jan. "Human Rights and Decolonization: New Perspectives and Open Questions." *Humanity* 1, no. 1 (2010): 111–135.
Eckel, Jan, and Samuel Moyn. *The Breakthrough: Human Rights in the 1970s*. Pennsylvania Studies in Human Rights. Philadelphia, PA: University of Pennsylvania Press, 2014.
Ehrlich, Paul R. *The Population Bomb*. NewYork: Ballantine Books, 1968.
Eisenberg, Jaci Leigh. "Butler, Harold Beresford." In *IO Bio: Biographical Dictionary*, edited by Reinalda, Kille, and Eisenberg, www.ru.nl/fm/iobio.
Eisenberg, Jaci Leigh. "Jenks, Clarence Wilfred." In *IO Bio: Biographical Dictionary*, edited by Reinalda, Kille, and Eisenberg, www.ru.nl/fm/iobio.
Eisenberg, Jaci Leigh. "Laquelle était la vraie France? France and the ILO During the Second World War." In *ILO Histories*, edited by Van Daele et al., 341–364.
Esping-Andersen,Gøsta. *The Three Worlds of Welfare Capitalism*. Princeton, NJ: Princeton University Press, 1990.
Evju, Stein. "Labour Is Not a Commodity. Reappraising the Origins of the Maxim." *European Labour Law Journal* 4, no. 3 (September 2013): 222–229.
Farré, Sébastian. "Trois experts, une visite, un rapport. L'Organisation internationale du travail et la liberté syndicale en Espagne franquiste." In *L'Organisation internationale du travail*, edited by Lespinet-Moret and Viet, 121–130.
Feiertag, Olivier. "Réguler la mondialisation: Albert Thomas, les débuts du BIT et la crise économique mondiale de 1920–1923." *Les cahiers Irice* 2, no. 2 (2008): 127–155.

Ferreras, Norberto Osvaldo. "Europe–Geneva–America: The First International Conference of American States Members of the International Labour Organization." In *Beyond Geopolitics*, edited by McPherson and Wehrli, 83–96.

Fink, Leon. "A Sea of Difference: The ILO and the Search for Common Standards, 1919–1945." In *The ILO from Geneva to the Pacific Rim*, edited by Jensen and Lichtenstein, 15–33.

Follows, John W. *Antecedents of the International Labour Organization*. Oxford: Clarendon Press, 1951.

Frey, Marc, Sönke Kunkel, and Corinna R. Unger, eds. *International Organizations and Development, 1945–1990*. Basingstoke: Palgrave Macmillan, 2014.

Frey, Marc, Sönke Kunkel, and Corinna R. Unger. "Introduction: International Organizations, Global Development, and the Making of the Contemporary World." In *International Organizations and Development*, edited by Frey, Kunkel, and Unger, 1–22.

Gallo, Stefano. "Dictatorship and International Organizations: The ILO as a Test Ground for Fascism." In *Globalizing Social Rights*, edited by Kott and Droux, 153–171.

Gatrell, Peter. *The Making of the Modern Refugee*. Oxford: Oxford University Press, 2013.

Gaudier, Maryse. *The International Institute for Labour Studies: Its Research Function, Activities and Publications 1960–2001*. Geneva: ILO, 2001.

Gernigon, Bernard, Alberto Odero, and Horacio Guido. *ILO Principles concerning the Right to Strike*. Geneva: ILO, 2000; initially published in *International Labour Review* 137, no. 4 (1998).

Gerry, Chris. "The Theoretical Basis of the World Employment Programme: A Note on Pragmatism, Social Democracy and Ideology," *Manpower and Employment Research* 10, no. 2 (1977): 25–31.

Geyer, Martin H., and Johannes Paulmann, eds. *The Mechanics of Internationalism. Culture, Society, and Politics from the 1840s to the First World War*. Studies of the German Historical Institute, London. Oxford: Oxford University Press, 2001.

Ghébali, Viktor-Yves. *The International Labour Organization: A Case Study on the Evolution of UN Specialised Agencies*. Dordrecht: Martinus Nijhoff, 1989.

Gilman, Nils. *Mandarins of the Future: Modernization Theory in Cold War America*. Baltimore, MD: Johns Hopkins University Press, 2003.

Goddeeris, Idesbald. "The Limits of Lobbying: ILO and Solidarność." In *ILO Histories*, edited by Van Daele et al., 423–442.

Gorman, Daniel. *The Emergence of International Society in the 1920s*. Cambridge: Cambridge University Press, 2012.

Guérin, Denis. *Albert Thomas au BIT, 1920–1932: De l'internationalisme à l'Europe*. Euryopa Études. Geneva: Institut Européen de l'Université de Genève, 1996.

Guieu, Jean-Michel. "Albert Thomas et la paix. Du socialisme normalien à l'action internationale au BIT." *Les cahiers Irice* 2, no. 2 (2008): 65–80.

Guinand, Cédric. *Die Internationale Arbeitsorganisation (ILO) und die soziale Sicherheit in Europa (1942–1969)*. Bern: Peter Lang, 2003.

Guthrie, Jason. "The ILO and the International Technocratic Class, 1944–1966." In *Globalizing Social Rights*, edited by Kott and Droux, 115–136.

Gzoyan, Edita. "The League of Nations and Armenian Refugees: The Formation of the Armenian Diaspora in Syria." *Central and Eastern European Review* 8, no.1 (2014): 89–101.

Haas, Ernst B. *Beyond the Nation-State: Functionalism and International Organization*. Stanford, CA: Stanford University Press, 1964.

Hagtvedt Vik, Hanne. "How Constitutional Concerns Framed the US Contribution to the International Human Rights Regime from Its Inception, 1947–1953." *International History Review* 34, no. 4 (2012): 887–909.

Hagtvedt Vik, Hanne. "Indigenous Internationalism." In *Internationalisms. A Twentieth Century History*, edited by Sluga and Clavin, 315–339.

Hagtvedt Vik, Hanne. "Taming the States: The American Law Institute and the 'Statement of Essential Human Rights'." *Journal of Global History* 7, no. 3 (2012): 461–482.

Hansenne, Michel. *Un garde-fou pour la mondialisation. Le BIT dans l'après-guerre froide*. Chêne-Bourg: Editions ZOE, 1999.

Hauf, Felix. "The Paradoxes of Decent Work in Context: A Cultural Political Economy Perspective." *Global Labour Journal* 6, no. 2 (2015): 138–155.

Heerma van Voss, Lex. "The International Federation of Trade Unions and the Attempt to Maintain the Eight-Hour Working Day 1919–1929." In *Internationalism in the Labour Movement, 1830–1940*, edited by Frits Van Holthoon and Marcel van der Linden, 518–542. Leiden: Brill, 1988.

Helleiner, Eric. *Forgotten Foundations of Bretton Woods: International Development and the Making of the Postwar Order*. Ithaca, NY: Cornell University Press, 2014.

Henrÿ, Hagen. "The Contribution of the ILO to the Formation of Public International Cooperative Law." In *Globalizing Social Rights*, edited by Kott and Droux, 98–115.

Herren, Madeleine. "Fascist Internationalism." In *Internationalisms: A Twentieth Century History*, edited by Sluga and Clavin, 191–212.

Herren, Madeleine. "Global Corporatism after the First World War – The Indian Case." In *Globalizing Social Rights*, edited by Kott and Droux, 137–152.

Herren, Madeleine. *Hintertüren zur Macht: Internationalismus und modernisierungsorientierte Außenpolitik in Belgien, der Schweiz und den USA*. Munich: Oldenbourg, 2000.

Herrera González, Patricio. "El pacto por la unidad obrera continental: sus antecedentes en Chile y México, 1936." *Estudios de historia moderna y contemporánea de México* 46 (July–December 2013): 87–119.

Hidalgo-Weber, Olga. "Dimensions transnationales des politiques sociales britanniques: Le rôle de la Grande-Bretagne au sein de l'Organisation internationale du Travail, 1919–1946." PhD diss., Université de Genève, 2015.

Hidalgo-Weber, Olga. "Femmes britanniques et pratiques internationales de justice sociale dans la première moitié du XXe siècle." *Le Mouvement Social* 263, no. 2 (2018): 77–92.

Hidalgo-Weber, Olga. *La Grande-Bretagne et l'Organisation internationale du travail (1919–1946). Une nouvelle forme d'internationalisme*. Louvain-la-Neuve: Academia-L'Harmattan, 2017.

Hidalgo-Weber, Olga. "Social and Political Networks and the Creation of the ILO: The Role of British Actors." In *Globalizing Social Rights*, edited by Kott and Droux, 17–31.

Hilson, Mary. *The Nordic Model: Scandinavia since 1945*. London: Reaktion Books, 2008.

Hodge, Joseph Morgan. *The Triumph of the Expert. Agrarian Doctrines of Development and the Legacies of British Colonialism*. Athens, OH: Ohio University Press, 2007.

Hoehtker, Dorothea, and Sandrine Kott, eds. *À la rencontre de l'Europe au travail. Recits de voyages d'Albert Thomas*. Paris: Publications de la Sorbonne; Geneva: ILO, 2015.

Hoffmann, Stefan-Ludwig. "Human Rights and History." *Past & Present* 232, no. 1 (2016): 279–310.

Hoffmann, Stefan-Ludwig. ed. *Human Rights in the Twentieth Century*. Cambridge: Cambridge University Press, 2010.
Hooper, Paul F. "The Institute of Pacific Relations and the Origins of Asian and Pacific Studies." *Pacific Affairs* 61, no. 1 (1988): 98–121.
Hu, Aiqun. *China's Social Insurance in the 20th Century: A Global Historical Perspective*. Leiden: Brill, 2015.
Huberman, Michael. *Odd Couple: International Trade and Labor Standards in History*. Yale Series in Economic and Financial History. New Haven, CT: Yale University Press, 2012.
Hughes, Stephen, and Nigel Haworth. "A Shift in the Centre of Gravity: The ILO under Harold Butler and John G. Winant." In *ILO Histories*, edited by Van Daele et al., 293–312.
Hutchinson, John F. "Rethinking the Origins of the Red Cross." *Bulletin for the History of Medicine* 63, no. 4 (1989): 557–578.
ILO, *Constitution and Standing Orders of the International Labour Organisation*. Geneva: ILO, 1934.
ILO, ed. *Edward Phelan and the ILO. The Life and Views of an International Social Actor*. Geneva: ILO, 2009.
ILO. *Employment, Incomes, and Equality: A Strategy for Increasing Productive Employment in Kenya*. Geneva: ILO, 1972.
ILO. *Freedom of Association*. Studies and Reports, Series A, Nos. 28–32. 5 vols. Geneva: ILO, 1927–1930.
ILO. *Indigenous Peoples: Living and Working Conditions of Aboriginal Populations in Independent Countries*, Studies and Reports, New Series, No. 35. Geneva: ILO, 1953.
ILO. *The ILO and Africa*. Geneva: ILO, 1960.
ILO. *The ILO and Asia*. Geneva: ILO, 1962.
ILO. "The I.L.O. Manpower Programme." *International Labour Review* 59, no. 4 (April 1949): 367–393.
ILO. *The Role of the ILO in the Promotion of Economic Expansion and Social Progress in Developing Countries*. Geneva: ILO, 1961.
ILO. *The Role of the ILO in the Promotion of Economic Growth*. Geneva: ILO, 1961.
ILO. *Social Policy in Dependent Territories*. Geneva: ILO, 1944.
ILO. "Voices for Freedom of Association." *Labour Education* 112, no. 3 (1998).
ILO. *World Employment 1995. An ILO Report*. Geneva: ILO, 1995.
ILO and Walk Free Foundation. *Global Estimates of Modern Slavery: Forced Labour and Forced Marriage*. Geneva: ILO, 2017.
Imber, Mark F. *The USA, ILO, UNESCO and IAEA. Politicization and Withdrawal in the Specialized Agencies*. New York: St. Martin's Press, 1989.
Jacobson, Harold Karan. "The USSR and ILO." *International Organization* 14, no. 3 (1957): 402–428.
James, Harold. *Rambouillet, 15. November 1975. Die Globalisierung der Wirtschaft*. Munich: Deutscher Taschenbuch-Verlag, 1997.
Jensen, Jill M. "From Geneva to the Americas: The International Labor Organization and Inter-American Social Security Standards, 1936–1948." *International Labor and Working-Class History* 80, no. 1 (2011): 215–240.
Jensen, Jill M. "US New Deal Social Policy Experts and the ILO, 1948–1954." In *Globalizing Social Rights*, edited by Kott and Droux, 172–189.

Jensen, Jill M, and Nelson Lichtenstein, eds. *The ILO from Geneva to the Pacific Rim. West Meets East.* Basingstoke: Palgrave Macmillan; Geneva: ILO, 2015.
Jensen, Jill M. "Negotiating a World Trade and Employment Charter: The United States, the ILO and the Collapse of the ITO Ideal." In *The ILO from Geneva to the Pacific Rim*, edited by Jensen and Lichtenstein, 83–109.
Jensen, Steven L. B. *The Making of International Human Rights: The 1960s, Decolonization, and the Reconstruction of Global Values.* Human Rights in History. New York: Cambridge University Press, 2017.
Jolly, Richard, Louis Emmerij, Dharam Ghai, and Frédéric Lapeyre. *UN Contributions to Development Thinking and Practice.* United Nations Intellectual History Project Series. Bloomington, IN: Indiana University Press, 2004.
Josephson, Harold. *James T. Shotwell and the Rise of Internationalism in America.* Rutherford, NJ: Fairleigh Dickinson University Press, 1974.
Kaufmann, Christine. *Globalisation and Labour Rights. The Conflict between Core Labour Rights and International Economic Law.* Oxford: Hart Publishing, 2007.
Kelly, Patrick William. *Sovereign Emergencies: Latin America and the Making of Global Human Rights Politics.* Human Rights in History. Cambridge: Cambridge University Press, 2018.
Kennedy, Paul M. *The Parliament of Man: The Past, Present, and Future of the United Nations.* New York: Random House, 2006.
Kent, Ann. *Beyond Compliance: China, International Organizations, and Global Security.* Palo Alto, CA: Stanford University Press, 2007.
Kettunen, Pauli. "The ILO as a Forum for Developing and Demonstrating a Nordic Model." In *Globalizing Social Rights*, edited by Kott and Droux, 210–232.
Kévonian, Dzovinar. "Enjeux de catégorisations et migrations internationales. Le Bureau international du Travail et les réfugiés (1925–1929)." *Revue européene des migrations internationales* 21, no. 3 (2005): 1–23.
Kévonian, Dzovinar. "Les juristes et l'Organisation internationale du Travail 1919–1939. Processus de légitimation et institutionnalisation des relations internationales." *Journal of the History of International Law* 12, no. 3 (2010): 227–266.
Kévonian, Dzovinar. "La légitimation par l'expertise: le Bureau international du travail et la statistique international." *Les cahiers Irice* 2, no. 2 (2008): 81–106.
Kleinöder, Nina, Stefan Müller, and Karsten Uhl, eds. *Humanisierung der Arbeit. Aufbrüche und Konflikte in der rationalisierten Arbeitswelt des 20. Jahrhunderts.* Bielefeld: Transcript Verlag (forthcoming 2019).
Klose, Fabian. *Human Rights in the Shadow of Colonial Violence: The Wars of Independence in Kenya and Algeria.* Pennsylvania Studies in Human Rights. Philadelphia, PA: University of Pennsylvania Press, 2013.
Konkel, Rob. "The Monetization of Global Poverty: The Concept of Poverty in World Bank History, 1944–90." *Journal of Global History* 9, no. 2 (2014): 276–300.
Kott, Sandrine. "Constructing a European Social Model: The Fight for Social Insurance in the Interwar Period." In *ILO Histories*, edited by Van Daele et al., 173–196.
Kott, Sandrine. "Dynamiques de l'internationalisation: L'Allemagne et l'Organisation internationale du Travail (1919–1940)." *Critique internationale* 52 (2011): 69–84.
Kott, Sandrine. "Fighting the War or Preparing for Peace? The ILO During the Second World War." *Journal of Modern European History* 12, no. 3 (2014): 359–376.
Kott, Sandrine. "From Transnational Reformist Network to International Organization: The International Association for Labour Legislation and the International Labour Organization,

1900–930s." In *Shaping the Transnational Sphere. Experts, Networks and Issues from the 1840s to the 1930s*, edited by Davide Rodogno, Bernhard Struck and Jakob Vogel, 239–259. New York: Berghahn Books, 2015.

Kott, Sandrine, ed. *La justice sociale dans un monde global. L'Organisation internationale du Travail*. Special issue of *Le Mouvement Social* 263, no. 2 (2018): 3–14.

Kott, Sandrine. "OIT, justice sociale et mondes communistes. Concurrences, émulations, convergences." *Le Mouvement Social* 263, no. 2 (2018): 139–151.

Kott, Sandrine. "Towards a Social History of International Organizations: The ILO and the Internationalisation of Western Social Expertise (1919–1949)." In *Internationalism, Imperialism and the Formation of the Contemporary World. The Pasts of the Present*, edited by Miguel Bandeira Jerónimo and José Pedro Monteiro, 35–57. Basingstoke: Palgrave Macmillan, 2018.

Kott, Sandrine, and Joëlle Droux, eds. *Globalizing Social Rights. The International Labour Organization and Beyond*. Basingstoke: Palgrave Macmillan; Geneva: ILO, 2013.

Kott, Sandrine "The Forced Labor Issue between Human and Social Rights, 1947–1957." *Humanity* 3, no. 3 (2012): 69–84.

Kott, Sandrine. "Competing Internationalisms: The Third Reich and the International Labour Organization." In *Nazism across Borders. The Social Policies of the Third Reich and their Global Appea*l, edited by Sandrine Kott and Kiran Klaus Patel, 29–52. Oxford: Oxford University Press, 2018.

La Hovary, Claire. "A Challenging Ménage à Trois? Tripartism in the International Labour Organization." *International Organizations Law Review* 12, no. 1 (2015): 204–236.

Lake, Marilyn. "The ILO, Australia and the Asia-Pacific Region: New Solidarities or Internationalism in the National Interest?" In *The ILO from Geneva to the Pacific Rim*, edited by Jensen and Lichtenstein, 33–54.

Lapeyre, Jean. *Le dialogue social européen. Histoire d'une innovation sociale (1985–2003)*. Brussels: European Trade Union Institute, 2017.

Laqua, Daniel, ed. *Internationalism Reconfigured: Transnational Ideas and Movements between the World Wars*. International Library of Twentieth Century History. London: I.B. Tauris, 2011.

Latham, Michael E. *Modernization as Ideology: American Social Science and 'Nation Building' in the Kennedy Era*. Chapel Hill, NC: University of North Carolina Press, 2000.

Lauren, Paul Gordon. *Power and Prejudice: The Politics and Diplomacy of Racial Discrimination*. Boulder, CO: Westview, 1988.

Lee, Eddy. "The Declaration of Philadelphia: Retrospect and Prospect." *International Labour Review* 133, no. 4 (1994): 467–484.

Leimgruber, Matthieu. "The Embatteled Standard-bearer of Social Insurance and Its Challenger: The ILO, the OECD and the 'Crisis of the Welfare State', 1975–1985." In *Globalizing Social Rights*, edited by Kott and Droux, 293–309.

Lee, Eddy, and Matthias Schmelzer, eds. *The OECD and the International Political Economy since 1948*. Basingstoke: Palgrave Macmillan, 2017.

Lerner, Abba P. "Mr. Keynes' 'General Theory of Employment, Interest and Money'." *International Labour Review* 34, no. 4 (1936): 435–454.

Lespinet-Moret, Isabelle. "Promouvoir la santé au travail comme droit social (1919–1940)?" *Le Mouvement Social* 263, no. 2 (2018): 61–76.

Lespinet-Moret, Isabelle, and Vincent Viet, eds. *L'Organisation internationale du Travail: origine, développement, avenir*. Rennes: Presses Universitaires de Rennes, 2011.

Lichtenstein, Nelson "The ILO and the Corporate Social Responsibility Regime in East and South Asia." In *The ILO from Geneva to the Pacific Rim*, edited by Jensen and Lichtenstein, 277–296.

Liebeskind Sauthier, Ingrid. "Modern Unemployment: From the Creation of the Concept to the International Labour Office's First Standards." In *Globalizing Social Rights*, edited by Kott and Droux, 67–84.

Liebscher, Daniela. *Freude und Arbeit. Zur internationalen Freizeit- und Sozialpolitik des faschistischen Italien und des NS-Regimes*. Italien in der Moderne, vol. 16. Cologne: SH-Verlag, 2009.

Lieten, G.K. "The ILO Setting the Terms in the Child Labour Debate." In *ILO Histories*, edited by Van Daele et al., 443–460.

Linnik, Marianna, and Sune Skadegaard Thorsen. "ILO and CSR – Minimum Human Rights Standards for Croporations." In *Governance, International Law and Corporate Social Responsibility*, edited by ILO and International Institute for Labour Studies, 105–127. Geneva: ILO, 2008.

Lorenz, Edward C. *Defining Global Justice: The History of U.S. International Labor Standards Policy*. Notre Dame, IN: University of Notre Dame Press, 2001.

Louis, Marieke. "La diplomatie sociale des multinationales." *La vie des idées*, 9 October, 2018, www.laviedesidees.fr.

Louis, Marieke. "Hansenne, Michel." In *IO Bio: Biographical Dictionary*, edited by Reinalda, Kille, and Eisenberg, www.ru.nl/fm/iobio.

Louis, Marieke. "The ILO, Social Partners and the G20: New Prospects for Social Dialogue at the Global Level?" *Global Social Policy* 16, no. 3 (2016): 235–252.

Louis, Marieke. "Women's Representation at the ILO: A Hundred Years of Marginalization." In *Women's ILO*, edited by Boris, Hoehtker and Zimmermann, 202–225.

Maier, Charles "The Politics of Productivity: Foundations of American International Economic Policy after World War II." *International Organization* 31, no. 4 (1977): 607–633.

Massart, Sylvie. "Les voyages d'Albert Thomas, directeur du Bit (1919–1932)." Master's thesis, Université Paris-I, Sorbonne, 1993.

Matera, Marc, and Susan Kingsley Kent. *The Global 1930s: The International Decade*. London: Routledge, 2017.

Maul, Daniel Roger. "'Help Them Move the ILO Way': The International Labour Organization and the Modernization Discourse in the Era of Decolonization and the Cold War." *Diplomatic History* 33, no. 3 (2009): 387–404.

Maul, Daniel Roger. *Human Rights, Development, and Decolonization: The International Labour Organization, 1940–70*. Basingstoke: Palgrave Macmillan; Geneva: ILO, 2012.

Maul, Daniel Roger. "The ILO, Asia and the Beginnings of Technical Assistance, 1945–60." In *The ILO from Geneva to the Pacific Rim*, edited by Jensen and Lichtenstein, 365–400.

Maul, Daniel Roger. "The International Labour Organization and the Globalization of Human Rights, 1944–1970." In *Human Rights in the Twentieth Century*, edited by Stefan-Ludwig Hoffmann, 301–320.

Maul, Daniel Roger. "The International Labour Organization and the Struggle against Forced Labour from 1919 to the Present." *Labor History* 48, no. 4 (2007): 477–500.

Maul, Daniel Roger. "Morse, David Abner". In *IO Bio: Biographical Dictionary*, edited by Reinalda, Kille, and Eisenberg, www.ru.nl/fm/iobio.

Maul, Daniel Roger. "The 'Morse Years': The ILO 1948–1970." In *ILO Histories*, edited by Van Daele et al., 365–400.

Maul, Daniel Roger, Luca Puddu, and Hakeem Ibikunle Tijani. "The International Labour Organization". In *General Labour History of Africa: Workers, Employers and Governments, 20th–21st Centuries*, edited by Stefano Bellucci and Andreas Eckert. Martlesham: James Currey; Geneva: ILO, 2019.

Maupain, Francis. *The Future of the International Labour Organization in the Global Economy.* Oxford: Hart Publishing, 2013.

Maurel, Chloé. "OIT et responsabilité sociale des sociétés transnationales depuis 1970." In *L'Organisation internationale du travail*, edited by Lespinet-Moret and Viet, 179–192.

Mazower, Mark. *Governing the World: The History of an Idea.* New York: The Penguin Press, 2012.

Mazower, Mark. *No Enchanted Palace: The End of Empire and the Ideological Origins of the United Nations.* Lawrence Stone Lectures. Princeton: Princeton University Press, 2009.

McPherson, Alan, and Yannick Wehrli, eds. *Beyond Geopolitics: New Histories of Latin America at the League of* Nations. Albuquerque, NM: University of New Mexico Press, 2015.

Mechi, Lorenzo. "Du BIT à la politique sociale européenne: Les origines d'un modèle." *Le Mouvement Social* 244, no. 3 (2013): 17–30.

Mechi, Lorenzo. "Economic Regionalism and Social Stabilisation: The International Labour Organization and Western Europe in the Early Post-War Years." *International History Review* 35, no. 4 (2013): 844–862.

Mehrotra, Santosh, and Richard Jolly, eds. *Development with a Human Face: Experiences in Social Achievement and Economic Growth.* Oxford: Oxford University Press, 1998.

Monteiro, José Pedro. "'One of Those Too-Rare Examples': The International Labour Organization, the Colonial Question and Forced Labour (1961–1963)." In *Internationalism, Imperialism and the Formation of the Contemporary World. The Past of the Present*, edited by Miguel Bandeira Jerónimo and José Pedro Monteiro, 221–251. Basingstoke: Palgrave Macmillan, 2018.

Morse, David A. "The Employment Problem in Developing Countries." In *Prospects for Employment Opportunities in the Nineteen Seventies: Papers and Impressions of the Seventh Cambridge Conference on Development Problems, 13th to 24th September 1979 at Jesus College, Cambridge*, edited by Ronald Robinson and Peter Johnston, 5–13. Foreign and Commonwealth Office, Overseas Development Administration. Cambridge University Overseas Studies Committee. London: HMSO, 1971.

Morsink, Johannes. *The Universal Declaration of Human Rights: Origins, Drafting, and Intent.* Philadelphia, PA: University of Pennsylvania Press, 1999.

Moyn, Samuel. *The Last Utopia: Human Rights in History.* Cambridge, MA: Belknap Press of Harvard University Press, 2010.

Moyn, Samuel. *Not Enough: Human Rights in an Unequal World.* Cambridge, MA: Belknap Press of Harvard University Press, 2018.

Moynihan, Daniel P. "The United States and the International Labor Organisation, 1889–1934," PhD diss. Fletcher School of Law and Diplomacy, Medford, MA, 1960.

Natchkova, Nora, and Céline Schoeni. "The ILO, Feminists and Expert Networks: The Challenges of a Protective Policy." In *Globalizing Social Rights*, edited by Kott and Droux, 49–66.

Neunsinger, Silke. "The Unobtainable Magic of Numbers: Equal Remuneration, the ILO and the International Trade Union Movement, 1950s–1980s." In *Women's ILO*, edited by Boris, Hoehtker, and Zimmermann, 121–148.

Nolan, Mary. *Visions of Modernity: American Business and the Modernization of Germany.* Oxford: Oxford University Press, 1994.

Normand, Roger, and Sahra Zaidi. *Human Rights at the UN: The Political History of Universal Justice.* Bloomington, IN: Indiana University Press, 2008.

Norsky, K.K. *The Influence of the International Labour Organization on Principles of Social Policy in Non-Metropolitan Territories*. Oxford: Oxford University Press, 1951.
O'Higgins, Paul. "'Labour Is Not a Commodity' – An Irish Contribution to International Labour Law." *Industrial Law Journal* 26, no. 3 (1997): 225–234.
O'Sullivan, Kevin. "'A Global Nervous System': The Rise and Rise of European Humanitarian NGOs, 1945–1985." In *International Organizations and Development*, edited by Frey, Kunkel, and Unger, 196–219.
Oechslin, Jean-Jacques. *The International Organisation of Employers. Three-Quarters of a Century in the Service of the Enterprise (1920–1998)*. Geneva: IOE, 2001.
Okia, Opolot. *Communal Labor in Colonial Kenya: The Legitimization of Coercion, 1912–1930*. Basingstoke: Palgrave Macmillan, 2012.
Olesen, Thorsten Borring, Helge O. Pharo, and Kristian Paaskesen, eds. *Saints and Sinners: Official Development Aid and its Dynamics in a Historical and Comparative Perspective*. Issues in Contemporary History. Oslo: Akademika Publishing, 2013.
Orenstein, Mitchell A. "Pension Privatization: The Transnational Campaign." In *Globalizing Social Rights*, edited by Kott and Droux, 280–292.
Orenstein, Mitchell A. "Transitional Social Policy in the Czech Republic and Poland." *Czech Sociological Review* 3, no. 2 (1995): 179–196.
Ortuño Anaya, Pilar. *European Socialists and Spain: The Transition to Democracy, 1959–77*. Basingstoke: Palgrave Macmillan, 2002.
Packenham, Robert A. *Liberal America and the Third World: Political Development Ideas in Foreign Aid and Social Science*. Princeton, NJ: Princeton University Press, 1973.
Patel, Kiran Klaus. *The New Deal. A Global History*. Princeton, NJ: Princeton University Press, 2016.
Pécoud, Antoine. "What Do We Know about the International Organization for Migration?" *Journal of Ethnic and Migration Studies* 44, no. 10 (2018): 1621–1638.
Pedersen, Susan. "Back to the League of Nations." *American Historical Review* 112, no. 4 (2007): 1091–1117.
Pedersen, Susan. *The Guardians: The League of Nations and the Crisis of Empire*. Oxford: Oxford University Press, 2015.
Pernet, Corinne A. "Developing Nutritional Standards and Food Policy: Latin American Reformers between the ILO, the League of Nations Health Organization, and the Pan-American Sanitary Bureau." In *Globalizing Social Rights*, edited by Kott and Droux, 249–261.
Phelan, Edward. "The ILO Sets up its Wartime Centre in Canada." In *Edward Phelan and the ILO. The Life and Views of an International Social Actor*, edited by ILO, 259–279. Geneva: ILO, 2009; initially published in: *Studies: An Irish Quarterly Review* 44, no. 174 (1956): 151–170.
Phelan, Edward. "Some Reminiscences of the International Labour Organization." In *Edward Phelan and the ILO. The Life and Views of an International Social Actor*, edited by ILO, 227–257. Geneva: ILO, 2009; initially published in: *Studies: An Irish Quarterly Review* 43, no. 171 (1954): 241–270.
Piguet, Laure. "La justice sociale par les statistiques? Le cas des accidents d'attelage des wagons de chemins de fer (1923–1931)." *Le Mouvement Social* 2 (2018): 31–43.
Plata-Stenger, Véronique. "Europe, the ILO and the Wider World (1919–1954)," *EGO – European History Online*, Mainz: Leibniz-Institut für Europäische Geschichte, 2016.
Plata-Stenger, Véronique. "L'OIT et le problème du sous-développement en Asie dans l'entre-deux-guerres." *Le Mouvement Social* 263, no. 2 (2018): 109–122.

Plata-Stenger, Véronique. *Social Reform, Modernization and Technical Diplomacy: The ILO Contribution to Development (1930–1946)*. Berlin: De Gruyter Oldenbourg, forthcoming 2020.

Plata-Stenger, Véronique. "'To Raise Awareness of Difficulties and to Assert Their Opinion'. The International Labour Office and the Regionalization of International Cooperation in the 1930s." In *Beyond Geopolitics*, edited by McPherson and Wehrli, 97–113.

Plata-Stenger, Véronique. "Une voie sociale pour le développement. Le Bureau international du Travail et les débuts de la coopération technique (1919–1949)." PhD diss. Université de Genève, 2016.

Plesch, Dan. *America, Hitler and the UN: How the Allies Won World War II and Forged a Peace*. London: I.B. Tauris, 2011.

Pohrt, Oliver. *Die internationale Gewerkschaftsbewegung zwischen Einheitswunsch und Kaltem Krieg. Der Weltgewerkschaftsbund (WGB) von der Gründungsphase bis zu seiner Spaltung (1941–1949)*. Regensburg: S. Roderer Verlag, 2000.

Polanyi, Karl. *The Great Transformation*. New York: Rinehart & Company, 1944.

Prashad, Vijay. *The Darker Nations: A People's History of the Third World*. A New Press People's History. New York: New Press, 2007.

Prince, Charles. "The U.S.S.R. and International Organizations." *The American Journal of International Law* 36, no. 3 (1942): 425–445.

Public Papers of the Presidents of the United States: Jimmy Carter, 1980–81. 3 Books. Washington, DC: U.S. Government Printing Office, 1981–1982.

Raphael, Lutz. "Die Verwissenschaftlichung des Sozialen als methodische und konzeptionelle Herausforderung für eine Sozialgeschichte des 20. Jahrhunderts." *Geschichte und Gesellschaft* 22, no. 2 (1996): 165–193.

Reinalda, Bob. "Organization Theory and the Autonomy of the International Labour Organization: Two Classic Studies still Going Strong." In *Autonomous Policy Making by International Organisations*, edited by Bob Reinalda and Bertjan Verbeek, 42–61. London: Routledge, 1998.

Reinalda, Bob. *Routledge History of International Organizations: From 1815 to the Present Day*. London: Routledge, 2009.

Reinalda, Bob, Kent Kille, and Jaci Leigh Eisenberg, eds. *IO Bio: Biographical Dictionary of Secretaries-General of International Organizations*, Nijmegen, The Netherlands: University of Nijmegen, www.ru.nl/fm/iobio.

Reynaud, Emmanuel. *The International Labour Organization and Globalization. Fundamental Rights, Decent Work and Social Justice*. ILO Research Paper Series No. 21. Geneva: ILO, 2018.

Reynaud, Emmanuel. *The International Labour Organization and the Living Wage: A Historical Perspective*. Conditions of Work and Employment Series No. 90. Geneva: ILO, 2017.

Ribi Forclaz, Amalia. "A New Target for International Social Reform: The International Labour Organization and Working and Living Conditions in Agriculture in the Inter-War Years." *Contemporary European History* 20, no. 3 (2011): 307–329.

Richards, Peter J. "Preserving Jobs under Economic Stabilisation Programmes: Can there be an Employment Target?" *International Labour Review* 125, no. 4 (1986): 423–433.

Robertson, Thomas. *The Malthusian Moment: Global Population Growth and the Birth of American Environmentalism*. Studies in Modern Science, Technology, and the Environment. New Brunswick, NJ: Rutgers University Press, 2012.

Rodgers, Gerry. "Decent Work as a Development Objective." *The Indian Journal of Labour Economics* 44, no. 1 (2001): 15–26.
Rodgers, Gerry. "India, the ILO and the Quest for Social Justice." *Economic and Political Weekly* 46, no. 10 March (2011): 45–52.
Rodgers, Gerry, ed. *The Poverty Agenda and the ILO. Issues for Research and Action*. Geneva: International Institute for Labour Studies, 1995.
Rodgers, Gerry, Eddy Lee, Lee Swepston, and Jasmien Van Daele. *The ILO and the Quest for Social Justice, 1919–2009*. Ithaca, NY: Cornell University Press; Geneva: ILO, 2009.
Rodgers, Gerry, J. Krishnamurty, and Sabyasachi Bhattacharya. "India and the ILO in Historical Perspective." *Economic and Politcal Weekly* 46, no. 10 (5 March 2011).
Rodogno Davide, Liat Kozma, and Magaly Rodriguez, eds., *The League of Nations' Work on Social Issues. Visions, Endeavours and Experiments*. New York: United Nations Press, 2016.
Rodríguez García, Magaly. "Conclusion: The ILO's Impact on the World." In *ILO Histories*, edited by Van Daele et al., 461–478.
Rodríguez-Piñero, Luis. *Indigenous Peoples, Postcolonialism, and International Law: The ILO Regime, 1919–1989*. Oxford: Oxford University Press, 2005.
Rosado Marzán, César F. "The Limits of Human Rights for Labour Rights: A Retrospective Look at the Case of Chile." In *The ILO from Geneva to the Pacific Rim*, edited by Jensen and Lichtenstein, 206–230.
Rosental, Paul-André. "Géopolitique et État-providence. Le BIT et la politique mondiale des migrations dans l'entre-deux-guerres." *Annales.Histoire, Sciences Sociales* 61, no. 1 (2006): 99–134.
Royle, Tony. "The ILO's Shift to Promotional Principles and the 'Privatization' of Labour Rights: An Analysis of Labour Standards, Voluntary Self-regulation and Social Clauses." *International Journal of Comparative Labour Law and Industrial Relations* 26, no. 3 (2010): 249–271.
Rupp, Leila J. *Worlds of Women: The Making of an International Women's Movement*. Princeton, NJ: Princeton University Press, 1997.
Sanchez Bajo, Claudia. "Work and Cooperatives: A Century of ILO Interaction with the Cooperative Movement." In *Cooperatives and the World of Work*, edited by Bruno Roelants, Hyungsik Eum, Simel Esim, Sonja Novkovic, and Waltteri Katamajaki. London: Routledge, forthcoming 2020.
Saunier, Pierre-Yves. "Borderline Work: ILO Explorations onto the Housing Scene until 1940." In *ILO Histories*, edited by Van Daele et al., 197–220.
Schenk, Catherine R. *International Economic Relations since 1945*. London: Routledge, 2011.
Schild, Georg. *Bretton Woods and Dumberton Oaks. American Economic and Political Postwar Planning in the Summer of 1944*. London: St. Martin's Press, 1995.
Schmelzer, Matthias. *The Hegemony of Growth: The OECD and the Making of the Economic Growth Paradigm*. Cambridge: Cambridge University Press, 2016.
Schot, Johan, and Vincent Lagendijk. "Technocratic Internationalism in the Interwar Years: Building Europe on Motorways and Electricity Networks." *Journal of Modern European History* 6, no. 2 (2008): 196–217.
Scodeller, Gabriela. "Educar in derechos laborales: politicas y acciones desplegadas por la OIT en América Latina durante los años 1950–1970." In *Una historia regional de la OIT: Aportes sobre regulación y legislación del trabajo latinoamericano*, edited by Laura Caruso and Andrés Stagnaro, 213–254. La Plata: Universidad Nacional de La Plata. Facultad de Humanidades y Ciencias de la Educación, 2017.

Seekings, Jeremy. "The ILO and Welfare Reform in South Africa, Latin America and the Caribbean, 1919–1950." In *ILO Histories*, edited by Van Daele et al., 145–172.

Serra, Narcís, and Joseph E. Stiglitz. *The Washington Consensus Reconsidered: Towards a New Global Governance*. The Initiative for Policy Dialogue Series. Oxford: Oxford University Press, 2008.

Servais, Jean-Michel. *International Labour Organization (ILO)*. Alphen aan den Rijn: Kluwer Law International, 2005.

Shotwell, James T. "The International Labor Organization as an Alternative to Violent Revolution." *Annals of the American Academy of Polical and Social Science* 166, no. 1 (1933): 18–25.

Shotwell, James T., ed. *The Origins of the International Labor Organization*. 2 vols. New York: Columbia University Press, 1934.

Sikkink, Kathryn. *Mixed Signals: U.S. Human Rights Policy and Latin America*. Ithaca, NY: Cornell University Press, 2004.

Sinclair, Guy Fiti. *To Reform the World: International Organizations and the Making of Modern States*. The History and Theory of International Law. New York: Oxford University Press, 2017.

Skran, Claudena. *Refugees in Interwar Europe. The Emergence of a Regime*. Oxford: Clarendon Press, 1995.

Slobodian, Quinn. *Globalists: The End of Empire and the Birth of Neoliberalism*. Cambridge, MA: Harvard University Press, 2018.

Sluga, Glenda. *Internationalism in the Age of Nationalism*. Philadelphia, PA: University of Pennsylvania Press, 2013.

Sluga, Glenda, and Patricia Clavin, eds. *Internationalisms: A Twentieth Century History*. Cambridge: Cambridge University Press, 2017.

Sluga, Glenda, and Patricia Clavin. "Rethinking the History of Internationalism." In *Internationalisms: A Twentieth Century History*, edited by Sluga and Clavin, 3–14.

Smith, Mark B. "Social Rights in the Soviet Dictatorship: The Constitutional Right to Welfare from Stalin to Brezhnev." *Humanity* 3, no. 3 (2012): 385–406.

Snyder, Sarah B. *Human Rights Activism and the End of the Cold War: A Transnational History of the Helsinki Network*. Human Rights in History. New York: Cambridge University Press, 2011.

Standing, Guy. "The ILO: An Agency for Globalization?" *Development and Change* 39, no. 3 (2008): 355–384.

Steiner, Zara, *The Lights that Failed. European International History 1919–1933*. Oxford: Oxford University Press, 2005.

Stegmann, Natali. "The ILO and East Central Europe. Insights into the Early Polish and Czechoslovak Interwar Years." *Acta Universitatis Carolinae. Studia Territorialia* 17, no. 1 (2017): 11–34.

Stricker, Yann. "'International Migration' between Empire and Nation. The Statistical Construction of an Ambiguous Global Category in the International Labour Office in the 1920s." *Ethnicities* (7 March 2019), 469–485.

Studer, Brigitte, Regina Wecker, and Gaby Sutter, eds. *Die "schutzbedürftige Frau." Zur Konstruktion von Geschlecht durch Mutterschaftsversicherung, Nachtarbeitsverbot und Sonderschutzgesetzgebung*. Zurich: Chronos, 2001.

Supiot, Alain. *The Spirit of Philadelphia: Social Justice vs. the Total Market*. Trans. Saskia Brown. London: Verso, 2012.

Süss, Dietmar. "Der Sieg der grauen Herren? Flexibilisierung und der Kampf um Zeit in den 1970er und 1980er Jahren." In *Die Vorgeschichte der Gegenwart. Dimensionen des Strukturbruchs nach dem Boom*, edited by Anselm Döring-Manteuffel, Lutz Raphael, and Thomas Schlemmer, 109–127. Göttingen: Vandenhoeck & Ruprecht, 2016.

Tapiola, Kari. "Die 'Multis': Ein Thema für die Vereinten Nationen." *Vereinte Nationen* 5 (1978): 151–154.

Tapiola, Kari. "The ILO System of Regular Supervision of the Application of Conventions and Recommendations: A Lasting Paradigm." In *Protecting Labour Rights as Human Rights: Present and Future of International Supervision*. Proceedings of the International Colloquium on the 80th Anniversary of the ILO Committee of Experts on the Application of Conventions and Recommendations, Geneva, 24–25 November 2006, edited by George P. Politakis, 29–36. Geneva: ILO, 2006.

Tapiola, Kari. *The Teeth of the ILO. The Impact of the ILO Declaration on Fundamental Principles and Rights at Work*. Geneva: ILO, 2018.

Thébaud, Francoise. "Difficult Inroads, Unexpected Results: The Correspondence Committee on Women's Work in the 1930s." In *Women's ILO*, edited by Boris, Hoehtker, and Zimmermann, 50–74.

Thomas, Albert. *A la recontre de l'orient. Notes de voyage 1928–1929*. Geneva: Societé des amis d'Albert Thomas, 1959.

Thomas, Daniel C. *The Helsinki Effect: International Norms, Human Rights, and the Demise of Communism*. Princeton, NJ: Princeton University Press, 2001.

Thörn, Håkan. *Anti-Apartheid and the Emergence of a Global Civil Society*. Basingstoke: Palgrave Macmillan, 2006.

Tosstorff, Reiner. "Albert Thomas, the ILO and the IFTU: A Case of Mutual Benefit?" In *ILO Histories*, edited by Van Daele et al., 91–114.

Tosstorff, Reiner. "The International Trade Union Movement and the Foundation of the International Labour Organization." *International Review of Social History* 50, no. 3 (2005): 399–433.

Tosstorff, Reiner. "Leuschner gegen Ley. Die Abfuhr für die Nazis auf der Internationalen Arbeitskonferenz im Jahre 1933 in Genf." *Jahrbuch für Forschungen zur Geschichte der Arbeiterbewegung* 3 (2004): 70–90.

Tosstorff, Reiner. *The Red International of Labour Unions (RILU) 1920–1937*. Leiden: Brill, 2016.

Tosstorff, Reiner. *Workers' Resistance against Nazi Germany at the International Labour Conference 1933*. Geneva: ILO, 2013.

Toye, John. *Dilemmas of Development: Reflections on the Counter-Revolution in Development Economics*. 2nd ed. Cambridge, MA: Blackwell, 1993.

Treu, Tiziano. "Labour Flexibility in Europe." *International Labour Review* 131, no. 4–5 (1992): 497–512.

Tsogas, George. "Labour Standards in International Trade Agreements: An Assessment of the Arguments." *The International Journal of Human Resource Management* 10, no. 2 (1999): 351–375.

Unger, Corinna R. *International Development. A Post-War History*. London: Bloomsbury Academic Publishing, 2018.

United Nations. *Report of the World Summit for Social Development, Copenhagen, 6–12 March 1995*. New York: United Nations, 1996.

United Nations. *The United Nations and Apartheid 1948–1994*. New York: United Nations, Department of Public Information, 1994.

United States Department of Health, Education, and Welfare, Office of Education. *Work in America. Report of a Special Task Force to the Secretary of Health, Education, and Welfare* (December 1973).

Valticos, Nicolas. *International Labour Law*. Deventer: Kluwer, 1979.

Valticos, Nicolas. "Fifty Years of Standard-Setting Activities by the International Labour Organisation." *International Labour Review* 135, no. 3–4 (1996): 393–414.

Van Daele, Jasmien. "Engineering Social Peace: Networks, Ideas and the Founding of the International Labour Organization." *International Review of Social History* 50, no. 3 (2005): 435–466.

Van Daele, Jasmien. "The International Labour Organization in Past and Present Research." *International Review of Social History* 53, no. 3 (2008): 485–511.

Van Daele, Jasmien, Magaly Rodríguez García, Geert Van Goethem, and Marcel van der Linden, eds. *ILO Histories: Essays on the International Labour Organization and Its Impact on the World During the Twentieth Century*. Bern: Peter Lang, 2010.

Van der Linden, Marcel. "Trade Unions." In *Handbook Global History of Work*, edited by Karin Hofmeester and Marcel van der Linden, 551–568. Berlin: De Gruyter Oldenbourg, 2018.

Van Goethem, Geert. *The Amsterdam International: The World of the International Federation of Trade Unions (IFTU), 1913–1945*. Aldershot: Ashgate Publishing, 2006.

Van Goethem, Geert. "Labor's Second Front: The Foreign Policy of the American and British Trade Union Movements During the Second World War." *Diplomatic History* 34, no. 4 (2010): 663–680.

Van Goethem, Geert. "Phelan's War: The International Labour Organization in Limbo (1941–1948)." In *ILO Histories*, edited by Van Daele et al., 313–340.

Verbruggen, Christophe. "Intellectual Workers and Their Search for a Place within the ILO during the Interwar Period." In *ILO Histories*, edited by Van Daele et al., 271–292.

Vosko, Leah. "Decent Work. The Shifting Role of the ILO and the Struggle for Global Social Justice." *Global Social Policy* 2, no. 1 (2002): 19–46.

Weber, Petra. *Gescheiterte Sozialpartnerschaft – Gefährdete Republik? Industrielle Beziehungen, Arbeitskämpfe und der Sozialstaat. Deutschland und Frankreich im Vergleich (1918–1933/39)*. Munich: Oldenbourg, 2010.

Wehrli, Yannick, and Fabián Herrera León. "Le BIT et l'Amérique latine durant l'entre-deux-guerres: Problèmes et enjeux." In *L'Organisation internationale du Travail*, edited by Lespinet-Moret and Viet, 157–166.

Weindling, Paul. "Social Medicine at the League of Nations Health Organisation and the International Labour Office Compared." In *International Health Organisations and Movements, 1918–1939*, edited by Paul Weindling, 134–153. Cambridge: Cambridge University Press, 1995.

Weisband, Edward, and Edward Singleton. "ILO Industrial Committees and Sectoral Activities: An Institutional History." Working Paper SAP 2.53/WP.100. ILO: Geneva, 1996.

Weissbrodt, David, and Maria Luisa Bartolomei. "The Effectiveness of International Human Rights Pressures: The Case of Argentina, 1976–1983." *Minnesota Law Review* 75 (1991): 1009–1035.

Whelan, Daniel J., and Jack Donnelly. "The West, Economic and Social Rights, and the Global Human Rights Regime: Setting the Record Straight." *Human Rights Quarterly* 29, no. 4 (2007): 908–949.

Wikander, Ulla. "Demands on the ILO by Internationally Organized Women in 1919." In *ILO Histories*, edited by Van Daele et al., 67–90.

Winter, Jay, and Antoine Prost. *René Cassin and Human Rights: From the Great War to the Universal Declaration*. Cambridge: Cambridge University Press, 2013.

Wobbe, Theresa. "Das Globalwerden der Menschenrechte in der ILO: Die Umdeutung von Arbeitsrechten im Kontext weltgesellschaftlicher Strukturprobleme von den 1930er bis 1950er Jahren." In *Menschenrechte in der Weltgesellschaft. Deutungswandel und Wirkungsweise eines globalen Leitwerts*, edited by Bettina Heintz and Britta Leisering, 283–316. Frankfurt am Main: Campus Verlag, 2015.

World Commission on the Social Dimension of Globalization. *A Fair Globalization: Creating Opportunities for All*. Geneva: ILO, 2004, https://bit.ly/2HFKk2o.

Yifeng, Chen. "The International Labour Organization and Labour Governance in China 1919–1949." In *China and ILO Fundamental Principles and Rights at Work*. Special isssue of *Bulletin of Comparative Labour Relations* 86, edited by Roger Blanpain, Ulla Liukkunen, and Chen Yifeng, 19–54. Alphen aan de Rijn: Kluwer Law International, 2014.

Zaragori, Aurélien. "Missions et Organisation internationale du Travail (OIT): Quelles collaborations pour le développement? Une étude historique (1920–1970)." *Social Sciences and Missions* 29 (2016): 310–342.

Zaragori, Aurélien. "L'OIT, le Saint-Siège et les milieux catholiques africains et latino-americaine dans les années 1950 et 1960." *Le Mouvement Social* 263, no. 2 (2018): 123–138.

Zimmermann, Susan. "'Special Circumstances' in Geneva: The ILO and the World of Non-Metropolitan Labour in the Inter-War Years." In *ILO Histories*, edited by Van Daele et al., 221–250.

Index

https://doi.org/10.1515/9783110650723-014

Bei Fragen zur Produktsicherheit wenden Sie sich bitte an:
If you have any questions regarding product safety,
please contact:

Walter de Gruyter GmbH
Genthiner Straße 13
10785 Berlin
productsafety@degruyterbrill.com